FILM AND RISK

Film AND RISK

EDITED BY METTE HJORT

Wayne State University Press   Detroit

Library of Congress Cataloging-in-Publication Data

Film and risk / edited by Mette Hjort.
    p.   cm. — (Contemporary approaches to film and media series)
    Includes bibliographical references and index.
    ISBN 978-0-8143-3463-8 (pbk. : alk. paper) — ISBN 978-0-8143-3611-3 (e-book)   1. Motion pictures—Production and direction.   2. Motion picture industry—Economic aspects.   3. Motion picture industry—Finance.   I. Hjort, Mette.
PN1995.9.P7F45 2012
384'.80681—dc23

2011030705

Typeset by Newgen North America
Composed in Warnock Pro and Meta

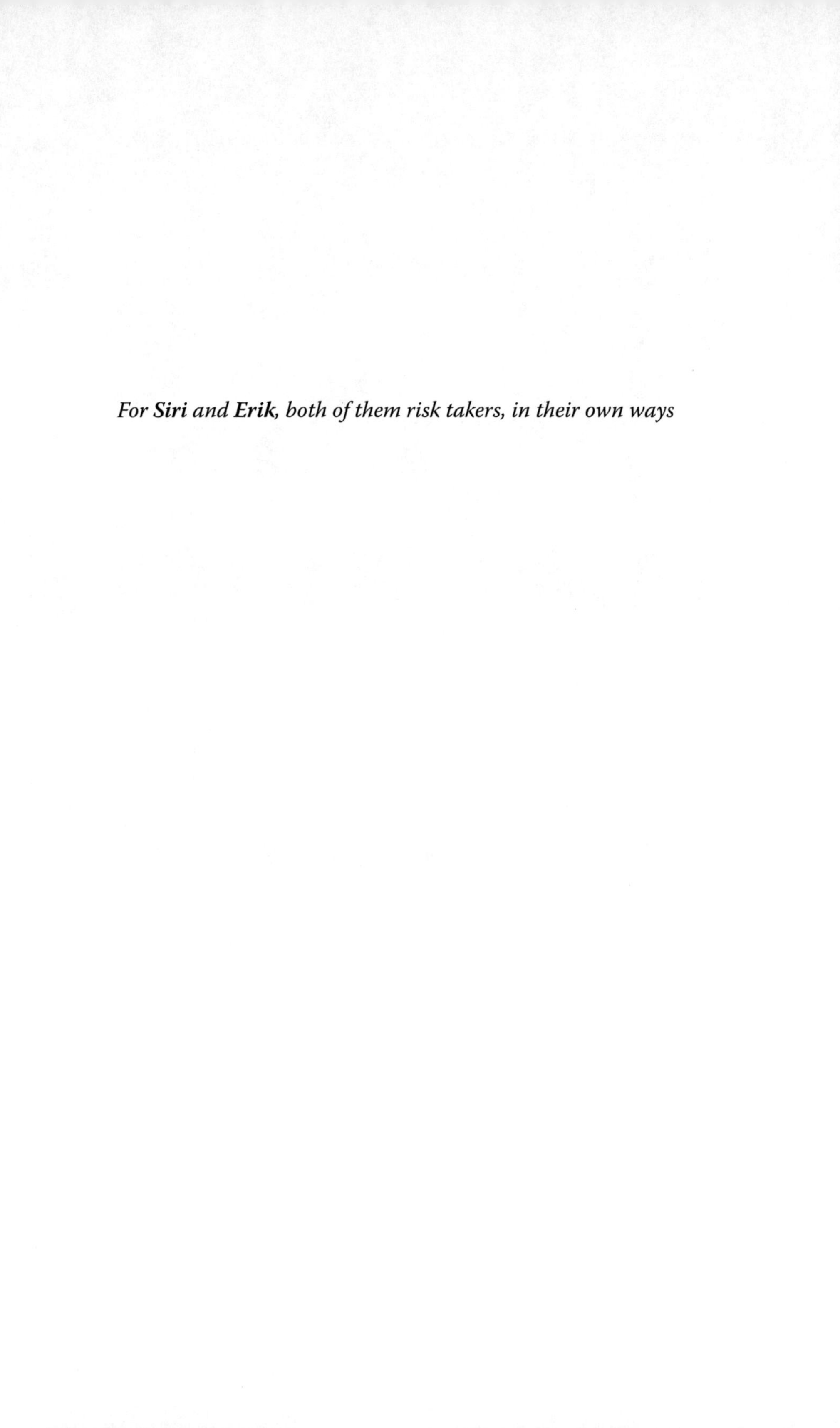

*For **Siri** and **Erik**, both of them risk takers, in their own ways*

Contents

Acknowledgments

I am grateful to Cheung Tit Leung for meticulous help with the preparation of the manuscript for publication and for research assistance. Martine Beugnet, Carol Hart, Jimmy Choi, Emily Yueh Yu Yeh, Richard Freadman, Peter Schepelern, Niels Bjørn, Darrel Davis, and David Bordwell all provided relevant examples and references along the way. Comments by two anonymous readers and by series editor Barry Keith Grant helped to improve the book. Annie Martin's enthusiastic support for the volume is especially appreciated, as is Robin DuBlanc's fine copyediting. The authors deserve my warmest thanks, for having been such a delight to work with throughout.

Film and Risk was fully supported by a Lingnan University direct grant (project no. DA08A7—Art and Risk). I am happy to acknowledge this generous support, and that of the colleagues who recommended funding for the project.

My interest in risk was prompted by a serious illness in 2004. I am grateful to Benjamin Lee for long discussions about risk at the time, for they helped me to see that worrisome thoughts about probabilities could be reframed and put to good use.

METTE HJORT

Introduction

The Film Phenomenon and How Risk Pervades It

The language of risk is common coin these days, informing virtually all areas of our lives. Parent/teacher discussions, whether in Asia or the West, make reference to learner profiles, and these often include the idea of being a "risk taker." Thus, for example, a child may be encouraged proudly to report that the recent class excursion with Outward Bound allowed her to meet one of her learning targets, to become "more of a risk taker." Discourses related to health, whether journalistic or medical, draw attention to long-term risks accompanying lifestyle choices. Phenomena such as Severe Acute Respiratory Syndrome (SARS), climate change, and the most recent financial meltdown all offer opportunities to reflect on the extent to which life in the twenty-first century is shaped by global risks, by the threat of different kinds of harm, some of them with remote originating causes. The ease with which many of us "speak" the language of risk is itself an indication of the extent to which highly sophisticated studies of risk, by economists, sociologists, and medical professionals, among many others, have been absorbed into the language of everyday life.

That risk should be a pervasive feature of contemporary life is anything but surprising. As Peter L. Bernstein argues persuasively in his intriguing study *Against the Gods: The Remarkable Story of Risk,* "The revolutionary idea that defines the boundary between modern times and the past is the mastery of risk: the notion that the future is more than a whim of the gods and that men and women are not passive before nature. Until human beings discovered a way across that boundary, the future was a mirror of the past or the murky domain of oracles and soothsayers who held a monopoly over knowledge of anticipated events." Bernstein's is a fascinating story about the thinkers, many of them passionate gamblers, who showed "the world how to understand risk, measure it, and weigh its consequences." While Bernstein sees the "Hindu-Arabic numbering system that reached the West seven to eight hundred years ago" as having facilitated probabilistic reasoning about the future, he understands the "serious study of risk" to have begun in the seventeenth century, as a result of two French thinkers' mathematical study of "a seventeenth-century version of the game of Trivial Pursuit." Blaise Pascal and Pierre de Fermat's findings, claims Bernstein, "led to the discovery of the theory of probability" and this in turn made possible "the capacity to manage risk, and with it the appetite to take risk and make forward-looking choices," that is, the very "energy that drives the economic system forward."[1] According to Bernstein, then, the ability to think in terms of risk, and the inclination to do so are, quite simply, defining features of modernity. And while modernity is now often held to be a plural phenomenon, admitting of different types and paths,[2] Bernstein's view that probabilistic reasoning about possible damage or harm pervades contemporary life is difficult to dispute. The global risk-focused debates prompted by the collapse of the 2009 Copenhagen Climate Change Conference clearly suggest the extent to which the language of risk is a lingua franca that is understood all around the world.

What is striking is that while the study of risk has become a veritable industry over the last few decades, film scholars have had very little to say about the topic. Yet, risk has not been entirely ignored, either, for many film scholars do gesture toward risk or make passing reference to it. For example, in her book on the remake phenomenon, *Encore Hollywood: Remaking French Cinema*, Lucy Mazdon points to risk management, or risk aversion, as a possible way of understanding the remake strategy.[3] And in his chapter "Gangsters, Cannibals, Aesthetes, or Apparently Perverse Allegiances," Murray Smith suggests that when we experience pleasure as a result of engaging with such characters as Hannibal Lecter (*Silence of the Lambs*, dir. Jonathan Demme, 1991), we do so in part because we are afforded the opportunity to explore "the extremes of possible or conceivable experience that we lack the opportunity or *courage* (emphasis added) to experience in reality."[4] Drawing on Greg Currie to weigh the advantage of imagination over actual experience, Berys Gaut chooses to foreground risk and the related questions of courage and danger:

> The great advantage of imagination over experience is that it is relatively costless: I could discover that I am brave through undergoing some terrible misfortune, which I rise above, but it would be better not to have to suffer. "Imagination trades reliability for

                                                        Mette Hjort

risk . . ." as Currie notes. Yet the lesser epistemic authority of imagination compared to experience should not be exaggerated. In choosing between a medical and a philosophy career, for instance, I cannot experience both in full, for I cannot live the rest of my life twice over, once entirely as a doctor, once entirely as a philosopher. However, I can imagine the rest of my life spent entirely as a doctor and can also imagine the rest of my life spent entirely as a philosopher. So there are some epistemic respects in which imagination is superior to experience. And a motivation actually to put myself in danger merely to find out whether I really am courageous calls into question whether I really am courageous, as opposed to reckless, even when I do not flinch from danger.[5]

Cinematic fictions offer viewers an opportunity to engage in make-believe that may well bring epistemic gains, and this without the costs involved in actually engaging in risky behavior. In *Chávez: The Revolution Will Not Be Televised; A Case Study of Politics and the Media,* Rod Stoneman returns to the issue of risk on several occasions, but without making it the focus of his discussion. Thus, for example, he refers critically to the now-dominant preferences for a "convenient, comfortable production base which eliminates much of the risk, unpredictability and danger of commissioning from small independents." Evoking the role played by "the recreation of a national film agency in Ireland in 1993," Stoneman praises the film board for consistently taking "risks with new directors," encouraging "them to transcend any residual insularity in relation to subjects and ideas."[6]

As is the case with most generalizations, the one that I have articulated here, which concerns film scholars' tendency to make only passing reference to risk, if at all, does have its exceptions. Not surprisingly, the exceptions occur in the area of economic approaches to film, economics being the discipline, as Bernstein rightly indicates, that pioneered thinking about risk. John Sedgwick and Mike Pokorny have, for example, coauthored a number of fine, empirically based articles over the years focusing on the ways in which filmmaking is caught up with economic risk. An early, oft-cited article of theirs is "The Risk Environment of Film-making: Warner in the Inter-war Period."[7]

Film and Risk is a response to what I see as a lacuna best thought of as an opportunity to engage in concept development and to propose some new ways of thinking about film that will articulate some of the pretheoretical intuitions with which film scholars appear to be working. It is quite simply the case that for the most part risk is overlooked in connection with the study of film. At the same time, many of those who write about film do seem to be working with intuitions about how various forms of risk taking shape aspects of the filmmaking or film-viewing process, and this in important ways. It is my firm conviction that risk is absolutely central to film, and that various conceptual approaches to risk, as well as different types of risk, warrant serious study by film scholars. Today, cinephiles, students, and scholars have at their disposal any number of very fine handbooks that usefully articulate the key concepts and terms of the still-young discipline of film studies. Examples include Susan Hayward's *Key Concepts in Cinema Studies* and *Complete A–Z Media and Film Studies Handbook*, by Vivienne Clark, Peter Jones, Bill Malyszko, and David Wharton.[8] However, in line with my argument thus far, these handbooks do not include entries on risk, although Susan Hayward does "welcome suggestions for further entries from readers," with reference to a possible revised edition.[9] *Film and Risk* is a collectively undertaken attempt to show that paying attention to risk in the context of film is well worth the effort. It is my hope that the volume will make this point, in such detail and so persuasively, that in future the term *risk* will become a well-established conceptual resource, one readily available to anyone with an interest in how films come into being and make their way into our lives.

In what follows I aim, in as straightforward a way as possible, to motivate the reader's interest in the topic of film and risk, to give the reader a sense of how the volume is organized, and, very importantly, to impart a clear understanding of the research questions to which the book is a response. Instead of reviewing the theoretical literature on risk, the introduction focuses on what I see as thought-provoking, real-world examples of how risk pervades the phenomenon of film. The task of defining "risk," and of situating a preferred definition in relation to competing approaches to risk, is thus taken up not in the introduction but on an "as-needed" basis in the chapters that follow. Instead of concluding with the once-obligatory synopses section, this introduction identifies the central research questions to which *Film and Risk* provides a response, organized into broad categories and keyed to specific contributors.

One of the advantages of this very direct approach, which eschews metatheoretical commentary, among other things, is that students, at various stages of their studies can be drawn into the conversation that this edited volume is meant to foster. Having taught English-language writings on film to students who are nonnative speakers of English for half a decade in Scandinavia and a full decade in Asia, I am increasingly interested in articulating research questions and results in as communicatively inclusive a way as possible. But my interest in inclusiveness is by no means motivated by pedagogical concerns alone, by the strong desire to enable capable and highly motivated students with fluency in languages other than English (some of them significantly harder to master than English) to engage more easily with the issues that are central to film studies today. Inclusiveness is also about trying to create the conditions for the kind of interdisciplinary discussion that is likely to be necessary if we are to make progress on some of these very issues. If, for example, we are to bring colleagues from economics, sociology, anthropology, and philosophy into our debates about film—which indeed we must if we are genuinely to understand risk and its place in the world of film—then the reasons for embarking on a project on film and risk have to be as clear as possible. Conversations spanning the theory/practice divide are also likely to be fruitful if we wish to grasp the ways in which filmmaking is informed by thinking about risk. And in my experience such conversations are best facilitated not by careful and detailed historical, theoretical, or interpretive discursive moves but by succinct accounts of the *issues* that are deemed to be key, and by telling anecdotes or relating specific cases that highlight the ways in which these issues are genuinely a matter of shared interest to both scholars and practitioners.

In what follows, then, I take up four specific tasks. I seek: (1) to make a case for seeing research on risk as central to film studies; (2) to articulate the methodological principles governing the volume's conception, and thereby its underlying aims; (3) to articulate the research questions to which *Film and Risk* provides the beginnings of answers; and (4) to suggest reasons why the study of risk is capacious, in the sense of capable of accommodating a wide range of methodological and theoretical commitments and a broad spectrum of interests. The aim is to accomplish these tasks in a way that will motivate cinephiles, scholars, students, film practitioners, policy makers and institution builders, and many other readers to begin to engage with the thought-provoking contributions that *Film and Risk* encompasses.

Why Risk Is Key: Some Telling Cases

Each of the chapters in *Film and Risk* evokes a significant number of empirical cases that illustrate the particular type or aspect of cinematic risk under discussion. The point, then, of the following examples is not to identify the full range of film's involvement with risk, for it is the task of the book as a whole to do this. Rather, the aim is simply to show that risk arises in many of the different areas that tend to be thought of as central to film studies. The idea is to encourage readers to recall the no doubt numerous cases that are known to them of the phenomenon of film being infused with risk. The examples canvassed here serve to suggest that our understanding of film can only be deepened, and this in genuinely rewarding ways, by taking risk seriously.

Screen Acting

On March 8, 1935, International Women's Day, Chinese actress Ruan Lingyu killed herself, at the age of twenty-five, prompting an outpouring of grief not only in Shanghai, where she was based, or in China, but around the world. Indeed, according to Kristine Harris, Ruan's funereal procession drew over one hundred thousand mourners.[10] Why did Ruan, at the height of her career at the time, kill herself?[11] This question, scholars generally agree, is one to which it is possible to give a more than plausible response. And the answer points directly to risks related to the activity of screen acting in China in the 1930s, and to risks linked to a particular approach to acting. Writing about movie actresses and public discourse in Shanghai in the 1920s and 1930s, Michael Chang argues persuasively that the classificatory system used to categorize courtesans and prostitutes during the late Qing dynasty and early republican years informed the public's understanding of the profession of actress. To the extent that actresses escaped opprobrium, Chang argues, they did so not because they acted well but because they "act[ed] good and act[ed] like 'themselves'"[12] The narrative of Ruan's personal life is intricate and cannot be fully explored here. Suffice it to say that her personal life did not meet the standards of goodness that Chang sees as potentially exempting actresses from censure during the early republican period. Indeed, Ruan was the object of considerable notoriety in the tabloid press as a result of vicious charges laid against her and her lover, Tang Jishan, by her common-law husband, Zhang Damin. Journalists writing for the tabloids were particularly happy to capitalize on the details of her personal life because of her role in Cai Chusheng's film *New Woman* (1934). Unable to censor Cai's film, which drew on a real-life suicide case to present a highly critical picture of the press's rumormongering, the journalists appear to have conspired with Zhang to attack Ruan and Tang publicly instead.

In addition to incurring risks simply by virtue of pursuing a career as a screen actress while refusing restrictive standards of authentic goodness, Ruan courted risk because she tended to relive such tragic experiences as her own suicide attempts through roles that involved similar actions, and to be generally consumed by the roles she played. Bérénice Reynaud puts the point as follows: "Ruan—who started her film career as a teenager to avoid the abuse and humiliation of her situation as a maidservant's daughter—did

Mette Hjort

not 'act,' but really experienced the feelings she projected on screen. Hence the unaffected charge, poignancy and feistiness of her performance—unable to separate acting from reality, she was consumed by the tragic dimension of her roles."[13] Shu Kei, a well-known Hong Kong filmmaker and dean at the Hong Kong Academy of Performing Arts, sees a direct connection between Ruan's tragic fate and the tragic roles that she played: "She was imprisoned twice. In other films she suffered from melancholy or madness; in one [film] she was assassinated and in another she died of illness. My sense is that every time she played these tragic scenes, she experienced a series of emotional shocks, and very often she proved incapable of drawing a distinction between the film and reality."[14] Shu Kei's line of reasoning finds support in observations made by Ruan's fellow actress Li Lili. On set during the shooting of a key scene in *New Woman,* Li later provided the following description of Ruan's performance as Wei Ming, the real-life actress who committed suicide on account of the tabloid press's efforts to blacken her reputation:

> [S]he went very silent for a while and quickly went into character: tears started to fall from her eyes, and while she was crying she took the sleeping pills. What appeared on the screen was a close-up of her face: she didn't show much expression, she just gazed as she swallowed one pill after another. However, the look in her eyes underwent a subtle change, showing all the contradictory emotions of a suicide at the moment when her life hangs in the balance, and expressing her thirst for life and dread of death, her indignation and her sorrow. . . . she couldn't stop crying for most of the day.[15]

At the time, Ruan had herself attempted suicide more than once, and it is generally assumed that her extreme response to the shooting of the scene supports the idea that the boundary between her life and her roles was highly unstable and at times barely present at all, at least subjectively.

Risk, it would appear, is an unavoidable subject for discussion, if we are to understand Ruan and the contributions she made as one of Chinese cinema's finest actresses. And Ruan is by no means a singular case. What is more, even the most superficial look at the history of screen acting quickly brings to light many other ways in which risk—as deliberate risk taking, as an unknowing exposure of the self to possible harm, or as a way of acting that straddles that very boundary—affects the agency of actors. In Hong Kong, for example, actors work in an environment that is closely associated with the triads (the Chinese equivalent of the Mafia), making it difficult, I

discovered, to get them openly to discuss the question of film and its relation to risk. Actors, whether from Hong Kong or elsewhere, may run the
risk of being mistaken for the characters they play, as Paprika Steen discovered when her flight to her holiday destination suddenly involved reas-
suring a young fellow passenger that she was not in fact an alien. Having
seen Ole Bornedal's *Vikaren* (The Substitute, 2007), that young passenger
"knew" Steen to be the alien schoolteacher Ulla Harms and felt an urgent
need to inform all other passengers of this fact, thereby reiterating in real
life the very structure of the film's narrative: in the film the children are
onto Harms's true nature, whereas the adults are taken in by her pretense
of being human. Reporting on Gabourey Sidibe's award-winning film debut
in *Precious* (dir. Lee Daniels, 2009), Stuart Jeffries focuses on "one problem. Sidibe keeps getting mistaken for the girl she plays." And that girl is
"functionally illiterate," has "been repeatedly raped by her father," and has
"two children as a result of her father's abuse, one of them a baby with
Down's syndrome who has been taken into care."[16] One of the risks of acting, clearly, is the conflation of the person and the role, but there are many
others. Jackie Chan, with his trademark outtakes, also comes to mind in
connection with acting and risk,[17] as does Michelle Yeoh, whose star status similarly rests on her ability to carry out her own stunt work. In their
very insistence on doing their own stunt work we find an implicit reference to some central, but insufficiently studied, practices of risk taking in
film: those of the stuntwomen and stuntmen who themselves take serious
risks so that others can opt out of risk work. Sylvia J. Martin has much
to say about this topic in her chapter in this volume, "Stunt Workers and
Spectacle: Ethnography of Physical Risk in Hollywood and Hong Kong,"
and there is thus no need to say more about the issue here. Let me instead
move on to some quite different examples of how risk shapes phenomena
that are generally assumed to be central to film studies.

Film Style

A concept of style has been a core element in the analysis of film from
the earliest attempts to think systematically about the cinematic medium's
specificity and unique contributions as compared with rival arts, such as
the theater. In *On the History of Film Style,* David Bordwell provides a helpful definition of style:

> I take style to be a film's systematic and significant use of tech-
> niques of the medium. Those techniques fall into broad domains:
> *mise en scène . . .*; framing, focus, control of color values, and

other aspects of cinematography; editing; and sound. Style is minimally the texture of the film's images and sounds, the result of choices made by the filmmaker(s) in particular historical circumstances. . . . [Style may also involve] other properties, such as narrative strategies or favored subjects or themes.[18]

The concept of style can be thought of as encompassing, among other things, choices reflected within a given film, across a number of films, within a single practitioner's oeuvre or across the oeuvres of practitioners who are deemed to have something in common—the circumstances under which they work, for example, or their commitment to certain values. In an attempt to capture an idea of the possible scope of the stylistic analysis of film, and the role that concepts of risk might play in such analyses, I would like to provide two examples of how risk determines cinematic style.

In an interview-based article focusing on the work of film editor Adam Nielsen, Lars Movin discusses the principles governing the use of music in Eva Mulvad and Anja Al-Erhayem's award-winning documentary *Vores lykkes fjender* (Enemies of Happiness, 2006). The film follows then twenty-seven-year-old Malali Joya's courageous role in the parliamentary elections in Afghanistan in 2005, after having challenged the Grand Council of tribal elders in 2003 on the grounds of corruption. The film focuses on Joya's campaign for election at a time when her life is constantly at risk.[19] Movin points out that music is introduced early on in the film, signaling a departure from "a cinéma vérité–style minimalism to a more expressive formal language." In response to a question regarding the film's sound/image relations, Nielsen explains his choices as follows:

> In the case of *Enemies of Happiness* the challenge we faced was that the life of the main character was constantly being threatened, but it was difficult to show this by means of images only. She lived on one side of the street and worked on the other, and to enable her to walk from the one place to the other, the entire street was blocked off. But the takes just showed some guards. It didn't look especially dangerous. So we felt that we needed to assist the viewer's understanding a bit. How do you show something that you can't really see? Here music can be a good tool.[20]

A stylistic analysis of *Enemies of Happiness* would likely note the nature of the music in the film, the frequency of its use, and the kind of images that it accompanies. Because stylistic features arising from sound/image relations involving extradiegetic music are very much a matter of deliberate choices, exploring the practitioner's agency through an in-depth interview helps to deepen the stylistic analysis. In this case what is brought to light as a result of taking a practitioner's intentions and reflective awareness of his practices seriously is the extent to which sound-image relations are shaped by a perceived need to ensure that the viewer understands the film as being to a significant extent *about* risk taking, and thus *about* courage. What makes the film's story tellable is that it centers on a young woman who knowingly risks her life, again and again, for the sake of significant social and political change in Afghanistan.

My second example of how cinematic style may be shaped by some aspect of the phenomenon of risk brings a concept of collective style into play.[21] I have in mind here a number of films made in Lebanon in the 1980s during the civil war that are marked, stylistically, by the circumstances under which they were produced. In "Cinema in Lebanon, Syria, Iraq and Kuwait," Kiki Kennedy-Day draws a broad distinction between visually successful and unsuccessful films produced in Lebanon in the 1980s, noting that war-based—and thus risk-based—stylistic markers are a defining feature of the former:

> Those films that incorporated the war and worked with its unpredictable outcomes were the most visually successful. In them the failures of production (for example, the bursting shells seen through the living-room windows in *Ghazal al-Banat 2*) are merely read as part of the plot. If the lights go out, it is simply what is expected to happen in times of war. It was not possible in war-torn Beirut to make highly polished films, but that lack of polish became part of the success of films like *Hurub Saghira* or *Ghazal al-Banat 2*.[22]

To understand the salient formal and thematic regularities that define the category of films to which *Hurub Saghira* or *Ghazal al-Banat 2* belong, and to do this in stylistic terms, it is necessary to grasp the filmmakers' decision making within a context that, while constrained by war, nonetheless offered certain choices. The decision to incorporate the uncertainties of war into the films, and thereby to transform the impossibility of polish into an opportunity for creativity and innovation, is a stylistic choice. As that choice appears to inform not just one work but a series of works, it is the basis for something like a group style. To make sense of that style it is necessary to grasp the circumstances of the films' production, and especially the filmmakers' decision to revise the definition of what counts as a successful film in light of the inevitable risks associated with the ongoing war. Without a concept of risk—and thus of uncertainty, probability, and danger or harm—it is possible simply to *describe* the films' recurring and salient features in a purely formal way, but it is not possible genuinely to *explain* them. Stylistic explanations become possible once practitioner's agency is brought into the analysis, and thereby the filmmakers' reasoning about uncertainty, probability, and danger or harm—that is, about risk.

As will become evident, several of the chapters in *Film and Risk* take up the issue of risk in stylistic terms. In "Accented Filmmaking and Risk Taking in the Age of Postcolonial Militancy, Terrorism, Globalization, Wars, Oppression, and Occupation," for example, Hamid Naficy looks at a range of cases that in many ways resemble the Lebanese situation described above. And in "Flamboyant Risk Taking: Why Some Filmmakers Embrace Avoidable and Excessive Risks" I focus on the reasons filmmakers might have for trading favorable risk positions for unfavorable ones and for systematically drawing attention to their risk taking, to the point where the expression of risk by various means becomes a guiding principle and a stylistic marker, relative in the first instance to a given work, but finally also in relation to the entire category of works that share the relevant traits.

Film's Institutions, Broadly Construed

Films are made and seen in contexts that are structured by policies, laws, regulations, and the activities of individuals working for a wide range of film bodies and institutions. Film, that is, has an institutional existence, and here too we will find that thinking about risk is crucial. To illustrate this point, I shall refer to seven quite different examples. My first example takes us once again to Afghanistan, this time in connection with the extraordinary actions of Khwaja Ahmadshah. When a Taliban decree defined motion pictures as heretical in 1996 and called for their destruction, Ahmadshah rescued a significant number of Afghan productions. At the time of the decree's promulgation, Afghan Film, "the Kabul-based organization that both promoted Afghan cinema and housed the Asian republic's entire film and TV archive" had 120 employees on staff. In response to the decree, 118 of these employees fled, while Ahmadshah and a colleague remained behind, determined to hide as many films as possible. Erlend Clouston describes their activities:

> Over the course of two weeks, the two men slipped in through a back door (the front entrance to the office was patrolled by the Taliban), took off their shoes and smuggled cans of film up to a processing studio on the second floor of the building. They made decisions

about what film would survive and what was expendable—a surreal jury working in whispers and stockinged feet.

Foreign films, whose negatives were presumably safe elsewhere, stayed on the shelves. But Ahmadshah considered it vital to rescue homegrown work such as *The Suitor*, a 1969 tragicomedy about a poor boy meeting a rich girl, directed by Khaleq A'lil—a film that has the added anthropological value of revealing the widespread popularity of the miniskirt among Afghan girls 40 years ago. "*We felt it was worth taking the risk,*" the $50-a-month technician says [emphasis added]. "These films belonged to our culture." . . . By the time Ahmadshah's rescue operation was complete in 1996, no fewer than 100,000 hours of film had been stuffed into the studio. A blackboard was nailed over the door, painted and hung with posters. When the Taliban's heresy-hunters arrived, they burned a dozen lorry-loads of film—but missed Ahmadshah's secret cavity.

"The minister for information was there," he recalls. "He said to me, 'If I find one reel hidden in the building, I must kill you.'"[23]

In this moving story, the continued existence of films that are both a form of cultural heritage and a vehicle for cultural memory comes to depend on the outcome of probabilistic reasoning in relation to clearly defined threats. Engaged in by individuals working for one of the many institutions that exist around the world to somehow defend film, this reasoning occurred in a situation of considerable uncertainty, where death could have been the result.

The example of Ahmadshah and Afghan Film points to the fragility of film's institutions in some parts of the world, and to the courage and passion that may be needed to create and sustain them, or to defend their remains until such time as they can be revived or reconstituted, perhaps in a new form. But there are also many examples of film institutions being created as a means of facilitating risk avoidance, a reduction of risk, or a transfer of risk from private individuals to state-funded bodies that are able to offer employees some of the most risk-free work environments imaginable. The history of western European cinema in the wake of the advent of TV provides many such cases. Indeed, the government-subsidized filmmaking characteristic of many a western European cinema was a response to the assumption that the production of films involved economic risks so great that directors or producers could not be expected to shoulder them, and certainly not on a regular basis or in numbers sufficient to sustain a national film industry. Shifting some of the costs, and thereby some of the risks, of filmmaking from the private sector to the public sector, governments effectively redefined the economic risks (that is, losses) associated with national film production as the inevitable costs of sustaining national cultures.

A non-European example of the kind of risk-shifting process being evoked here can be found in Syria, where the National Film Organization was created in the mid-1960s. Kiki Kennedy-Day cites the risk aversiveness of private investors as one of the most important reasons for the establishment of the National Film Organization: "Since the private sector had an aversion to risk, the idea of a state-sponsored cinema that was willing to take a chance on unknown young directors was inspired."[24] One of the first films produced by the Syrian National Film Organization was *Sa'iq al-Shahinah* (The Truck Driver, 1967), directed by the Yugoslavian Bosko Vucinitch, with an all-Syrian cast and crew.

While state-funded film institutions in stable democracies are very much about transferring risk from the private to the public sector, and while the civil-servant-style employment conditions that such institutions offer are anything but risky, the concept of risk may nonetheless be very much on their employees' agenda. A case in point is that of New Danish Screen, a funding scheme administered by the Danish Film Institute. New Danish Screen was created with the intent of revitalizing and thereby sustaining a national cinema by fostering the conditions needed for artistic risk taking in contexts where film practitioners might be inclined to repeat previously successful formulas. Eva Novrup Redvall's chapter, "Encouraging Artistic Risk Taking through Film Policy: The Case of New Danish Screen," looks closely at this scheme, and makes a compelling case for seeing concepts of risk as pivotal in some instances—not only to the work of funding bodies but also of policymakers.

Filmmaking requires training of some kind, and this may be acquired in a number of ways, including the following: by completing the curriculum of a conservatoire-style institution with, typically, highly competitive admissions standards; through an apprenticeship model involving a series of jobs in the film industry; by becoming part of a network of practitioners where sociability based on friendship and shared interests and passions facilitates a generous sharing of knowledge and know-how. Film education, be it formal and structured or more fluid, ad hoc, and improvised, is also, much like archives and institutes, part of the institutional fabric of cinema. And in the area of film education thinking about risk is, once again, unavoidable. In the case of improvised arrangements made possible by passion, generosity, and a strong sense of shared purpose, risk is, much as in the case of Afghan Film evoked above, often a matter of probabilistic reasoning about life-threatening events. For example, in "Reel Challenges: Socially Conscious Afghan Filmmakers Brave Censorship, Poverty and Death Threats to Get Their Message Out," Anand Gopal draws attention to the death-defying activities of Asad Salahi, a police officer in Kabul and a filmmaker with a strong commitment not only to making films but to training others who might then go on to make them: "I even ran secret training courses for filmmakers in my office until one day the Taleban came and took everything, including the film and cameras."[25] Many other examples, from many other parts of the world, could be provided.

If we turn to some of the more stable institutional environments for film education, to such robust institutions as the Hong Kong Academy for Performing Arts, the National Film School of Denmark, the Huston School of Film & Digital Media, or the London Film School, we find that thinking about risk takes a different form. Here students are inevitably taught to think about the tensions between the kind of artistic risk taking that informs and drives personal filmmaking and the risk-aversive tendencies of the film industry in which the film school graduate will eventually have to make his or her way. In his chapter, "Chance and Change," Rod Stoneman draws on his experiences as a film commissioner (for Channel 4), as the CEO of the Irish Film Board and, currently, as the director of the Huston School of Film & Digital Media to make a case for the pursuit of certain types of risk. There are serious costs involved in conforming to the risk-aversive tendencies of the established film industries, and it is thus crucial, Stoneman argues, that budding film practitioners be encouraged to think deeply and systematically about the extent to which various forms of risk taking are essential to the process of producing meaningful cinematic works with some degree of authenticity.

Film festivals provide yet another example of how the phenomenon of film is supported by a dense institutional network, by iterated practices that are regularly engaged in within the context of established frameworks, or within situations that articulate an aspiration for such frameworks and thus an intent to take up the often difficult task of institution, used here to mean the act of instituting. The scholarly discussion of film festivals, beginning with Marijke de Valck's *Film Festivals: From European Geopolitics to Global Cinephilia*,[26] and continuing with Dina Iordanova's team-based *Dynamics of World Cinema* project, constitutes an unusually lively area of ongoing film research. The Film Festival Yearbook series, published by the Dynamics of World Cinema team, makes it impossible to ignore the many different and important roles that film festivals (increasingly) play in world cinema today. Of particular interest in the present risk-focused context is some of the research being conducted on a more individual basis by

Cheung Tit Leung at Lingnan University in Hong Kong. Based on empirical on-site research, and focused on Asian film festivals with a particular emphasis on documentary filmmaking, Cheung Tit Leung's project has taken him not only to such established festivals as the Yamagata International Documentary Film Festival but also to a little-known festival in mainland China called the China Documentary Film Festival (Beijing, Songzhuang Art Center; funded by Li Xianting's Film Fund). Founded in 2003, the festival is to some extent structured by the logic of discretion and secrets. Organizers maintain a low profile for the festival, thereby keeping it off the government's radar. Indeed, the program for the festival is released only one week in advance, a strategy designed to minimize the risk involved in screening "sensitive" films. That is, the festival's modus operandi is traceable to an awareness of risks arising from the nature of the films the organizers seek to show.

Risk may be less obviously present at the more established, and visible, film festivals, but it is by no means absent. Scholars who have devoted considerable energy to documenting the Sixth Generation phenomenon in the People's Republic of China (PRC) often note that labels such as "underground" or "independent," used with reference to filmmakers, have helped to fuel a festival-mediated international interest in such directors as Jia Zhangke, Wang Xiaoshuai, Zhang Yuan, Wang Quanan, and Lou Ye. Indeed, at times it almost seemed as if festival organizers' and festivalgoers' interest in PRC filmmakers correlated directly with the censorship of their work by PRC officials, with their status as underground filmmakers who knowingly take risks in order to make their censored films. Attributions (whether entirely accurate or not) of risk taking to filmmakers thus constitute, quite simply, one of the more salient bases for festival inclusion, for access to a global circuit, and for mediation to global audiences.

Spectatorship

Film spectators sometimes take risks when they see films. Some of the risks have to do with viewers' awareness of laws governing the conditions under which films may be seen, and with probabilistic reasoning about the likelihood of being caught and punished in connection with transgressions of the relevant codifications. Reporting from Berlin in 2006, Roger Boyes discusses "measures, some of the toughest in Europe," that were "announced after an aggressive campaign by the film industry in Germany, the largest market in the EU and [with] one of the most computer-literate populations." Boyes notes that the new law, which was to be introduced at the outset of 2007, threatened Germans who downloaded "films . . . for private use" with two years in prison, while anybody downloading "films for commercial use" faced "up to five years." The law "infuriated consumer groups" and prompted a response from Patrick von Braunmühl, from the Federation of German Consumer Organizations, who drew attention to the difficulties families faced in trying to monitor the downloading behavior of teenagers still residing at home.[27] Von Braunmühl's reasoning evokes the phenomenon of risk arising from the behavior of others, and this with reference to serious legal consequences. The rigors of the controversial German law, the thought appears to have been, are such that parents face (unknowingly) being at risk on account of the (possibly unacknowledged, possibly defiant) risk-taking behavior of their teenagers. Teenagers, it is often emphasized in the literature on risk, tend to reason poorly about risk. Indeed, they typically fail to recognize risks as risk, a common neurological explanation being that their brain development is still incomplete.

There are, of course, many other (far less obvious) ways in which spectators may be exposed to risks as a result of their decision to see a given film. The Danish filmmaker Lone Scherfig (known for her Dogma film *Italiensk for begyndere* [Italian for Beginners, 2000] and, more recently, *An Education* [2009]) recalls how her father once shared a room in the Copenhagen hospital commonly referred to as Riget (the Kingdom) with a patient who insisted on being treated by Dr. Moesgaard, the doctor (played by Holger Juul Hansen) in Lars von Trier's *Riget*.[28] While this particular spectator failed to distinguish competently between fiction and reality, and acquired false beliefs as a result, more competent viewers who do not succumb to illusion may also acquire attitudes or beliefs that are unlikely to serve them well in real-world contexts. Taking its name from Goethe's *Sorrows of Young Werther,* the "Werther effect" is a term used by psychologists and others to describe situations in which spectators' engagement with fictional depictions of suicide end up motivating actual suicides. There are also well-documented cases of successful fictional crimes serving as models for (typically unsuccessful) crimes in the real world: "The Godfather movies . . . also led to instances of life imitating art. Some organized criminals imitated behaviors from these films."[29] These examples of how spectatorship may be imbricated with either an inadvertent and unknown exposure to risk or with actual risk taking—a distinction explored at length by Paisley Livingston in "Spectatorship and Risk"—may seem remote from some of the more common or standard forms of film reception. Yet, it is not difficult to imagine far less exceptional examples of spectators' exposure to risk as a result of film viewing, beginning with the uncontroversial case of spectators' acquisition of false beliefs about smoking, as a result of the cinematic representation of this activity as appealing, and this

     Mette Hjort

in countless films produced over a significant period of time. In *Film and Risk,* the fascinating idea that spectators take risks when watching films is explored by a number of contributors. For example, in "The Financial and Economic Risks of Film Production" Michael Pokorny and John Sedgwick invite us to think of films as involving "risk environments," and to think of spectators as entering these environments when they opt to see a given film.

Cinematic Authorship

"Authorship" was once thought of by film scholars not in terms of a practitioner's agency or deliberative practices, but in terms of such forces as ideology or pan-cultural psychological constants and their manifestation at the level of textual structures. This situation has changed dramatically in recent years, with philosophers such as Paisley Livingston making a compelling case for renewed interest in cinematic authorship.[30] The proposals developed by Livingston and others acknowledge the collaborative dimensions of filmmaking, and thus in no wise involve a return to the wrongheaded ideas of cinematic authorship that film scholars once derived from literature, and which scholars influenced by Marxism, semiotics, and psychoanalysis rightly rejected. The new, more analytically oriented debates about cinematic authorship foreground such issues as collaboration, control, nonaccidental contributions to the filmmaking process, and the presence or absence of coercion. Drawing on V. F. Perkins's insistence on control as crucial, Livingston, for example, works with a noncoercion clause.[31] In the current context this is fascinating, for coercion can, of course, be a matter of threats and thus of risks.

In the present context, I am interested in what a focus on risk might bring to the discussion of cinematic authorship. I would like briefly to evoke three thought-provoking cases that point to risk as a decisive factor in cinematic authorship. The first case suggests that exposure to inevitable risks can weaken the articulations between the various collaborative dimensions of cinematic authorship. The second suggests that risk is unequally distributed across the filmmaking process, and that the distribution of risk may well have implications for how we go about identifying the (principal) authors of a film. The third case shows that a practitioner's risk environment, to borrow Pokorny and Sedgwick's term, can negate control to the point where it becomes difficult to think of that practitioner as genuinely authoring a given film.

Anders Høgsbro Østergaard's award-winning documentary film *Burma VJ* documents the "rebellion of Buddhist monks against Burma's military junta" in 2007 and the activity of the video activists whose images of the rebellion were the outside world's sole source of information about the unfolding events.[32] At the time of the rebellion Østergaard was already making a documentary about the Burmese video activists, who intrigued him on account of their risk taking:

> To begin with, I was mainly interested in my central character as a documentarian. . . . He and his friends have to film with their cameras concealed in bags, which obviously is a major restriction on what they are able to document. My interest, then, was more about why they were even doing what they were doing. Why do they expose themselves to such risk? What are their thoughts about it and how are they affected by what they do? I was fascinated by my protagonist's almost instinctive need to document the world, which apparently came before any considerations about what political goals they might serve. My film was a small, intimate, psychological affair. Then came the rebellion.[33]

At the time of the rebellion's eruption, Østergaard had virtually completed a short documentary portrait of the Burmese video activists. However, when images of the rebellion started flooding into Oslo, where the Voice of Burma (DVB) is based, the director decided to rethink his project. The rebellion aggravated the risks being taken by the video reporters, but it also had the effect of diminishing Østergaard's control over a filmmaking process that had involved collaboration with the Burmese video activists, especially the main protagonist, referred to as Joshua. The loss of control is clearly described by the film's editor, Billeskov Jansen, in an interview conducted by Lars Movin:

> The filmmakers faced the problem that the tapes they received in Denmark had been recorded over in Burma or Thailand, so there was no guarantee that the footage was in actual chronological order. Also, they didn't know how many photographers had been present at the different events. Finally, it seemed almost impossible to pin down what shots had been made on what days. Then help arrived from an unexpected place: "We discovered that we could log on to Google Earth and locate Rangoon, zoom in as far as we could go and still maintain relatively good resolution," Billeskov Jansen says, "much higher quality images than you get if you look at Copenhagen, for instance. At first, I wondered about that, but then I tried looking at other areas where you would expect the West

   Mette Hjort

to have military interests and the images of those places generally
looked better, too. That way, we were able to identify the locations
of buildings and streets we recognised from the videotapes."[34]

Billeskov Jansen's comments strongly suggest that an intensification or ag-
gravation of risks borne by some contributors to the filmmaking process
can have the effect of disarticulating it, and this in ways that make properly
coordinated, collaborative efforts difficult. If cinematic authorship does indeed admit of different types, as I believe it does, then the presence of particular kinds of risk may well be one of the factors determining the category
of cinematic authorship to which a given film belongs.

My second example of risk playing a role in the determination of cinematic authorship is a so-called Dogma film, that is, a film made in accordance with the rules specified in the "Vow of Chastity" that filmmaker
Lars von Trier flamboyantly announced in Paris in 1995. Lone Scherfig's
Italian for Beginners was the first Dogma film to be made by a woman,
and took Dogma in a new and interesting direction. In the spring of 2008 I
interviewed two of the actors who had worked with Scherfig on *Italian for
Beginners,* as well as the film's cinematographer, editor, and sound person.
The aim was to understand, through careful consideration of these practitioners' agency, what the differentiated impact of the Dogma rules was
on the different action roles that contribute to the filmmaking process.[35]
I was particularly struck by what Rune Palving, the sound person, had to
say about the rules' implications. One of the things he foregrounded is just
how risky a Dogma project is, from the perspective of the person in charge
of the sound. The rules, after all, specify that the sound must be recorded
at the same time as the image, and that no manipulations of the sound or of
the image can take place during the postproduction phase. What you have
once shooting is completed is essentially what you get. Palving described
his understanding of the risks of Dogma as follows: "It was my first film, so
for me it was really a big gamble. You could really put your whole career
at risk. If Dogma goes wrong, it goes really wrong. You can't save it. There
is nothing to be done in the postproduction phase." Palving went on to
note that he was convinced that he was given the opportunity to work on
Italian for Beginners because more established sound designers with more
of a reputation to lose had quite simply been unwilling to take the requisite
risks.[36] What is interesting is that Palving also identified the gains of the
Dogma process, from the point of view of the sound designer, as having to
do with enhanced control, power, and stature in connection with the filmmaking process. Because the sound can't be "fixed" during the postproduction phase, the sound person's authority and decision-making capacity are

considerably enhanced by the Dogma rules. Palving's reasoning suggests that there may be forms of risk taking that correlate with status, authority, and control; if this is so, then individuals occupying the relevant risk positions become prime candidates for consideration as cinematic authors—if, that is, we accept that control is indeed a decisive factor for cinematic authorship (which I do).

My last example of how risk can have an impact on cinematic authorship is that of Shin Sang-ok, a South Korean film director who was abducted in 1978 while filming in Hong Kong. North Korean Kim Jong-il is generally assumed to have orchestrated the abduction not only of Shin Sang-ok but of his wife, actress Choi Eun-hee (in a separate incident). Shin and Choi escaped from North Korea in 1986, but only after an earlier failed attempt that led to Shin's incarceration in a prison camp, where he claims to have survived on grass and tree bark. Shin's best-known North Korean film is *Pulgasari,* a monster movie resembling the Japanese Godzilla movies.[37] Shin and Choi "quoted Kim as telling them that he had ordered them 'brought' to North Korea to help develop its film industry." They described Kim as a "movie buff" and indicated that the North Korean leader had a particular fondness for "adventure movies, like 'Indiana Jones.'"[38] There can be little doubt that risk—risk of incarceration or death—overshadowed Shin's North Korean filmmaking career. The question is: What were the implications of this risk environment for his cinematic agency and for his capacity genuinely to author films? This is the kind of question to which a number of quite different *speculative* responses can be given. A persuasive response would be one that draws on empirical data of the kind that quite simply, at least to my knowledge, isn't available. So we cannot settle the question here. The story of the abducted filmmaker whose authorship was to some extent coerced does, however, remain instructive, for it points to a limit case where agency, and thus authorship, is eclipsed by threats and the risks that they evoke.

The Natural Environment

Up until this point, I have been exploring some of the ways in which risks and risk taking can be understood as relevant to broad areas that are usually thought of as central to film studies. I would like to conclude with some examples of film's involvement with risk that point not to established areas of interest but to a new area of concern requiring urgent attention: film and the environment. In 2006 Jiang Zhuqing and Wang Shanshan reported on the environmental impact and legal ramifications of established Fifth Generation filmmaker Chen Kaige's making of *The Promise:*

                                                                 Mette Hjort

Early this week, Vice-Minister of Construction Qiu Baoxing criticized the crew that filmed "The Promise" for damaging the pristine environment at Bigu Tianchi in Shangrila County, Southwest China's Yunnan Province. A reinforced concrete structure was left on the lake's shore, and more than 100 wooden posts were left in the water, Qiu said. The Beijing News reported on Friday that the crew [of] "The Promise" also damaged about 60 trees in the Yuanmingyuan Garden (Old Summer Palace) during the shooting of an autumn scene. They painted the trees yellow all of them over 10 metres high at the end of 2004, and many have since withered.[39]

The Promise is but one of countless cases of film production involving serious environmental risks. In the context of filmmaking in mainland China, *The Promise* is, however, a watershed case, for the controversy it generated produced significant mobilization in favor of a "green production code," with artists and critics calling for legislation designed to protect especially scenic spots. The initiative foregrounded the need to preserve "China's beautiful scenery . . . on film and in reality," and called "on producers to exercise self-discipline and government departments, news organizations and environmental groups to enhance supervision." Coverage of the initiative, in connection with the controversy of Chen's film, highlighted the extent to which *The Promise* is representative of standard filmmaking practices, rather than a deviation from an accepted norm. Thus, for example, environmental despoliation resulting from filmmaking was said to have been reported in "the famous Jiuzhaigou nature reserve in Sichuan province and Shennongjia nature reserve in Hubei province."[40] While the debate generated by *The Promise* focused on what analytic aestheticians with an interest in environmental aesthetics call "scenic nature,"[41] it did raise the issue of filmmaking's environmental footprint more generally:

Environmental activists welcomed the publicity of the event and its significance, according to Wang Ping, a member of the Chinese People's Political Consultative Conference (CPPCC), the national political advisory body. "The environmental impact of cultural and entertainment industries has long been an area covered by no laws and no regulations," said Wang, a professor of environmental engineering at Beijing University of Industry and Commerce. "Although they are mostly temporary projects, whether shooting a movie or having a festival celebration, they tend to subject the environment to risks," she said. "Sometimes the pollution of a temporary project can remain forever."[42]

In their contribution to *Film and Risk*, Richard Maxwell and Toby Miller provide a groundbreaking discussion of the environmental risks associated with filmmaking. Not only do Maxwell and Miller make it crystal clear that filmmaking has had serious environmental costs from the very beginning of film history, they convincingly claim that film spectators and film scholars have an important role to play in limiting the environmental risks of filmmaking, through judicious and informed viewing choices, among other things.

The risks evoked thus far, in this broad outline of film's imbrication with risk, have mostly involved various forms of harm—the threat, that is, of possible negative consequences being actualized. But risk is not necessarily negative, and there is considerable evidence to suggest that there are strong links between a highly valued phenomenon such as creativity and risk taking. One of the tasks that *Film and Risk* takes up is that of bringing into clear focus the more positive meanings of "risk" in the context of film. One clear thread running through the volume is that the growing insistence on risk management in film-related contexts has serious costs, one being that it is becoming more and more difficult for practitioners to work under circumstances that make meaningful artistic risk taking, and thus creativity, possible. In its own modest way, then, *Film and Risk* is an attempt to support those increasingly embattled individuals who remain committed to meaningful artistic risk taking. *Film and Risk,* I believe, makes a contribution along these lines because it helps us to see why it is important to defend those shrinking spaces—associated, for example, with the efforts of film schools and film institutes—where meaningful artistic risk taking is not only possible but encouraged and valued.

Organizing/Methodological Principles

Film and Risk fosters and provides a basis for the kind of interdisciplinary conversation that I see as being necessary, by bringing together the findings of scholars from such disciplines as philosophy, anthropology, film studies, economics, and cultural studies. Interdisciplinarity should not only be about eventually transcending the disciplinary demarcations of academic or theoretical knowledge, but also about working across the boundaries between theory and practice. As a result, *Film and Risk* includes contributions by a lawyer with expertise in entertainment law (Bill Grantham) as well as essays by practitioners with experience in the areas of filmmaking (Rod Stoneman) and photojournalism (Michelle L.

     Mette Hjort

Woodward). Although photojournalism involves still rather than moving images, an account of its norms and practices sheds valuable light on cultural preferences and tendencies that undoubtedly shape the contexts in which some (especially documentary) filmmakers operate.

As the categories of research questions identified below suggest, some of the contributions do converge on similar issues. Although the contributions have not been divided into categories, each with its own subheading, the order of the chapters is by no means arbitrary. Among other things, the first three chapters (by Hjort, Ponech, and Livingston) survey some of the conceptual terrain that is relevant to understanding risk and its relation to film. The next three chapters (by Martin, Ginsburg, and Naficy) focus intensely on risk as it arises in the context of the practice of filmmaking, on what I would like to call "practitioner's risk." Subsequent chapters by Choi, Pokorny and Sedgwick, and Grantham offer takes on economic risk in the context of film production. The concluding chapters, by Redvall, Woodward, Stoneman, and Maxwell and Miller, make it clear just how decisive a role thinking about risk has played, and continues to play, in the context of the development of film's institutional landscape.

Contributors' Research Questions

Conceptualizing Risk

1. What are the different available models for thinking about risk, and how is the multifaceted phenomenon of risk best approached in the context of film? (Hjort; Ponech)

2. What is the difference between running a risk and taking a risk? (Livingston)

3. What is the relation between contingency or chance and risk, in the context of film? (Stoneman)

4. Can artists' experimentations with chance help us to understand some of the more positive dimensions of risk? (Stoneman)

The Representation and/or Discernability of Risk in Film

5. Is the "imperfection" that often characterizes the "accented" style of exilic, diasporic, and ethnic filmmakers the mark of risks incurred or taken during the production process? (Naficy)

6. What role can films, especially documentaries, play in alerting spectators to the persistence of social and political dangers that place certain groups at serious risk? (Ginsburg)

7. What are some of the artistic risks arising from the representation of risk in cinematic works? (Livingston)

8. How do we explain the pervasiveness of representations of risk in the cinema? (Livingston)

9. Why do some filmmakers choose to relinquish favorable "risk positions" in order to take risks that are at once avoidable and excessive? And why do they choose to document this process?[43] (Hjort)

10. Can cinematic works focusing on risk inadvertence make a contribution to risk-perception studies? (Ponech)

11. How have the norms of photojournalism changed since the 1930s, with regard to the depiction of risk? (Woodward)

SPECTATORS' ENGAGEMENT WITH RISK

12. Can the appeal of cinematic spectacles of extreme risk be explained in terms of their offering the possibility of a relatively low-risk engagement with high risk? (Livingston)

13. What is the epistemic value to spectators of cinematic explorations of extreme risk taking and/or risk inadvertence? (Ponech)

14. Do film spectators have an obligation to think about the risks to the environment entailed by the films they see? (Maxwell and Miller)

15. What effect do photojournalistic norms emphasizing "visual drama" have on "what viewers learn about a given situation?" (Woodward)

16. In what sense can viewers be said to "enter a risk environment when choosing to view a movie"? (Pokorny and Sedgwick)

PRACTITIONERS: DIRECTORS, PROFESSIONAL AND NONPROFESSIONAL ACTORS, STUNTPERSONS, AND PHOTOJOURNALISTS

17. What are the different types of risk that arise in connection with film production? (Hjort)

18. Why is risk taking inevitable for exilic, diasporic, and ethnic filmmakers? (Naficy)

   Mette Hjort

19. What are the risk attitudes of stunt workers, and especially stunt doubles, and to what extent are these attitudes shaped by the priorities of the commercial film industries? (Martin)

20. What light do partnerships involving nondisabled filmmakers and disabled subjects shed on the differentiated distribution of risk within the filmmaking process? (Ginsburg)

21. What is the relationship between risk taking and activism? (Ginsburg; Hjort)

22. Can the now-dominant norms of photojournalism be seen as necessitating extreme risk taking on the part of photojournalists? (Woodward)

Money: Profits and Losses

23. What are the ways in which Hollywood financiers have sought, historically and more recently, to diminish the economic risks of producing films? (Maxwell and Miller)

24. How have models of film financing evolved over the last quarter of a century in the United States? (Grantham)

25. What roles do risk aversion and the disregarding of risk play in film-financing transactions? (Grantham)

26. How effective are transnational strategies as a means of managing financial risk within a globalized film industry? (Choi)

27. What is the risk environment of Hollywood film production? (Pokorny and Sedgwick)

The Institutional Dimension: Film Policies, Film Commissioners, and Photography Agencies

28. Should film policies be assessed partly in terms of their implications for environmental sustainability? (Maxwell and Miller)

29. Can artistic risk taking be fostered through film policies? (Redvall)

30. How essential is it to the survival of a small national film industry that filmmakers continue to take artistic risks? (Redvall)

31. How central have concepts of risk been to the work of such film-commissioning institutions as Channel 4 and the Irish Film Board? (Stoneman)

32. What is the difference, as a film commissioner, between being fearless and being reckless? (Stoneman)

33. What has the impact of the influential photography agency Magnum Photos, founded in 1947, been on the visual norms of photojournalism, particularly with regard to the depiction of risk? (Woodward)

Filmmaking and the Environment

34. What are the key environmental risks associated with filmmaking? (Maxwell and Miller)

35. What role did competitive capitalist practices play in the development of film production as a high-risk activity, in environmental terms? (Maxwell and Miller)

36. What are some of the central examples of environmental despoliation resulting from film production, and what conclusions are we warranted in drawing from the relevant production histories? (Maxwell and Miller)

37. What are the environmental risk implications of the growing tendency for filmmakers to embrace digital technology? (Maxwell and Miller)

38. Is it sufficient for film scholars to take up environmental issues uniquely in terms of the themes/representations of the films they study, or is an entirely different approach called for? (Maxwell and Miller)

The Capaciousness of Risk Studies

As the above list of research questions indicates, risk is a topic that invites exploration from a wide range of perspectives. There is still much work to be done on film and risk, and it is my hope that the present volume will inspire others to further deepen the discussion, or to take it in new directions. Far from being a topic that is likely to be of interest to only one of the factions to which film scholars belong, "risk," I believe, is an inclusive area of inquiry that can accommodate film scholars with quite different priorities and commitments. In taking up risk as a research topic, film scholars who draw on evolutionary psychology to understand film cognition, for example, might relate studies of human beings' genetic dispositions to perceive certain environments as risky to film cognition. Scholars whose interests in film are more cultural, social, and political may well find the concept of risk a useful means of pinpointing the effects of unequal distributions of power, as well as of identifying some of the strategies that have been adopted in response to such inequities. For scholars such as myself, who are interested in practitioner's agency (essentially the ways in which filmmakers subjectively understand their practices), the broadly institutional dimensions of film, and the ways in which these areas intersect, risk is a particularly fruitful research topic. This is so because risk invites us to think in terms of a wide range of factors: genetic endowments linked to evolutionary history, individual self-understandings and actions, social context and culture, and the combined effect, over time, of disparate and uncoordinated activities that nonetheless ultimately intersect.

It is my hope that *Film and Risk* will stimulate some interesting discussions and bring together interlocutors who might not otherwise be inclined to seek each other out. It is also my hope that *Film and Risk* will encourage film scholars to engage seriously with a number of increasingly urgent challenges relating to, among other things, the sustainability of film. Richard Maxwell and Toby Miller's chapter, "Film and the Environment: Risk Offscreen," is, in my view, agenda setting in this regard. To adopt risk as a framework for analysis, their chapter clearly demonstrates, is, potentially, to bring neglected issues warranting serious discussion and urgent attention into sharp focus. The question that *Film and Risk* ultimately asks is this: How credible will film studies, as a discipline, be if film scholars continue to ignore the many risks with which their objects of study are entangled?

Notes

1. Peter L. Bernstein, *Against the Gods: The Remarkable Story of Risk* (New York: John Wiley & Sons, 1998), 1, 3.

2. See Charles Taylor's work on multiple modernities, *Modern Social Imaginaries* (Durham: Duke University Press, 2004).

3. Lucy Mazdon, *Encore Hollywood: Remaking French Cinema* (London: British Film Institute, 2008).

4. Murray Smith, "Gangsters, Cannibals, Aesthetes, or Apparently Perverse Allegiances," in *Passionate Views: Film, Cognition and Emotion*, ed. Carl Plantinga and Greg M. Smith (Baltimore: Johns Hopkins University Press, 1999), 236.

5. Berys Gaut, *Art, Emotion and Ethics* (Oxford: Oxford University Press, 2007), 156.

6. Rod Stoneman, *Chávez: The Revolution Will Not Be Televised: A Case Study of Politics and the Media* (London: Wallflower, 2008), 10, 11.

7. John Sedgwick and Mike Pokorny, "The Risk Environment of Filmmaking: Warner in the Inter-war Period," *Explorations in Economic History* 35 (1998): 196–220.

8. Susan Hayward, *Key Concepts in Cinema Studies* (London: Routledge, 1996); Vivienne Clark, Peter Jones, Bill Malyszko, and David Wharton, *Complete A–Z Media and Film Studies Handbook* (London: Hodder Arnold, 2007).

9. Hayward, *Key Concepts in Cinema Studies,* vii.

10. Kristine Harris, "The New Woman Incident: Cinema, Scandal and Spectacle in 1935 Shanghai," in *Transnational Chinese Cinemas,* ed. Sheldon Hsaio-peng Lu (Honolulu: University of Hawaii Press, 1997), 277.

11. For a fuller discussion of Ruan Lingyu's acting and her contributions to the golden age of Chinese cinema, see Mette Hjort, "Ruan Lingyu: Reflections on an Individual Performance Style," in *Chinese Film Stars,* ed. Yingjin Zhang and Mary Farquhar (London: Routledge, 2010), 32–49.

12. Michael Chang, "The Good, the Bad, and the Beautiful: Movie Actresses and Public Discourse in Shanghai, 1920s–1930s," in *Cinema and Urban Culture in Shanghai, 1922–1943,* ed. Yingjin Zhang (Stanford: Stanford University Press, 1999), 136.

13. Bérénice Reynaud, "Glamour and Suffering: Gong Li and the History of Chinese Stars," in *Women and Film: A Sight and Sound Reader,* ed. Pam Cook and Philip Dodd (London: British Film Institute, 1993), 25.

14. Shu Kei, "La légende de Ruan Lingyu," in *Le cinéma chinois,* ed. Margoli Reclus and Marie-Claire Quiquemelle (Paris: Centre Georges Pompidou, 1984), 152–54.

15. Quoted in Richard Meyer, *Ruan Ling-Yu: The Goddess of Shanghai* (Hong Kong: Hong Kong University Press, 2004), 50.

16. Stuart Jeffries, "Bigger Issues," *Review: South China Sunday Morning Post,* February 21, 2010.

17. In "Out of Action," Clarence Tsui's interview-based article on Jackie Chan, risk taking is very much the thread lending cohesion to the performer's entire career: "His standing as one of the world's most inventive daredevils may be intact but he will be 55 next month; the end of his stunt-driven, high-wire existence is certainly nigh. Chan says he anticipated that a long time ago and that 'it's a miracle that I've survived.'" *PostMagazine, South China Morning Post* (2009), 25. See scmp.com/video for the interview with Jackie Chan as well as clips from his films. Working as I do at Lingnan, an unusually plucky university in Hong Kong, China, mention of Jackie Chan is inevitable: the gymnasium and pool that are prominent features of our institutional landscape were gifts to Lingnan from Chan. These gifts, I like to think, express the performer's recognition of Lingnan as somehow like-minded, as an institution that was built and sustained by especially courageous educators, many of them highly skilled risk takers.

18. David Bordwell, *On the History of Film Style* (Cambridge, MA: Harvard University Press, 1997), 4.

19. See "Women Make Movies" for more information about the film: http://www.wmm.com/filmCatalog/pages/c702.shtml.

20. Lars Movin, "Rum til reflektion," *FILM* 56 (April 2007): 16.

21. For a particularly influential discussion of "general style," to which collective style arguably belongs, see Richard Wollheim, "Pictorial Style: Two Views," in *The Concept of Style,* ed. Berel Lang (Philadelphia: University of Pennsylvania Press, 1979), 129–45.

22. Kiki Kennedy-Day, "Cinema in Lebanon, Syria, Iraq and Kuwait," in *Companion Encyclopedia of Middle Eastern and North African Film,* ed. Oliver Leaman (London: Routledge, 2001), 374.

23. Erlend Clouston, "If I Find One Reel, I Must Kill You," *Guardian,* February, 20, 2008; see http://www.guardian.co.uk/film/2008/feb/20/features.afghanistan.

24. Kennedy-Day, "Cinema in Lebanon, Syria, Iraq and Kuwait," 390.

25. Anand Gopal, "Reel Challenges: Socially Conscious Afghan Filmmakers Brave Censorship, Poverty and Death Threats to Get Their Message Out," *South China Morning Post,* February 5, 2009.

26. Marijke de Valck, *Film Festivals: From European Geopolitics to Global Cinephilia* (Amsterdam: University of Amsterdam Press, 2007).

27. Roger Boyes, "Two Years in Prison for Downloading Latest Film," *Timesonline,* March 24, 2006; see http://technology.timesonline.co.uk/article/0,,20409 –2100973,00.html.

28. *Politiken, FILM,* February 2, 2010. I am very grateful to Peter Schepelern for alerting me to this anecdote.

29. Mark Jones, "The Historical Impact of Organized Crime on American Society," in *Organized Crime: From Trafficking to Terrorism,* ed. Frank Shanty and Patit Maban Mishra (Santa Barbara: ABC Clio, 2005), 22.

30. See Paisley Livingston's *Cinema, Philosophy, Bergman: On Film as Philosophy* (Oxford: Oxford University Press, 2009), 63–83; and Berys Gaut, "Film, Authorship and Collaboration," in *Film Theory and Philosophy,* ed. Murray Smith and Richard Allen (Oxford: Clarendon, 1997).

31. Livingston, *Cinema, Philosophy, Bergman,* 72.

32. Lars Movin, "Barefoot Reporter in Burma," *FILM* 64 (November 2008): 3.

33. Cited in ibid.

34. Lars Movin, "Thank You, Google Earth," *FILM* 64 (November 2008): 6.

35. For a much more ample discussion of this material, see Mette Hjort, *Lone Scherfig's "Italian for Beginners"* (Seattle: University of Washington Press, 2010).

36. Ibid., 62.

37. Jon Herskovitz, "Abducted S Korean film director dies," *Indian express.com,* April 13, 2006, http://www.indianexpress.com/news/abducted-s-korean-film-director-dies/2299/0.

38. "Shin Sang Ok, 80; S. Korean Director Abducted by North," *Los Angeles Times,* April 14, 2006, http://articles.latimes.com/2006/apr/14/local/me-shin14.

39. Jiang Zhuqing and Wang Shanshan, "Filming Ban Aims to Protect Scenic Areas," *China Daily,* May 13, 2006, 1–2, http://www.chinadaily.com.cn/china/2006–05/13/content_589018.htm.

40. "Film Producers Make Green Pledge After Promise Incident," *People's Daily Online*, March 13, 2006, http://english.peopledaily.com.cn/200605/13/print20060513_265173.html.

41. See, for example, Yuriko Saito's "The Aesthetics of Unscenic Nature," in *Nature, Aesthetics, and Environmentalism: From Beauty to Duty*, ed. Allen Carlson and Sheila Lintott (New York: Columbia University Press, 2008), 238–53.

42. Jiang and Wang, "Filming Ban," 2.

43. For a discussion of risk positions, see Ulrich Beck, *Risk Society: Towards a New Modernity*, trans. Mark Ritter (Thousand Oaks, CA: Sage, 1992), 26.

METTE HJORT

Flamboyant Risk Taking

Why Some Filmmakers Embrace Avoidable and Excessive Risks

While many scholarly books and articles devoted to film make passing reference to risk, no attempt has been made systematically to explore filmmaking as a process involving the actual taking of risks as well as the depiction of risk taking. As a mostly cost-intensive, collaborative activity that spans the worlds of commerce and art and aims to engage large numbers of people—often in a range of different places—filmmaking is necessarily caught up with, at the very least, economic risks. That the phenomenon of risk should be rather neglected in the scholarly literature on film is in many ways surprising, given how central it is to any number of other disciplines, many of them relevant to the study of film. Risk, after all, is a concept that economists, sociologists, and anthropologists consider crucial, as their already voluminous and still growing literature on the topic clearly indicates.

"Risk" is not only a technical term used by experts and scholars, but one that figures centrally in the kinds of discourses that shape and inform everyday life. As John Tulloch and Deborah Lupton point out, risk has come to assume significance for "'non-experts' or 'lay people'" as a result of a "climate of heightened awareness and publicity about risk."[1] Filmmakers, it would seem, are well aware of the pervasive interest in risk that is a feature of life in most parts of the world today, for risks and risk taking are recurring themes in both fictional and nonfictional films. New Zealand director Roger Donaldson's biopic *The World's Fastest Indian* (2005) is a good example of a fully blown thematic treatment of risk through filmmaking. Focusing on the motorbike racer Burt Munro, Donaldson's film explores risk taking as a way of life and as a precondition for setting the racing records the New

Zealander achieved. In addition to the many films that foreground risk as the main theme, there are countless films that make passing—yet striking—reference to risk, some of them reflexively so, as a comment on the risks of filmmaking.[2] *Mr Bean's Holiday* (dir. Steve Bendelack, 2007) for example, concludes with the character played by Willem Dafoe narcissistically intoning the creative risks that filmmakers of a certain caliber necessarily and admirably take. And in *Sprængfarlig bombe* (Clash of Egos, dir. Tomas Villum Jensen, 2006), a parodic take on Lars von Trier, and especially his art-film attitudes, the filmmaker Claus Volter responds to the poor performance of his new film at the box office, and to his girlfriend's concerns about his producer's resulting financial problems, with a laconic, "That's the way it is. We risk ourselves artistically. He risks himself economically." It is not difficult to think of any number of other examples of cinematic depictions of risk, both reflexive and nonreflexive. The point, though, is that filmmakers' clear interest in risk has not prompted the scholarly uptake that is in fact warranted.

I am not interested in speculating about the reasons why risk has played a negligible role in film scholarship to date. More interesting, in my view, is the task of understanding what film scholars stand to gain by focusing some of their critical efforts on the complicated phenomenon of risk. In this chapter the intention is to begin to explore several research questions:

1. What are the different available models for thinking about risk, and how is the multifaceted phenomenon of risk best approached in the context of film?

2. What are the implications of relative degrees of risk discernability in various films? In some films the risks taken to produce them are indiscernible; in other cases the element of risk is manifestly present in the finished film, as a result of the film's "aboutness" or its visual style; and there are also cases of filmmakers working hard not only to take risks that are in fact avoidable but to foreground or even magnify them through a process of flamboyant risk taking.

3. What are the different types of risk that arise in connection with film?

4. Why do some filmmakers relinquish favorable "risk positions" in order to take up unfavorable risk positions involving what are in fact both avoidable and excessive risks?[3]

5. What are the ethical implications of risk taking in film?

　　　　　　　　　　　　　　　　　　　　　　　Mette Hjort

6. Have attitudes toward risk in filmmaking milieus changed significantly in the course of film's history, and what do any such changes tell us about cultural shifts regarding the understanding of risk?

7. Is there a conceptually precise way of distinguishing between meaningful risk taking that warrants affirmation and risk taking that is ultimately problematic and less than admirable?

I develop my argument in three stages. I begin by saying a few words about existing approaches to risk and how they might be relevant to work on film. I go on to consider the question of risk discernability in connection with documentary filmmaking. In the final section I look at the phenomenon of flamboyant risk taking and at the issue of risk positions as it arises in documentary films with a subjective or performative dimension. Flamboyant risk taking has ethical implications, as we shall see. An account of this particular kind of risk taking also brings into focus the extent to which attitudes toward risk have changed in the course of film's history and provides an opportunity to consider how we might distinguish between meaningful and less than admirable forms of risk taking. Finally, through its clear links to contexts of affluence, stability, and security, the phenomenon of flamboyant risk taking invites a comparative perspective on the realities of cinematic agency. It invites us to acknowledge the genuine diversity of cinematic agency and the extent to which practitioner's agency in the cinema is shaped by the constraints and opportunities of very specific cultural and political contexts.

APPROACHES TO RISK AND THEIR RELEVANCE FOR THE UNDERSTANDING OF FILM

Jens O. Zinn, a key figure in the University of Kent–based Social Contexts and Responses to Risk Network (SCARR), has provided useful literature reviews detailing different approaches to risk, and surveys of some of the same material are also available in Deborah Lupton's *Risk,* in John Tulloch and Lupton's *Risk and Everyday Life,* and in Pat Caplan's edited volume *Risk Revisited.*[4] While the research on risk involves many competing positions and nuanced arguments, it is fair to say that there is a divide between two quite different traditions of thought, one defined by a mix of economic, mathematical, and cognitive psychological models, and the other by various sociocultural and anthropological premises and approaches. For present purposes it suffices briefly to evoke the first of these two traditions, whereas a slightly more differentiated account is helpful in the case of the second. Zinn rightly notes, "Economic approaches are primarily based on rational actor models and the assumption that people make deliberative choices between alternatives. From this perspective, risk (where it is assumed that the alternatives can be understood as outcomes to which probabilities can be attached) is a special case of decision-making under uncertainty, where the probability of an event or the full range of outcomes is not known."[5] Though a comprehensive and critical examination of economic, mathematical, and cognitive psychological models is beyond the scope and purpose of this chapter (and indeed my competence), it is worth noting that such models do represent a tradition of thought that has contributed to what Lupton calls "technico-scientific approaches to risk."[6] In addition to bracketing what anthropologist Mary Douglas calls "the dirty side of the subject" of risk taking[7]—the activity's connections to politics and morals—these approaches are seen as favoring a model of individual agency and a highly normative concept of rationality. The latter supports a sharp distinction between expert and lay conceptions of risk and risk taking, with lay reasoning typically being found deficient. As Tulloch and Lupton remark, "[T]hose drawing on the work of Tversky and Kahneman . . . have tended to represent lay people as deficient in their abilities, [and as] drawing on 'irrational' assumptions when making judgements about such phenomena as risk."[8] Following Tversky and Kahneman, the deficiencies are caused by the layperson's allegedly irrational use of heuristic principles (such as "representativeness" or "availability") when deliberating about risk.[9]

Aspects of the decision-theoretical, econometric, and game-theoretical models of risk perception and risk taking have been called into question by influential anthropologists, sociologists, and cultural theorists who contend that the complexities of risk are best understood by emphasizing social structures, social processes, and culture. Thus, for example, the German sociologist and systems theorist Niklas Luhmann has argued that whereas agents are able actually to recognize some real risks, and thus to deliberate about the extent to which they are worth taking, they entirely overlook or ignore other real risks, and this in a way that is systematically correlated with social frameworks.[10] According to Luhmann, narrowly individualistic models of human agency and rationality do not allow us to grasp the reasons why some risks are perceivable, and possibly even salient, while others remain invisible. Following this line of reasoning, decisive factors influencing the very discernability of risks are to be sought at the level of social contexts.

                                                                Mette Hjort

Mary Douglas similarly claims that "it is impossible to make sense of the concept of risk in the compartmentalized, individualistic frame of analysis normally employed."[11] Douglas and her coauthor Aaron Wildavsky are credited with having articulated one of the "central theories of sociological risk research," what Zinn calls the "Risk and Culture approach." The "grid/group scheme" associated with Douglas and Wildavsky emphasizes "the degree to which an individual's life is circumscribed by externally imposed descriptions" and "the extent to which people are driven by or restricted in thought and action by their commitment to a social unit larger than that of the individual."[12]

The "Risk Society approach" developed by Ulrich Beck provides another influential sociological account of risk. Beck's research focuses on the specificity of risk in a postindustrial age. The claim, more specifically, is that the project of modernity, which found expression in various processes of industrialization, produced a new type of risk: border-defying "global" and "glocal" risks. These risks are the negative and unintended consequences of the pursuit of scientific and instrumental rationality, and are seen to define a genuinely new historical situation: "It is . . . true that risks are not an invention of modernity. Anyone who set out to discover new countries and continents—like Columbus—certainly accepted 'risks.' But these were *personal* risks, not global dangers like those that arise for all of humanity from nuclear fission or the storage of radioactive waste. In that earlier period, the word 'risk' had a note of bravery and adventure, not the threat of self-destruction of all life on Earth."[13] Whereas industrial society was concerned with the "distribution of goods," risk society is necessarily focused on the "distribution of 'bads' or dangers."[14] Risk society, Beck argues, is necessarily a "world risk society" and a "catastrophic society" where "the focus is more and more on hazards . . . that require the 'sensory organs' of science . . . *in order to become visible or interpretable as hazards at all.*" In Beck's analysis risk is caught up with what he calls "reflexive modernization": "*Risk* may be defined as a *systematic way of dealing with hazards and insecurities induced and introduced by modernization itself.* Risks, as opposed to older dangers, are consequences which relate to the threatening force of modernization and to its globalization of doubt. They are *politically reflexive.*" According to Beck, risk society generates its own affective dispositions, most importantly a "commonality of anxiety" and "solidarity from anxiety," the latter being constitutive of a new political force that is unique to risk society.[15] In spite of his insistence on the global and glocal dimensions of contemporary risk formations, Beck does acknowledge the continued relevance of socioeconomic differences, especially in connection with risk positions, the latter being shaped, in his view, by such factors as geographic location, income, race, gender, and so on.

As Zinn points out, Lupton and Tulloch's contributions to the understanding of risk can be seen as building on some of the insights of the "Risk and Culture" approach.[16] At the same time, it is important to note that much of their work is informed by a productive rejection of some of Beck's central theses. Beck, for example, tends to portray the "human actor" as "anxious about and fearful of risk,"[17] and while this conception makes sense in the context of an exclusive focus on global risks, it cannot ultimately do justice to the full range of risk behaviors or risk perceptions, and certainly not in the context of film. With its emphasis on attributions of positive value to risk, and on risk taking as a genuinely agential phenomenon involving decisions and a degree of control, Tulloch and Lupton's empirical investigation of "the [positive] meanings that people give to voluntary risk-taking" charts a research path that departs from the one explored by Beck.[18] Another point of disagreement with Beck concerns the continued pertinence of concepts of class, nation, race, and gender to the understanding of risk. Although Beck claims that risk and wealth are both "the object of distributions" and "constitute positions—risk positions and class positions respectively," and although he recognizes that "extreme poverty and extreme risk" are systematically connected, the very concept of a risk society is one that gives priority to global risks that cut across divides.[19] Tulloch and Lupton are among a growing number of researchers who see what Beck calls "the old categories . . . of the normal world of nation-state modernity" as necessary elements in a comprehensive understanding of the phenomenon of risk.[20]

In the present context, where the aim is ultimately to shed some light on what I call "flamboyant risk taking," and this in the context of (especially contemporary) documentary filmmaking, the following insights derived from the theoretical paradigms on offer are helpful:

- Reasoning about risk is *anticipatory* and *probabilistic* and involves an element of *uncertainty*.

- "As mathematical calculations . . . risks are related directly and indirectly to cultural definitions and standards," making it difficult to discuss risk without considering norms and values.[21]

- Nonexpert or lay reasoning about risk is worthy of study, in part because such reasoning affords insight into the cultural and normative dimensions of risk.

- There are different types of risk, global as distinct from personal risks,[22] but also environmental risks, lifestyle risks, medical risks, interpersonal risks, economic risks, and criminal risks,[23] among many others.

                                                              Mette Hjort

- Risks may be constitutive of negative emotions, such as anxiety,[24] but may also be causally linked to a number of positive emotions,[25] to a sense of self-efficacy and creativity.

- Agents' exposure to and ability to cope with risk are to some extent determined by risk positions, which positions are themselves shaped by socioeconomic factors, among others.[26]

With this composite picture of risk in place, it is now appropriate to take up the next task on the agenda, which is to consider the matter of risk and its discernability in the context of documentary film. I am interested, more specifically, in the degree to which risk taking, on the part of one or more of the various film practitioners who count as a given film's coauthors, is discernible in the relevant film. My aim in evoking a number of quite different cinematic examples is to highlight two distinct issues: the role that concepts of risk play in the process of understanding and evaluating certain films; and the extent to which risk has emerged as a kind of "virtue" concept in the course of the history of film. With regard to the first of these two issues, I have a spectrum ranging from (a) through (e) in mind:

(a) Films that do not explicitly refer to risk taking on the part of the film's author or coauthors, and that do not display or represent any risk taking on their part. Contextual information regarding the production histories of these films will not bring to light any unusual forms of risk taking on the part of the films' makers, and thus a concept of risk can be deemed irrelevant to both the viewer's ability to make sense of the films and to the viewer's assessment of these films according to aesthetic but also moral or ethical norms.

(b) Films that do not explicitly call attention to risk taking on the part of the film's author or coauthors, although contextual information regarding the production histories of these films is likely to bring to light unusual or significant degrees of risk taking. A concept of risk is thus irrelevant to the viewer's ability to make sense of the films, but not to the viewer's assessment of these films according to especially moral or ethical standards.

(c) Films that do not foreground risk taking on the part of the film's author or coauthors, but do require viewers to *infer* real risk taking in order properly to understand the films, and to appreciate the achievements of their makers.

(d) Films that *foreground* risk, often through explicit commentary, thereby requiring viewers to work with a concept of risk taking in the course of the cognitive, affective, and evaluative processes of cinematic reception. The pursuit of contextual information regarding the films' production histories establishes consonance between the levels and types of risks that are foregrounded and those that were actually taken. A concept of risk is relevant both to the viewer's capacity to understand the films and to his or her assessment of them in terms of especially moral or ethical standards.

(e) Films that (like [d]) *foreground* risk, often through explicit commentary, thereby requiring viewers to work with a concept of risk taking in the course of the cognitive, affective, and evaluative processes of cinematic reception. The pursuit of contextual information regarding the films' production histories fails (in contrast to [d]) to establish consonance between the levels and types of risks that are foregrounded and those that were actually taken. A concept of risk in these cases is relevant both to the viewer's capacity to follow the films, and to his or her (presumably to some degree negative) assessment of them in terms of especially moral or ethical standards

In the next section, devoted to the discernability of risk in film, I shall focus on the questions of inference (c) and foregrounding (d), before briefly considering an example in which the failure to display or represent real and serious risks can be said to count as a significant ethical failing (b).

Risk Discernability in Film

Case Type (c)

While some films do not require a *focal awareness* of the realities of cinematic risk to be fully understood or appreciated, the intended effects of others quite clearly depend on viewers' ability to grasp the connections between cinematic images and the often physical risks that accompanied their production, and to do so through inferential reasoning based on an understanding of the basic principles of filmmaking. A much-acclaimed documentary by emerging Danish filmmaker Asger Leth makes the point. In *Ghosts of Cité Soleil* (2006), Leth—the son of veteran filmmaker Jørgen Leth—documents the activities of vigilante militias in Cité Soleil, a slum just outside the Haitian capital, and events leading to and following the ousting of President Aristide in 2004.[27] Risk of death is a recurrent theme in the discourse that now accompanies Leth's noteworthy film. Mediating the film to audiences, the "Director's Note" foregrounds extreme physical risk as a key element in its production history and, by implication, as a factor relevant to viewers' responses: "The film was shot during the most tumultuous times of 2004 and would never have been possible without the immense talent, heart and raw courage of Miloš Lonćarevič, the film's young Serbian co-director and cinematographer who would risk his life again and again in one of the most dangerous and fascinating places anywhere."[28] Comments in *Variety* similarly foreground risk, and in a way that explicitly

                                                        Mette Hjort

links Leth's achievement as a filmmaker to the physical risks that he took, and survived: "There has never been anything quite like Asger Leth's film *Ghosts of Cité Soleil;* it's amazing it even exists and that the director is still alive."[29]

During the first moments of *Ghosts of Cité Soleil* an intertitle informs the viewer that Cité Soleil is a site of extreme danger. This point is not explicitly made, however, throughout the film, and the discernability of extreme risk thus depends on audiences' capacity to reason effectively about the causal history of the images they see. Risk discernability in this instance arises in a process of *explicitation* in the context of reception. Yet there are also many examples of filmmakers explicitly *foregrounding* the element of risk that is constitutive of their projects. In cases where risk has become a defining feature of what David Bordwell calls the "biographical legend" of filmmakers,[30] we are often dealing with risks that are excessive in the sense that they clearly lie beyond the threshold of acceptable risks for most film practitioners. This kind of risk taking has a willful quality to it and is, at some important level, very much what the filmmaking is all about. In the context of film, then, it is helpful to distinguish between *inevitable risks, avoidable risks,* and *excessive risks,* the point being to draw attention to those film practitioners who, for whatever reason, gravitate toward both avoidable and excessive risks with the intention of calling attention to a strong preference for risk. I take the term "inevitable risks" to refer to risks that tend to be recurrent across different film productions in specific cultural contexts, and thus a matter of common knowledge among particular communities of filmmakers—the risk of adverse weather conditions, illness, and escalating costs in one part of the world, the risk of government interference in another. "Avoidable risks" and "excessive risks," by contrast, signal filmmaking situations in which filmmakers have opted to pursue projects that bring a range of additional risks to the standard situation. These risks count as excessive to the extent that the probabilistic reasoning involved in their assessment would lead most filmmakers within a given community to eschew them and to opt for a different kind of film project. In this sense "excessive" signals a departure from a norm.

Case Type (d)

It is almost impossible not to mention Werner Herzog in this context, for as Paul Cronin points out in his remarkable interview book, *Herzog on Herzog,* this key contributor to the New German Cinema has developed over the years a "reputation as a risk-taker, [as] someone who goes to extremes."[31] To some extent this reputation is based on production anecdotes such as this:

Some years ago when I [Werner Herzog] was directing an opera, I wanted to have a stuntman crashing down from the rigging twenty-two metres above the stage, as if a mountain climber had fallen from a rock face. The problem was that he had to hit a very narrow space: an opening in the floor with a large cushion underneath. It was proving to be very difficult to hit this spot from such a height. We could not afford a stuntman, and as *nobody wanted to take responsibility of testing this fall* [emphasis added], I had myself hoisted up. From an altitude of about thirty-five feet I jumped down and got severe whiplash in my neck. I realized that it was just ridiculous to try from fifty feet, and immediately scrapped the whole idea of the jump.[32]

Herzog's reputation as a risk taker is, however, also based on films that make *salient* the director's preference for the category of avoidable and excessive risks. In response to Herzog's insistence on the acute need to confront what he regards as the dangers involved in a serious "lack of adequate imagery" in contemporary image culture, Cronin says, "And there are few filmmakers who are willing to take the necessary risks."[33] Herzog's concurrence with this remark helps to explain a film such as *La Soufrière*, a thirty-minute documentary from 1977 in which Herzog and his cinematographer, Edward Lachman, explore, at times with themselves in the frame, an island that awaits a volcanic explosion that experts at the time called an "inevitable catastrophe."

The Herzog example prefigures an important, and in my view insufficiently explored, *recent* development in documentary filmmaking, *flamboyant risk taking*, a defining feature of which is the *display* of the film practitioner's subjective involvement with avoidable and excessive risks. A well-known example of what I have in mind is the Oscar-nominated indie film directed and produced by Morgan Spurlock, *Supersize Me*. In this 2004 film, viewers watch the effects of Spurlock's attempt to prove a thesis about the current epidemic of obesity by following rules of his own devising: for thirty days the filmmaker will eat and drink only from the McDonald's menu; he will eat three meals a day; he will try everything on the McDonald's menu at least once; if asked whether he wishes to "supersize" his meal, he will respond in the affirmative; and finally, he will move his body only as much as the average American body moves per day. As is well known, the film documents the impact of Spurlock's self-imposed junk food regime—the dramatic weight gain, the stress on internal organs, and the impairment of bodily functions to the point of serious medical concern.

Case Type (b)

We begin to get a sense of just how different contemporary attitudes toward risk are from those of the earliest filmmakers if we recall some of the controversies that now surround what is typically considered the first feature-length documentary, Robert Flaherty's *Nanook of the North* (1922). Allegedly documenting the life of the Inuit Nanook, Flaherty staged much of the action of the film. In doing so, he drew on many of the suggestions proposed by Nanook himself, who thus counts as one of the coauthors of the film, following a collective model of cinematic authorship. Some of the relevant stagings involved exposing Nanook and his fellow Inuit to considerable risks, and in some instances the risk taking also encompassed the director and cameraman Flaherty. For example, although the Inuit relied on rifles for hunting by the time Flaherty made his film, the decision was made to stage and document earlier, more traditional, and far more dangerous methods. In a text titled *"How I Filmed Nanook of the North,"* Flaherty remembers that Nanook and his fellow huntsmen expressed anxiety about being pulled into the water while hunting with a harpoon, and that they urged the filmmaker to allow the hunt to be concluded by rifle: "For a long time it was nip and tuck—repeatedly the crew called to me to use the gun—but the camera crank was my only interest then and I pretended not to understand."[34] Flaherty has been much criticized in recent times for exposing the Inuit in his film to excessive risks, and for obscuring this aspect of his film.[35] The point is that risks qualifying as both avoidable and excessive made *Nanook of the North* possible, and these risks were *obscured* rather than *foregrounded* by the film's director. The authorial attitude evident in this earliest of feature-length documentary films is, in short, the very antithesis of that of flamboyant risk taking. When contrasted with the clear discernability of risk in a film such as *Supersize Me,* the indiscernability of risk in *Nanook of the North* tells us something about how cultural attitudes toward risk have shifted in the course of time. In a contemporary context, the *spectacle* of risk taking based on avoidable and excessive risks is potentially a source of various goods—influence, prestige, fame, money, and, not trivially, social change. The tendency today, at least in some cultures, is not to obscure or hide risks, but to foreground them.

I would like now to turn to three quite different examples of flamboyant risk taking in the context of documentary film: *Living with Hunger, Ethiopia* (dir. Sorious Samura, 2004), *Smiling in a Warzone: The Art of Flying to Kabul* (dir. Simone Aaberg Kærn and Magnus Bejmar, 2005), and *Get a Life* (dir. Michael Klint, 2003). To varying degrees, these films involve a contrived setup, a mix of expert and nonexpert understandings of risk, and a display of risk that is subject to assessment in ethical terms. Within the more general context of interdisciplinary research on risk, these films offer precious insight into the ways in which filmmakers understand the *display* of risk as a means of achieving certain goals. These films further highlight the relevance of assessing risk taking in terms that are not merely a matter of *logical* precision, as theorists such as Tversky and Kahneman would have it, but of *ethical* principles and cultural norms. A risk-focused analysis of these films also has something to contribute to a quite different area of research, that of the theory and history of documentary film. Concepts of risk make it possible, for example, to identify certain (emerging) regularities in the landscape of documentary filmmaking, and to illustrate and clarify central problems pertaining to the ethics of documentary filmmaking. When discussed comparatively, that is, in relation to each other, and with passing reference to other films and filmmakers, these three films also help us to see that the desire to be seen as a risk taker—to the point, perhaps, of passing off trivial risk taking as genuine and meaningful risk taking—may well have a sociocultural, socioeconomic, or sociopolitical basis.

Risk Taking and Activism

I want to begin by looking at flamboyant risk taking as a form of cinematic activism, and in this connection the work of Sierra Leonean director Sorious Samura is of interest. In addition to *Living with Hunger,* to be considered here, Samura has directed *Cry Freetown, Return to Freetown, Out of Africa, Living with AIDS, Living with Refugees, Living with Corruption,* and *Living with Illegals,* and in each case it has been a matter of the filmmaker taking considerable risks for the sake of his film, and for the sake of the social and political project to which the film contributes. An Insight News Television Production of 2004 *Living with Hunger,* winner of Emmy and Bafta awards, shows Samura preparing to leave the comforts of his London life to join families who are just barely managing to survive in Ethiopia. Much as in the case of *Supersize Me,* this fifty-minute documentary involves a self-imposed framework of rules or constraints. Samura pledges to eat only what his almost starving host families eat, and this for a period of one month. Although the host families receive food aid, the meager supplies last only two weeks rather than the two months that official schedules dictate. Like the families with which he lives, Samura thus finds himself surviving on wild cabbage, a local weed with virtually no nutritional content. The filmmaker loses nineteen kilograms (almost forty-two pounds) in a few weeks by eating what his host families eat. During a thirty-seven-kilometer (almost twenty-three-mile) walk in which he accompanies two

　　　　　　　　　　　　　　　　　　　　　　　　　

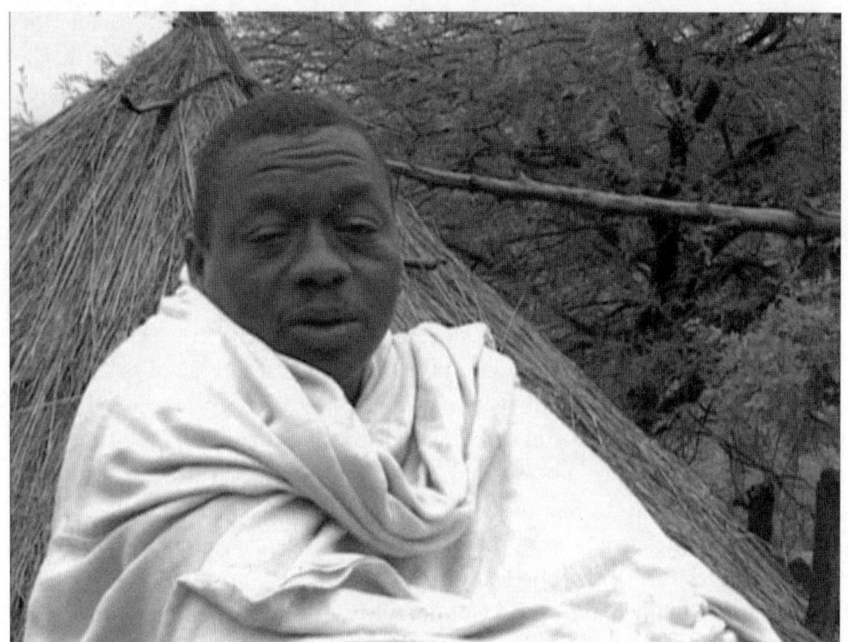

Sorious Samura on the verge of collapse after "living with hunger" in Ethiopia.

Ethiopians in search of work, he collapses and experiences a medical crisis that initially looks like a heart attack to his producer, Charlotte Metcalf.

Metcalf, who had been making films in Africa for a decade by the time she produced *Living with Hunger,* explains that the point of the film was to draw attention to the kind of food crisis that is rarely recognized—not to an *acute* food crisis leading to widespread death (and therefore widespread news coverage), but to the plight of millions who survive while facing hunger on a daily and long-term basis. Metcalf does not see *Living with Hunger* as a picture of hopelessness, but as an action-motivating image of tenacity and resourcefulness under virtually unimaginable but by no means unchangeable circumstances. According to Metcalf, she wanted to tell an important story about hunger that would be compelling to viewers by making the documentary filmmaker Samura "the story itself." Reflecting on Samura's physical distress in the course of the filmmaking process, Metcalf notes: "I did worry, but there wasn't really a lot we could do, except go with it because it was all part of the story. And it was one of those terrible dilemmas you get in films sometimes. . . . The more dehydrated and ill and uncomfortable he got, the better it was for the film, because [we understood] what those people were going through every single day of their lives."[36]

With these prefatory and descriptive remarks in place, let us cast a more analytic look at risk and its function within the overall project that *Living with Hunger* constitutes. In this film Samura chooses to exchange a favorable risk position, linked to his life in the West as a successful documentary filmmaker, for a risk position that is highly unfavorable and associated with extreme poverty. The main risks entailed by this new risk position are personal and physical, linked to the impact of hunger. While it is possible to predict the hunger itself, it is impossible to know for sure how the filmmaker's body will respond to it, especially over a thirty-day period. And it is in this "peculiar, intermediate state between security and destruction"[37] that we find the element of uncertainty that is characteristic of risk and risk taking. While the trading of risk positions cannot be fully achieved within the adopted framework—inasmuch as Samura, his producer, and the members of the film crew all know that medical interventions and assistance are ultimately available to Samura—the risks taken by the filmmaker *are* real. Not only are these risks real, they are also unnecessary and thus excessive when viewed in terms of the far more favorable risk position that is in fact available to the filmmaker, and is indeed his under normal circumstances.

Samura's adoption of an unfavorable risk position brings to mind some of the techniques described by Bill Nichols in connection with the documentary filmmaker who seeks to move "from a position of separation from those he or she represents to a position of commonality with them" for the purposes of achieving a more appropriate documentary ethics.[38] In *Living with Hunger* that commonality is achieved through a process of physical transformation with genuine risks, and as a result the gains achieved by moving from a position of "*I* speak about *them* to *you*" to "*I or We speak about us to you*" are significant.[39] In addition to an empathetic perspective that overcomes the ethically troubling aspects of what Susan Dwyer calls a "rabidly third person perspective,"[40] Samura's risk taking produces an argument for social and political change. The force of this argument, its capacity to persuade and thus motivate action, derives to a very significant extent from the filmmaker's willingness to put himself in harm's way. In the context of *Living with Hunger,* Samura's body is very much a sacrificial body, and it is the filmmaker's willingness to sacrifice health, and possibly even his life, that lends rhetorical force to the activist cinematic argument in favor of change. Sacrifice, in the form of unnecessary personal and physical risk taking, underscores the filmmaker's commitment to his thesis and challenges the viewer, if not to match this commitment, then at least to respond appropriately to it by undertaking actions that follow logically from witnessing suffering.

Because flamboyant risk taking draws attention to the *person* who opts to make a performance of his or her risk taking, this type of filmmaking is open to charges of narcissism and self-indulgence. In the case of *Living with Hunger* the filmmaker is shielded from such charges by the film's actual effects. Equally relevant is the filmmaker's track record over a significant period of time. *Living with Hunger* is part of a much larger "living with" project in which Samura has taken significant life-threatening risks again and again. This longer-term project, it is fair to say, provides indisputable evidence of the sincerity of the activist commitments to which the filmmaker lays claim in *Living with Hunger.*

Let me turn now to my next example, Simone Aaberg Kærn and Magnus Bejmar's *Smiling in a Warzone: The Art of Flying to Kabul.* As we shall see, the charges of narcissism and self-indulgence have some real purchase in this case.

Risk Taking as Narcissism

The role played by risk in performance artist Simone Aaberg Kærn and radio and TV journalist Magnus Bejmar's *Smiling in a War Zone: The Art of Flying to Kabul* is quite different. This film documents the couple's flight in a small, canvas-covered Piper Colt from Copenhagen to Kabul in 2002, a journey taking several months. The Kabul project was conceived in the wake of 9/11, when airspace became heavily militarized. Having previously made the skies her field of artistic practice,[41] Aaberg Kærn decided to reclaim the skies as a performance project when she read about Farial, a sixteen-year-old girl in Kabul who expressed her dream of becoming a fighter pilot to a Danish journalist working in Afghanistan.[42] Aaberg Kærn determined to fly to Kabul, her intention being to broker permission to enter various militarized airspaces along the way in order ultimately to give Farial the opportunity to fly the Piper Colt. The 6,000-kilometer (3,728-mile) trip and the proposed flight with the sixteen-year-old are framed as performance art throughout. As Aaberg Kærn puts it: "If Farial flies over her town in this plane, it will be a performance, an artwork, a statement for the power of the free story in a U.S. Air Force war zone."

Aaberg Kærn sees *Smiling in a Warzone* as an instance of what she calls "extreme expressionism," with the term "extreme" referencing risk.[43] Risk is made salient from the moment of the project's conception through to the arrival in Kabul. At the outset of the film we hear Aaberg Kærn saying: "I have to go now before things stabilize in Kabul" and "We must go now before the war is over." We hear an exchange between Aaberg Kærn

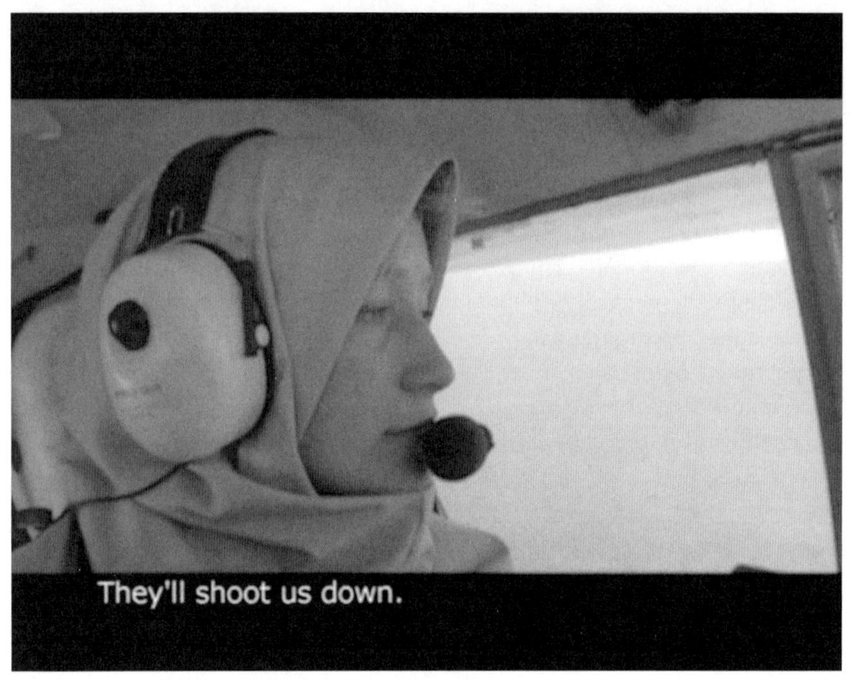

Simone Aaberg Kærn flies into Afghan airspace without permission.

and her partner, who would have liked to bring along both a parachute and a bulletproof vest. Aaberg Kærn's voice-over remarks that both had to be left behind, since a Piper Colt can carry only forty kilos' (eighty-eight pounds') worth of luggage. Commenting on a performance project with some Turkish pilots, which is "nested," to use Paisley Livingston's term,[44] within the larger project, Aaberg Kærn foregrounds the risk of death: "Interception flying with fighter planes is just as prohibited as it is lethal. So if we succeed it's instant art." The most crucial sequence, however, focuses on Aaberg Kærn's attempts to leave Iran, where she has overstayed her welcome, and to enter Afghanistan, where U.S. military personnel refuse to grant her permission to enter the airspace under their control. Her American interlocutor, whose voice is heard by the viewer, explains that if she opts to enter Afghan airspace without permission, she will be classified either "as an unknown or as a hostile," both classifications involving considerable danger. With no option but to leave Iran, and nowhere else to go but Afghanistan, Aaberg Kærn devises a high-risk exit strategy that ultimately succeeds. In sum, if a theme constitutes a film's essential aboutness, then the theme of *Smiling in a Warzone* is the extreme (and thus unusual) risks taken by its two cinematic coauthors.

Mette Hjort

The theme of personal and especially physical risks prompts a question that the filmmakers do attempt to answer: Why? That is, what makes the risk taking subjectively rational to these filmmakers? What do they hope to achieve with their extreme risk taking? The answer that is actually articulated by the filmmakers resembles the one given in connection with *Living with Hunger,* but this putatively activist intent is called into question by other aspects of the film. Referring to the performance concept that structures the film, Bejmar evokes the goal of somehow changing reality: "if you prod reality a bit by adding a new element to it, it shifts, which forces you to look at it differently. So it is with Simone, the flyer. She is the object we add to the world, that people have to relate to as we go along."[45] In the course of the film, Aaberg Kærn articulates various self-understandings: as an artist intent on challenging militarized realities, as a feminist intent on providing Muslim girls with a positive role model, and as a generous and courageous altruist willing to carry gifts of opportunity and freedom halfway around the world without expecting anything in return. Yet the returns on Aaberg Kærn's project of personal risk taking have been considerable. Of these, artistic recognition, in the form of numerous awards, is no doubt particularly significant inasmuch as it considerably enhances the opportunities for further artistic pursuits.

The sincerity of the film's rhetoric of virtue is called into question by the filmmakers' consistent manifestation of seriously deficient reasoning about central ethical issues of documentary filmmaking. And the doubts that the film itself prompts about the filmmakers' intentions only intensify when contextual knowledge concerning the absence of a track record of serious and effective activism is brought into the evaluative picture. While numerous ethical deficiencies are apparent in the film, one is particularly salient by virtue of its direct relation to the flamboyant thematic of risk. Involving as it does a commitment to the performance concept of "prod[ding] reality," Aaberg Kærn's project includes a troubling interpersonal dimension that requires strangers to take risks that they themselves see as unwarranted, irresponsible, and unnecessary—in short, as both avoidable and excessive. The manipulative and instrumental aspect of Kærn's flamboyant risk taking is particularly evident in a painful exchange between the pilot and an official who refuses to grant her permission to enter Sarajevo:

KÆRN: This is a cultural flight. It's in your interest to let it go through. . . .

MILITARY OFFICIAL: Try to understand. I have my job. I have my life. I have my family. I need to work correctly with my duty. I reject your flight. Your request.

This poignant rejoinder to what is perceived as a self-indulgent request brings some of the potential problems of flamboyant risk taking into clear focus. In its more narcissistic incarnations, flamboyant risk taking is troubling because the risk taker's actions generate new and unnecessary risks for *others*—for individuals who do not have the luxury of deciding that it might be socially and politically fruitful, or quite simply interesting and self-affirming, to step outside the risk position that is normally theirs.

BANAL RISK TAKING AND FALSE DISPLAY

My last example of flamboyant risk taking is Michael Klint's *Get a Life*, a film made according to Lars von Trier's documentarist code for so-called dogumentarism. A spin-off of the Dogma 95 concept and its "Vow of Chastity" (requiring filmmakers to abide by ten rules), the dogumentary idea was announced by Lars von Trier in 2001. The dogumentary manifesto imposed nine rules on filmmakers, including "All clips must be marked with 6.12 frames of black (Unless they are a clip in real time, that is a direct clip in a multi-camera filming situation)" and "The end of the film must consist of two minutes of free speaking time by the film's 'victim.' This 'victim' alone shall advise regarding the content and must approve this part of the finished film. If there is no opposition by any of the collaborators, there will be no 'victim' or 'victims.' To explain this, there will be text inserted at the end of the film."[46] Like *Smiling in a Warzone, Get a Life*, produced by Zentropa Real, allows us to identify some of the ways in which a project of flamboyant risk taking can fail. In this case the failure has to do with the foregrounding of risks that are in fact minor, given the risk taker's favorable risk position.

Get a Life is framed by sequences showing cameraman Claus Bie and director Michael Klint in Copenhagen, first preparing and later reflecting on their documentary. Most of the film concentrates on their efforts to record the effects of a devastating disease called noma, which afflicts approximately four hundred thousand Africans, mostly young children. The film begins with a shot of the dogumentary code being signed by von Trier and a shot of Klint speaking to the camera. The terms used produce a rather strange and unfocused rhetoric of social change and making a difference: "This film is about appreciating life in comparison with people who may lead cursed lives. This film is about helping other people and making a difference. It's about giving a life to others. I have to warn you. Some of the images in this film look like they stem from our worst nightmares or our fear of death. These are images from a remote part of the world. . . . I hope the film will make a difference. Enjoy the film."

 Mette Hjort

In Nigeria, the filmmakers initially have trouble locating victims of noma, allegedly on account of taboos surrounding the illness, but they eventually focus their documentary efforts on a children's hospital devoted to the treatment of the disease. Here they film the medical assessments and operations of numerous noma patients as well as their own responses to the world in which they now find themselves. These deeply problematic responses are the antithesis of flamboyant risk taking. In fact, they foreground the extent to which affluence and parochialism shield these first world filmmakers from physical risks endemic to their location and from the risks of genuine involvement. Examples of the filmmakers' complacent exchanges include Klint informing Bie that his room lacks hot water and that he knew this would be the case; Bie providing guidance on the amount of sunscreen that Klint should be using as the latter contemplates his image in the mirror with satisfaction; and Klint and Bie complaining about the food that they are served and proffering off-the-cuff analyses of Africa's problems. The distanced, cold, ill-informed, and ultimately tasteless perspective evident here is further manifested in a series of inserts with the words of the title—"Get a Life." This phrase is inscribed with chalk on a wall, appears written on the dusty arm of an impoverished Nigerian child, and on one occasion has been spelled out with shells arranged on reddish soil. The phrase is apparently intended to make viewers "who complain unduly about life's petty problems here in the rich part of the world" appreciate their own good fortune.[47] Contrasting as they do with horrific scenes of poverty-induced illness, these inserts prioritizing the first world viewer's ability and need to enjoy life are entirely wrongheaded.

Flamboyant but ultimately banal risk taking enters the picture when it becomes apparent that one of the noma patients, three years old, requires an O-positive blood transfusion. Klint, dimly aware that he might have the requisite blood type, volunteers to give blood, and his gesture provides the basis for a series of comments about risk. Bie, for example, sardonically expresses the hope that the needles are clean, speculating that they may well be dropped on the floor in the course of the procedure but used nonetheless, and wonders how many times the doctor's gloves have been recycled. When Klint is told that his blood is indeed of the right type, he waves his arms in superhero fashion, and his sense of having taken serious risks becomes evident when he begins to fret about the bruise that has emerged where the needle penetrated his arm, to the point of consulting a visiting German doctor about possible causes. Klint also notes the number of mosquito bites he has sustained and expresses a semiserious worry that the malaria pills he has been taking might be defective. Far from underscoring the reality of Klint's risk taking, these scenes draw attention to his first world panic about conditions elsewhere and, by extension, to the comforts and securities of the privileged risk position that is his, even in the context of his Nigerian film project. That project, after all, does not sever the film-maker from the vast array of medical and other services that are potentially available to him elsewhere, should the need arise.

The discourse that has emerged about *Get a Life* through practitioner interviews with the film's makers makes much of the transformation that is allegedly signaled by Klint's blood donation: "The filmmakers assume they will simply portray reality professionally, as they usually do. Instead, they are *personally* [emphasis added] drawn into the struggle to save the children."[48] Klint, it is clear, is invested in embracing the self-concept of one who is willing to take significant personal risks in order to diminish the distance separating privileged and far-from-privileged risk positions. His flamboyant performance of what is ultimately banal risk taking drives home the extent to which the willingness to take risks counts as a virtue, as a source of admiration and prestige, in today's first world, Western cultural landscapes. *Get a Life* also draws attention to the unfortunate but by no means uninteresting phenomenon of risk display as a performative self-contradiction, with the putative reality of serious risks being called into question by the very gesture of display. Whatever the goals, flamboyant risk taking becomes incoherent if viewers are likely to consider the risks on display banal, in the sense of falling well within the range of what is reason-able and acceptable.

Let us return, in conclusion, to the categories of films, (a) through (e), that were proposed at the outset, as a means of understanding key aspects of film practitioners' risk taking. More specifically, to which of our two cat-egories of flamboyant risk taking should our three examples—*Living with Hunger, Smiling in a Warzone,* and *Get a Life*—be assigned? My sense is that *Living with Hunger* belongs to category (d) by virtue of what appears to be a high level of consistency between the reality of the filmmaker's risk taking and its display. Another reason for assigning *Living with Hunger* to category (d) would be the apparent continuity between the filmmaker's stated goals and his actual goals. Contextual information, in the form of interviews with the director and his producer, but also in the form of a consistent track record over an extended period of time, make this conti-nuity clear. *Smiling in a Warzone* and *Get a Life,* on the other hand, belong in category (e). There are scenes in *Smiling in a Warzone* that suggest that the risks actually taken by Aaberg Kærn and Bejmar were not quite as great as they claim, and the same is true of *Get a Life.* Inconsistency between the filmmakers' stated intentions with their risk displays and the apparent deeper motivations for these displays provides an additional reason for assigning these films to what is essentially a category of failure.

Filmmaking in Contexts of Persistent and Pervasive Risk

I would like to conclude by taking a step back from my chosen examples in order to situate them, very briefly, in relation to documentaries that are being made by filmmakers who are known to take serious risks again and again, and who do so without calling attention to this risk taking through any kind of flamboyant display. The work of Ai Xiaoming, a professor in the Department of Chinese Language and Literature at Sun Yat Sen University (Zhongshan University) in Guangzhou, China, contrasts, in a thought-provoking way, with the films emphasizing a display of risk, especially those belonging to category (e). One of the most important human rights activists in China, Ai Xiaoming has made documentaries about tainted blood and AIDS (*The Epic of Central Plains,* 2006; *Care and Love,* 2007), about date rape (*Garden in Heaven,* with Hu Jie, 2005), and about conflicts over land and corruption (*Tai Shi Village,* 2006), among other things.[49] At the time of writing she was working on a film focusing on the shoddy construction of the many schools that collapsed during the Sichuan earthquake, and on the corruption that helps to explain why some buildings collapsed while others did not. Ai Xiaoming is a filmmaker who is constantly on the government's radar and who has had to keep a very low profile from time to time. In 2009, for example, she was to have attended the Chinese Documentary Film Festival organized by Tammy Cheung and Visible Record in Hong Kong but was prevented from doing so on account of the risks to which her film about the Sichuan earthquake had exposed her, and her need as a result to be out of the public eye for a while.

Like many of the films belonging to the "new documentary" movement in the People's Republic of China,[50] Ai Xiaoming draws on traditions of documentary filmmaking generally associated with Direct Cinema, on practices, that is, that are entirely at odds with the idea of any kind of flamboyant display on the part of the filmmaker. Filmmakers like Ai Xiaoming and Hu Jie (with whom Ai has collaborated) take significant risks on a regular basis, but leave these risks to be inferred from the images, or from the absence of images, as the case may be. When one's daily commitments and whole way of life are caught up with risk taking, of the kind that results in unwanted attention from government officials or thugs, flamboyant displays of risk have little appeal, as Zhao Liang's *Petition* (2009), about those who travel to Beijing to report grievances, makes clear. What the contrast between Chinese directors' practices and those of Aaberg Kærn and Klint suggests is that flamboyant risk taking is more likely to arise when the everyday, taken-for-granted risk position of the risk taker is highly favorable. What this in turn suggests is that risk-taking displays correlate with affluence and privilege, and with the parts of the world where these "goods" are widely enjoyed. The *Jackass* films, for example, all banal rather than meaningful instances of flamboyant risk taking, are very much a Western phenomenon. *Smiling in a Warzone* and *Get a Life* can be understood in terms of such Western specificities, but even within the West there are differences, some of them relevant to the examples under discussion. There is another factor that might help to explain the risk flamboyance that these films display: it can be hard to be creative in contexts that are *pervasively* safe. This, at least, is what filmmakers in welfare-state Denmark, safe nation-state par excellence, tell me. Uncertainty, a defining feature of risk and risk taking, is also an important creative element. Some film practitioners see certain forms of uncertainty as a means of stimulating their creativity and in some instances the desire to move into a space that is charged with risks is accompanied by another kind of desire, the desire to have the reality of the risk taking be acknowledged. Here, perhaps, in this mix of needs arising within worlds marked by social safety nets, and by the risk-aversive attitudes and pervasive affluence that to some extent have produced them, we find yet another possible explanation for flamboyant risk taking. Films that fail in the way that *Smiling in a Warzone* and *Get a Life* do have a kind of "novice" quality about them. Unused to living with risk, and with risk taking anything but a kind of second nature, the filmmakers make choices that can only seem strange, even deeply objectionable, when viewed from the perspective afforded by life worlds where social safety nets and the highly favorable risk positions that they offer cannot be taken for granted.

Notes

I am grateful to Professor Emilie Yueh-yu Yeh for giving me the opportunity to present my work on film and risk to an engaged and thoughtful audience at Hong Kong Baptist University, and for probing comments received on that occasion.

1. John Tulloch and Deborah Lupton, *Risk and Everyday Life* (Thousand Oaks, CA: Sage, 2003), 1.

2. On the process of thematization and the distinction between primary and secondary themes, see Mette Hjort, "Themes of Nation," in *Thematics: Interdisciplinary Studies,* ed. Max Louwerse and Willie van Peer (Amsterdam: John Benjamins, 2002), 301–20.

   Mette Hjort

3. For a discussion of risk positions, see Ulrich Beck, *Risk Society: Towards a New Modernity*, trans. Mark Ritter (Thousand Oaks: Sage, 1992), 26.

4. Jens O. Zinn, "Literature Review: Sociology and Risk," SCARR Working Paper 1 (2004), 1–25, www.kent.ac.uk/ . . . /Sociology%20Literature%20 Review%20WP1.04%20Zinn.pdf; Jens O. Zinn, "Literature Review: Economics and Risk," SCARR Working Paper 2 (2004), 1–17, www.kent.ac.uk/ . . . / Economics%20Lit%20Review%20WP2%20.04Zinn.pdf; Deborah Lupton, *Risk* (New York: Routledge, 1999); Tulloch and Lupton, *Risk and Everyday Life*; Pat Caplan, ed. *Risk Revisited* (London: Pluto, 2000).

5. Zinn, "Literature Review: Economics and Risk," 14.

6. Lupton, *Risk*, 17.

7. Mary Douglas, *Risk and Blame: Essays in Cultural Theory* (London: Routledge, 1992), 11.

8. Tulloch and Lupton, *Risk and Everyday Life*, 7–8.

9. Amos Tversky and Daniel Kahneman, "Judgment under Uncertainty: Heuristics and Biases," *Science* 185, no. 4157 (1974): 1124–31, psiexp.ss.uci.edu/ research/teaching/Tversky_Kahneman_1974.pdf.

10. Niklas Luhmann, *Risk: A Sociological Theory* (New York: Walter de Gruyter, 1993), 4.

11. Douglas, *Risk and Blame*, x.

12. Mary Douglas and Aaron Wildavsky, *Risk and Culture* (Berkeley: University of California Press, 1982); Zinn, "Literature Review: Sociology and Risk," 9.

13. Beck, *Risk Society*; Ulrich Beck, *World Risk Society* (Cambridge: Polity, 1999), 20.

14. Scott Lash and Brian Wynne, introduction to Beck, *Risk Society*, 3.

15. Beck, *Risk Society*, 23, 24, 27, 21, 49.

16. Zinn, "Literature Review: Sociology and Risk."

17. Tulloch and Lupton, *Risk and Everyday Life*, 10.

18. Ibid., 11.

19. Beck, *Risk Society*, 26, 41.

20. Ulrich Beck, "Risk Society Revisited: Theory, Politics and Research Programmes," in *The Risk Society and Beyond: Critical Issues for Social Theory*, ed. Barbara Adam, Ulrich Beck, and Joost van Loon (Thousand Oaks, CA: Sage, 2000), 211.

21. Ibid., 215.

22. Beck, *Risk Society*, 20.

23. Lupton, *Risk*, 13–14.

24. Beck, *Risk Society*.

25. Tulloch and Lupton, *Risk and Everyday Life*.

26. Beck, *Risk Society*, 26, 41.

27. Lars Movin, "The Ballad of Billy and 2Pac," *FILM* 53 (2006): 12–14.

28. Asger Leth, "Director's Note," *FILM* 47 (2005): 10.

29. Todd McCarthy, "Ghosts of Cité Soleil," *Variety*, September 27, 2006, http://www.variety.com/review/VE1117931713.html?categoryid=31&cs=1.

30. David Bordwell, *The Films of Carl-Theodor Dreyer* (Berkeley: University of California Press, 1981).

31. Paul Cronin, *Herzog on Herzog* (London: Faber & Faber, 2002), 19.

32. Ibid., 20.

33. Ibid., 67.

34. Robert J. Flaherty, "How I Filmed *Nanook of the North*," *World's Work*, October 1922, 632–40, www.cinemaweb.com/silentfilm/bookshelf/23_rf1_2.htm.

35. William Rothman, "The Filmmaker as Hunter: Robert Flaherty's *Nanook of the North*," in *Documenting the Documentary: Close Readings of Documentary Film and Video*, ed. Barry Keith Grant and Jeannette Sloniowski (Detroit: Wayne State University Press, 1998), 23–39.

36. Interview with the producer, *Living with Hunger, Ethiopia*, DVD, directed by Sorious Samura (London: Insight News TV, 2004).

37. Beck, "Risk Society Revisited," 213.

38. Bill Nichols, *Introduction to Documentary* (Indianapolis: Indiana University Press, 2001), 18.

39. Ibid., 13, 18.

40. Susan Dwyer, "Romancing the Dane: Ethics and Observation," in *Dekalog 01: On "The Five Obstructions"*, ed. Mette Hjort (London: Wallflower, 2008), 1–14.

41. Annemarie Hørsman, "The Art of Flying to Kabul," *FILM* 47 (2005): 3.

42. On performance art, see Kathy O'Dell, *Contract with the Skin* (Minneapolis: University of Minnesota Press, 1998); Linda Weintraub, Arthur Danto, and Thomas Mcevilley, *Art on the Edge and Over: Searching for Art's Meaning in Contemporary Society, 1970s–1990s* (Litchfield, CT: Art Insights, 1997).

43. Hørsman, "The Art of Flying to Kabul," 5.

44. Paisley Livingston, "Artistic Nesting in *The Five Obstructions*," in Hjort, *Dekalog 01*, 57–75.

45. Hørsman, "The Art of Flying to Kabul," 5.

46. For all the rules, see Michael Klint, "Drop That Film!" *FILM* 39 (2004): 15, www.dfi.dk/English/~/media/Sektioner/Nyheder/ . . . /PDF . . . /FILM39 .ashx.

47. "Crucial Dilemmas," *FILM* 39 (2004): 14, www.dfi.dk/English/~/media/ Sektioner/Nyheder/ . . . /PDF . . . /FILM39.ashx.

48. Ibid.

49. Ai Xiaoming's films are available through Visible Record in Hong Kong. See http://www.visiblerecord.com/en/.

50. For information about the new documentary movement and the related Sixth Generation phenomenon in the People's Republic of China, see Paul G. Pickowicz and Yingjin Zhang, eds., *From Underground to Independent: Alternative Film Culture in Contemporary China* (Lanham, MD: Rowman & Littlefield, 2006). See also Chris Berry, Lu Xinyu, and Lisa Rofel, eds., *The New Chinese Documentary Film Movement: For the Public Record* (Hong Kong: Hong Kong University Press, 2010).

TREVOR PONECH

True Stories of Risk Inadvertence

Risk Inadvertence

A troubling feature of our lives is the apparent pervasiveness of risk. So risky is life that individuals could not possibly keep track of all the risks they run. Nor do they necessarily care all that much about the ones they do identify, save for those somehow discovered to be, for a time, particularly salient or disturbing. People in fact often appear cavalier or oblivious to the risks they face. I am not referring to apathy toward alarmist predictions that terrorists will someday detonate a dirty bomb in one's city or that junk food is everywhere increasing the incidence of morbid obesity. No, what I have in mind are instances in which the danger is a good deal more personal and imminent. The cow's in water up past her knees, the official begs me to get in the boat, but I barricade myself inside the house to ride out the flood. Cycling on urban streets, I weave through traffic, never use hand signals, and race down sidewalks, whisking past unsuspecting pedestrians; I am an accident in the making. Having little income and no assets, yet still wanting to own a home, I happily accept the broker's offer of an adjustable-rate subprime mortgage. Cognizant of some good evidence, I form the belief that smoking is carcinogenic; still, I do nothing to try to break my habit because, hey, if one thing doesn't kill you, another will.

Perhaps even before the worst happens, other parties are bound to react to the aforementioned scenarios by wondering, *"What was he thinking?"* To ask that question is to venture into the terrain of risk psychology. Within that field, one cardinal lesson is that people can be quite bad at judging their own vulnerability to life's intricate tapestry of attendant mishaps and traumas. The public usually overestimates the frequency of high-consequence, low-probability catastrophes and underestimates the hazards of daily life.[1] People often discount the riskiness of activities like smoking, in which the effects are cumulative or delayed.[2] Psychologists, economists, public-health researchers, safety experts, and others who study risk have assorted terms to refer to potentially distorted risk perceptions. Chief among these is the "optimistic bias," that is, the psychometrically demonstrated tendency of individuals to guess their personal susceptibility to a representative sample of garden-variety risks to be less than that of other people.[3]

There are countless ways somebody might come to be, or fail to stop being, inattentive to a risk. Not all involve irrationality, imprudence, or blameworthiness. Finding fault with the agent depends on understanding the conditions underlying instances of what I shall call risk inadvertence. Studies of differential risk perceptions have posited battalions of influences on laypersons' judgments of and attitudes toward risks. Explanations range across the spectrum of theorizable cognitive, personality, sociocultural, and psychodynamic causes. I do not critically survey the proffered explanatory frameworks, electing instead to operate on a much smaller scale. Thus I also eschew all but the present allusion to critical social theories of how and why rationalistic conceptions of risk have since the Enlightenment emerged alongside science and modern social institutions and have on a global scale permeated modern peoples' consciousness of the circumstances under which they lead their lives. Rather than a world-historical perspective, my own narrow focus is on personal risk: risk that some individual (or group of individuals) takes: risk that is invited, bidden, if not exactly voluntary. Central here is a topic standard in philosophical psychology but given only glancing treatment in the risk literature. Though conducive to all sorts of gratifications and payoffs, the hotter, more passionate springs of human action frequently impair processes of rational cognition. Wants, desires, and fantasies can preempt or short-circuit prudential reason and action. My task, then, is to consider the effects of motivated irrationality in episodes of risk inadvertence.

In what follows, I make philosophically oriented use of a work of documentary cinema, Werner Herzog's *Grizzly Man* (2005). I assume this movie and others like it can serve as illustrations of and commentaries on real peoples' bouts of motivated irrationality. These agents are subsequently less attentive to live, subjectively important risks than they might otherwise have been. Interpreted in relation to the pertinent bodies of philosophical and psychological inquiry, *Grizzly Man* is apt to help us challenge and clarify some of our ideas about risk perception. Later I will elaborate a bit on the commingling of epistemic and artistic merit in filmmakers' nonfictional, character-driven stories. At this early stage, though, I should say something of how I understand the concept of risk.

An Agential Concept of Risk

My notion of risk is nontechnical and partakes of an overall concern with agency, practical reason, and action. "Agent" refers to a being endowed with subjectively meaningful psychological properties causally networked with one another and with outward behavior. Such beings have a capacity for practical reason, that is, for asking themselves, if only implicitly, "What do I do now (or later)?" and undertaking deliberations that involve weighing the pros and cons of conflicting goals or routes to achieving them. "Action" designates overt as well as mental behavior motivated and steered by some of an agent's beliefs, desires, plans, and intentions. I have a plan, that is, my own recipe, committed to memory, for making a *ragù alla bolognese.* Wanting to eat pasta, I undertake the mental act of deliberating over what kind of sauce to make; I settle on executing that plan later today. My Sunday afternoon sauce making counts as an action, or course of actions, insofar as the aforementioned mental items and events make a profound difference to my eventual culinary activities and their outcome.

Here is one way to connect risk with agency. The concept of risk applies perspicuously, but not exclusively, to an expectable disvalued consequence of some prospective or ongoing action or course of actions. Some such risks are trivial. It is easy to overcook my ragu's red onion, carrot, and celery *sofritto* base, a possible gastronomic failure that would at worst annoy me. On the other hand, the losses associated with high-speed car crashes seem grievous to me so, given the ubiquitous black ice, I am especially cautious when driving on rural Quebec highways in the winter. What makes over-cooked sofritto or a car crash an expectable consequence of some action? Expectability implicates something about ways the world is along with something about ways an agent is. The causally operative properties of the tender vegetables, olive oil, skillet, and high heat have the power to react to and upon one another so violently as to produce desiccated, scorched vegetables. I, on the other hand, know something of the properties and forces at play on the stove. That knowledge gives me the capacity to anticipate certain effects—and prevent them by stirring constantly while observing texture and color changes.

I think of valuation as having, forming, or acquiring beliefs about the goodness or badness of a particular or typical state of affairs. Value is always relative to some category or categories of interests: moral, economic, epis-temic, hedonic, instrumental, aesthetic, health related, and so on. Valuation is personal and perspectival. It makes essential reference to the goodness of some state of affairs for some agent(s) in a certain context. Likewise, the idea of value-bearing consequences opens space for subjective, imaginative appraisals of how good or bad some eventuality could be and what it would be like to experience it. If by "perceive" one includes something along the lines of appreciate from the perspective of an emotionally hued concern with one's welfare or that of others, then to perceive a risk is not just to know what can or likely will happen, it is also to have "realistic knowledge" of what it would be experientially like for that situation to come to pass.[4]

Let's not forget that "risk" is also a verb. People risk their money, their reputations, their lives; they risk disappointment, injury, heartache, failure, "everything." Usually risking is for the sake of attaining a subjectively valued end, one that somehow mitigates a corresponding danger or one's appreciation of it. Generally, then, the verb applies to situations in which an agent opts to satisfy a given desire and embarks on corresponding actions despite expectable disvalued consequences of so acting. Although the etymology of "risk" is much disputed, its connection with the Vulgar Latin *risicare*, a nautical term meaning "to navigate amongst cliffs," carries forward the sense of daring to pursue a parlous course of action.[5]

Mine is predominantly an agential, psychological approach to risk—one that treats risk as both target of awareness and as action, including willfully risky action. We should acknowledge a more objective, impersonal angle on risk, too. The idea is to accommodate situations in which agents do not or could not construe their actions as having a particular baneful outcome, as well as encounters with risk having little if anything to do with intentions and volition. Hence, a more agent-neutral concept would associate risk in general with disvalued states of affairs that are within nature's powers to bring about. Throughout the nineteenth and into the mid-twentieth century, the Foré people of New Guinea's Eastern Highlands were liable to develop a mysterious fatal trembling disease. Before the 1960s, neither the Foré nor anyone else suspected that *kuru* comes from eating human brain tissue containing proteinaceous infectious particles.[6] Until epidemiologists arrived to investigate, tribe members had neither reason to expect their ritual mortuary cannibalism might hurt them nor the epistemological wherewithal to discover kuru's underlying causes. The only risks they believed in were dangers to soul and community entrained by failure to practice transumption. But sometimes risk is not only undetectable but profoundly unbidden. Certain Foré beliefs and practices systematically put agents in harm's way. In other cases, causal relations between agents' doings and their disvalued consequences are increasingly distal, arational, wayward, and aleatory. It frequently suffices to be in the wrong place at the wrong time—breakfasting in your oceanfront Phuket hotel room on December 26, 2004—to get yourself into trouble. If tomorrow a cosmic black swan event annihilates most life on Earth, nobody will have made any psychological contribution at all to producing humanity's imperilment.

The business of individuating and identifying risks—judging when and where they begin and end, differentiating them from one another and from nonrisks—is hideously complex. As a rough guide, I posit that a state of affairs stands out as a risk when it seems apt to bring about or comprise a given disvalued consequence. While doing so could strike some readers as counterintuitive, I yoke this premise to an ontological preference for risk realism.

Winter conditions, black ice, high speed, worn tires, and driver inattention are apt to produce sudden loss of vehicular control and subsequent damages to life and property. Roughly described, the risk, R, just is: the aptness of winter weather, black ice, worn tires, high speed, and driver inattention to produce sudden loss of vehicular control and subsequent damages to life and property. R is one way reality is—whichever particular motorists, speedings, ice patches, and so on are involved. It has been that way at innumerable spatiotemporal locations in the past; it presumably will continue to be thus in the future. Most drivers in the northern hemisphere know something of R. Highway safety experts have vast empirical knowledge of how come R is the case.

The *aptness* of a state of affairs, or a congeries of states of affairs, to produce a certain result is not its likelihood. Aptness pertains to an actual state of affair's extant causal powers, to what it is ready to do. Winter conditions being apt or ready to produce damages means that when certain entities exist and stand in the relevant relationships, they have in causal partnership the capacity to bring about certain effects. Like saltwater's capacity to corrode metal, the collaborative power of certain entities to cause loss of vehicular control is real, be it eventually exercised or somehow inhibited. We are often uncertain whether, or unaware that, a state of affairs is apt to produce or comprise a disvalued consequence. Recall the Forés' predicament. We are often uncertain as to whether a situation's aptness to produce a disvalued outcome will (now, later) manifest itself. We often try to calculate the probability that, say, winter conditions will collaborate to manifest their known aptness for auto wrecks. That we do not know if or when entities will come together to produce a certain outcome does not, as Ulrich Beck thinks, consign risk to an unreal "permanent state of virtuality."[7] A risk exists if and when the right entities are brought together in the right relations, such that their capacity to produce an undesired outcome is ready to be exercised. Whether it will be exercised, this particular time or sometime in the future, could be anyone's guess.

My risk concept makes essential reference to some agent's or population of agents' evaluative attitudes toward an actual or prospective state of affairs. Risk antirealists would say I thereby concede their point, namely, that it is up to us what counts as a risk. In the words of one psychologist, "Hazards and risks are socially constructed, though founded on material objects."[8] Evaluative attitudes might change historically, culturally, contextually, and across personal perspectives. The Foré no longer believe cannibalism an unqualified good thing. For some people, the terrorist bombing's expectable consequences are cause for jubilation. I love Parmesan cheese, though it nauseates others. If nothing possesses (dis)value intrinsically, then maybe riskhood is ultimately something we project onto the world. The premise, though, is not that badness is "in" R as one of its component parts or properties, the way the sugar (and more debatably sweetness) is in the chocolate bar. All a risk realist need believe is that there exist states of affairs that possess intrinsically the aptness to produce on the part of some agent(s) a particular psychological uptake: disvaluation of some of R's consequences, including unwelcome subjective experiences R is liable to cause. Even when disvaluations are highly contextual, perspectival, or idiosyncratic, they might nonetheless be held with good reason. Moreover, the perspectival, differential nature of valuation does not show that something's desirability is ultimately conventional or up to us. Sufferers of acute lactose intolerance choose neither to disvalue milk, for what it can do to them, nor to disvalue the symptoms it causes. They might prefer not to be disgusted by dairy products, yet be powerless to change.

Which risks (now) matter to a population of agents is at least partially a social construct. So too is the stock of existing risks, technology, for instance, continually adding novel risks even as it alleviates old ones. The concept of risk is anthropic, cut to the measure of human concerns and preferences. As for the fundamental anthropism of risk itself, consider the following. Very simple organisms noncognitively detect and react self-protectively to things that can annihilate them. We are not merely projecting onto lowly *Paramecium* when we say that it is at risk from *Dileptus*. Its rudimentary self-steering motivational system is unequivocally disposed to be against contact with that organism. In the course of its proper functioning, a *Paramecium* approached by a food-seeking *Dileptus* launches harpoonlike trichocysts at its predator, a not always successful defensive response. The *animal rationale* has an infinitely richer experience of its world

                                                   Trevor Ponech

of risks and its vulnerability to them. Then again, compared to *Paramecium* our reactions to risk can be remarkably ambivalent.

A Cinematic Model of Irrational Risk Inadvertence

Werner Herzog's *Grizzly Man* introduces viewers to amateur naturalist Timothy Treadwell, who for thirteen summers communed with the omnivorous grizzly bears of the Alaska Peninsula. At the end of that last season, despite or because of his intimate acquaintance with their species, a bear or bears killed and partially ate Treadwell and his girlfriend.

Much of *Grizzly Man* is composed of the remnants of Treadwell's sojourns in Katmai National Park and Preserve—a cache of over a hundred hours of video the self-styled bear expert recorded during his expeditions. Herzog adapts this found footage to craft the story that he wants to present. That story at once conveys what he thinks Treadwell was really doing out there in the wild—and Herzog's artistic response to his subject's "ecstasies," as he calls them. Treadwell's ostensible mission, for which he attained a measure of celebrity, was to study the bears, protect them from poachers, raise their profile as an endangered species, and educate the public about these misunderstood and wrongly feared creatures. Yet his eco-warrior mission, if not entirely spurious, appears to Herzog to have been subordinate to needs of which Treadwell himself was only dimly aware.

Amid the found footage and in interviews with Treadwell's friends, associates, and parents, Herzog finds intimations of what he refers to in his voice-over narration as Treadwell's "natural tendency toward chaos." After a tumultuous young adulthood of alcohol and drug abuse, the erstwhile would-be television actor seeks out the wilderness, as if in retreat to a mythic state of nature free and clear of bad habits and unnatural desires born of civilization. For months at a time, usually though not always alone, he insinuates himself into the lives of Katmai's grizzlies, exploiting an isolated species' relative lack of wariness of human contact. Disregarding park regulations to keep a hundred yards' distance from bears and move camp once a week, he would closely stalk these creatures, even touch them, and ordinarily stationed his tent for weeks on end at their trails' busy intersections. Although Treadwell carries neither firearms nor bear repellants, he does, by his eighth visit, come equipped with video cameras. Filming at close range, he captures, sometimes provokes, extraordinary displays of grizzly behavior, occasionally reaching from behind his camera into the frame to caress or tap a surprised bear on its snout. Whether alone in the shot or sharing the screen with fauna, Treadwell routinely focuses the audiovisual recording on himself. In some of the resultant sequences, he

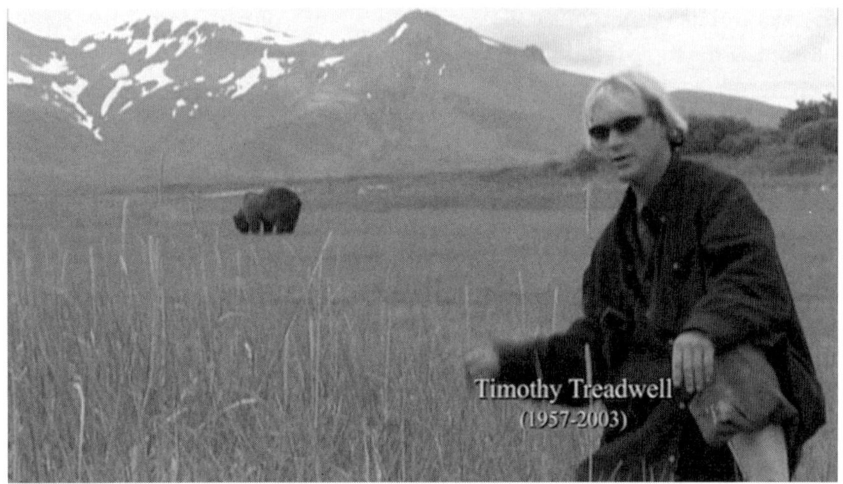

Timothy Treadwell: "If I show weakness, if I retreat, I may be hurt, I may be killed."

pretends to be an action hero saving his animal friends from poachers and other unspecified perils. Alternatively, he tries to adopt the role of onscreen host of a wildlife film. Cajoling mild-mannered beasts, sternly admonishing edgier ones, his host persona often slides into baby talk and childish excitement. There are still more effusive moments, like when a teary Treadwell professes his devotion to the grizzlies and foxes: "I'm in love with my animal friends. . . . I'm so in love with them, and they're so f——ed over, which so sucks." Sometimes his addresses to the camera veer toward dark thoughts of his willingness to die for the bears, or turn into paranoia about hunters and interlopers, or escalate into rage toward park wardens whom he believes to be ineffective, uncaring, and condescending.

Grizzly Man makes plain that Treadwell, however troubled a person, learned much about certain bear populations and how to comport himself around them so as to avoid or defuse their aggression. A grizzly's disposition and capacity to maul a human might never be manifested, might under some circumstances be inhibited. Yet these traits can neither be wished away nor altered by acts of human compassion. Thus, Herzog's narrative implies that a form of risk inadvertence accompanied the amateur naturalist's survival and demise.

Risk-perception studies are not especially focused on risk inadvertence per se. It is more common to examine, on the one hand, the cognitive processes by which laypeople estimate the extent, probability, and severity of risk; and, on the other hand, the social psychology of differential risk perception, that is, how concern with assorted kinds of actual or perceived risks (crime, economic instability, environmental disaster, genetic engi-

                                                    Trevor Ponech

neering, and the like) varies across individuals or categories of individuals.[9] Moreover, psychologists tend to treat risk perception and active, voluntary risk taking as two separate topics. This separation is somewhat arbitrary, both phenomena pertaining to agent rationality. "Risk inadvertence" usefully regroups them in order to designate potential breakdowns of rationality: in particular, agents' motivated failures to turn their minds to actual, subjectively relevant risks.

A broad overview of the varieties of risk inadvertence might distinguish: (1) failure of agent(s) A at space-time location L to detect R; (2) A's failure at L to ascertain R's magnitude or seriousness for A; (3) A's failure to gauge A's vulnerability to R; (4) A's affective indifference to R; (5) A's mistaken willingness to take or face R. Not every episode of any of these varieties of inadvertence tokens an instance of irrationality. That issue turns on how the agent came to be inadvertent.

Herzog's Treadwell is hardly oblivious to the existence of genuine, mortal dangers associated with the teeming "grizzly sanctuary" and "grizzly maze." The found footage shows him discriminating between bears he believes approachable and those he deems untrustworthy. In one of his final recordings, he avows that "camping in grizzly country is dangerous. . . . I am right on the precipice of great bodily harm or even death." During a shot woven into the documentary's opening sequence, Treadwell, posing in a field while a pair of grizzlies forage in the background, says defiantly that if he shows weakness, the bears will "take me out, they will decapitate me, they will chop me into bits and pieces." He knows what harm these beasts can inflict and has a strong, albeit unexpected, emotional response to the dangers. To whatever degree Treadwell is risk inadvertent, it is in relation not merely or even mostly to his sense of invulnerability, but to his volition.

Maybe the real Timothy Treadwell was an impulsive sensation-seeking risk taker. Were this true, we could hypothesize that it was psychobiologically so—if indeed some habitual risk takers are sent in that direction by their neurochemistry.[10] We should still ponder how an alternative developmental history, comprising different affiliations, experiences, and beliefs and greater self-understanding, could alter the details of and extent to which someone's disposition for sensation seeking expresses itself in risky undertakings. Insofar as they have any effects whatsoever on mental life and outward behavior, personality traits and intractable biological or subintentional forces presumably combine reciprocally with other persistent as well as rather more transitory psychological items. Whether talking about actual agents or characters in narratives, individuating personalities and explaining behavior normally require that we refer to quite large clusters of causally networked perceptions, beliefs, desires, plans, and propensities in order to figure out what the agent was thinking and doing within a particular situation. Privileging one or another type of personality trait or primary motivational mechanism, including psychoanalytic doctrine's subconscious anxiety-reduction defense mechanisms, seems to miss most of the ingredients, the intermeshing attitudes, reasoning styles, and motivations generating episodes of risk inadvertence.[11]

Apropos, cognitive psychology has made important contributions to the study of risk, many of these being organized around the concept of unrealistic risk optimism. People often estimate their own risk vulnerability as lower than average. This bias is especially pronounced when individuals are asked to assess their susceptibility to voluntary risks. It is exacerbated by habituation, too. Familiar risks are judged less risky than novel ones; the longer one practices a risky behavior without experiencing its disvalued consequences, the more likely one is to acquire an impression of subjective immunity.

Standard accounts of how the optimistic bias arises gesture toward two general sources.[12] On the cognitive side, there is the overreliance on various quick, efficient, yet highly fallible judgmental strategies, such as the availability heuristic. When making inferences—including ones about likelihood, frequency, severity, causes, and consequences associated with a given risk—agents typically draw heavily upon presuppositions, personal experiences, and what seems obvious to them under the circumstances. Instead of seeking out and sorting through detailed information, they make top-of-the-head judgments based on perceptual vividness, accessibility to memory, and what is readily imagined.[13] Treadwell seems as prone as any lay reasoner to misuse this heuristic. His assertion that "no one in the history of the world" has lived so closely with bears unwittingly implies that, in assaying his prospects for ongoing fraternal relations with grizzlies, he has been extrapolating from too egocentric and small a sample of successful encounters. It turns out that, in the long run, bears don't always show their sweet side.

The optimistic bias is also held to have a motivated side. One perennial idea is that defensive denial plays a role in its emergence. Coupled with the obscurity of the notion of denial and doubts about the reality of defensive and other psychodynamic mechanisms, data showing that more fearsome, life-threatening hazards elicit no more optimism than minor ones tell against this postulate.[14] Alternatively, there is some empirical support from social comparison theory that the optimism bias meets a need for self-esteem or satisfies a desire to be better or stronger than others.[15] It is unclear whether Treadwell was low on self-esteem; Herzog's story makes it equally if not more plausible that inflated self-confidence vitiates his

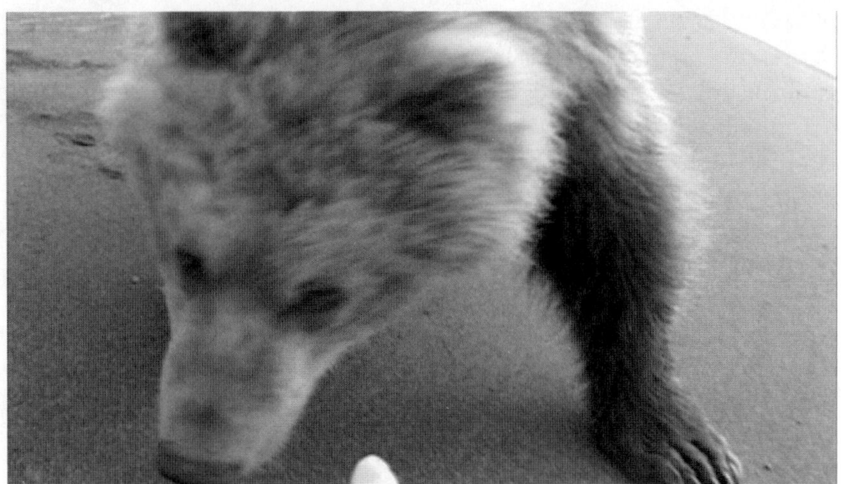

Treadwell reaches from behind the camera to touch a bear's nose.

attentiveness to danger. In any case, rather than evoking risk optimism and its generation by some fairly linear, direct causal chain of cognitive and motivational factors, *Grizzly Man*'s model of risk inadvertence suggests a less tidy, more tumultuous etiology.

Tending toward chaos, Treadwell the narrative character manifests conflicting attitudes toward himself, bears, and the risks he courts. Treadwell's candid camera catches him in flights of puerile sentimentality—giving the bears twee names, cooing at them, confabulating about their personalities and lives. At the same time, often during the same shot, his camera records flashes of grizzly ferocity near or nasty enough to make the observer automatically recoil and retreat. That he possesses and self-protectively adverts to knowledge regarding the grizzlies' unsympathetic dispositions is apparent across Herzog's selections from the audiovisual archive. Images of fights between rival males, of the remains of cannibalized cubs, and of predatory old grizzlies huffing indifferently at the lens supplement Treadwell's explicit pronouncements on the dangers the bears pose to him. Yet he also slips into and fixes upon thoughts of his special invulnerability. The site of his imminent death pictured in the background, he warns his prospective audience: "Come here and do what I do. You will die. You will die here. . . . They will frickin' get you. . . . I found a way to survive with them. . . . I'm just different." However ambivalent his optimistic bias, his overall risk inadvertence remains strong.

The Treadwell of *Grizzly Man* understands himself as someone who wholeheartedly cares about bears and who effectively devises and implements plans consistent with a life project of wildlife advocacy. It is less obvious that he also has a lucid understanding of himself as one whose desires and fantasies are liable to distort his judgment and self-control. It is intrinsically gratifying to disappear into Katmai's refuge to act out what Treadwell calls his "kind warrior" persona. In an unintentionally *cinéma vérité* style, he records his ecstasies: directing himself in make-believe scenarios constructed around the bears; enacting a wishful fantasy of reciprocal, sympathetic bonds between the bears and himself, bonds facilitating their mutual recognition of shared goodness. At the same time, Treadwell fabricates a myth of himself as the grizzlies' lone protector, his mere presence repelling poachers. Handheld shots of him indicate that he was not always alone. Park wardens and naturalists contend the poaching threat was more imagined than real. Treadwell's desirous self-concept also meshes with his feelings about the animals. When a drought causes mothers to eat their cubs, his anthropocentric notions of the grizzlies' perfection become harder to indulge. So he bare-handedly tries to build a salmon run to replenish their withered fishing stream with food in the ultimate hope of directing his cast of grizzly actors to be more like the creatures he wants them to be.

The cinematic portrait of Treadwell suggests a motivated breakdown of agent rationality. Desires and their gratification potentially steer agents away from thinking carefully about risk. They could, for example, mitigate a dangerous situation's psychological burdens, including fear, anxiety, and imaginative engagement with what it would be like to experience the worst were it to transpire. Or they could motivationally outweigh the foregoing with their own more subjectively pressing burdens on attention, practical reasoning, and action. Preoccupied as he is with realizing his grizzly-man dream, Treadwell is less attentive than he would otherwise be to the readily apparent aptness of astonishingly close contact with bears to turn out badly for their fragile human admirer.

Philosophical discussions of motivated irrationality posit that desires can bias agents toward acquiring false or unwarranted beliefs.[16] I expect Treadwell, for instance, routinely engages in "selective evidence-gathering" and "positive misinterpretation," energetically looking for instances of placidity and subsequently interpreting these as supporting belief in the bears' hitherto underappreciated inherent gentleness. Absent an investment in the wishful fantasy of sympathetic bonding with bears, he might have been less focused on exhibitions of seemingly benign conduct and not as inclined to count nonaggressive behavior as evidence of goodwill toward him.

Maybe wishful thinking impedes Treadwell's ability to settle on cogent judgments of his susceptibility to harm, the likelihood of mishap, and the

                                                   Trevor Ponech

overall value of the risky venture. Here the malign influence of desire generates a volitional species of risk inadvertence, inasmuch as it distorts the processes by which his will is formed and sustained. People often voluntarily take risks because they lack the quantity or quality of information needed to dissuade them. Another path to an agent's willingness to take a risk is the motivationally distorted route. In the teeth of the evidence, so to speak, that the grizzlies are an imminent danger to him and his companion, Treadwell nonetheless does not, perhaps cannot, will himself to take a more cautious approach to the bears.[17] The narrative invites the thought that a self-destructive aspect of his temperament exacerbates Treadwell's recklessness. Yet Herzog's characterization evinces that he wanted and expected to continue his work; and that he had more than a modicum of concern for his own life and that of his girlfriend, Amie Huguenard, concern accompanied by the normal aversions to being mauled or helplessly watching a loved one's mauling. Hence the possibility that Treadwell's risk inadvertence involves volitional incoherence. Bear attacks were not only a live possibility but, from Treadwell's own point of view, expectable if not a 100 percent certainty. He had good reason to take precautionary actions and knew which ones would do the trick.[18] Had his practical reasoning not been burdened by his unique complement of motivationally biased beliefs and runaway desires, it would have been within his power to settle upon and execute effective measures to remove himself and his companion from harm's way, thereby acting according to a large cluster of long-standing, subjectively important values, plans, and desires predicated on his continued survival.

Cognitive failures to detect or accurately size up a risk—sometimes called "risk blindness"—can also exhibit motivational springs.[19] Consider Treadwell's risk-inadvertent conspecific, Fred Leuchter, in Errol Morris's documentary, *Mr. Death: The Rise and Fall of Fred A. Leuchter, Jr.* (1999). Leuchter isn't risk blind in the way the Foré were; it is difficult to charge that the latter could or should have known better, this charge being the retrospective quiddity of irrational risk inadvertence. Leuchter, a self-taught engineer who designed execution systems for U.S. prisons, becomes a star defense witness in a Holocaust denier's trail. Chiseling away like an imp of the perverse at the walls of Auschwitz, he removes proof hidden below the surface, in the form of cement samples uncontaminated by chemicals, that Crema 1 could not have been a gas chamber. But Leuchter is mistaken. Such chemicals penetrate only a few microns and their residue would have long ago vanished.

Near the movie's end, Morris speaks from behind the camera to ask Leuchter if he ever worried he might be wrong. "No," he answers, "I'm past that." Leuchter seems oblivious to the specifically epistemic risks of his amateur sleuthing. As well as being optimistic about his capacity to avoid error, he is disinclined to attend to or look for his mistakes. Not even in the most disciplined research contexts is there any getting past the expectable, disvaluable consequences of inquiry, chiefly believing falsely and without good enough justification. Yet in a strange way, he is profoundly averse to the risk of error. Morris's film characterizes Leuchter as fancying himself a prodigiously gifted investigator, a kind of Sherlock Holmes. Wishing to maintain this self-conception, it helps to ignore disconfirming evidence of error's pervasiveness and one's own nescience. Best, then, to minimize exposure to the risks of heavy "investigative investments"—Bernard Williams's phrase for the frustrations, costs, and potential losses accompanying truth seeking.[20]

RISK, NARRATIVE, AND PHILOSOPHY

Grizzly Man is what I regard as a risk narrative, one that happens also to be a work of nonfiction. Risk in the sense of *risicare,* daring, is obviously a staple of narrative cinema. Granted, popular cinematic representations of riskings are frequently little more than accelerants for exciting escapist fantasies, often incorporating a supreme hero who displays enviable Bondlike self-control and affective inadvertence in the face of danger. More generally, risk depictions reliably spark visceral thrills, help create suspense, and promote sympathetic responses to characters. It could be, moreover, that active risk simply is part of what makes a story a story; that depicting risk in one or another form, of greater or lesser magnitude, is elemental to narrative. Indeed, one strategy for making an utterance or representation that is readily identifiable as a story is to present an agent who in pursuing a goal or trying to satisfy a desire embarks on corresponding actions despite their expectable disvalued consequences. Most such strivings seem naturally to involve the agent's risking something, if only failure to realize sought-after ends.[21] This description could be modified so as to highlight instances in which it is the narrator or audience who expect disvalued consequences to which the character is oblivious.

Grizzly Man is a documentary because, in making this film, Herzog and his collaborators ably pursued the appropriate sorts of generic objectives, ones very similar to the intentions governing the linguistic activity of uttering felicitous assertions. They readied a progression of images and sounds as a vehicle for representing the actual historical agent, Timothy Treadwell, expressing beliefs about him, and encouraging their audience to form beliefs about Treadwell. This representation is not a transparent win-

                                                          Trevor Ponech

dow onto the man and what he was thinking. It is, rather, a cinematically constructed characterization of this agent's temperament, desires, and actions: by watching the movie, we learn how Herzog conceives of Treadwell. Yet this Treadwell-concept is hardly vacuous or nonreferring. Not least of *Grizzly Man*'s virtues is that some of its content is truth indicative, when understood to be about certain actual, particular historical individuals and events. In turn, this content is conducive to the audience's acquisition of true beliefs about said referents. This is not the end of its epistemic value, however.

Grizzly Man is also an exemplary work of cinematic art. From traces of his subject's existence, Herzog gleans fodder and inspiration for an imaginatively conceived, skillfully wrought, thematically complex movie. As this movie begins, he speaks of finding "dormant" in Treadwell's wildlife footage "a story of astonishing beauty and depth." Awakening that story means shaping, elaborating, and responding to the found footage. Consider the treatment of one powerful piece of the historical record. Although its lens was capped, a camera ran while the killer grizzly invaded Treadwell and Huguenard's camp. Without explaining to us all the factors in his decision, the director chooses not to insert into his own film the resultant audio recording of the horrific attack, instead taking a more oblique approach to describing the tragedy's gory details. Stoically donning headphones, he listens to the evidence—then recommends to its owner that she destroy it. Here, the problem with the facts is that they carry a risk of nihilistic sensationalism. The brute historical record could overpower Herzog's own idiosyncratic nature film, the goal of which is not to gawk at a troubled man's gruesome death but to contemplate the fundamental furies of human nature. In Herzog's view, such eruptions of *homo demens,* especially those provoked by the movie camera, are the inventive, imaginative stuff of art, if not unto themselves sufficient for the production of art.

The preponderance of stories involves, as if by default, representations of risk. A full-blown risk narrative affords the extra benefits of an interesting commentary or perspective on risk that meshes with existing theoretical and philosophical approaches to this topic. *Grizzly Man* meets this requirement. My claim is not that this movie supplies raw empirical evidence for some theory. Nor do I suppose it to be a vessel of prepackaged knowledge to be extracted in an interpretive exercise of disambiguation and amplification. Its principal epistemic virtue is that it equips us conceptually and imaginatively to ponder in depth its protagonist's dispositions and attitudes toward risk. It openly encourages audiences to wonder why on earth Treadwell would act as he did, and offers the wherewithal to explore solutions in terms of breakdowns of agent rationality. In this manner, the documentary lends itself to the heuristic function of prompting and guiding philosophical reflection on standard accounts of what it is that blocks people from perceiving subjectively important threats.

Risk psychologists occasionally puzzle over why removing agents' optimistically biased estimate of personal invulnerability to risk often fails to bring about their undertaking, or even deciding to undertake, self-protective measures.[22] More vividly than the usual studies, surveys, and forests of data, *Grizzly Man* models this puzzle while suggesting a solution to it. The optimistic bias is but one possible manifestation of the underlying agential phenomenon of risk inadvertence. "Risk inadvertence" picks out instances of an agent's lacking, to some degree, a disposition or capacity to turn his or her mind to subjectively expectable, disvalued consequences of an actual or anticipated course of action. From the standpoint of an interest in agency and practical reasoning, the most intriguing varieties of this phenomenon have a potentially intractable motivational dimension, the agent's cognition and volition succumbing to desires that run contrary to cogent perceptions, the emergence of more prudent choices of what to do, and the power to put those judgments into action.

Notes

1. Paul Slovic, Baruch Frishhoff, and Sarah Lichtenstein, "Cognitive Processes and Societal Risk Taking," in *The Perception of Risk,* ed. Paul Slovic (London: Earthscan, 2000), 32–50.

2. William D. Diamond, "Effects of Describing Long-Term Risks as Cumulative or Noncumulative," *Basic and Applied Social Psychology* 11 (1990): 405–19; Neil D. Weinstein, "Unrealistic Optimism about Susceptibility to Health Problems: Conclusions from a Community-wide Sample," *Journal of Behavioral Medicine* 10 (1987): 481–500.

3. Neil D. Weinstein, "Optimistic Biases about Personal Risks," *Science* 246 (1989): 1232–33.

4. Paul Slovic, "Do Adolescent Smokers Know the Risks?" in Slovic, *The Perception of Risk,* 365.

5. Ernest Klein, *A Comprehensive Etymological Dictionary of the English Language* (Amsterdam: Elsevier, 1967), 2:1350.

6. For background on the kuru medical mystery in relation to Foré culture, see Ricki A. Lewis, *Discovery: Windows on the Life Sciences* (Malden, MA: Blackwell Sciences, 2001), 63–74.

7. Ulrich Beck, "Living in the World Risk Society," *Economy and Society* 35 (2006): 322.

8. Glynis Breakwell, *The Psychology of Risk* (Cambridge: Cambridge University Press, 2007), 11.

                                                                                      Trevor Ponech

9. Ibid., 44–77; Karl Dake and Aaron Wildavsky, "Theories of Risk Perception: Who Fears What and Why?" in *Risk,* ed. Edward J. Burger (Ann Arbor: University of Michigan Press, 1993), 41–60.

10. Marvin Zuckerman, "The Psychobiological Model for Impulsive Unsocialized Sensation Seeking: A Comparative Approach," *Neurobiology* 34 (1996): 125–29.

11. Hélène Joffe, *Risk and "the Other"* (Cambridge: Cambridge University Press, 1999) takes a social-psychological approach to risk reliant in part on the usual psychoanalytic repertory of drives and defenses.

12. Weinstein, "Optimistic Biases about Personal Risks," 1232–33.

13. Amos Tversky and Daniel Kahneman, "Judgement under Uncertainty: Heuristics and Biases," *Science* 185 (1974): 1124–31.

14. Weinstein, "Optimistic Biases about Personal Risks," 1232.

15. Joanne V. Wood, Shelley E. Taylor, and Rosemary R. Lichtman, "Social Comparison in Adjustment to Breast Cancer," *Journal of Personality and Social Psychology* 49 (1985): 1169–83; Shelley E. Taylor, Margaret E. Kemeny, G. M. Reed, and Lisa G. Aspinwell, "Assault on the Self: Positive Illusions and Adjustment to Threatening Events," in *The Self: Interdisciplinary Approaches,* ed. Jaine Strauss and George R. Goethals (New York: Springer-Verlag), 239–54.

16. Alfred Mele, *Self-Deception Unmasked* (Princeton: Princeton University Press, 2001), 26–27.

17. *Among Grizzlies,* Treadwell's published account of his early adventures in the Alaska Peninsula, concludes with his acknowledging that many of his previous interactions with bears had been reckless and resolving henceforth to take a more "conservative and respectful approach." In the same paragraph, he expresses his "greatest fear": that other people might imitate his "past dangerous style of study and become injured or killed." Timothy Treadwell and Jewel Palovak, *Among Grizzlies: Living with Wild Bears in Alaska* (New York: Ballantine, 1997), 191.

18. Per Sandin discusses the rationality of precautionary action and the prospects for formulating a coherent principle or rule—grounded in something akin to an everyday, commonsense idea of precaution—applicable to decision making about risk within such spheres as public health and environmental policy. See Sandin, "The Precautionary Principle and the Concept of Precaution," *Environmental Values* 13 (2004): 461–75; Sandin, "Common-sense Precaution and Varieties of the Precautionary Principle," in *Risk: Philosophical Perspectives,* ed. Tim Lewens (New York: Routledge, 2007), 99–112.

19. I take this term from Marc Gerstein with Michael Ellsberg, *Flirting with Disaster: Why Accidents are Rarely Accidental (*New York: Stirling, 2008), 63.

20. Bernard Williams, *Truth and Truthfulness: An Essay in Genealogy* (Princeton: Princeton University Press, 2002), 87.

21. One defensible approach to analyzing the concept of narrative is that suggested by Paisley Livingston, *Literature and Rationality: Ideas of Agency in Theory and Fiction* (Cambridge: Cambridge University Press, 1991), 54–55. His

minimal definition is predicated on the idea that narrative discourse involves representation of "an agent or agents as they strive to achieve some goal, usually encountering some unusual—or otherwise pertinent—form of difficulty." My remarks here are intended to be consistent with the type of narrative theory Livingston proposes.

22. Neil D. Weinstein, Peter M. Sandman, and Nancy E. Roberts, "Perceived Susceptibility and Self-Protective Behavior: A Field Experiment to Encourage Home Radon Testing," *Health Psychology* 10 (1991): 25–33; Breakwell, *The Psychology of Risk*, 84.

PAISLEY LIVINGSTON

Spectatorship and Risk

Cinematic fictions often depict characters who face a remarkable variety of natural and otherworldly dangers, such as attacks by aliens, dinosaurs, zombies, killer puppets, and swarms of insects. The risk of physical injury and death is the staple of the horror, crime, war, and action genres, while in art films, the focus tends to be on psychological and moral perils. Risk is such a pervasive subject in film that one is tempted to conjecture that this is the main attraction of that seemingly low-risk activity, film spectatorship.[1] In what follows I investigate several issues related to this conjecture, beginning with the problem of identifying and classifying risk, both in the actual world and as it is represented in cinematic works. In my first section I introduce a distinction between taking and running risks and discuss epistemic problems related to the classification of events as risks or rewards. Next I discuss some of the challenges—and artistic risks—that filmmakers confront as they attempt to represent risks in works of fiction. With regard to artistic tradeoffs related to the representation of risk, in the third section I provide a more detailed discussion of two cases: *Pleasantville* (dir. Gary Ross, 1998) and *La visione del sabba* (Sabbath Vision, dir. Marco Bellocchio, 1988). Finally I ask how we might explain why risk is such a pervasive subject in the cinema. What is at stake in the spectator's seemingly low-risk engagement in spectacles of extreme risk?

Identifying and Classifying Risks

As I shall use the term in this chapter, "risk" refers to a possible event that would be bad or harmful.[2] Some risks are *run,* while others are *taken.*

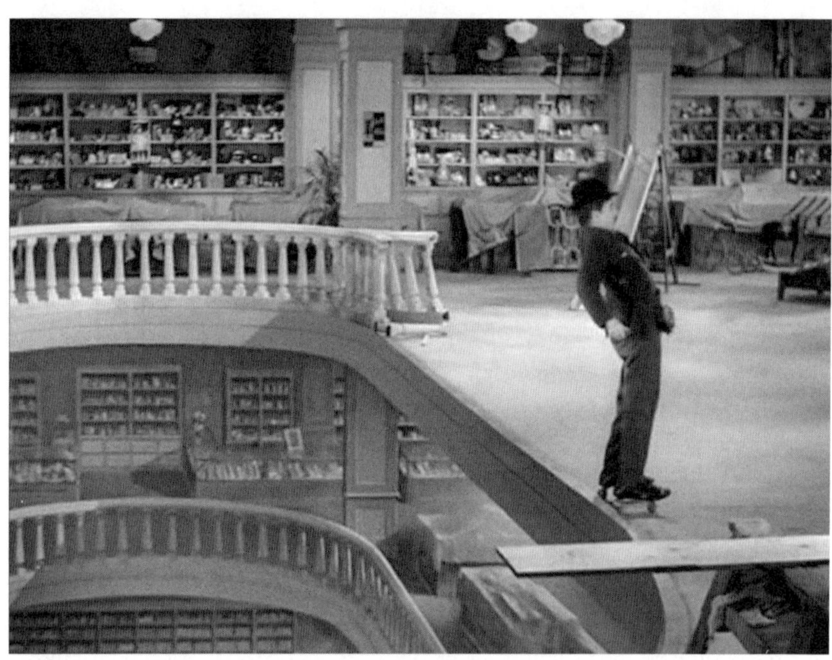

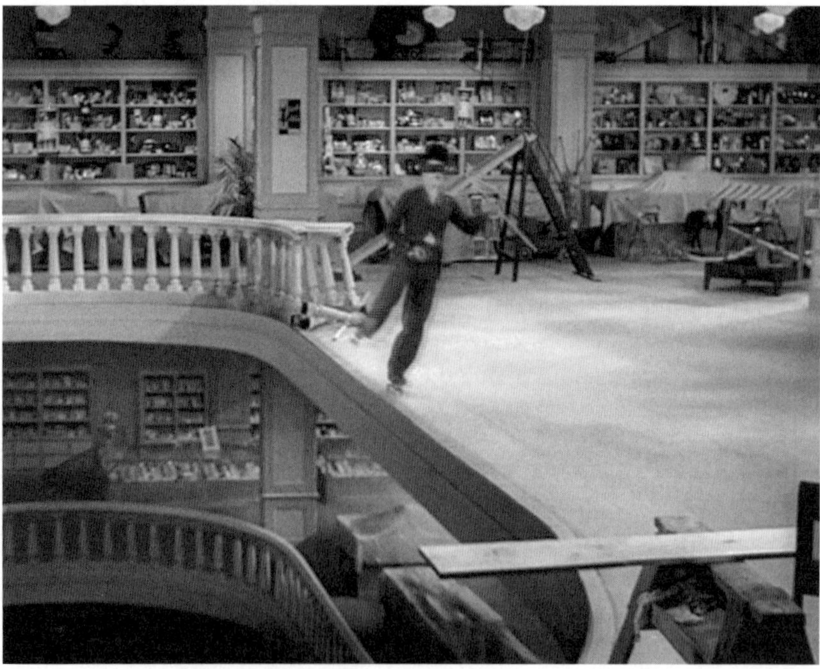

Unwittingly running a risk: Chaplin's *Modern Times*.

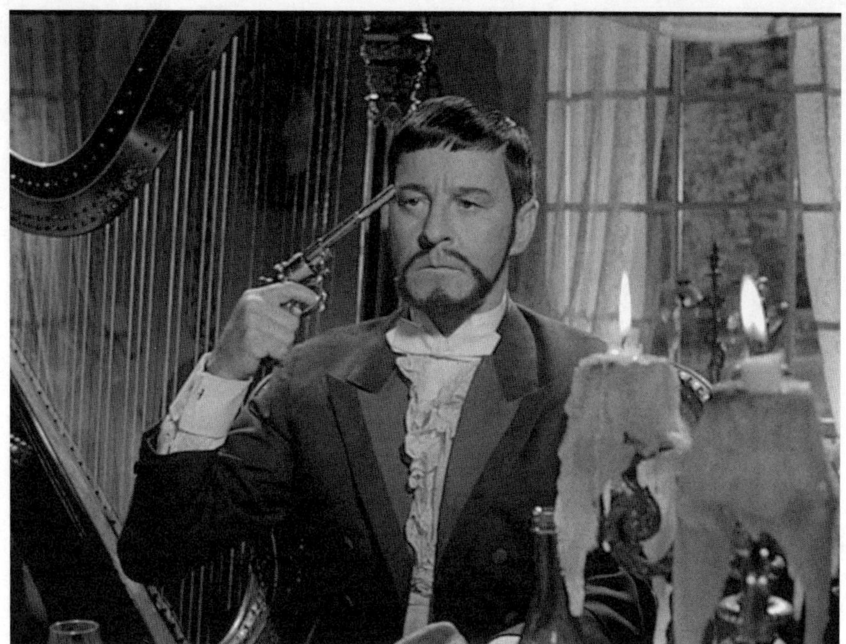

Bravely taking an imagined risk in Bergman's *Smiles of a Summer Night.*

Someone *runs* a risk in a situation just in case a possible outcome would be harmful or bad for that person, whether or not the person knows it. To *take* a risk, on the other hand, is to perform some action while believing, rightly or wrongly, that doing so makes a bad outcome more likely. While only agents can *take* risks, we can meaningfully speak of the risks *run* by objects and artifacts. For example, it is cogent to say that when a masterpiece is placed within Mr. Bean's reach in *Bean* (dir. Mel Smith, 1997), it runs the risk of being damaged. Arguably, attributions of risk are always relative to the preferences of sentient beings, but I shall not pursue this issue here, except to say that even if this point is granted, it does not follow that risks are somehow unreal, or that statements about them cannot be true or false.

The distinction between running and taking a risk is illustrated in various films. For example, in Charles Chaplin's *Modern Times* (1936), the tramp finds some roller skates in a department store. He skates well, and in an attempt to show off to his companion, puts on a blindfold and continues skating. It is apparent that he has not noticed that part of the railing is missing behind him. In skating blindfolded, he *runs* but does not *take* the risk of falling to his death.

Similar judgments apply whenever someone has skewed estimates of the likelihood of negative events. In *Fearless* (dir. Peter Weir, 1993), a crash

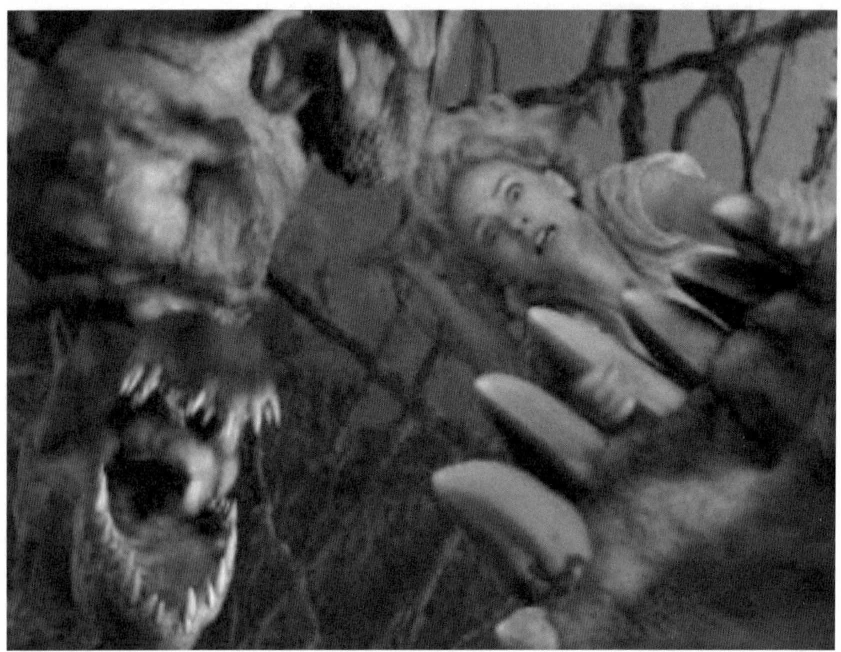

Obvious danger in Jackson's *King Kong.*

survivor suffers from a temporary delusion of invincibility. When he intentionally walks on the ledge of a tall building, he runs, but does not knowingly take, serious risks. In Ingmar Bergman's *Sommarnattens leende* (Smiles of a Summer Night, 1955), Count Malcolm challenges Fredrik Egerman to play Russian roulette, but secretly puts only blank cartridges in the revolver. As Egerman lifts the gun to his temple, he wrongly believes that he is risking his life, unaware that the actual risk he runs is only that of being ridiculed by the count. Egerman courageously takes but does not actually run the risk of losing his life when he pulls the trigger.

A difficult issue concerns the basis of the judgments whereby we classify some possible events as risks and others as rewards. In all cases of risk *taking,* it is the risk taker's attitude toward the possible events that would appear to settle the matter. This is also the case in many instances where risks are *run.* For example, in a scene in *King Kong* (dir. Peter Jackson, 2005), it is obvious that Ann Darrow does not want to be devoured by a dinosaur, so as she dangles precariously above its open jaws, she is clearly at risk. Yet other cases of risk running do not work this way. In *Modern Times,* the tramp is oblivious to the drop-off. As he has formed no opinion regarding the possible event of skating over its edge, his actual evaluation of the possible event cannot be the basis for classifying it as a risk.

                                                        Paisley Livingston

With this issue in mind, one might propose that it is the agent's *conditional* assessment of the outcome that determines whether there was a prior risk or not, where the conditional assessment is one that answers the question: "If the event were to occur, how would the agent evaluate it?" This works fine in the case of the tramp's reckless skating, as we have no doubt that he would consider falling to his death a negative outcome. Unfortunately, as a principled solution to the problem, the proposal is open to devastating counterexamples.[3] In extreme cases, such as brainwashing, a person can wrongly reclassify a prior risk as an opportunity, or a prior opportunity as a risk, because the event in question brings with it a change of evaluative attitudes. One might try to repair the conditional analysis by indexing the counterfactual assessment to a time prior to the possible event's occurrence: if, prior to the brainwashing, a person would have evaluated the event negatively, then it constitutes a risk. Yet such a condition does not handle cases where the person's prior judgment was faulty. For example, when Bill, the character portrayed by Richard Gere in *Days of Heaven* (dir. Terrence Malick, 1978), conspires to have his girlfriend marry the rich farmer, he seriously miscalculates his own future evaluation of the very events he is scheming to bring about. Only an assessment of those events that transcends his poor understanding of his own interests could identify the actual risks he runs. More generally, whenever someone has a distorted evaluation of the relevant outcomes, it would be wrong to say that there is a risk only if the agent would evaluate the event negatively. Attributions of risk should rest, finally, on warranted assessments of the values of events.[4] Such an assessment may take into account the agent's own evaluations and evaluative dispositions, but these are not in all cases decisive. When uncertainty arises with regard to such an assessment, as is often the case, it carries over to the corresponding judgments about risk. This is a problem that emerges in one of the cinematic examples discussed at greater length below.

Risks can be classified in terms of the types of negative events involved. One of the greatest sources of risks and risk-related behavior, in film and elsewhere, is human conflict or rivalry. Yet not all cinematic and other risks derive from either the actual or imaginary scarcity that fuels the unending struggles between human beings. Disaster films, and some recent movies involving climate-change scenarios, are a case in point. In *Flood* (dir. Tony Mitchell, 2007), a raging storm in the North Sea causes a tidal surge that inundates London, claiming many lives. As is often the case in stories in the disaster genre, some interpersonal conflicts are introduced during the first part of the film. Yet these familial and romantic conflicts are forgotten or happily resolved as everyone faces the risks brought by the storm. In many disaster films, a wonderful new harmony is achieved because the catastrophe conveniently extirpates the bad guys.

The Cinematic Representation of Risk as an Artistic Challenge (and Risk)

The representation of risk in fiction films constitutes a type of artistic challenge that can lead to creative solutions and failures, the assessment of which can contribute to the spectator's appreciation of the art of film. One aspect of this challenge can be described as follows: given that possible future outcomes cannot normally be seen, how are they to be gotten across to the spectator? And when the spectator is meant to know that a given character is aware of a particular risk, or that a character has faulty beliefs about actual risks, how are such story facts to be conveyed?

Filmmakers' solutions to these problems depend upon some of the most basic strategies that can be used to express determinate content by means of an audiovisual display. Such strategies begin with the array of cinematographic techniques for producing individual shots having specific *depictive* contents. For example, a focused, well-lit shot of sufficient duration can successfully represent a baby in a baby carriage as seen from a certain angle and distance. The contents of such a shot can readily be identified by most viewers, who in so doing draw upon their basic perceptual capacities and beliefs about the world. On some accounts of how this works, spectators "imagine seeing" the baby in the carriage, possibly through the imaginative mediation of some kind of motion picture–like images that reliably track the objects and events. What they imagine seeing, on this account, is not the baby in the carriage *simpliciter,* but a transparent *image* of the baby in the carriage.[5] A rival view has it that the viewer's basic uptake of cinematic content does not involve imagining seeing: spectators actually see the audiovisual display and then draw more or less spontaneous inferences about the depictive and other contents of the images. I will stay neutral on the debate over imagining seeing here, and simply observe that on all viable accounts, the audiovisual display has determinate *depictive* contents (that is, what is audiovisually represented) recognizable by competent, sufficiently informed spectators.

How, then, does the filmmaker manage to use the contents of the images and soundtrack to convey certain kinds of thoughts and feelings about possible negative outcomes? The question may seem trivial, but it should be recalled that, in many cases, these outcomes do not end up being realized as the story unfolds. It is not finally true in the fiction that the dinosaur devours Ann Darrow, because King Kong protects her. Yet it is certainly

Paisley Livingston

true in the story that she was at great risk of being eaten by the hungry dinosaur. What is it, then, that grounds such story truths pertaining to possible but nonactual fictional events? What makes it correct to say that, had King Kong not intervened, Ann Darrow would probably have been killed? Although a quick and casual response to that sort of question might run, "It certainly looked like it would happen," it is important to remember that this casual response is best understood as shorthand, since it is not literally the case that the conclusion follows directly from the specifically visual properties of the previous story events. The reader who has doubts about this point is invited to imagine a story in which a character has been unknowingly endowed with perfect "dinosaur proofing." Such a character, who is not at risk, could be depicted as being futilely stalked by a ferocious dinosaur. Visually identical shots could be used in a different story context to depict a character genuinely at risk of being devoured by a dinosaur. It follows that the determination of risk in a story is not achieved by purely visual means.

A more careful response to the question about the fixation of fictional content refers to the expressive or rhetorical strategies filmmakers can successfully use to cause competent spectators to have warranted imaginings that run along certain lines and not others. As we survey some of these strategies, it will emerge that their use involves certain kinds of artistic tradeoffs—or, in other words, risks and rewards.

A first family of devices that can be used to lead spectators to draw specific inferences about unseen but possible future events in a story, including risks run by characters, can be labeled "verisimilitude." A straightforward and historically influential example can be found in the Odessa steps sequence in Sergei Eisenstein's *Battleship Potemkin* (1925), which has been imitated or alluded to in several other films—most elaborately and notoriously, Brian De Palma's 1987 *The Untouchables*. I will briefly describe how this relatively straightforward example works so as to set the stage for a discussion of other kinds of strategies.

Once it has been established that the setting is a massacre taking place on a long, steep flight of steps, the montage presents the viewer with shots of a baby carriage. One close-up shows its wheels teetering at the edge of the step. Drawing upon salient beliefs about the ways and means of the world, abetted perhaps with a thought about the rhetorical aims of the filmmakers who are responsible for the making of the sequence, the competent spectator quickly and effortlessly draws the inference that the carriage may roll off the edge and go tumbling down the steps. A basic assumption warrants an imaginative conjecture to the effect that, should this happen, the carriage could very well overturn, in which case the baby

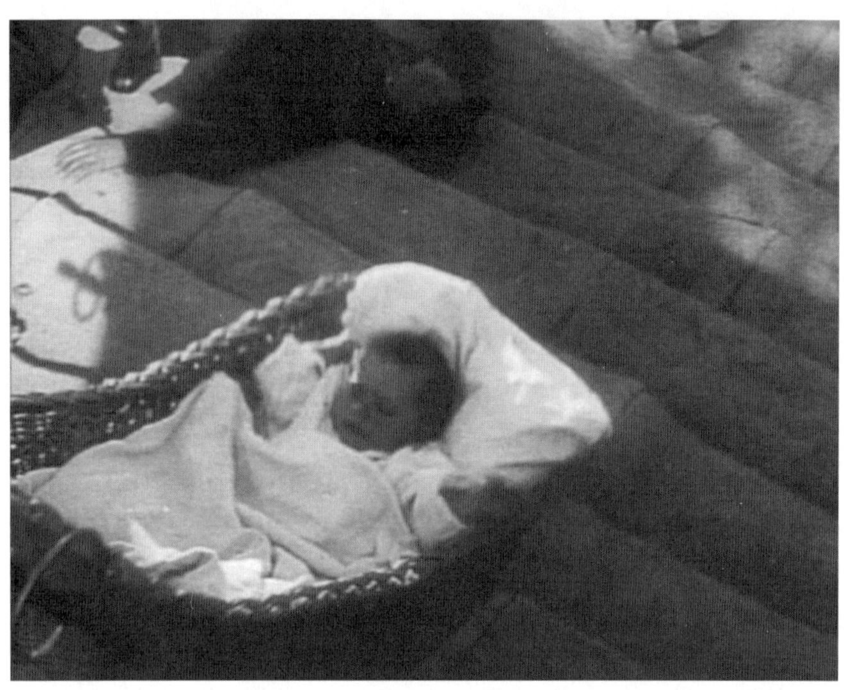

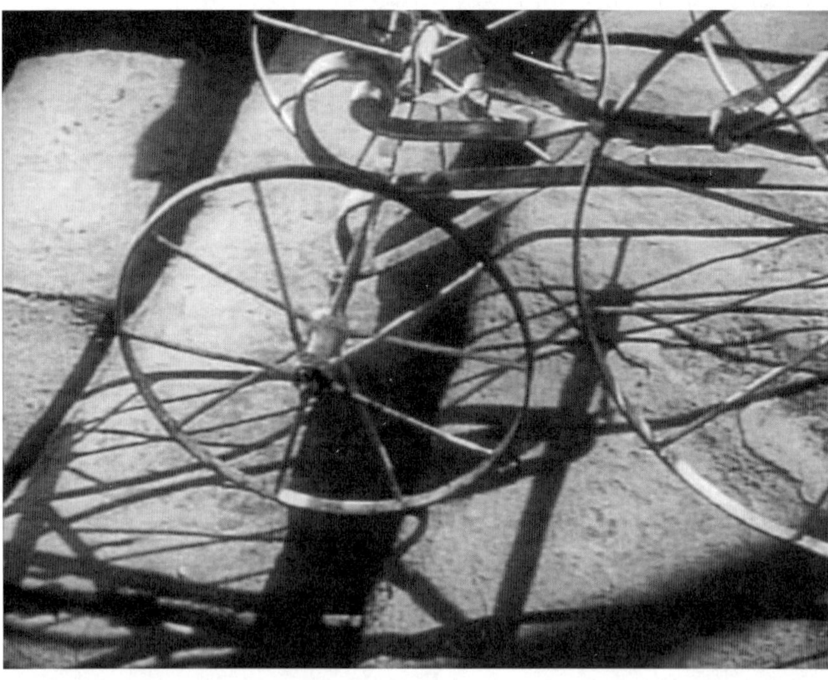

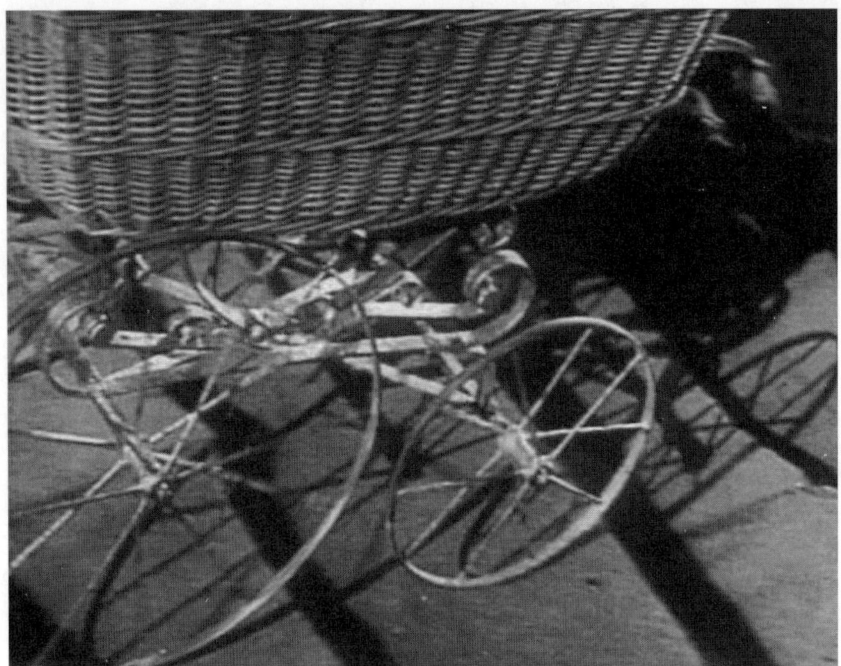

Inferred risk in Eisenstein's *Battleship Potemkin*.

would probably be injured. The spectator who understands that this baby shares a basic human aversion to painful injury can in principle classify this as a risky situation for the child. For normal spectators, the sight of an infant being injured is an unwelcome one, so some kind of negative affect can be expected to accompany the imaginative apprehension of the child's risk.

In this example, the rhetorical design of the montage relies upon commonsensical ideas about the actual world's causal regularities. More specifically, one of the unfilmable but essential story premises is that in general baby carriages are highly unlikely to roll safely down a long flight of steps. Eisenstein and De Palma both play upon this premise by having the carriage roll straight down the steps without turning over. As the carriage descends, it accelerates, thereby raising the anticipated likelihood of its overturning. As people watch the Odessa steps sequence on a first viewing, one question that may come to mind, then, is "When will the carriage tip over or crash into something?" and this concern can heighten the desired emotional impact of the scene.

The more general point illustrated by this basic but telling example is that the intended activation of *obvious,* actual-world premises can make

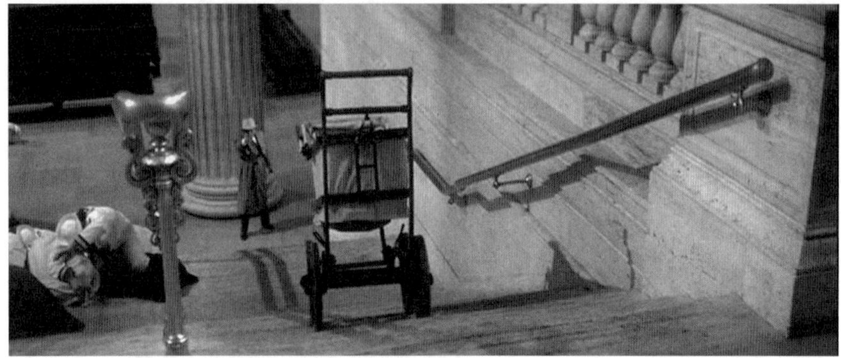

Precarious descent in De Palma's *Untouchables*.

possible the expression of specific risks in a fiction film, even though the risk-related events are not visually represented and are, finally, imaginary. An effective way to evoke specific risks, then, is by drawing upon the spectators' assumptions about the ways and means of the actual world. More schematically, the inference to this sort of implicit fictional content works as follows. First of all, some event that belongs to type X is made salient in the story, for example, by figuring among the obvious depictive contents of a shot. Second, part of the audiovisual content of the film intentionally evokes an obvious premise: whenever there is an event of type X, an event of type Y is likely to happen. It follows that an anticipation of a Y event is warranted, and this imaginative inference is meant to be drawn by attentive and competent viewers.[6]

Another, related strategy worth mentioning in this context is to show the characters talking about the relevant dangers. On the assumption that at least some of what they say is truthful, the contents of these statements, which are grasped by the spectator, handily carry over into viewers' understanding of the story. For this to work, however, the reliability of a given character's forecasts has to be established. For example, a character is portrayed as highly competent and effective, and some of his predictions are confirmed as the story develops. It may then be inferred that some of this character's other statements about possible negative outcomes are also credible. Since characters' speeches about risks may be well crafted and can contribute to the dramatic interest of a work, the use of dialogue is not per se a bad solution to the artistic problem. On the other hand, filmmakers who overwork this strategy risk slowing down the action and making things too obvious.

Another strategy is to sidestep or overrule the actual-world premise that future and/or possible events cannot literally be seen. For example, an

                                                                                   Paisley Livingston

explicit visualization of the realization of a harmful event can be implicitly framed as the contents of some character's imaginative anticipation of danger, or even as a vivid and accurate premonition experienced by someone with special powers. To make this work, the filmmaker needs to find an effective way to signal this framing of the depicted events, such as using slow motion to represent the content of the character's anticipatory imaginings or vision.

Violations of verisimilitude in the ordering of story events is another option that can be taken up in an effort to signal future negative outcomes to the spectator. This device is central to *Premonition* (dir. Mennan Yapo, 2007), a film in which a woman inexplicably begins to live her days out of their usual temporal order. In *Memento* (dir. Christopher Nolan, 2000), a "reverse" narrational strategy is meant to be vaguely evocative of the central character's cognitive disorder.[7] Spectators who have early on in the film witnessed the reverse images of Teddy's murder may be expected to figure out that Teddy is at risk as he interacts with Leonard, the man who has already been seen killing him.

Another way in which spectators can be led to anticipate dangers faced by characters is by prompting their expectations about what sorts of things tend to happen in works belonging to a particular genre. For example, in thrillers and horror films, really tough monsters or killers often seem to have been finally subdued near the end of the film, but spring back to life for one last vicious assault. A viewer who reckons that a film is converging on this pattern (the killer is down and the surviving lovers are about to embrace) may thereby anticipate an attack that will take the survivors by surprise. Insofar as this sort of inference involves a metafictional attitude, it may conflict with the aim of maximizing the viewer's imaginative and emotional engagement with the story events.

A tradeoff is faced by filmmakers who take up the problem of indicating the risks taken by fictional characters: either the filmmaker works with the most familiar and commonplace story premises, and thereby enhances the likelihood of the spectators' convergence on the desired story truths, or the filmmaker works with unusual and unrealistic story premises, and thereby reduces the likelihood of achieving the intended uptake. At stake in this tradeoff are two important artistic goals: successful communication of a story, and making an innovative and artistically valuable use of the art form or medium. The sorts of strategies I have discussed so far tend to maximize the likelihood of communicative success, yet they also tend to purchase this success at the cost of diminished artistic novelty and emotional impact. The question that arises, then, is whether and how determinate fictional content pertaining to risk can be expressed in the absence of heavy recourse to verisimilitude and/or conventions, and this without sacrificing communicative success. In other words, what are the options for filmmakers who want to convey an unusual fictional story that deviates significantly from conventions as well as from reliance upon explanatory dialogue and obvious, widely shared assumptions about the ways and means of the actual world?

One device that is sometimes employed in such a context is a stepwise, retrospective revelation of risked events. The viewer is shown strange calamity after strange calamity, which can have the desired effect of generating an overall sense of foreboding or "impending doom." For example, the viewer has no real grasp of any implicit causal regularities subtending the particular fictional events; a series of vividly depicted misfortunes nonetheless supports the inference that the surviving characters are seriously at risk. That the specific risks in question remain highly unpredictable makes surprise effects possible but vitiates any engaged reasoning about the dangers faced, or about the means the characters use to avoid them. One risk for the filmmaker who takes this approach is that the story can take on a random and arbitrary quality, which can detract from the spectator's imaginative engagement.

Another option is to deploy a comprehensive rhetorical design that makes it possible for viewers to come up with fairly detailed propositions regarding what is going on in a story that is relatively unfamiliar, unconventional, and unrealistic. As before, risks are revealed stepwise, but in the process, a causal pattern emerges, allowing the spectator to hit upon an unfamiliar law that obtains in the imagined domain of the story. Having grasped this general story premise, the spectator can begin to form reliable inferences about specific as-yet-unseen events, including risks and rewards. As a result, it becomes possible for the spectator to have a better appreciation of the strategies characters use in dealing with the inferred risks. The spectator is thereby in a position to understand which characters do and which do not accurately foresee the dangers, and this can make possible certain effects, such as tragic irony or the pathos of watching an overly self-confident figure march blindly into a trap.

As these claims are fairly schematic, it may be helpful to illustrate and develop them by referring to examples. The two cases I discuss in what follows have been chosen to illustrate some of the artistic tradeoffs mentioned above. A first example achieves a fairly high degree of communicative success in the expression of implicit content in a novel fictional context, but does so at the cost of reliance upon a fairly obvious rhetorical contrast. In the second example, communicative success and related artistic desiderata are to a greater degree sacrificed to novelty.

	

In *Pleasantville* two contemporary teenagers are astounded to find themselves transported magically into the colorless world of a 1950s American
black-and-white television series. The other characters of this series have
limited belief systems and very predictable behavior. In spite of the fact
that they are the denizens of a 1950s fiction, it turns out that these people
have untapped human potential. They are quickly influenced by the unconventional newcomers. As they begin to change, some of the things in their
world suddenly take on color. The newly emergent colors are visible to all
of the characters who, strangely, refer to them as "real colors."[8] Initially, the
conditions under which these colors burst forth remain mysterious to the
spectator and characters alike. As the transformation of the fictional town
Pleasantville unfolds, the spectator tries to resolve this mystery by discov-
ering a causal pattern. At first it would appear that only when a character has an erotic experience is color released in the surroundings; in some
cases, when someone has an orgasm, that person's skin permanently takes
on "real color." But this conjecture about the unfamiliar causal mechanism
is falsified when a character's newfound passion for the art of painting has
the same type of consequence. Later on, it is a powerful outburst of anger
that does the trick. The hypothesis that eventually covers the data is that
colors are released whenever people have some kind of passionate, deeply
engaging, and intrinsically valued experience (as opposed to experience
that merely conforms to the conventions). Once the spectator has arrived
at this hypothesis, he or she is in a position to observe which of the characters have a similar understanding of what is going on. The protagonist
has figured it out, while the moralistic and accusatory mayor has not. We
can easily anticipate that the mayor is in danger of learning the lesson the
hard way. When the protagonist baits him, he too experiences the color-
provoking emotions of self-discovery.

Although many of the story events in this film are not only unusual but
literally impossible given the target viewers' basic assumptions about the
laws of nature, many fictional truths about the goings-on in *Pleasantville*
are perfectly uncontroversial. Spectators can easily form the needed inferences about risks and rewards by activating assumptions they would deem
blatantly false in actuality. This is the case because the spectator's reasoning
about implicit story events is guided by a highly obvious and stereotypical
rhetorical contrast between "black-and-white" conformism and "colorful"
authenticity. This evaluative contrast is firmly anchored in the character-
izations and corresponds to a well-marked difference between characters

who act upon their authentic desires and those who are too conventional and repressed to do so. This straightforward rhetorical design guarantees communicative success in a context where the constraints of verisimilitude have been seriously loosened. I turn now to a discussion of a case that illustrates issues that emerge when recourse to such obvious rhetorical structures is eschewed.

In Marco Bellocchio's *La visione del sabba,* the central character is a young psychiatrist, Davide, who has recently finished his training. Davide and his beautiful wife drive to a town where he is to serve as an expert witness on a panel dealing with an unusual murder case. The accused killer is a woman, Maddalena (portrayed by Béatrice Dalle), who has apparently claimed that she is a three-hundred-year-old virgin, and that the devil made her kill the man. Neither Davide nor the spectator has any idea about the dangers the young psychiatrist may face when he meets this woman. Bellocchio begins the sequence in which they meet with a shot in which Davide and another psychiatrist are seen in focus in the foreground; out of focus in the background can be glimpsed a corridor and a glass door through which Maddalena has emerged in the company of two police officers and a doctor. As Maddalena approaches in her red dress, she comes into focus and is greeted by the other psychiatrist. She then turns to face Davide. She smiles seductively, her eyes holding and caressing his gaze. It is clear that Davide finds her striking. As he looks at her intently, something very strange happens. The right half of the scene darkens unnaturally, and as Maddalena continues to stare into Davide's eyes, smiling flirtatiously, her body begins to rotate upward, to the left, around the implicit axis of her head. She giggles playfully, holding his attention, spinning about her head a full seven times, faster and faster, as though drawing him into some kind of vortex, at the center of which are her laughter and inviting gaze. The discordant violin and electronic effects on the sound track reinforce the strangeness of this unusual scene.

Although viewers can immediately admire Bellocchio's ingenious mise-en-scène, at this point in the film the spectator is hardly in a position to say what has happened to Davide. The other persons in the corridor have not noticed anything unusual. Once Maddalena stops rotating in thin air, Davide looks stunned, but it is impossible to know, just yet, what impact this real or imagined event may have had on him. As the story unfolds, it becomes tempting to conclude that Davide has quite literally been bewitched. He suddenly loses all interest in his wife and makes this indifference perfectly apparent. When Maddalena asks him for his wedding ring, he hands it over. When the panel meets to interrogate her about the murder, he takes her side. He disrupts the meeting by kissing her passionately

    Paisley Livingston

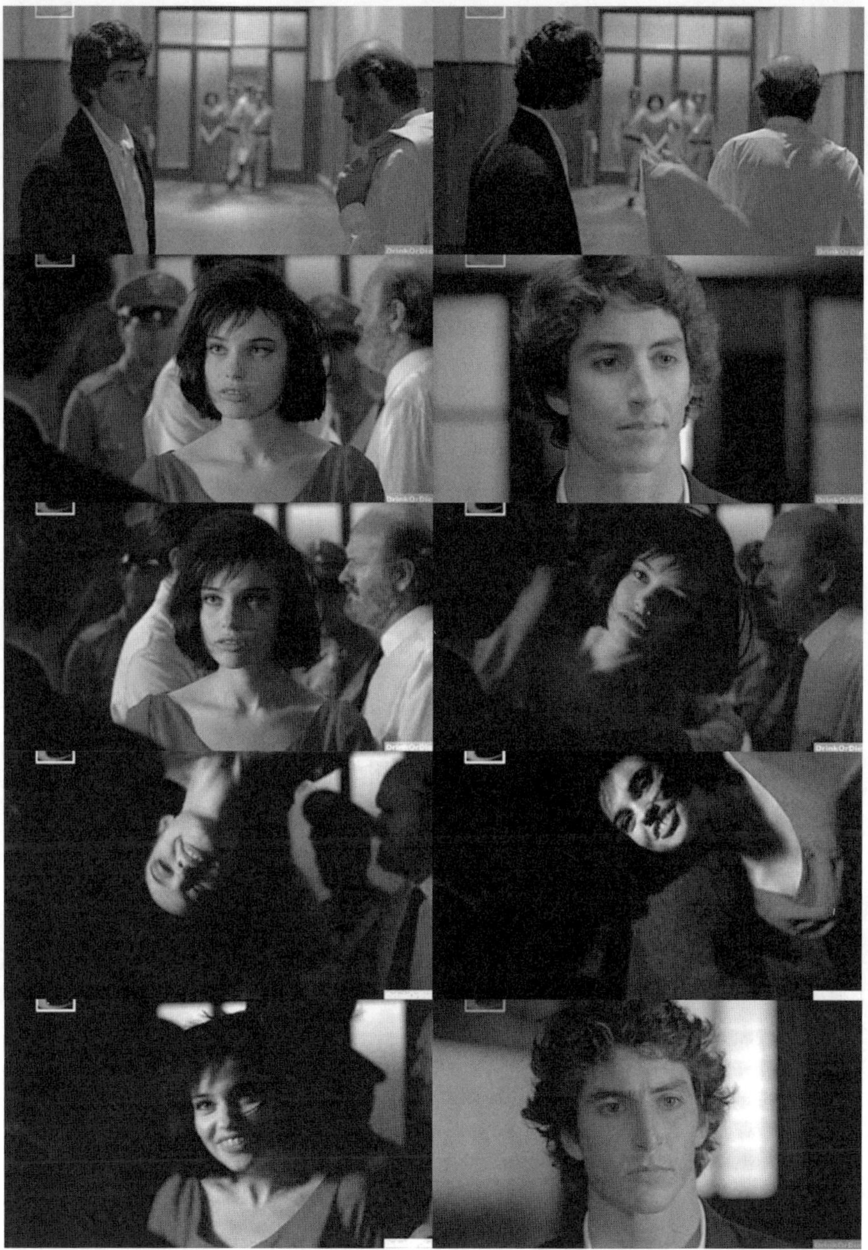

The doctor is bewitched by the patient in Bellocchio's *La visione del sabba*.

as the astounded and shocked officials look on. It seems correct, then, to say retroactively that when Davide was on his way to meet Maddalena, he unwittingly ran the risk of enchantment. Magic is real in the story; the woman really is a witch, in league with the devil.

Yet matters are not so simple, for at least two reasons. First of all, it is far from apparent that the director intends for us to take the witchcraft motifs in such a literal fashion; instead, his stated intention was to have the apparently magical events stand in symbolically for the woman's erotic power, understood along broadly psychoanalytical lines. In a published interview, the director refers to the character as representing "the dimension of seduction" and vacillates between referring to Maddalena as "the witch" and as "a schizophrenic." With regard to the characterization of Davide, Bellocchio comments: "From the moment the psychiatrist loses his professionalism, his professional coldness, his fantasies open up and he begins to see things he never saw before. He has the 'Vision of the Sabbath.' It's about someone who was a very good psychiatrist, in a normal situation with a family, with kids, and yet, for complicated reasons, he risks losing everything."[9] Various elements of the film support this line of thought. What Davide risks in being seduced by Maddalena is not demonic possession but a divorce and some serious professional and psychological problems.

Yet even this is only part of the picture. Various aspects of the film diverge sharply from the mission of presenting any kind of plausible or realistic story. For example, there is a lengthy sequence in which Davide goes out at night and spontaneously joins a highly erotic and quasi-satanic dance ceremony with a troupe of performers who were glimpsed earlier rehearsing in the town. The music and dance, which are like a highly eroticized *Le sacre du printemps,* heighten the sense of allegorical stylization. The viewers' attention is drawn to the musical qualities of the original score, composed by Carlo Crivelli, and the striking choreography by Raffaella Rossellini. At another point in the film, the accused witch is burned at the stake by Davide and a group of medieval soldiers and clergymen, but she emerges unscathed and smiling. The director comments convincingly about this aspect of the film: "Some of the appearances of the witch have no believability, no verisimilitude about them at all. She's in prison, then she shows up at the lake, and so on. In a certain sense, I was trying to destroy, or at least to avoid, a very classical novelistic structure, and instead to follow certain paths that lead to the unconscious rather than to the conscious mind."[10] Many features of the film mesh perfectly with these stated intentions. It should also be observed, however, that even if the viewer accepts that the work is to be understood as a kind of psychoanalytic allegory, the allegory must have some basis in the depiction of specific story events. This

                                                    Paisley Livingston

entails that even the spectator who is highly attuned to the director's intention to break with verisimilitude is not simply relieved of the imaginative task of trying to figure out what Davide is doing, and what dangers and rewards he faces.

Another reason why it is hard to make confident statements about the risks the character Davide runs in this story is that it is far from apparent that there is a clear and straightforward scheme of values expressed in this work. Given that verisimilitude has been rejected (if not "destroyed"), it is far from obvious which, if any, of our actual-world evaluations are pertinent. One searches in vain for rhetorical devices decisively indicating that Maddalena is to be imagined as a genuinely evil figure. At the same time, there is some evidence suggesting that we are invited to align ourselves with Davide in his "rebellious" discovery of the immense value of the erotic pleasure Maddalena offers. I have in mind the lengthy sequence in which Davide and Maddalena make love, a sequence that focuses the spectator's gaze on the lovers' faces as they are transported by the pleasure they give each other. Nothing about this scene suggests that we are invited to imagine that this transaction is evil, or that Davide is letting Maddalena lead him off to eternal damnation. And if the spectator is to pursue this lead, it follows that Davide did not in fact risk anything like "bewitchment" when he encountered Maddalena. Perhaps what he faced in the vortex of her seductive wiles was a rare opportunity to free himself from repression by experiencing a vision of his own unconscious mind. A conjecture that comes to mind in this connection is that what Bellocchio is trying to evoke in his characterization of Davide is a fantasized inversion of the familiar Freudian maxim: "Wo Es war, soll Ich werden" (Where the id was, I shall be).

Such a reading, however, ignores other important aspects of the film, starting with the obvious reflection that to attempt the inverted psychoanalytic "liberation" would be disastrous for any actual human being as well as for those misfortunate enough to come into contact with such a person. In keeping with this point, Bellocchio clearly portrays the suffering of Davide's rejected wife, who simply cannot fathom how he could suddenly begin to treat her with such cruelty and indifference. There is no indication that the Davide who has been transformed by Maddalena is in any real sense a better person, and it is hard to imagine that he faces a successful career in psychiatry once he has allowed himself to be publicly seduced by the accused murderess. Earlier in the film Davide is shown interacting with a disturbed patient who tries to seduce him. He resists this attractive young woman's advances and does his best to cope with her psychotic behavior in a caring yet professional manner. This scene stands in perfect contrast to his zombielike behavior once his lust for Maddalena has taken over. Such elements of the work support the thought that the encounter with the seductive patient was indeed a risky one for the young psychiatrist—if not a supernatural event, then at least an appalling eclipse of reason.

How do such sharply contrasting elements fit together? My tentative response to that question is that the overall attitude targeted by the filmmaker is one of ambivalence. By "ambivalence" I mean that the tension between contrasting evaluative attitudes is meant to remain unresolved. While we are meant to imagine that Davide indeed risks "losing everything" he previously valued as a result of his pursuit of the enchanting woman, we are also meant to align ourselves at times with contrasting perspectives on his wanton pursuit of pleasure. There is ample evidence in support of this manner of reconstructing the director's overall intentions, and it is this ambivalent position on the fictional course of events that corresponds best to the various elements in the audiovisual display, such as an oscillation between scenes that consecutively underscore the contrasting (and ultimately incompatible) valences of Davide's adventure.

It is possible that some spectators can at least provisionally adopt Bellocchio's ambivalent perspective, and these viewers may find that this strange, stylized *visione* is skillfully crafted and highly innovative. For this to work, however, the artistic value of the ingenious artistry would have to be taken as outweighing the lack of a clear story with a straightforward evaluative framework and a determinate content pertaining to fictional risks. Yet it is likely that many viewers will find it impossible or inappropriate to adopt a perfectly ambivalent attitude with regard to the depicted events, specific aspects of which clearly have a positive or a negative value. Here we come back to the general theme of artistic tradeoffs. In the absence of any warranted evaluations, the spectator's response cannot move along spontaneous emotive and imaginative lines. If Maddalena is not consistently identifiable as a moral threat, then we cannot fear or despise her; if she is not an alluring and admirable figure, we cannot align ourselves with Davide in his passion for her. If Davide is not wrong to abandon his wife for Maddalena, we cannot correctly feel discomfort or moral disapproval over his behavior. More generally, if the moral import of Davide's transformation is wholly uncertain or lacking, what attitude should spectators have with regard to the overall trajectory of the story? Should we be indifferent? Does the intended spectator remain undecided and in a state of tension between two contrasting evaluative attitudes? Yet how could such a spectator even begin to say what risks and rewards were experienced by the characters? In sum, one complaint about this film runs as follows: having eschewed verisimilitude as well as reliance on stable generic conventions, Bellocchio's film gives us too few inferential resources to work with as we attempt to make

                                                                 Paisley Livingston

sense of the story and point of the film, including the nature of the risks the character faces. As parts of the film read like a straightforward promotion of wanton behavior and sexual obsession, the intended overall ambivalence is disquieting, as least for the many spectators who think moral content is relevant to one's reaction to a film.[11] It is likely that this ambivalence and uncertainty concerning the film's representations of risks and rewards help to explain its commercial failure. It is clear, in any case, that the director took this risk quite deliberately in his desire to express his own rebellious "vision."

Explaining the Representation of Risk

At the outset of this chapter, I broached the conjecture that while going to films is not itself a risky matter, one of its main attractions is the representation of risk. Supposing that this conjecture is worthy of consideration, one may go on to ask how such a fact could be explained. Why would spectators gravitate toward cinematic displays of risk?

A first answer to this question surfaced in the last two sections of this essay. By appreciating the cinematic artistry manifested in the solution of problems related to the representation of risk, spectators can have valuable aesthetic experiences. It strikes me as uncontroversial to observe that at least some part of the public has a genuinely aesthetic interest in the art of film, and I hope to have established that some specific and interesting storytelling challenges arise with regard to risk. Yet such an answer hardly promises to tell us why so many spectators are eager to consume lurid spectacles built around thrilling risks and violent mayhem, even when the films in question can hardly be counted as artistically sophisticated or innovative works.

Another line of thought that arises in response to our conjecture appeals to the viewers' various cognitive interests, at least some of which pertain to the various risks and rewards that might be encountered in life. The movies respond to these interests by providing an imaginative tour of risks, which makes it possible for spectators to learn about these dangers without incurring the actual losses. This elementary point about the rewards of observational learning, or what the psychologist Albert Bandura called "modeling" can be reinforced by referring more generally to the important role of testimony as a source of knowledge.[12] Someone whose knowledge of the world was entirely based on direct acquaintance or immediate experience would have a severely impoverished system of beliefs. In many cases, the price to be paid for knowledge by acquaintance is simply too high. To mention but one example, a fictional work such as *The Panic in Needle*

Park (dir. Jerry Schatzberg, 1971) must have been instructive for at least some young persons curious about the risks of heroin addiction. Without themselves having to become destitute addicts, spectators can easily learn something from this film about what that sort of trajectory is like.

A third line of thought that arises with regard to my central conjecture appeals to the spectators' hedonic motivation. Many of the spectators' imaginative experiences at the cinema are best characterized as fantasy, where this term is used to single out imaginings having a primarily hedonic orientation. It is pleasurable, for example, to experience in one's imagination what it is like to be far more skillful or lucky than one really is in the actual world, just as it is pleasurable, at least for some people, to imagine doing transgressive things that, if carried out in actual life, would likely incur punishment or moral condemnation.[13] Revenge is a case in point. Many people who do not believe that violent retribution is appropriate are sometimes inclined to go along with the contrary proposition for the sake of the feelings stirred up by a skillfully conveyed story.

It is generally correct to say that in the mainstream cinema, the very enormity of the risks that are evoked or represented is often matched by the enormous gap between the characters' abilities and those of the average spectator or human being. To mention but one relatively recent example, in *Taken* (dir. Pierre Morel, 2008), a former CIA agent travels to Paris to rescue his daughter from the vicious slave traders who have abducted her. In order to save the girl, he displays a truly awesome ability to outsmart and defeat the scores of criminals he encounters. For example, unarmed, he boldly enters a house occupied by a gang of experienced, determined, and heavily armed thugs. He easily tricks these suspicious and cruel fellows, then swiftly kills or subdues them. Taking their leader prisoner, he tortures this culprit into revealing the information he needs, murders him, and then leaves the house unscathed.

In comedies, such epic displays of unmatched strength are on the whole absent. What takes their place is inordinate luck. The comic hero runs all sorts of risks, often without taking any. After making various sorts of inept attempts to cope with these dangers, the comic figure ends up, by perfect happenstance, the champion. A good example is Pierre Richard in *Le grand blond avec une chaussure noire* (dir. Yves Robert, 1972), a farce in which a clueless musician is misidentified as a dangerous secret agent and thereby becomes embroiled in a conflict between rival police factions. The many risks he runs all come to naught, of course, and this without any especially skillful or intelligent actions on his part.

These three lines of thought regarding the raison d'être of the cinema's representation of risk are compatible with regard to the cinematic medium taken as a whole, yet with regard to specific aspects of particular films, there is a definite tension between them. I have already discussed the tension between a justified admiration of Bellocchio's cinematic artistry and worries one might have about the content of the work and its capacity to give rise to warranted emotional responses.[14] In other cases, there is a conflict between the spectators' different interests in risk. Using fiction films as prompts for pleasurable fantasies is in general at odds with lucid appreciation of cinematic artistry. Moreover, a film's function as a more or less artfully produced prop for fantasy may directly detract from its quality as a reliable or useful source of observational learning or testimony, especially with regard to the way in which risk is represented and understood. Are the spectators really lucidly experiencing a given type of risk *as a risk* when the warranted imaginings about dangers are but a shadowy prompt for pleasurable thoughts of an all-too-predictable mastery? Although it may seem paradoxical to say so, under certain conditions, it is the very representation of risky situations that allows spectators to avoid authentic thinking about possible negative events *as such*. A hypothesis to consider, then, is that the risks imaginatively "taken" in the film are so totally inconsequential for the fantasizer that the possibility of any genuine observational learning is vitiated.

What is more, the successful functioning of a film as a prompt for fantasies can come at the cost of severe cognitive and moral limitations (and one can say this without taking on the burden of establishing that all fantasy is somehow immoral). The film *Taken* provides an excellent example of the sorts of limitations I have in mind. As he ferociously fights his way through Paris, hell-bent on saving his daughter, the former CIA agent puts any number of innocent bystanders at serious risk. Spectators who imaginatively share the hero's desire to save the innocent girl from being sexually exploited by the nasty criminals are likely to be indifferent to the issue of collateral damage. They may also disregard the implicit fact that, with the exception of his daughter's victimization, the hero blatantly disregards all questions of legality and justice. This could tend to reinforce the thought that in the just war against alien threats, American interests warrant the use of extreme violence. For example, at one point, the hero intentionally shoots the innocent wife of a corrupt French official who stands in his way. As is typical of films in the action genre, where the focus is on the astounding skill with which the protagonists chase down and thwart their enemies, no rhetorical emphasis whatsoever is placed on the implications of such behavior. We are invited to sit back and enjoy ourselves while the professional killer does the job for us, and although the shadowy risks are certainly thrilling, we can be confident that our surrogate will win out in the end. It does not look, then, like there is much to be learned from films of this sort, and it is not a great leap of faith to predict that they can at the very least reinforce, if not promote, dubious ways of thinking about the actual world. And if this is the case, the avid consumer of such fantasies is running a serious risk after all.

NOTES

1. It is true, of course, that film going has on occasion proved deadly, an early example being the deaths of seventy-one children in the 1929 Glen Cinema disaster in Paisley, Scotland. Yet such cases are relatively rare, and the risks involved are hardly specific to watching films, as there have been similar disasters in theaters, lecture halls, and other crowded places. Filmgoers do, of course, run a small risk every time they buy a movie ticket, as the expectations that motivated this purchase may be disappointed.

2. For background and references, see Sven Ove Hansson, "A Philosophical Perspective on Risk," *Ambio* 28, no. 6 (1999): 539–42; and "Risk," in *The Stanford Encyclopedia of Philosophy*, www.plato.stanford.edu. I survey related decision- and action-theoretical topics in my *Literature and Rationality: Ideas of Agency in Theory and Fiction* (Cambridge: Cambridge University Press, 1991).

3. These counterexamples are inspired by a type of philosophical problem that cropped up as objections to conditional analyses of dispositions; a key reference is C. B. Martin's "Dispositions and Conditionals," *Philosophical Quarterly* 44 (1994): 1–8. For background, see Michael Fara, "Dispositions," in *The Stanford Encyclopedia of Philosophy*.

4. It follows that in the absence of commitment to evaluative judgments, including moral ones, talk of "risk" is ultimately unfounded and incoherent. I leave it to the skeptic to try to establish that this is a problem for our ordinary and scholarly discourses about risk and related phenomena, but doubt that any such demonstration will be forthcoming.

5. My principal source here is George M. Wilson, *Seeing Fictions in Film: The Epistemology of Movies* (Oxford: Oxford University Press, 2011). For additional background, see Paisley Livingston and Carl Plantinga, eds., *The Routledge Companion to Philosophy and Film* (London: Routledge, 2009).

6. This is obviously an intentionalist approach to the determination of fictional content, but it is a "partial" or moderate one. I provide a broader perspective on, and justification of, such an approach in my *Art and Intention* (Oxford: Clarendon, 2005).

7. In this regard I fully concur with David Bordwell, who parenthetically deems the tie between short-term memory loss and the reverse structure of the film "fairly arbitrary." This point can be reinforced by observing that any film that induced temporary anterograde amnesia in spectators would thereby render them incapable of following even a moderately complicated story. For Bordwell's insightful characterization of the narrative design of *Memento*, see

    Paisley Livingston

The Way Hollywood Tells It: Story and Design in Modern Movies (Berkeley: University of California Press, 2006), 89–91. For discussions of the film's philosophical implications, see Andrew Kania, ed., *Memento* (London: Routledge, 2009).

8. I call this puzzling because these statements suggest that the denizens of Pleasantville previously had some kind of idea about what would have to be called "unreal" colors. Could this have been a matter of more or less able manipulation of color terms in the absence of the distinctive phenomenological qualities labeled by those terms? How could this work, and how could such people have had meaningful thoughts about something called "real colors"? It is hard, given the meager evidence provided in the film, to work out the details.

9. Peter Brunette and Marco Bellochio, "A Conversation with Marco Bellocchio," *Film Quarterly* 43, no. 1 (1989): 50.

10. Ibid., 52.

11. An anonymous reader of this essay worried that my interpretation of this film is "moralistic" in some unspecified but negative sense. In response to this criticism, I would like to point out that I espouse only a moderate form of moralism, that is, the thesis that moral content, such as the ethical attitudes promoted by a filmmaker in a work, is relevant to an overall artistic evaluation of that work's merit. For reasons outlined in the first parts of this chapter, thinking about risk, in fictional and other contexts, depends crucially on assigning values, including moral values, to actions and events. Given the prevalence of risk-related topics in cinematic works, the chances for a comprehensive, "immoralist" perspective on film look bleak.

12. For background to this paragraph, see Albert Bandura, *Social Learning Theory* (Englewood Cliffs, NJ: Prentice-Hall, 1977); and Jennifer Lackey, *Learning from Words: Testimony as a Source of Knowledge* (Oxford: Oxford University Press, 2008).

13. I elaborate on this and a few rival conceptions of fantasy in my *Cinema, Philosophy, Bergman: On Film as Philosophy* (Oxford: Oxford University Press, 2009), 187–92.

14. For more on the problem of warranted response, see Paisley Livingston and Alfred R. Mele, "Evaluating Emotional Responses to Fiction," in *Emotion and the Arts,* ed. Mette Hjort and Sue Laver (Oxford: Oxford University Press, 1997), 157–76.

SYLVIA J. MARTIN

Stunt Workers and Spectacle

Ethnography of Physical Risk in Hollywood and Hong Kong

This essay examines physical risk in the commercial film industries of Hollywood and Hong Kong. Many of the films that emerge from commercial industries and garner profits in the hundreds of millions of dollars are composed of spectacular images of action and death.[1] Through the anthropological method of ethnographic fieldwork, including on-site observation and interviews, I illustrate that the production of spectacle acquires a logic of its own, in which a range of commercial media personnel adhere to the industrial dictum that spectacle reaps profit. Most commercial film industries are engaged in an endless quest for spectacle, mirroring capitalism's infinite pursuit of profit. Profit making in these industries is dependent, in part, on the ceaseless quest for spectacle, since many of the global blockbusters are films that feature stunning action sequences that transcend language barriers. Thus, these industries are sustained by the various physical risks that the production of spectacle involves. Inasmuch as stunt work is integral to bodily spectacle, I explore stunt workers' attitudes toward risk, what I call "risk attitudes," as well as the practices in which such attitudes find expression. I focus on the labor of stunt doubles, since stunt doubles are hired to perform the most dangerous sequences of stunts, such as the impact of a car crash, in order to protect actors. The risk-taking practices of stunt doubles, I posit, also connote the uncanny of the double as representative of the dangerous and the deadly.

My argument is comprised of three points: first, that for stunt workers, and stunt doubles in particular, physical risk in the filming process is mediated by socio-professional concerns; in other words, physical risk is rarely perceived within a purely physical context. As Faye Ginsburg has demonstrated, media production is a matter of both cultural products and social *processes*.[2] The ways in which people perform their jobs in commercial media production emerge out of interactions with a range of other people and ideologies. This is demonstrated through the work of stunt doubles, who must carefully negotiate with actors in order to create a unified sequence of dangerous bodily spectacle in the course of what is essentially a fragmented labor process. Second, a decisive reason for the risk taking of stunt workers is the drive for spectacle from within the commercial film industries. Third, I claim that physical risk taking can be "productive."[3] Although physical risk taking can destroy the body of individual stunt workers, it nourishes the commercial film industries and contributes to their profits. I conclude by looking at various affective techniques that stunt workers employ for managing physical risk.

This essay is part of a multisited ethnographic study of commercial film/TV production processes, which includes interactions between the production sites of Hollywood and Hong Kong. Highly prolific commercial media hubs, Hollywood and the "Hollywood of the East" (as Hong Kong has been described by media scholars and professionals) have over the decades converged in stunt styles and labor as well as coproductions and financing. As with other transnational studies that emphasize interactivity[4] and connections over commonalities,[5] I shift between the stunt workers of Hollywood and Hong Kong in order to talk about the theme of spectacular physical risk that is pertinent to both sites, yet articulated in different ways due to the trajectory of each industry. It is not my intention here to situate Hollywood as the standard by which physical risk is measured. A notable difference within this transnational ensemble of stunt workers is that Hong Kong's stunt labor is not presently unionized, unlike much of Hollywood's. As a result, Hong Kong stunt workers commonly experience more fluid hiring and remuneration arrangements whereas stunt work in Hollywood features more segmentation through job specialization. The stunt population in Hollywood is more extensive than that of Hong Kong, with a more sizeable female population.[6] Despite these disparities, I contend that by examining the range of engagements with physical risk across these key sites of production we gain a richer understanding of what it is to perform dangerous bodily labor. I turn now to the concept of physical risk.

RISK CONCEPTUALIZED

The concept of risk that has emerged in modernity refers to "conditions in which the probability estimates of an event are able to be known or

                                                    Sylvia J. Martin

knowable."[7] Individualized calculative behaviors have come to be promoted under liberal governance and modern forms of reflexivity.[8] In the social sciences, risk-taking practices surrounding the physical body have been steeped within the rationality/irrationality discourse that proliferated in fields such as economics, psychology, and cognitive science, with the dominant discourse framing bodily risk taking as irrational. Yet diverging from the emphasis on risk avoidance is what Deborah Lupton refers to as the "counter discourse" of risk and risk taking as a positive undertaking. This alternative scholarship explores risk taking as intentional and valued for its potential in self-cultivation.[9] Stephen Lyng borrows Hunter S. Thompson's term *edgework* to illustrate the phenomenon of people who intentionally undertake perilous activities for a liberatory, even pleasurable, experience in which one's physical and mental stamina is tested and aspirations to self-actualization are achieved. Edgework lushly conveys the intoxicating and transportive experience of skirting the boundaries between life and death, order and disorder, armed with uneven combinations of skilled control and chance. Yet, unlike the communities in these studies, my research focuses on a workforce that does not pursue risk taking as a leisure activity but as a labor practice in the context of capitalist industries. While Giddens posits that risk taking in the economic sector (and I include here the commercial media industries) hinges on flirtations with uncertainty,[10] stunt workers strive to reduce unpredictability regarding their survival. In her ethnography of traders at the Chicago Board of Trade and their risk-taking practices in the financial futures market, anthropologist Caitlin Zaloom points out that earlier ethnographic analyses have depicted risk taking as unsettling the regularity of an "ordered existence" associated with a modern social condition. Working in a different direction, Zaloom argues that risk should be recognized as productive in that its pursuit actually engenders the infrastructure and organization of the financial futures market.[11] Although the film industry is emblematic of modernity, as it proffers novel perspectives on the world and thus the opportunity to rework one's life in relation to those newly envisioned prospects,[12] my discussion of risk follows Zaloom's in emphasizing that risk-taking practices are productive. As with the traders that Zaloom studied, the intentional risk-taking practices of stunt workers generate the spectacle that the commercial film industries of Hollywood and Hong Kong market. The bodies of these women and men are their instruments for physically risky labor. I define physical risk as the potential for bodily harm from external dangers and examine how risk is constitutive of spectacle.

Studios and production companies sell the illusion that car crashing, bungee jumping, and action fighting stunts are performed by the actors themselves. Yet production executives have a stake in maintaining the safety of these star commodities and are therefore reliant upon a labor sector to protect the bodies of their stars. Many of the stunt performers I observed and interviewed have worked over the decades as stunt doubles under contracts and agreements that stipulated their anonymity so as to protect this illusion. In this section I shall examine the complex labor of stunt doubles and how their physical risks are constitutive of spectacle.

The stunt double merits attention inasmuch as the image of the stunt is among the most valorized within spectacular films, just as, conversely, the labor of the double who performs the most crucial and dangerous component of the stunt is among the most veiled. A stunt double is a stunt worker who is hired to perform certain physical activities for an actor, those activities being considered a risk to the actors' "health and good looks," even in cases where an actor is not recognized as a valuable commodity.[13] What is at stake in this process can be evoked by considering an example of a star who injured herself while performing a stunt. The film I have in mind is Ann Hui's Hong Kong film *Ah Kam* (1996). In outtakes that play over the end credits, star Michelle Yeoh, known for performing her own stunts, is seen immediately after she sustained an injury from a fall taken from a bridge. The dazed look of pain in Yeoh's eyes as she turns her face to the camera attests to the serious physical risks courted in the creation of dazzling stunts. These outtakes also serve as an industrial cautionary tale about the necessity of stunt doubles for star commodities.[14]

Stunt doubles typically absorb the physical risks for actors. In the photo below of a Hollywood female stunt worker named Courtney,[15] we see the injuries that can result from stunt doubling on a film. Courtney's injuries included a skull fracture in four places, an eye socket fracture, and two black eyes. In observing this stunt double's bloody visage, we are confronted with the effects of the hazards of the shadowy labor of stunt doubles, effects that are rarely displayed in the celebratory "making of" industrial narratives of stunt work. Yet if, as Toby Miller et al. claim, a film is a commodity the value of which results from the labor that creates it,[16] an analysis of film and risk must attend to the labor that comprises cinematic spectacle, particularly its gendered dimensions. Even with the growth of computer-generated imagery in film, action sequences primarily rely on bodily labor. To contextualize the risks of such bodily labor, I will discuss the general labor conditions of stunt doubles.

    Sylvia J. Martin

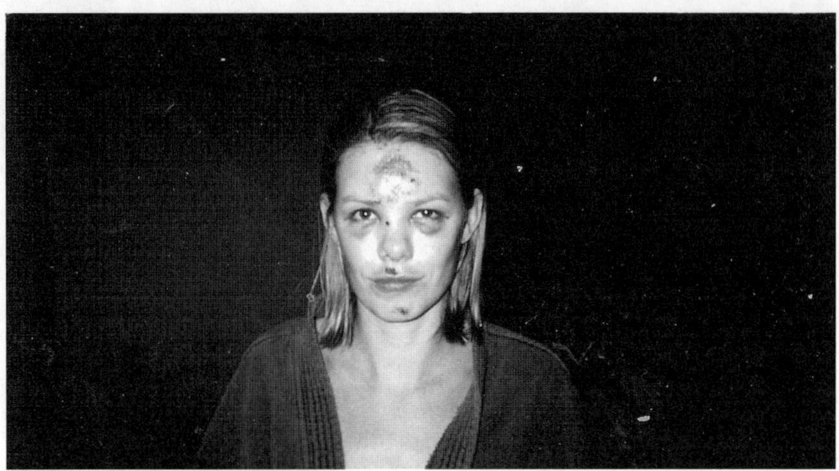

Courtney after one of her stunts.

The use of a stunt double is essentially a form of visual trickery on the part of filmmakers in the Hollywood and Hong Kong film industries. In most cases, the actor appears in shots leading up to or immediately after the actual stunt. In the effort to accomplish a visually seamless performance to assist the editing process, the wardrobe, hair, and makeup departments may also be involved. Since the double must be of similar height, body build, and coloring as the actor, attending to physical risk is only one of the tasks that confront the stunt double. There is greater attention to the correspondence between the contours of the bodies of actors and doubles in Hollywood, whereas in Hong Kong stunt coordinators allot less time to searching for an exact match since production schedules for filmmaking in Hong Kong are generally much shorter. I discovered that among Hollywood stunt doubles, staying fit is important not only for the agility needed to perform stunts safely but also to stay competitive in an industry in which executives increasingly demand taut bodies, particularly in the case of female actors. Ideally, stunt doubles should be slimmer than the actors they double: a double must be able to wear the same size costume as the actor in order to maintain the same silhouette, even with protective padding underneath.

It is important to point out here that the stakes for physical risk for male and female stunt workers differ. The sexualized spectacle that female actors constitute in commercial film increases the physical risk for female doubles. For instance, the frequently revealing costumes and greater display of skin for female actors means that their stunt doubles are unable to wear as much protective clothing and padding as male doubles, whose actors are usually more fully clothed and therefore padded.[17] A female double who must jump out of a moving vehicle in a short, tight-fitting dress while wearing high heels is left little room for padding, and she is likely to incur more broken bones, ripped ligaments, and bruises in this situation than if she wore jeans and a jacket.

In some cases, more permanent measures than weight loss are taken by doubles. Stunt workers who are contracted to double for a star for a series of films may undergo plastic surgery in an effort to shore up disparities between their image and that of the actor they are doubling. Calf implants and rhinoplasty are not uncommon surgeries among contracted doubles, since legs and noses are among the features with the most prominent outlines in silhouette; the faces of stunt doubles are rarely filmed from a full frontal position.

Yet even ostensibly minor cosmetic details enable and constrain the labor of stunt doubles. Although stunt work requires physical strength and agility, several female stunt doubles in Hollywood commented that they had won jobs over other potential doubles partly because of their hair's similarity to that of the actor. With increasingly sophisticated camera technologies such as Hi-Definition, cosmetic details such as hairstyles undergo unprecedented scrutiny. Hair, especially for female actors, is considered one of the most obvious identifiers, and the more similarity there is between actor and double without wigs, the lower the hair department can keep its budget, as expensive wigs should only be budgeted for actors, not doubles. One stunt double who works in Hollywood told me that her employment on a film was due to the hair supervisor's approval as much as the director's. "For the *Kill Bill* job, the reason I got that was because Quentin liked me, and my hair was right. The hair guy liked my hair—all he had to put on was a cheap fall, because my hair in front was right, light and fine like hers. And the hair guy was a famous, famous hair guy. He told the stunt coordinator to hire me, so I was hired."

I return now to Courtney and her on-set accident. In the course of doubling on a Hollywood film for a female actor in 2000, she sustained the worst injury of her career. A scar still lingers on her forehead and asphalt remains embedded in her head from where it split open. This episode of how physical risks are realized and managed reveals the tremendous personal cost of spectacle for commercial purposes and the potentially infinite substitutability of the stunt double's individual labor.

For this job, Courtney was hired to double for an actor whose character was supposed to jump out of a moving semitruck, yet the execution of the stunt did not go smoothly. "They decided I would get swung out of the truck. But when we did the shot, instead of facing the vehicle in the direction it is moving, which you need to do to hit the ground in the tuck position, I was straight up and down, so when I landed it was like getting pushed down at forty miles an hour and then I bounced off the pavement and there was a bright flash of light. I remember this hideous horrible pain and everyone yelling, 'Call an ambulance!'"

Although Courtney was taken immediately to a hospital, saving her costume for *her* replacement double was of paramount concern to the production team in its bid to stay on schedule. The stunt coordinator and members of the hair department were unable to remove the bloody wig Courtney had been wearing because the pins attached to her hair had become embedded in her scalp on impact. Her wig was finally removed at the hospital, whereupon it was rushed back to the set, washed clean of blood, and pinned to the scalp of the next stunt double who had been called up in the meantime so that the stunt could be reshot and completed that same day.

Of the physical pain, Courtney said, "I never lost consciousness, which was horrible because I've never been in pain like that. I cried finally when they told me my neck wasn't broken." Regarding the importance of maintaining the integrity of the wig so that the filming of the stunt could be completed, Courtney spoke of another painful realization. "It taught me a lesson. Stunt people can be carted off and die. Bottom line is, we are expendable. Because the actress can't even get bruised. I fractured my skull, and my actress didn't come to see me in the hospital." Despite Courtney's comment, many stunt doubles would not expect a hospital visit from the actor they double. In Hollywood, due in part to the division between above-the-line and below-the-line labor, many stunt doubles are expected by production management to refrain from talking to the actors they double except to communicate technical information, their very presence an imposition on the actor.[18] Yet some stunt doubles, such as Courtney, recognize the power relations that configure their protective labor and the transference of the risk of physical injury onto their persons.

Thus it becomes apparent that while the spectacle of stunts can reap enormous profits for media conglomerates and production executives, the labor it requires can be deadly for the stunt performers involved. In the next section, I explore how stunt doubles, frequently denied onscreen credit and on-set speaking rights while absorbing danger and injury for actors, constitute a spectral form of labor.

THE UNCANNY LABOR OF THE STUNT DOUBLE

As suggested by the title of the job, there is an uncanny aspect to shadowing an actor's violent actions, in many cases anonymously duplicating the original in the service of spectacle. In his discussion of the uncanny, Freud noted that the double represents "the uncanny harbinger of death."[19] In Freudian scholarship and literature, glimpsing one's own double, or Doppelgänger, portends something sinister, such as the death of the person who sees his or her own double. Setting aside psychoanalytic implications of the double, I am concerned here with the socio-professional and ontological dimensions of the relevant film-production practice. The stunt double indeed signifies death in that the double performs dangerous stunts that can go horribly wrong (such as evidenced by Courtney's injuries). Yet unlike the specter of the double, in performing the stunt, the stunt double transfers the physical risk from the actor onto him- or herself, thus protecting the actor by absorbing the potential for deadly injury. According to stunt workers (and financiers who demand the use of completion bonds), the stunt double, unlike the actor—and particularly a star—is considered expendable. In a dialectical sense, then, the double, who represents mortality, actually bestows the promise of *im*mortality on the actor. Hence Courtney's fraught relationship with stunt doubling in the production process.

The double may additionally protect his or her actor through other on-set tasks such as providing padding to avoid any potential discomfort or incidental injury. An actor will generally perform the beginning or end shots of a stunt, such as delivering the first blow in a fight or lying on the ground after the stunt double has filmed the shot of being hit. Doubles may guide their actors by suggesting how to position themselves and where to pad themselves so that they remain comfortable and avoid getting sore or bruised. Observing, coaching, and physically assisting the actor is a task that the stunt coordinator usually delegates to the double.

Stunt doubling in Hollywood is a largely silent form of labor; in addition to the on-set etiquette of minimal conversation with the actor unless it regards safety precautions, the double utters no onscreen dialogue. In both Hollywood and Hong Kong films, the labor of the stunt double is visible yet invisible: the stunt that the double performs is the essence of the bodily spectacle, yet that performance should not be discernible as distinct from the actor's performance.[20] To maintain the illusion, many stunt workers in both Hollywood and Hong Kong doubled for years without receiving screen credits. While since the mid-1990s more doubles in Hollywood are publicly asserting their labor, there are celebrities who claim to perform all their own stunts and who are contractually promoted as doing so. Yet Courtney's experience (and the implementation of completion bonds) highlights the endless, expendable supply of doubles for the irreplaceable source, the actor.

    Sylvia J. Martin

The challenges of the stunt double aligning him- or herself with the actor illustrate the extent to which the physical risks of doubling are linked to social and professional risks. The interface between actor and double is supposed to be seamless. Yet the stunt double disrupts the coherence of the actor's performance. In Freud's conceptualization, the double is the subject's substitute, and thus "there is a doubling, dividing and interchanging of the self."[21] In Hollywood in particular, where there is in some situations a discernible division between above-the-line and below-the-line labor, an ensemble of stratified labor constitutes the supposed unity of the performed stunt.

Thus, although their terms of employment and status on a film project differ, the relationship between the actor and the stunt double, particularly in Hollywood, is characterized by uneasy interdependence. For example, the stunt double is expected to mimic the actor to whom he or she is assigned. "You have to study the actor to convey him, to mimic the way he moves and acts," a stunt coordinator and former double remarked. This point was also expressed by many other stunt doubles. Managing one's relationship with one's actor, it turns out, is integral to retaining one's job, and it is a relationship that can take time to nurture. As Courtney said, "If you have a good relationship with your actor, it's like a marriage; they trust you." Yet while some actors are grateful that doubles take their fall for them, others want to be seen as able to do their own stunts. In fact, for some actors, there is a fear of being usurped by their double, recalling Freud's claim that the double can exercise agency over its source, surmounting it. Particularly on low-budget films with unknown actors, an actor's tenuous hold on his or her own job status may be further unsettled by an attractive stunt double. The line can be further blurred if the actor has an athletic history. The use of a double in this case may, from the perspective of the actor, represent personal inadequacy, and stunt doubles speak of actors who try to perform their own stunts. One time, when an actor she doubled attempted to sabotage Courtney's onscreen visibility, Courtney disciplined her actor by actually increasing the risk of physical injury to her. "She was rude to me so people told me, 'You know what you do to actors like that? You forget to give them a couple of kneepads. Let her hit her knees, see how it feels.' It's kind of a dirty trick but sometimes they need to be humbled. I've been snubbed by actors and it's like, 'I'm getting hit by a car for you!'"

It becomes apparent that risks of a physical nature coexist alongside risks of a socio-professional character. These risks are all constitutive features of the spectacular imagery so desired by studios and production executives. Physical risk is, however, of particular importance, for it generates the socio-professional risks in this instance, and is causally linked to the profits pursued by the commercial film industries.

SPECTACLE AT ALL COSTS

Spectacle has become emblematic of commercial film, and film sets as well as bodies are routinely set ablaze with the intention of thrilling audiences with astonishing catastrophes. While conducting ethnographic fieldwork on the production processes of commercial media, I observed that risks of a physical nature are necessitated by commercial media industries' perceived need to manufacture and market spectacle. I also found that the production of spectacle is an affective and even visceral experience for a range of media workers.

One night in February 2004, while working as an "extra" on the set of a Hollywood television drama, I observed the burning of the set on which I was working at the Warner Bros. studio lot. According to the show's producers, the promotion of such a spectacle would increase viewer ratings. It was the end of a late-night shoot, around 11 p.m., and chilly. I huddled with the other extras for warmth as we watched the special-effects personnel assemble the pyrotechnic materials to set the restaurant on fire. Although the shot did not require any of the cast, setting the restaurant ablaze was nevertheless a risky operation because of the production members' proximity to the flames. After the special-effects team prepared the restaurant for the explosion, the assistant directors yelled at us to stand further back. On cue, the structure exploded, orange blazes shooting into the air. The studio's fire department extinguished the flames, which could have burned out of control in the winds. Even though this contrived catastrophe—this glowing inferno of a spectacle—was designed for purely fictional purposes, we all experienced the actual effects of it, such as the acrid smoke that made most of us cough and our eyes tear up. The physical destruction of the set also elicited an affective response from many involved in the production. They expressed a sense of awe and achievement at the destruction of the structure: applauding, cheering, exclaiming, and high-fiving one another. Later I asked one of the assistant directors, Ron, about the potential dangers to everyone in the vicinity of filming such an explosion, and he responded, "Well, that's part of the excitement!" Several of the other crew members echoed his sentiment.[22] As was evident from the display of victory that accompanied the assault on the built environment, media workers engage dynamically with such visual and affective stimulation, the set becoming a sensorium of sorts as a result. Thus we see that the affective dimension of risk taking in the production of spectacle is interwoven with physical risk in the form of bodily hazards.

The human, bodily dimension of risk has persisted in some of the most dangerous film-production practices such as stunt work, even though techniques such as computer graphics are increasingly being used. As Yau, a veteran stunt worker and action director of dozens of Hong Kong films, remarked, producers and directors have over the past several decades called for increasingly dangerous stunts, the rationale being that such astonishing visual displays will lure more viewers to the cinemas. Yau recalled a conversation he had recently had in which a fight choreographer on a film asked his advice on how to film, in one take, a close-up, slow-motion shot of a man being hit by a car wherein the tires drove over the man's body and his body rolled underneath the car. The film director insisted that an actual body be used for the close-up instead of animatronics or computer graphics. Surprised by the director's insistence on the graphic extremity of the stunt, Yau told the fight choreographer, "Here's how you do the stunt: you find a guy with a terminal disease, and he can do it!" He laughed as he recounted this exchange, but then grew serious as he contemplated the director's demand, commenting that it is only since he has become an action director with a team of stunt workers to manage that he has found himself wondering why there is such a demand for realistically brutal stunts. Of this pressure, he commented, "When I was a stunt guy, I'd do anything. I didn't want to lose face. I didn't worry about myself. But now I have more of a responsibility than that. I have to protect the guys." Yau's half-joking remark to his colleague that the performance of extreme stunts requires a double already facing imminent death is a stark reminder that the likelihood of a body's surviving such labor is small. Consequently, Yau grapples with the implications of computer technologies: the use of computer graphics protects the lives of stunt workers, just as the widespread deployment of such graphics threatens to render stunt work obsolete.

For some stunt workers, the physical risks that filmic spectacle entails are offset by a sense of control over the material conditions under which stunts are performed. As a stunt coordinator insisted, "Filming a stunt involving a motorbike race, we are in a controlled environment, versus a bike racer really racing in the canyons." Yet even the film set's "controlled environment" cannot adequately protect workers from risk. Wanda, a female Hollywood stunt worker, suffered severe injuries from a motorcycle stunt she performed in which she missed the ramp for a jump and lost control of her bike. Wanda broke both sides of her jaw and lost several teeth; her remaining teeth were hanging from their roots. In the ten hours of reconstructive surgery she underwent, Wanda had her teeth wired through her gums, a titanium plate inserted into her chin, screws implanted into her jawbone, and her mouth wired shut. She was compensated for the time she lost working and the surgeries were paid for by the insurance that the production company had purchased, but Wanda had to adjust to the surgical results of her injuries. "I hated my new smile. I loved my old teeth, loved my old dimple, but that's gone now because of the reconstructive surgery," she reminisced, fingering her reconstructed jawline. As Wanda's experience attests, the death-defying stunts that are the staple of filmic spectacle are dangerous work practices, no matter how "controlled" the process.

A female stunt worker who had broken her back while doubling for an actor spoke of the change in her previously nonchalant attitude toward the dangers of stunts. "I had a different philosophy when I went back. I learned a respect I never had before. There is no 'little' stunt. You need to understand that anything can go wrong. So don't blow it off. There is no 'just' falling down, no 'just' getting a glass at your head."

Given the commercial film industries' relentless grind of spectacular imagery that demands physical risk taking from its personnel, I next examine the socially mediated ways in which stunt workers attempt to manage risk. These techniques include embracing a sense of adventure and teamwork as well as fostering reliance upon family networks.

Affective Management of Physical Risk

Sitting in an office from nine to five, that would kill me.

In the quote above, a stunt double who has worked on dozens of Hollywood blockbusters wryly expressed the fear of bodily stagnation that is widespread among stunt workers, who consider the high falls and car crashes of stunt doubling an opportunity to pursue physical activity and thrill seeking in the form of a job. Attitudes toward physical risk convey the continual battle for affective and physical control over chance that jumping out of moving vehicles, crashing cars, and enduring explosions entail. Here I look at affective techniques, including the transformation of fear qua negative experience into a positive process and the optimization of kinship ties. The point here is to underscore the extent to which physical risk, at least in the context of stunt work, is mediated by social processes.

For some stunt workers, a kind of alchemy occurs in which the fear of physical risk is converted into adrenaline, frequently culminating in a feeling of exhilaration after the completion of a dangerous stunt with minimal

                                    Sylvia J. Martin

or no injury. While reveling in the freedom from desk-bound toil, these thrill seekers also offer their bodies up to be hurled and hit for the benefit of the commercial film industries, whose profits far outweigh those of the stunt workers. As a female stunt worker said of the physical risks that she faces before taking a hundred-foot dive off a building, "I don't think of it as fear, I think of it as adrenaline. If you start thinking about it as fear, you will be scared. It's like tricking yourself into believing you can do something." Another stunt worker told me, "There are nerves and butterflies but I feel it more as adrenaline, not fear. I see stunts as an adventure, not a risk."

Many stunt workers honed this transformative attitude through prior training and skills acquisition in circus work, Chinese opera performance, or competitive sports. One stunt coordinator attributed his skill at performing high jumps of a hundred feet or more off buildings to his years of experience in circus acrobatics, which trained him in "aerial awareness." The Hong Kong action director Yau, who studied in one of the private academies of Beijing Opera in Hong Kong in the late 1950s, was trained to overcome his childhood fear of performing backflips and jumps through instruction and peer pressure. Yau studied under his *sifu* (master) from the age of seven to seventeen, following a strict schedule of training with other children. Whenever he hesitated to perform a stunt, his *sifu* would admonish him that his peers had successfully performed the stunt and they remained intact, and thus he should follow suit. The idea that his fears deserved special consideration was summarily dismissed. The repetitive discipline, combined with the team-building support from the other students that greeted him after he completed a dreaded move, helped Yau to start viewing the physical risks as minimal and to trust his training and expertise, to the point of his being able to enjoy the opera performances and, later, film stunt work.

Many stunt workers are self-acknowledged thrill seekers who engage in calculative practices. Kelly explains it thus:

> Stunt people are thrill seekers, not daredevils. I don't like being called a daredevil. A daredevil looks at a cliff from seventy feet up and says, "Wow, that would be fun to jump off of!" But he can land wrong. He may jump off the cliff into the water without checking the depth of water first, which can change from week to week. He won't take precautions. A stunt person—a thrill seeker—would practice jumping off at a low level first, then work their way up to sixty feet; they would check the depth of the water first; they would work themselves up to that level; they would practice. We're

trained professionals. We make calculations and we practice and rehearse.

On many Hollywood and Hong Kong film sets, there is limited time budgeted in which to rehearse a stunt (unless, as with big-budget Hollywood films, there is a second unit devoted solely to action), so precautions such as the ones described by Kelly sometimes have to be taken in one's personal time. Kelly credits her circus experience as a flying trapeze artist with teaching her how to perform under the pressure of live audiences when there is no second take, as is often the case with stunt filming. Others also emphasized that the physical expertise they had acquired through prior live performance—whether it be circus work, Chinese opera performance, or competitive sports—was excellent training for stunts that require precision and coordination on a rushed film-production schedule with little time to rehearse. As a veteran stunt double who toured with a circus for several years said, "Anyone can jump off a building, but they'll only do it once in life: they'll die. It's the precision that's required that makes it hard. Anyone can crash a car, but to do it at a certain speed, a certain angle, with the camera nearby and not hit anyone, and make it look authentic, is hard. It's a skill."

Other considerations shape attitudes toward physical risk, such as kinship ties. On a cloudy February day in 2006 in Hong Kong, the production coordinator for a film shoot invited me to observe a Hong Kong stunt coordinator direct a car crash. As I stood behind the protective barrier with other members of the production unit, the stunt coordinator, Wong, gave a few words of instruction to the young stunt worker who was assigned to take the hit from the car that Wong was going to drive. Wong then climbed into the car, backed up several yards, stopped, and started to drive forward. The young man ran toward the oncoming car and was then struck. The car immediately halted as the man's body rolled up the hood of the car, slammed against the windshield, and rolled off onto the cement ground. The action director called, "Cut!" and the young man picked himself up off the ground to applause from the spectators. Wong jumped out of the car and clapped the young man on the back.

As we applauded from the sidelines, the production coordinator informed me that the car crash was performed by a father-son stunt team. When I asked Wong later that day how it felt to hit his son with a car, it became apparent that the physical risks of a car crash to an individual family member were outweighed by the risk of the loss of a family practice and profession. Wong emphasized that striking his son with a car represented the continuation of a family tradition of action and stunts, illustrating how physical risk should be understood alongside social practices. Physical risk is a productive element here through which not only a film industry but also a kin-based network are maintained.

Kin-based networks are a discernible feature among stunt workers in Hollywood and Hong Kong. For a craft whose practitioners seek to create an atmosphere of trust and reliability, family hiring practices are a prime strategy. Hollywood "stunt dynasties" are legendary, and as a Hollywood stunt double and wife of a stunt coordinator told me, "I was a bit nervous the first time I was set on fire, but my [stunt coordinator] husband had worked with his fire specialist a hundred times, so I felt in good hands." Lee, a Hong Kong stunt worker and fight choreographer, comes from three generations of Cantonese opera performers and was trained as a child to perform onstage by his father, grandfather, uncle, and older brother. His fear of performing onstage was assuaged by his grandfather. Years later, when his uncle and brothers performed in televised and filmed adaptations of Cantonese operas, they recruited him as a trusted performer.

Stunt coordinators and action directors who rehire the same team members remark that working with the same team—particularly family members—is a common tactic for reducing physical risks, since members of the network are familiar with the individuals' limitations as well as their strengths, and directions are thus more easily conveyed. As with many industries, family hiring practices are maintained not only to pool economic resources but also to instill a sense of trust.[23] While family hiring practices involve complex dynamics and are exclusionary,[24] the kinship ties in the Hollywood and Hong Kong film industries should be understood as a strategy for avoiding physical risk.

CONCLUSION

As I have argued, the precise nature of physical risk varies according to the specificity of contexts of labor, and this in turn highlights the extent to which physical risk is mediated by socio-professional concerns. Ultimately, the risk attitudes and risk-taking practices of stunt workers, and stunt doubles in particular, cannot be abstracted from the processes through which their work is put into operation by the commercial film industries of Hollywood and Hong Kong—industries that hinge on the twin pillars of spectacle and profit. While storylines are considered important, spectacle—which still entails physical labor despite the increasing use of computer graphics—is assumed by diverse media personnel to be desirable, and therefore profitable. Physical risk is thus "productive" in that it generates spectacular images and profits for the commercial film industries even as it is destructive of stunt workers' bodies, particularly those of stunt doubles. We might conclude with a question that is well worth pondering: If there is no limit to the production of spectacle, is there no limit to the physical risks incurred in its pursuit?

Notes

1. By spectacle, I refer to the visual form intended to stun and thrill viewers that is evident in many contemporary film genres and television programs and that originated in the American and French pre-1906 silent film era. See, for instance, John T. Caldwell, *Televisuality: Style, Crisis, and Authority in American Television* (Piscataway: Rutgers University Press, 1995), 5; Tom Gunning, "The Cinema of Attractions: Early Film, Its Spectator, and the Avant-Garde," in *Early Cinema: Space, Frame, Narrative,* ed. Thomas Elsaesser and Adam Barker (London: British Film Institute, 1990), 61; Thomas Elsaesser, "Early Cinema: From Linear History to Mass Media Archaeology," in Elsaesser and Barker, *Early Cinema,* 4.

2. Faye Ginsburg, "Indigenous Media: Faustian Contract or Global Village?" *Cultural Anthropology* 6 (1991): 93.

3. Caitlin Zaloom, "The Productive Life of Risk," *Cultural Anthropology* 19 (2004): 365.

4. Mei Zhan, "Does It Take a Miracle? Negotiating Knowledges, Identities and Communities of Traditional Chinese Medicine," *Cultural Anthropology* 16 (2001): 453–80.

5. Inderpal Grewal and Caren Kaplan, *Scattered Hegemonies: Postmodernity and Transnational Feminist Practices* (Minneapolis: University of Minnesota Press, 1994).

6. In the Hong Kong film industry, action directors and fight choreographers sometimes hire Hong Kong male stunt workers or mainland Chinese female stunt workers to double for female actors. Doubling across gender occurs in Hollywood as well, including short female stunt workers doubling as boys.

7. Deborah Lupton, *Risk* (London: Routledge, 1999), 7.

8. Ulrich Beck, *Risk Society: Towards a New Modernity* (London: Sage, 1992); Anthony Giddens, *The Consequences of Modernity* (Cambridge: Polity, 1990); Anthony Giddens, *Modernity and Self-Identity* (Cambridge: Polity, 1991); Nikolas Rose, "Governing 'Advanced' Liberal Democracies," in *Foucault and Political Reason: Liberalism, Neoliberalism and Rationalities of Government,* ed. Andrew Barry, Thomas Osborne, and Nikolas Rose (Chicago: University of Chicago Press, 1996), 37–64.

9. Stanley Cohen and Laurie Taylor, *Escape Attempts: The Theory and Practice of Resistance to Everyday Life,* 2nd ed. (London: Routledge, 1992); Stephen Lyng, "Edgework: A Social Psychological Analysis of Voluntary Risk Taking," *American Journal of Sociology* 95 (1990): 851–86; Lupton, *Risk,* 152.

10. Giddens, *Modernity and Self-Identity*, 132.

11. Zaloom, "The Productive Life of Risk," 365.

12. Arjun Appadurai, *Modernity at Large: Cultural Dimensions of Globalization* (Minneapolis: University of Minnesota Press, 1996), 31; Walter Benjamin, "The Work of Art in the Age of Mechanical Reproduction," in *Illuminations*, ed. Hannah Arendt (New York: Schocken Books, 1968), 236; Giddens, *Modernity and Self-Identity*, 133.

13. Scott Siegel and Barbara Siegel, *The Encyclopedia of Hollywood* (New York: Facts on File, 1990), 412.

14. In addition to the preservation of actors by the hiring of stunt doubles, many films in Hollywood and Hong Kong require completion bonds, which protect financiers from the loss of what is referred to as an "essential element" from the production, such as an injury to or death of the film's star, which can bring production to a standstill.

15. In accordance with the regulations for research on human subjects stipulated by the Institutional Review Board for the larger anthropological project from which this piece draws, all names have been changed to protect confidentiality.

16. Toby Miller, Nitin Govil, John McMurria, Richard Maxwell, and Ting Wang, *Global Hollywood 2* (London: British Film Institute, 2005), 5.

17. For more on female Hollywood stunt doubles, see M. Banks, "Bodies of Work: Rituals of Doubling and the Erasure of Film/TV Production Labor" (PhD diss., UCLA, 2006), 175–237. I discovered Banks's dissertation after the manuscript for this chapter was completed; therefore, it was not incorporated into my analysis of risk and the uncanny labor of Hollywood and Hong Kong stunt doubles in the service of spectacle. Nevertheless, our independent studies of female Hollywood stunt doubles share several similar findings, attesting to some of the commonalities of their labor experience.

18. Usually after a period of time (which differs according to the length of the project and the dynamic between the actor and double), the double may approach his or her actor for increased instruction and conversation, unless the stunt coordinator mediates between the two. This dynamic is not as evident in Hong Kong production practices, where relationships are generally more casual.

19. Sigmund Freud, "The 'Uncanny,'" in *Writings on Art and Literature* (Stanford: Stanford University Press, 1997), 211.

20. There are varying levels of transparency as to who doubles for whom. In the past ten years in both Hollywood and Hong Kong, stunt doubles have increasingly made their identities known, despite NDAs (nondisclosure agreements), although many of the old guard consider this dishonorable.

21. Freud, "The 'Uncanny,'" 210.

22. Although I focus on film production, I include ethnographic fieldwork of television production since many contemporary film and television industry production practices have become entangled in one another, such that the

genres, spaces of filming, networks of personnel, and emergent technologies of both commercial industries intersect and overlap with each other.

23. Tejaswini Ganti, *Bollywood: A Guidebook to Popular Hindi Cinema* (New York: Routledge, 2004), 55. This point was also emphasized to me by a former stunt double whose father, uncle, and brother doubled for the same character played by different actors over time in a long-running film franchise.

24. Susan Greenhalgh, "De-Orientalizing the Chinese Family Firm," *American Ethnologist* 21 (1994): 746–75; Sylvia Junko Yanagisako, *Producing Culture and Capital: Family Firms in Italy* (Princeton: Princeton University Press, 2002).

FAYE GINSBURG

The Canary in the *Gemeinschaft?*

Disability, Film, and the Jewish Question

In the nineteenth century, canaries were taken into British mines to detect the potential risk to humans of methane gas, which is odorless but lethal. The sensitivity of this small, delicate bird to an invisible but deadly substance meant that if it died, a risk was present that humans would not have been able to detect. My title plays with the phrase "the canary in the mineshaft" that evolved from this poignant interspecies situation; in this chapter, I explore how scientific and documentary images of disability have served as visible evidence (the "canaries," if you will) of a kind of risk lurking in the Jewish community over the course of the twentieth and into the twenty-first century. The toxic element, in this case, is the stigmatization of the Jewish/disabled body within a particular *Gemeinschaft* (community), a development in which biomedical discourses are deeply implicated.[1] This process is an example of how "Otherness" becomes associated with the risk of danger or marginality, as discussed by cultural studies scholar Deborah Lupton in her book on the ways in which risk is understood in modernity.[2]

As a counterpoint to this process of exclusion, I examine recent works—primarily documentary films—that are reversing that trend through a different understanding of risk, one associated with the epistemological vertigo that comes with the breaking of social barriers by rendering visible alternative kinds of relationships with those conventionally regarded as "Other" through a process I call "mediated kinship." In these projects, relationships among family members with disabilities—which often require rethinking the normative frameworks of the taken-for-granted Gemeinschaft world—are reimagined on their own terms, and in ways that take the risk of recruiting relationships outside the biological family into a kinship arena. We might think of these as "unnatural family histories," made public through documentaries that become "parables of possibility" through the alternative cultural scripts that they offer viewers. I argue that these films, most of them quite recent, take the important step that is required in the contemporary era to reverse a long-standing stigma by taking the risk of visibility with those identified as disabled. Such films work through a logic of the embrace and reversal of stigma strongly identified with the new social movements of the postwar era (often reductively called identity politics). They speak back to the social and biomedical regimes that have too often defined the lives of people and their families who are living with a difference in ways that are far more flexible and inclusive than that of prior generations. In the case of films that are a partnership between a nondisabled filmmaker and a disabled subject, it is important to acknowledge that the risks involved in these media projects are different for each party, despite the depth of their collaboration. For an able-bodied person who makes a film about someone with a disability is not exposing him- or herself to the potential ridicule of less enlightened audiences. In my own interviews with disabled protagonists in these films, the risk of exposure to a potentially discriminatory gaze is eclipsed by the pleasures of gaining visibility on their own terms and on behalf of others also identified as disabled.

I focus much of this chapter on the work of filmmakers whose documentaries are diagnostic of the shifting meaning of disability in different Gemeinschaften from the 1930s to the present.[3] In particular, I examine recent works that address the human costs of the exclusion and denial of people with disabilities in the past by practitioners of Nazi "science," not only during the Third Reich but for decades beyond that, even into the 1990s. Other films focus on the denial of disability in the Jewish community in the postwar period. And, finally, the most recent works reveal the capacity of Jewish tradition to embrace different modes of embodiment as part of a more inclusive Gemeinschaft in the future, a position supported through idioms of kinship and human rights.

A Note on the Jewish Question and the Question of Technology[4]

My choice of the German word Gemeinschaft—in addition to its punning effect in the title—stresses a feature that distinguishes Jews from members of other religious communities. While Judaism as a faith draws on particular theology(ies) and practices, the category of "the Jew" also indexes a kin-based cultural world—a Gemeinschaft—as well as a shared (and seemingly inescapable) genetic heritage. As such, the question of Jewish identity

                                                                      Faye Ginsburg

problematizes more bounded definitions of religion as a community organized around shared belief and rituals.

To encompass that range associated with Jewish identity, I draw upon Foucault's understanding of technologies as methods that can "permit individuals to effect by their own means or with the help of others a certain number of operations on their own bodies and souls, thoughts, conduct, and way of being, so as to transform themselves in order to attain a certain state of happiness, purity, wisdom, perfection, or immortality . . . through which human beings produce an ethical self-understanding": what some scholars of his work have called "technologies of personhood."[5]

I suggest that the place of disability within the Jewish world has been shaped by recent profound changes in two key technologies that have played expanding roles over the last century in reframing contemporary personhood and in shifting our understandings of risk: biomedicine and documentary media. My work interrogates how transformations in these fields shaped ideas about the boundaries of Jewish identity—who is in and who is out—in ways that have inspired members of this community to take the risks involved in becoming "moral pioneers."[6]

In the case of biomedicine, we are living in what some have called the second "age of biology," an era dominated by new knowledge of things molecular and genetic. Its impact on daily life is felt through the routinization of prenatal genetic testing.[7] As historians of science have cautioned us, the new genetics of the late twentieth and twenty-first centuries exists in the shadow of the last century's eugenics, haunting the present like a "ghost in the machine," to use Sander Gilman's appropriation of the phrase.[8] Gilman elaborates on this idea in an article addressing questions of Jewish genetic disease: "[T]hose who see in genetic manipulation, alteration or selection the potential for the elimination of genetically transmitted diseases are constantly forced to confront a history that they claim not to be their own."[9]

Over the last two decades, assisted reproductive technologies (ARTs) have supported a growing potential for individualized "neoeugenics" in the technologically advanced West, where we find the routine use of genetic testing by individual couples and their choice to abort fetuses with genetic anomalies diagnostic of particular disabling conditions. Although U.S. genetic counselors are trained to express neutrality about the choices a pregnant woman and her partner may make around amniocentesis testing, the very existence of such a technology and the offer of such tests under the terms of consumer choice are premised on the desire for normalcy and fear of unknown abnormalities.[10] As my colleague Rayna Rapp and I have argued elsewhere, this normalizing discourse about disability that has emerged with the proliferation of reproductive technologies stands in distinction to the one accompanying the expansive, democratizing language of civil rights that has shaped the disability rights movement in particular. As a result, almost all "modern parents" might find themselves facing the contradictions created by progress in both biomedicine—premised on selecting against certain disabling conditions—and social movements founded on expanding democratic inclusion of all citizens, regardless of bodily condition.[11]

This is a circumstance faced more frequently by Jews of Ashkenazi descent—whether secular or religious—because of the high incidence of genetic disease in this population. For that reason, Ashkenazi Jews are strongly encouraged to have carrier or fetal screening for the eleven genetic disorders for which we are considered to be particularly at risk.[12] Debates about the implications for action based on this form of knowledge run deep in this community, motivating religious innovations in the management of such knowledge. Dor Yeshorim, for example, is an ultra-Orthodox Jewish genetic testing service that succeeds because of its ironclad policy of complete anonymity for its clients, whose genetic profiles are checked for compatibility even before a match is arranged, thus screening for potential genetic disease while avoiding abortion.[13] For less Orthodox and secular Jews, the technology of genetic testing has produced a kind of collective recognition of a community at risk, a social fact given form in the emergence of organizations in the United States such as the Jewish Genetic Disease Consortium and its constituent support groups. Indeed, many who know they carry one of the mutations for these diseases see themselves as linked in a kind of "imagined community" in which the medium is not the vernacular novel or the newspaper, as Benedict Anderson discussed, but mutated DNA.[14] For example, those who know they share this mutation but who are related in no other way may refer to each other as "cousin" on Internet support groups. As Gilman notes regarding genetic disease: "Those labeled as 'ill' in complex ways accept the label and turn it into a mark of identity. For is there nothing more redolent of 'identity' in the age of the human genome than our biological code? In an age of biologization, have not our genes become the ultimate definition of who we believe we are? . . . In the nuclear family, the desire is to construct a world beyond the nuclear family into which the illness can be projected and given meaning."[15] Awareness of the ghostly presence of even a single ancestral mutation that first occurred centuries ago, Gilman suggests, has particular consequences. "The phantom in the machine here is the story of the cohort [the genetic disease community] into which the family must insert itself."[16]

The process of constructing that "story of the cohort" brings us to the second technology: media. Over the last seventy years, exhilarating transformations have occurred in visual media technologies as an extension of the human capacity for witnessing, testifying, and storytelling, all forms for the production and circulation of new social facts as well as narrative invention. These changing "techne," marked by shifts from 16 mm film to analog video to the proliferation of the digital, are identified with particular forms of evidence, historicity, narrative, and poetics.[17] Photography and film were used to document and justify eugenics projects in prewar Europe and the United States, and they continued to play a significant role in the Nazi era (and beyond), in particular as evidence used by the infamous Dr. Mengele (among others). Since the 1940s, this visual legacy has not only been claimed and resignified as evidence of a horrific period but has also, more recently, been appropriated by documentary makers as part of the retelling of the intimate histories of survivors for whom such footage, ironically, may be one of the few fragile forms of material connection to their former lives, even as they hope to destroy this artifact representing profound humiliation.[18] In this process of reclamation, witnessing, and the creation of counternarratives, it is impossible to underestimate the impact of small-format, inexpensive, widely available media-making technologies—beginning with analog video in the 1980s, and Internet and other digitally based forms that first emerged in the 1990s. These have had remarkable effects as technologies (in the Foucauldian sense) that enabled the expansion of documentary to encompass new cultural subjects whose lives previously had been stigmatized and/or rendered invisible in public space.[19]

As some have argued regarding the impact of this form of media practice, the mediated subject does not emerge out of thin air.[20] Nor does it remain singular, for it is, rather, "subjectified" through a series of discursive regimes—religion, culture, and ethnicity being perhaps the most pronounced—that some have called attention to as the first-person plural.[21] In other words, the filmmaker does not simply reflect on his or her life and culture through the filmic text but uses these media technologies as forms of cultural intervention that extend beyond the "I" to the "we," and that can reach through time and space beyond the immediacy of face-to-face interaction. These works become meaningful in new ways as they enter into social worlds in their creation, exhibition, circulation, consumption, and resignification, as a constantly evolving cultural practice.

In tracing the transformative trajectory of the changing place of disability in Jewish life through documentary works, I rely on an understanding of media objects as polysemic, gaining new meanings as they follow unruly and constantly transforming paths over historical time, and as they enter into unanticipated social and cultural domains and take on new and different forms of authority. Once unleashed from their historical moment and original intention, media forms often promiscuously violate social and epistemological boundaries; they can move rapidly from the domain of scientific records to that of legal evidence or to the realm of personal narrative, in each case constituting new forms of visible evidence that have the potential to shape new understandings of personhood.[22]

The first set of films I want to discuss serve, loosely, as "cautionary tales." I borrow that term from its use in folklore studies to describe a traditional story meant to warn the audience of particular kinds of risk—the taking for granted of apparent normalcy, for example—as a danger that can be destructive not only to the individual but to a whole community. The 2004 documentary *Gray Matter*, made by American filmmaker Joe Berlinger, cautions against the dangers of genocidal practices masquerading and documented as "science" in photography and film. He also demonstrates how film and photographic archives can be powerfully reanimated in a new historical moment, serving purposes that subvert their original intention. Berlinger, who early in his voice-over of the film confesses to being "obsessed with the brutality of the Holocaust," traveled to Vienna in 2002 to witness a funeral for the remains (mostly preserved brains) of hundreds of infants and children who had disabilities such as epilepsy, diabetes, or Down syndrome, or who were orphaned or the "wrong" religion—many of them Jewish—and who died from brutal treatment in the 1940s, after being experimented upon by forensic psychiatrist Dr. Heinrich Gross (notoriously nicknamed "the Austrian Dr. Mengele").[23] Evidence suggests that Gross oversaw their killing at the Spiegelgrund hospital in Vienna, when it served as a Nazi-era "euthanasia" clinic. Once the children were dead, Gross had their brains preserved in glass pickle jars and labeled with their names, diagnosis, and the dates of their very short life spans. They were used as data in scientific papers published by Gross and others as late as the 1990s. For Berlinger, and most viewers, far more shocking than the grim story of the facts of Nazi "medicine" was the fact that these brains were considered legitimate scientific evidence for so long after the war, and that Gross continued to work in Austria as a medical expert for the court system well into the late twentieth century. As we see in the documentary, Gross—who was alive and around ninety years old at the time of filming in 2004—was never successfully prosecuted despite several efforts to do so and despite the existence of definitive proof of his activities. Several Austrian historians in the film suggest that Gross had been protected by the many Nazi sympathizers who remained in the Austrian establishment after World War II. He lived freely in Austria and—perhaps most shockingly—was awarded the Honorary Cross for Science and Art in 1975 (although he was eventually stripped of that honor in 2003) and collected a comfortable pension until his death in 2005. In the film, despite his best efforts, Berlinger does not succeed in finding Gross, but he does meet survivors of Spiegelgrund whose compelling and tragic stories are far more significant in underscoring the danger at the heart of this cautionary tale than the confrontation that never happens.

This film is relevant to my argument in at least two ways. First, its opening sequence shows the compelling appropriation by Austrian citizens of enlarged archival photographs of the faces of the disabled children killed by Dr. Gross: photos they hold in their arms in an effort to honor and remember these victims. In ways that Gross could never have imagined, the photos are not displayed as scientific specimens but are resignified in a context of repentance and memorialization. Removed from their original context of stigma, these images are now literally embraced in the arms of those protesting Gross's work and its link to Austria's Nazi legacy, as part of the ritual accompanying the burial of the human remains in Vienna. The documentary thus captures the way the photos are sacralized in this public demonstration of kinship, insisting on their common humanity.

Second, the film generates a clear case for the power of film and photography as a technology of governmentality in the construction of "scientific" arguments that supported the Nazi project. We see not only the photos of the children but documentary footage used in Nazi propaganda about Jews and those with disabilities used to "normalize" genocidal campaigns through medical, economic, and public-health discourses that anchored these images as frightening, polluting, and dangerous. They were an essential part of the Nazi program to rid the society of genetically impure people considered *lebensunwertes Leben*—life unworthy of life. One of the speakers at the funeral, Dr. Werner Vogt, a physician who had gathered evidence against Gross in the 1970s, said the ceremony "destroys a secret Austrian proclamation that goes as follows: 'Let's forget the murders; let's forgive the perpetrators and thousands of silent confidants; let's defame and hide the survivors.'"[24] The cautionary tale focuses on Austria's collective denial of its own participation in such atrocities, suggesting that those who fail to come to terms with their past continue to harbor this toxic sensibility.

I now want to turn to a second documentary cautionary tale in which the resignification of genocidal "biomedicine" and archival footage—and the continued work beyond the war of Nazi scientists who had been involved in experimenting with those with disabilities—play a central role. The film *Liebe Perla* is an astonishing 1999 documentary by Israeli filmmaker Shahar Rozen structured around the relationship between two women linked by their size and their histories. Hannelore Witkofski, a short-statured German woman and disability advocate born in the postwar period, sets out on a quest to understand the fate of people like herself during the Nazi era.[25] During the process, she tracks down and befriends Perla Ovitz, the only survivor of her ten-member family. Seven of the family members were little people and before World War II they had formed the Lilliput Troupe, performing music throughout eastern Europe. Because of their genetic condition, her family had been of interest to Dr. Josef Mengele, who ran the infirmary at Auschwitz-Birkenau, where he carried out human experimentation on identical twins and people with genetic abnormalities. In Perla's view, the Ovitz family survived Auschwitz only because Mengele chose to keep them alive for his "experiments." As she explained in a 1999 interview, "We were the only family who entered a death camp and emerged together. If I ever questioned why I was born a dwarf, my answer must be that my handicap, my deformity, was God's way of keeping me alive."[26]

At the time of filming Perla was eighty years old and living in Israel. When she tells Hannelore, her new German friend, about the humiliating experience that she and her family endured in 1944 when they were filmed naked for Mengele's research archives, Hannelore initiates her project: to go from archive to archive in Germany, and then to Auschwitz-Birkenau in Poland, to find this footage and restore it to Perla, whom she regards as the rightful owner of her image.[27] As Hannelore expresses it in the film, reading aloud one of her letters to Perla: "Today is our last day in Auschwitz. We did not find the film. Often I hoped that if I do find it, as soon as I open the box, it would crumble into dust. I'm afraid that someone in some archive or other or in some attic would find it and show it. . . . The film belongs to you, and you alone."

At one archive, Chronos Films, Hannelore succeeds in finding other Mengele footage. In a remarkable moment in the film, as the archivist runs the film for her, she recognizes a face among the anonymous bodies in striped clothing, restoring personal identity and history to this dehumanizing footage. Yet she is unable to locate the footage Perla remembers. Toward the end of the film, Perla receives word from Yad Vashem, the Holocaust memorial in Jerusalem, that members of the organization have found something of hers. She and Hannelore arrive there to find that it is not the missing footage: far better, it is a box containing her family's handmade musical instruments—adjusted to their small size—that they had used on their European tours.

In a meditative analysis of this film, Holocaust scholar Sara Eigen writes: "*Liebe Perla* itself manages much of the work that would be demanded of the lost film, if found: it deftly manages some creative play with archival exposure to serve history and to re-open the case against the Nazi-era and post-war German medical communities, all without exploiting the lost film's actual images as historical evidence. Hannelore's assertion of Perla's rights seem right and good; history has been served by *Liebe Perla*, and historians should return the favor by allowing the film to remain lost."[28] Hannelore's journey through the archives shapes the documentary, inviting us to witness what can happen when such documents, produced under the most racist and oppressive conditions, are taken up and transformed in a kind of ritual process of restoring the humanity of their victims.

Yet *Liebe Perla* also operates as a cautionary tale. It does not leave us with an assured sense that these problems are safely behind us, as we see some of the prejudices toward people with disabilities that Hannelore encounters in contemporary Germany. Additionally, Hannelore's archival work reveals the links between Germany's Nazi past and the present. In one scene, shot in the library at the Max-Planck-Gesellschaft in Berlin (formerly the Kaiser Wilhelm Institute), she pores over archives that make clear that Mengele and his mentor, Dr. Otmar Freiherr von Verschuer—the wartime director of the Institute for Anthropology, Human Hereditary Teaching and Genetics—had collaborated around Mengele's Auschwitz "research." After the war, rather than being punished as a war criminal, Verschuer went on to lead the Institute for Human Genetic Research at the University of Münster. As Hannelore reads aloud from his obituary in 1969, more than twenty years after the war, she notes, ironically, that he was celebrated "for his contributions toward humanistic eugenic research."[29] Indeed, it was only in 2001, two years after this film was made and more than six decades after the war, that the Max Planck Institute issued an apology to the few remaining survivors of Mengele, Verschuer, and other Nazi scientists. While Hannelore hopes to bring back the film footage Mengele had shot to Perla, she also seems to be fulfilling the desire Perla and other survivors have to see their stories help prevent future atrocities. In his speech at the Max Planck Institute on the occasion of the apology, Auschwitz survivor Jona Laks made clear that revelation is not sufficient insurance against the possibility of recurrence. "It was inside our planet and a part of it, perpetrated by human beings against the lives of other human beings. It was here, among us. There is no guarantee that it will not return again.[30]

While *Gray Matter* and *Liebe Perla* alert us to the histories of dangers to the community—threats that may continue in new form—other films have focused on the troubling questions raised by the erasure of disability *within* the Jewish community during the postwar period. Susie Korda's 1999 documentary, *One of Us,* focuses not on Nazi campaigns against Jews and the disabled but on the lack of public acknowledgment of disability in the postwar American Jewish community, bringing the cautionary tale closer to home. Korda chronicles long-kept secrets of her troubled American Jewish family. Tracing the family history, she discovers the existence of an unknown sister born with Down syndrome who was sent away after her father, a Holocaust survivor, abandoned the family after the birth of this child. To make matters even more complex, her brother develops neo-Nazi obsessions while her mother remains emotionally distant. The filmmaker eventually finds her long-lost sister living happily as a young adult in a large non-Jewish family. As other work has shown, the case of the Korda family, while distinctive, is not unique, as disabled children were routinely institutionalized during this period—a practice that was considered appropriate and humane well into the 1970s.[31] The film raises questions about where, and by whom, the boundaries of kinship and communities are drawn, while suggesting a radical generational change in attitude toward disability, as represented by the filmmaker.

Korda's parents might be considered an extreme instance of a sociohistorical situation shaping attitudes toward disability in the postwar American Jewish Gemeinschaft. For Ashkenazi Jews, particularly after the horrendous losses suffered in Europe (beginning with the period of intense anti-Semitic pogroms in the late nineteenth and early twentieth centuries up through the Holocaust), a cultural ethos amplified the biblical imperative to go forth and multiply. In the twentieth century, and especially the post-Holocaust era, for middle-class Jewish North Americans, having Jewish children was the foundation for rebuilding lives and communities, seen by many as an answer to the genocidal policies against Jews.

In a peculiar inversion of the eugenic policies practiced against Jewish and other populations, postwar Jewish survival was not just about having progeny. Children were needed to demonstrate the capacity of Jews not only to survive efforts to exterminate them but also to succeed in society. Building on a long cultural tradition that has always valorized religious study as the highest form of accomplishment—at least for men—postwar Jewish cultural life has continued to place particularly high value on intellectual prowess, in or out of the synagogue. While certainly not written in Jewish theology, the emphasis on having children who were intelligent and high achieving across a number of fields where brains and creativity count—such as medicine, law, science, business, scholarship, the arts—was a built-in assumption of Jewish cultural life. "Smart genes" were imagined to be part of the inalienable cultural and genetic capital that Jews assumed they carried with them; even impoverished immigrants and refugees whose material lives had been shattered could hold onto their DNA.[32] Children born with disabilities interfered with that narrative. Until relatively recently, Jewish children with such conditions were routinely institutionalized, fostered out, or hidden from view.

In ultra-Orthodox communities, where arranged marriages are essential to biological and social reproduction, a "stain" on the lineage is seen as damaging to both immediate and extended kin, who will inevitably bear the stigma of being known to carry a "hereditary disease." For those unable to avoid the birth of children with genetic disease through the use of a service like Dor Yeshorim (as discussed above), the question of how to care for loved ones while still keeping their status a secret can exact a serious toll. This does not mean that families would not seek the best possible medical care for sick children, even if they never told them the name of their condition for fear that they might further damage chances of marriage for themselves or other close relatives.[33]

Hidden Blessings, being made by Andrea Eisenman, is a documentary in progress that addresses this situation. Born with the genetic disease cystic fibrosis (CF), a life-threatening lung condition with a high incidence in the Ashkenazi population, Eisenman received a life-saving bilateral lung transplant in 1998 and since then she has competed in the Transplant Olympics and is involved in organ-donor awareness through public speaking.[34] Because of her outreach work for CF, Eisenman—a secular Jew—was contacted by ultra-Orthodox Hasidic Jews living in Brooklyn who have kept their cystic fibrosis hidden from their community and loved ones (even spouses) for years but who now recognize the need to change that circumstance. She was so astonished by their efforts that she decided to make *Hidden Blessings* to address this issue. As Eisenman explained: "There is a conflict in many closed communities, particularly the Orthodox and Hasidic, between secrecy and health, privacy and disclosure. A genetic disease results in the stigmatization of an entire family in the crucial matters of matchmaking, where kinship is the primary source of cultural capital and marriage. This leads to underreporting of illness and medical noncompliance. There is no emotional support for them in their isolation."[35]

Hidden Blessings follows the journeys of several people, including a Hasidic man, Josef. As he explains in one scene from her work in progress:

"When you suffer from something like cystic fibrosis, it's painful as is. But what makes it even much harder: the secret. That you have to keep it a secret that you have CF. You can't tell anybody that you have cystic fibrosis. I know nobody understands. I know nobody understands what I'm going through, because they don't have CF." Eisenman decided to make this film as a cautionary tale, warning the audience of the physical and emotional complications caused by this culturally imposed secrecy surrounding so serious a physical condition.

Does the question of disability and its lack of cultural acceptance suggest a disturbing disconnect between the two dimensions of being Jewish discussed in the opening section of this chapter? How do we understand the tension between the restrictive Gemeinschaft of culture and kinship described by Josef in the quote above and religious concepts guided by ideas of social justice and theological injunctions to accept all those rendered "in God's image"? This question was central to an essay with that title written by Rabbi Dianne Cohler-Esses, published in 2006 in the *Jewish Week.* While she is not ultra-Orthodox, her words eloquently describe the tensions between the realities of a particular exclusionary Jewish Gemeinschaft and the possibilities of an inclusive Jewish theology as well as her desire to close that gap through what she calls a "search for a new story." She writes:

> I am the parent of three children, two of whom have learning disabilities. Besides Eli, [my son with developmental delays], our eldest daughter Ayelet (almost eight) has language processing difficulties. . . . As a parent of children with learning disabilities I find myself resisting the powerful emphasis on educational achievement in the Jewish community and in our culture at large. What to do with those who can't live out this particular script? Are they somehow exiled from the hierarchy of Jewish communal values? Sometimes I feel like my own family members are strangers in our own land. At others, like we are a family searching for a new story. I believe it is time for us, the Jewish community, to expand this script, to create new stories where other kinds of children also become stars. And to begin by asking ourselves the following questions: Have we put so much emphasis on achievement, intellectual and otherwise, that we haven't left room for other modes of being? Other values? Are we so concerned with excelling that we've forgotten our simple humanity? Have we eclipsed, perhaps, the very fullness of the face of God? . . . Our children, those with diagnosed disabilities or those with the more typical struggles of life, are all created in the Divine image not in the human image of

mastery and perfection. There is nothing at all they have to do to achieve this state of being. No fancy nursery schools, no scores on tests, and no Ivy League Schools will attest to the indisputable fact of their divine image.[36]

THE SEARCH FOR A NEW STORY: PARABLES OF POSSIBILITY

What might that new story look like? The 2007 documentary *Praying with Lior* (dir. Ilana Trachtman) is emblematic of what Cohler-Esses is seeking and of what I call "parables of possibility." In the literature on folklore, parables are defined as stories that ask us to examine our everyday assumptions about the usual order of things, "a traditional technique for coping with problematic [or risky] social situations" providing "a microcosm of the life situation and a projected resolution."[37] I think of films such as *Praying with Lior* as parables because they indeed ask us to rethink our assumptions about disability, offering models of possibility rather than limits. In this case, the risk involves taking a leap beyond the usual order of things—of risking a relationship of recognition with someone who has been ruled "Other" in the conventional categories. *Praying with Lior* focuses on Lior Liebling, a Jewish boy with Down syndrome, and the way his special capacity for prayer has shaped his own life as well as that of his family and community. The documentary's director, Ilana Trachtman, was drawn to Lior's life when she first heard him pray. As she explains:

> I was not looking for a film subject, and I wasn't particularly interested in disability. I'm not sure I ever thought about disability. What I was doing had no connection to my career as a producer/director of TV documentaries. I was actually trying to pray. Searching for spiritual inspiration outside the stale synagogue experience of my childhood, I attended a retreat for the Jewish New Year. As I sat in the service, anxious, distracted, counting the pages until I'd be free, I heard Lior's unabashed, off-key, ecstatic voice. When I turned to look at the source of this sound, I was struck to see a boy with Down syndrome. And I was surprised to find myself envious of this "disabled" child, who could pray as I wished I could. Over the course of this retreat, I stalked Lior, looking for the secret to his prayer. When I heard he was having a Bar Mitzvah, I pictured the movie version. And then I realized that I could make it.[38]

The film mirrors the experiential process that led filmmaker Trachtman to take that risk. She chronicles the four months leading up to Lior's anxiously anticipated bar mitzvah. With intimacy and patience, the film illuminates what it means to be "praying with Lior" through the eyes of the diverse community nurturing him: his father, who is a Reconstructionist rabbi (Mordechai Liebling); his stepmother, Lynne Iser; his three siblings; an embracing liberal Reconstructionist Jewish community; his late mother; and his twelve-year-old classmates at the Orthodox yeshiva where he goes to school. His school peers' acceptance of him demonstrates how these young people use religious teachings to understand the value of difference. As one of the yeshiva students explains to the camera: "Let's say there are two baseball players. One could easily hit a home run, and one works very hard. The person who works very hard to hit a home run, he gets more credit than the person who could easily hit a home run. Same way with Lior. It counts double."

The film opened at the San Francisco Jewish Film Festival in July of 2007 and has had a robust run of festival screenings since then, including a theatrical run in New York City in February 2008 at the Cinema Village theater, with lines around the block for every screening, earning it the distinction of highest-grossing independent film that weekend. After one of the opening screenings, Lior's extraordinary, loving, and involved stepmother took questions from the audience. When asked how the film had changed her family's perspective, she answered: "While it had been fun and exciting during the making of the film, now that it is out in the world, it has changed my children. They understand they have a role to play helping other families, as activists, something they never understood before. Getting out in the world with the film has brought them a second life."[39]

Similarly, Trachtman is clear that in the process of making and then circulating this film with Lior and his family, she has taken the risk of exposing them to those who might not share his community's willingness to embrace Lior and what he represents. Thus, she found herself becoming "an accidental activist" as she worked to position the film as "the centerpiece of an ambitious outreach campaign to change the way people with disabilities are perceived and received by faith communities."[40] Despite the extraordinary way in which Lior's life had been integrated into his religious community, Trachtman points out that this is the exception rather than the rule, not only for the Jewish community but for communities of faith more broadly:

According to the National Organization on Disability, over 54 million Americans are disabled. Less than half of our houses of worship are handicapped accessible. This number alone speaks to the abandonment of the disabled in faith communities. In a society that literally "worships" perfection and sameness, individuals with physical and cognitive disabilities are dismissed and discriminated against everywhere. In the place where they should receive the most welcome and derive the most comfort—their faith communities—parents of children with special needs often hear "Your child shouldn't be here."[41]

Praying with Lior shows how different parts of the Jewish community—broadly defined from secular to Orthodox—might take the simple risk of rendering visible all of its possible members. Trachtman's film and the others discussed above take the risk of visibility to challenge the hegemonic cultural narratives that marginalize the lives of those who have not been valued, and in this way provide parables of possibility. All the films (and the Cohler-Esses editorial) offer chronicles of lives imagined in a new register. The filmmakers have all taken the risks associated with articulating alternative disability narratives, narratives that are foundational steps toward the integration of disability not only into everyday life in the United States but also into the filmmakers' particular communities of belief and practice. Authorized by those with disabilities and/or their family members and friends, these media offer revised, phenomenologically based understandings that at times also anchor substantial analyses of the social, cultural, and political construction of these conditions in Jewish life. Some articulations, such as that of Rabbi Cohler-Esses, summon theology to underscore the ontological value of all who are rendered in God's image.

Pushing the wordplay of the title a bit (and perhaps beyond its endurance), I want to suggest that these filmmakers and activists who are interrogating the place of disability in Jewish life are acting as "cultural canaries," using image-making and storytelling technologies to reframe the boundaries of acceptance regarding who is in and who is out of this particular community. The cultural and social labor these kinds of media practices represent in the Jewish community is part of a modest but growing movement that began a little over two decades ago, very much in step with the growth of both the disability rights movement and the emergence of "the New Jews," a group that more generally is identified with being flexible and inclusive, reversing the exclusionary practices of prior generations.[42] Exemplifying this trend, Yad Ha Chazakah (Hand of Strength), the Jewish Disability Empowerment Center, was catalyzed by Orthodox Jewish disability activist Sharon Shapiro in October 2005 and inaugurated in January 2008. Shapiro, who has a background in the Independent Living movement,[43] explained in an interview in the *Jewish Week:* "I wanted to know where all the Jews with disabilities are. It couldn't be that no Jews except me and a handful of people had a disability."[44]

Anita Altman, who founded the United Jewish Appeal's (UJA) Task Force on People with Disabilities in the mid-1990s, has now turned to film as a powerful vehicle for humanizing the experience of living with disabilities, inaugurating a disability film festival, Realabilities, in 2008. Commenting on the new film work that is emerging from the community, Altman said, "I feel like we're riding the crest of a wave. This is all part and parcel of trying to change societal attitudes about people with disabilities, trying to open up not only the Jewish community but the larger community to realize people have a lot to contribute, whatever their level of ability."[45]

In God's Image: You, Me, and Everyone We Know

Before I continue, allow me to take a risk and provide full disclosure about how I got into this. I am part of this story. In 1989, my daughter Samantha was born with a rare Jewish genetic disorder, one so uncommon that even I, an anthropologist and daughter of a geneticist, had never heard of it. Familial dysautonomia (FD) is so infrequent that only a little over six hundred people have ever been diagnosed with it; approximately half that number is alive today. Through the efforts of the parent-run Dysautonomia Foundation, for which I serve on the board of directors, the "FD gene" was discovered and it is now routinely part of prenatal testing for Ashkenazi couples.[46] The diagnosis of FD, based on a random mutation that probably occurred around five hundred years ago in a Jewish shtetl near Minsk (what in genetics is called genetic drift, enhanced by generations of Jewish endogamy), accounted for a range of inexplicable and bizarre symptoms (linked, it turned out, by a dysfunctional autonomic system) that had landed us in the hospital with great frequency from the time Samantha was two weeks old. To allow her to live with a disorder that can make every basic function a struggle—swallowing, breathing, regulating blood pressure—Sam has had multiple surgeries and manages daily life thanks to medical technologies such as feeding tubes and pumps, oxygen concentrators, and a strict regime of daily medications.

By the time she was ten, Sam had grown tired of having to explain herself to her classmates and friends and wondered why there were no others like herself on the kids' shows she watched on television. A notable exception was *What Are You Staring At?* an innovative, Emmy Award–winning special produced by Linda Ellerbee's Nick News in 1998 and aired repeatedly during 1999. The half-hour program featured a group of kids and teens with

Faye Ginsburg

a range of disabilities—Down syndrome, hearing and visual impairments, cerebral palsy, polio, burn injuries—as well as "celebrity crips": journalist John Hockenberry and the late actor Christopher Reeve. In the summer of 1999 in New York City, Samantha surfed onto *What Are You Staring At?* and was riveted. When the final credits ended, she had come up with a solution to her problem. She announced that she wanted to talk about her disability on television. She found the Web site for the Make-a-Wish Foundation, a group that grants "wishes" to children with life-threatening diseases, and e-mailed the foundation, explaining that her wish was to go on Nick News and talk about her life with FD.[47] Within two weeks, she was working with a friend and a Make-a-Wish volunteer making a pitch book with Polaroid photos and handwritten text about her life and disability. Sam's inventory of her life included pictures, reminiscent of crime-scene photos, all her medical equipment as well as photos of her dog, friends, and relatives.

By her eleventh birthday, she was working with a producer from Nick News, and by late April of 2000, the show was broadcast. Of greatest significance to Sam was that so many FD kids were able to see another child like them on television. She was deluged with e-mail from families with FD children around the country who were thrilled to see an image and story that for once included their experience. As a result, Sam has been invited to show her tape and to talk to a number of groups, ranging from scientists working on medical interventions for her disorder to those interested in how synagogues can become more inclusive. Two years later, Samantha used the occasion of her bat mitzvah to raise awareness and over $10,000 for research on FD.[48]

The media world into which Sam surfed at the end of the twentieth century is evidence of a transforming public culture—religious and otherwise—in which disability is becoming a more visible presence in daily life, albeit very slowly. This anecdotal evidence—Sam's immediate sense of kinship with the disabled kids and adults she saw and heard on television and her desire to join the process of making the reality of living with a disability part of public discourse—underscores the significance of such imagery for those with disabilities, who do not see themselves regularly in dominant forms of representation. Indeed, much of the early writing in disability studies focused not only on the need for changes in civil rights legislation but also on the absence of disabled people from literature and popular media—or, where present, the negativity of their portrayal, citing the legacy of freak shows, circuses, and asylums.[49] Meanwhile, activists were working to alter the media landscape itself.[50] Their work has become increasingly evident in the growing number of photography shows and film and video festivals devoted, in part or entirely, to the topic of disability.[51]

And, of course, the myriad Web sites, e-lists, blogs, and chat groups on the Internet have dramatically expanded the range of locations through which questions about disability and its public presence are being negotiated and communities of support are being formed.

The circulatory reach of electronic and digital media is a key factor in the creation of "mediated kinship," a term I coined with Rayna Rapp as a way of capturing how all the media practices I have been discussing can create a new sense of a Gemeinschaft among those who may be physically separated but who share the experiences of genetic or other diseases.[52] Emerging as a neighboring—and sometimes overlapping—field in relation to the formal, institutionalized discourse of disability rights, alternative forms of mediated kinship often offer a critique of normative American family life through everyday cultural practice. Encompassing many genres and identities, a common theme is an implicit rejection of the pressure to produce "perfect families" through the incorporation of difference under the sign of love and through intimacy in the domain of kinship relations. Mediated spaces of public intimacy such as the ones I have mentioned in Sam's case—documentaries, talk shows, online disability support groups, Web sites, and so on—are crucial to building a social fund of knowledge more inclusive of the fact of disability across a range of communities.[53]

An exemplary case of this within the Jewish Gemeinschaft took place in January 2007, in a series of film screenings and discussions organized by award-winning filmmaker and media activist Judith Helfand, a DES survivor (the drug diethylstilbestrol was given to her mother during pregnancy). Held as part of a four-day Limmud ("to learn" in Hebrew) in upstate New York, the activities were billed as a conference, a festival, a gathering, and "an opportunity to craft your own Jewish world." Then in its second year, the Limmud was modeled on a similar project that began in the United Kingdom twenty-five years ago.[54] Helfand had been approached by Limmud's planning committee to program something on Jews and film, and she chose to bring a group of innovative filmmakers and activists who are using their documentary work to reframe the question of who is a Jew in the context of disability. Pulling together this group, which included me and my daughter, the title for the session (playing on the name of a popular independent film from 2006), was *In G-d's Image: You, Me, and Everyone We Know.* The description in the Limmud program read as follows:

> This is a series of nine sessions focused on "non-fiction filmmaking & story-telling about inclusion and exclusion, abilities and disabilities, family and community. Expect humor, chutzpah, a lot of hope, serious fun, voices and points-of-view you've never heard

before and will want to hear from again. Our collective hope is that *In G-d's Image: You, Me, And Everyone We Know* will inspire Limmud–New York to talk openly about inclusion and exclusion. Long-term, we hope the series will be used as a resource to spark a necessary and mindful discussion within the institutions dedicated to an inclusive, human, kind and just Jewish community.[55]

A number of sessions focused specifically on independent film projects, including Trachtman's *Praying with Lior* and Eisenman's *Hidden Blessings*, both works in progress at that time. I call them projects rather than films, because they are much more than documentary texts. Each is part of a much broader campaign of outreach, education, and intervention in multiple sites. At the first session, the irrepressible Helfand looked up at the seventy or so participants gathered there—people who ran the gamut from Orthodox to secular—and exclaimed: "They wanted me to program Woody Allen! Look at this! This has never happened before! When have a bunch of Jews gotten together to look at movies that can make us think about these issues? What do we do when something has never happened before to bless this occasion?" Voices called back: "The Shehechiyanu!" And, without missing a beat, the group spontaneously joined together in reciting this most basic of Jewish prayers, the blessing for all new or special experiences, traditionally said to inaugurate joyous—and novel—occasions.[56]

CONCLUSION

It goes without saying that we are far removed from Mengele's film footage in the use of contemporary media technologies to include or exclude the disabled in the life of specific communities, whether these be national, local, or virtual. However, the deployment of media technologies—documents, documentaries, DNA karyotypes, or digital Web sites—is critical to the creation of a variety of Gemeinschaften in the contemporary world, whether it is the sense of relatedness that is built in online discussion groups among the dispersed Jewish families whose children share a rare mutation of chromosome 9 or the spirit of inclusion that embraces audiences who view the film *Praying with Lior,* as I have seen happen at countless screenings. The hegemonic power of "science" and "biomedicine" buttressed the interpretive frames that gave Nazi film and photography authority at a particular historical moment. The impossibility of tethering such media permanently to their *originary* frameworks—perhaps the foundational premise for what constitutes the risk of visibility—is part of the unruly productivity of these works, as future generations refuse to let unacceptable narratives shape their interpretation, no longer allowing them to objectify and dehumanize people—in this case, those with disabilities.[57] The passion with which archival footage is repositioned through idioms of kinship and human rights is an index of the continued power of these images, and of the fear that without their radical resignification, they can continue to wreak damage, like the half-life of nuclear toxins. In the hands of activists from Hannelore and Perla to Andrea and Josef to Ilana and Lior to Samantha, these images and the people they represent can have a second life.

Whereas phenotypic evidence, captured on film, was once used by eugenicists to make the case for an underlying pathology they imagined lurked within, the filmmakers discussed here refuse to allow such reductive interpretations of the body to separate the disabled from their social worlds. Instead they take the risk of visibility to assert what I call mediated kinship, creating relationships across a range of boundaries. Such forms of relatedness are not necessarily genealogical or familial. Consider the following:

1. The bond constituted between Hannelore and Perla in their shared status as little people who have suffered discrimination and join together in the search to reclaim Mengele's footage

2. The political performance of Austrian activists who resignified photos from the scientific archive of Heinrich Gross to claim kinship with the murdered disabled children they represent

3. The relationships created across different forms of Judaism by those with the genetic disease cystic fibrosis, who share the mission to break the unwritten code of silence surrounding chronic diseases in the Hasidic community

4. The extended family and community that finds itself (in both senses) praying with the Down syndrome teen Lior

In any polysemic tradition, there are always new ways to take the risk of imagining community where exclusion once existed. The media practices considered in this chapter provide a counterdiscourse—from cautionary tales to parables of possibility—to the naturalized stratification of membership within an ethno-religious community that for so long has marginalized those disabled from birth. It is not only the acceptance of difference within families but also the recognition of relatedness that makes these works potentially radical in their implications. As sites of information and free play of imagination, these cultural forms risk constituting new social landscapes that move embodied difference beyond the constraints of racialized hierarchies and medical diagnoses. The disjunction between the aspiration for democratic inclusion and the fantasy of bodily perfectibility through technological intervention—from eugenics to ARTs—has energized much of this cultural expression in documentary media, creating a growing sense of public intimacy with experiences of disability. And in the Jewish case, such narratives constitute a legacy both internal and external to a community, given a recent history that has too often denied the possibilities of such lives, at times with enormous violence, and more recently with culturally produced regimes of invisibility. The most recent disability narratives that I have discussed here involve agents taking the risks linked with visibility, as a counter to the narratives of loss and fear that too often accompany such stories; instead the alternative narratives offer models of lives lived against the grain of normalcy, with ingenuity, courage, and joy.

NOTES

I want to thank Mette Hjort for encouraging me to write this essay and for her thoughtful editorial suggestions. The essay was developed in a workshop organized by Jeremy Stolow, Deus in Machina, in Toronto in 2006, and a version of it is being published in an edited collection based on that conference. I want to thank Jeremy Stolow for his extremely helpful comments on earlier versions of this work. I am grateful to Gregg Mittman for inviting me in March 2008 to the Max Planck Institute in Berlin, where I gave a version of this essay—adding the material on Mengele—as a keynote speech for a conference there, The Educated Eye: Photographic Evidence in Scientific Observation. I am, as always, indebted to my long-standing colleague Rayna Rapp; many of the ideas of this essay emerged from our intertwined work together over the years on disability and its changing social framework. Thanks as well to extraordinary activists/filmmakers Judith Helfand and Ilana Trachtman for their insights, creativity, and commitments; to friends and scholars Barbara Kirshenblatt-Gimblett and Jeffrey Shandler for our conversations; and to Patsy Spyer for her thoughtful comments on the penultimate version. The ideas for this essay first started to develop in a workshop with the title The Canary in the *Gemeinschaft* that I organized jointly for the Working Group on Jews/Religion/Media and the Working Group on Bioethics and Religion, which I ran with Rayna Rapp in 2005–6 (as part of the activities of the Center for Religion and Media at New York University). Finally, I owe my interest in this area and perhaps my most important understandings to my daughter Samantha, who has opened up worlds for me that I had never known existed, and whose joyous exuberance, despite her complex life with familial dysautonomia, is a daily parable of possibility. The section in this essay on Samantha's excursions into media activism is drawn from a 2001 work written with Rayna Rapp: "Enabling Disability: Rewriting Kinship, Reimagining Citizenship," *Public Culture* 13, no. 3 (2001): 533–55.

1. According to Tönnies, who first introduced the categories of Gemeinschaft/Gesellschaft into sociological discourse in 1887, people living in a Gemeinschaft are linked by shared belief and kinship and a "unity of will." See Ferdinand Tönnies, *Community and Civil Society,* ed. José Harris (Cambridge: Cambridge University Press, 2001), 22.

2. Deborah Lupton, *Risk* (New York: Routledge, 1999).

3. If one were to date the inauguration of this work, it would be 1979, when Ira Wohl's direct cinema documentary *Best Boy*—focusing on the fate of his cousin, the developmentally disabled "Philly" Wohl who spent his first fifty years at home with Max and Pearl, his aging working-class Jewish parents in Queens—won the Academy Award for Best Documentary. The documentary, which follows Philly as he eventually moves to a group home, where he thrives, brought unexpected visibility to the hidden question of disability in the Jewish community. Twenty years later, Ira Wohl made a follow-up film, *Best Man,* focused on the story of Philly's bar mitzvah at age seventy. In the years since then, a number of landmark documentaries have been made that continue to explore the sometimes perplexing questions raised by disability in the Jewish American postwar culture, a Gemeinschaft that valorizes intelligence and middle-class achievement in its children.

4. Holocaust scholar Lucy Dawidowicz argues that the term the *Jewish Question* was not only associated with Nazi genocidal policy, it was a neutral expression for the negative attitude toward the apparent and persistent singularity of the Jews as a people against the background of rising political nationalisms and new nation-states. *The War against the Jews, 1933–1945* (New York: Bantam, 1975).

5. Michel Foucault, "Technologies of the Self," in *Technologies of the Self,* ed. L. H. Martin, H. Gutman, and P. H. Hutton (Amherst: University of Massachusetts Press, 1988), 12; Toby Miller, *The Well-Tempered Self: Citizenship, Culture, and the Postmodern Subject* (Baltimore: Johns Hopkins University Press, 1993).

6. Rayna Rapp, *Testing Women, Testing the Fetus* (New York: Routledge, 1999). The question "Who is in?" addresses biopolitics, while the second question ("Who is out?") raises questions about narrative invention, although one might argue that the same concerns are evident in both arenas. On biopolitics, see Deborah Heath and Paul Rabinow, "Biopolitics: The Anthropology of the New Genetics Immunology," introduction to special issue, *Journal of Culture, Medicine, and Psychiatry* 17 (1993): 1–2. On narrative invention, see Alisa Lebow, *First Person Jewish* (Minneapolis: University of Minnesota Press, 2008); Laura Levitt, *American Jewish Loss After the Holocaust* (New York: New York University Press, 2007); Mary Jo Maynes, Jennifer Pierce, and Barbara Laslett, *The Use of Personal Narratives in the Social Sciences and History* (Ithaca: Cornell University Press, 2008).

                                                    Faye Ginsburg

7. See Rapp, *Testing*, 5.

8. Sander Gilman, "The New Genetics and the Old Eugenics: The Ghost in the Machine," introduction to special issue, ed. Sander Gilman, *Patterns of Prejudice* 36, no. 1, (2002): 3–4. The phrase "the ghost in the machine" was first introduced by Gilbert Ryles to critique the Cartesian concept of mind in his 1949 book *The Concept of Mind* (Chicago: University of Chicago Press, 1949), then taken up by Arthur Koestler in his book *The Ghost in the Machine* (London: Penguin, 1967), where he discusses the human tendency to self-destruction.

9. Gilman, "The New Genetics," 2.

10. Eric Parens and Adrienne Asch, eds., *Prenatal Testing and Disability Rights* (Washington, DC: Georgetown University Press, 2000).

11. Rayna Rapp and Faye Ginsburg. "Enabling Disability: Rewriting Kinship, Reimagining Citizenship," *Public Culture* 13, no. 3 (2001): 533–56.

12. Of course, there are those who may not be aware that their ancestry is Ashkenazi, but who carry the genes associated with that community nonetheless, making the question of boundaries and categories particularly complex. For example, the British filmmaker Stephen Frears had no idea about his own lineage until his son, born in 1972, was diagnosed with familial dysautonomia. As Frears commented in a 2001 interview, "I may not have known I was Jewish, but I carried the gene." See http://www.jewishjournal.com/home/preview.php ?id=7499.

13. See Gina Kolata, "Nightmare or the Dream of a New Era in Genetics?" *New York Times,* December 7, 1993, http://www.nytimes.com/1993/12/07/health/ nightmare-or-the-dream-of-a-new-era-in-genetics.html. In the Ashkenazi Jewish population (those of eastern European descent), estimates suggest that one in four individuals is a carrier of one of nine genetic conditions for which genetic testing is now available. These diseases include Tay-Sachs disease, Canavan, Niemann-Pick, Gaucher, familial dysautonomia, Bloom syndrome, Fanconi's anemia, cystic fibrosis, and mucolipidosis IV. Some of these diseases may be severe and may result in the early death of a child. For those in the very Orthodox or Hasidic communities, for whom abortion is not an option, and for whom knowledge that a genetic disease runs in their family creates a profound reduction in their "kinship capital," creative alternatives to secular forms of genetic testing were developed. Rabbi Josef Ekstein, who had four of his own children die of Tay-Sachs disease, realized his community needed to take advantage of the testing available and founded Dor Yeshorim in the early 1980s. Hebrew for "generation of the righteous," Dor Yeshorim is a premarital genetic testing program for Ashkenazi Jews in Israel and the United States. This service is usually used by Orthodox Jewish couples whose marriages have been arranged by their families and the community's rabbi. The prospective partners are tested for carrier status. Individuals are tested anonymously, using a code. The rabbi compares the results by code, and if both people are carriers for the same disorder, the families are informed that the marriage may not take place. If only one person is a carrier, then the marriage can go forward, since the couple

cannot have a child with the disease. Which person is a carrier is not divulged, to avoid stigmatization. See rarediseases.about.com/od/geneticdisorders/a/doryeshorim.htm.

14. Benedict Anderson, *Imagined Communities* (New York: Verso, 1991).

15. Sander Gilman, "Private Knowledge," special issue, ed. Sander Gilman, *Patterns of Prejudice* 36, no. 1 (2002): 6.

16. Gilman, "New Genetics," 16.

17. In *The Question concerning Technology,* Heidegger draws on the etymology of *techne:* its roots are in the Greek *techne,* which is "the name not only for the activities and skills of the craftsman but also for the arts of the mind and the fine arts." For the Greeks, *techne* was intimately linked to *poiesis,* the poetic, and thus linked to the "bringing forth" so essential in the pursuit of aletheia/veritas/truth. See Martin Heidegger, *The Question concerning Technology, and Other Essays* (New York: Harper Perennial, 1982).

18. On Mengele and his practices, photographic and otherwise, see Robert Jay Lifton, *The Nazi Doctors: Medical Killing and the Psychology of Genocide* (New York: Basic Books, 2000). On the resignification and recirculation of photographs, see Susan Crane, "Choosing Not to Look: Representation, Repatriation, and Holocaust Atrocity Photography," *History and Theory* 47, no. 3 (2008): 309–30.

19. See Faye Ginsburg, "Screen Memories: Resignifying the Traditional in Indigenous Media," in *Media Worlds: Anthropology on New Terrain,* ed. F. Ginsburg, B. Larkin, and L. Abu Lughod (Berkeley: University of California Press, 2002), 39–56.

20. See, for instance, Lebow, *First Person Jewish;* Michael Renov, *The Subject of Documentary* (Minneapolis: University of Minnesota Press, 2004); Catherine Russell, *Experimental Ethnography: The Work of Film in the Age of Video* (Durham: Duke University Press, 1999).

21. See *First Person Plural,* DVD, directed by Liem Deanne Borshay (San Francisco: Center for Asian American Media, 2000); Lebow, *First Person Jewish.*

22. For a fuller discussion of this idea, and of "media worlds" more generally, see the introduction to Ginsburg, Larkin, and Lughod, *Media Worlds.*

23. or details, see Virginia Heffernan, "'Gray Matter': A Driven Filmmaker and His Grim Subject," *New York Times,* April 23, 2005, http://www.nytimes.com/2005/04/12/arts/television/12heff.html?pagewanted=print

24. Steve Erlanger, "Vienna Buries Child Victims of the Nazis," *New York Times,* April 29, 2002, http://www.nytimes.com/2002/04/29/world/vienna-buries-child-victims-of-the-nazis.html.

25. In her excellent article on the film, Barbara Duncan writes that "Hannelore Witkofski, in an interview for the film magazine, *Documenter,* www.documenter.com/issue04/041acgb.htm clarified her conditions for being filmed, drawing the line at the privacy of her home: 'I didn't want any type of "home story," because of my experiences with how disabled persons are presented in the media, how they are shown. So imagine, this cute . . . picture

         Faye Ginsburg

of a short-statured woman cooking on a very short oven with a small soup. It would be a kind of children's movie, like a fairytale. So it was for me, very important to save my privacy. . . . And on the other side, [I wanted] to bring my work to the center, because working people with disability, this is absolutely uncommon in the public view. Disabled people are poor, they suffer, but they don't work.'" Barbara Duncan, "*Liebe Perla:* A Complex Friendship and Lost Disability History Captured on Film," *Disability World: A Bi-monthly Webzine of International Disability News And Views* 9 (2001), http://www .disabilityworld.org/07–08_01/arts/perla.shtml.

26. Quoted in Yehuda Koren and Eilat Negev, *In Our Hearts We Were Giants: The Remarkable Story of the Lilliput Troupe* (New York: Da Capo, 2005), 274.

27. In a thoughtful and provocative essay that includes discussion of *Liebe Perla,* Susan Crane, writing from an ethical and historical-critical perspective, asks: "Have Holocaust atrocity photographs reached the limits of their usefulness as testimony?" She argues for their repatriation rather than for unconditional public access, given that "few of the victims of the Shoah pictured in either the best known or the least circulated images were willing subjects." "Choosing Not To Look," 309.

28. Sara Eigen, "*Liebe Perla,* Memento Mori: On Filming Disability and Holocaust History," *Women in German Yearbook: Feminist Studies in German Literature and Culture* 22 (2006): 1–20. Eigen ends her article with this eloquent articulation of closure around the question of the missing film. "Perla Ovici died in 2001, the last of her immediate family, the only known remaining witness to the film that she hoped to locate and destroy" (18).

29. Ibid. For an excellent overview of the role that the Kaiser Wilhelm/Max Planck Institute played in Nazi science before, during, and after the war, see William Seidman, "Science and Inhumanity: The Kaiser-Wilhelm/Max Planck Society," *If Not Now* 2 (2000), http://www.baycrest.org/journal/ifnot01w.html; revised February 18, 2001, http://www.doew.at/thema/planck/planck1.html. The apology for the institute's role in such projects occurred at a conference sponsored by the Max Planck Presidential Commission, which was established to investigate the institute's activities from 1933 to 1944. On June 7, 2001, Max Planck president Hubert Markl offered survivors of concentration camp experiments "the deepest regret, compassion, and shame at the fact that crimes of this sort were committed, promoted, and not prevented within the ranks of German scientists. . . . The Max Planck Society, as the Kaiser Wilhelm Society's 'heir,' must face up to these historical facts and its moral responsibility." Markl's admission was followed by emotional speeches by two victims of Nazi physician Josef Mengele's infamous "twins" experiments at the Auschwitz-Birkenau death camp. See Robert Koenig, "Max Planck Offers Historic Apology," *Science,* June 12, 2001, http://sciencenow.sciencemag.org/cgi/content/full/2001/612/3.

30. Quoted from Jona Laks's speech in his role as the chairman of the "Organization of the Mengele Twins" on the occasion of the opening of the symposium Biomedical Sciences and Human Experimentation at Kaiser Wilhelm

Institutes—The Auschwitz Connection, Berlin, June 7, 2001, http://www.mpg
.de/english/illustrationsDocumentation/documentation/pressReleases/2001/
bs_laks_e.htm.

31. Rapp and Ginsburg, "Enabling Disability," 544.

32. This particular myth played out in a *New York Magazine* article by
Jennifer Stout titled "Are Jews Smarter?" about a controversial 2005 study. As
Stout wrote, "[Did] Jewish intelligence evolve in tandem with Jewish diseases as
a result of discrimination in the ghettos of medieval Europe? That's the premise of a controversial new study that has some preening and others plotzing."
Jennifer Stout, "Are Jews Smarter?" *New York Magazine,* October 16, 2009,
http://nymag.com/nymetro/news/culture/features/1478/.

33. For example, Josef in the film *Hidden Blessings* is a case in point of this
situation.

34. The defective gene causes the body to produce unusually thick, sticky
mucus that clogs the lungs and leads to life-threatening lung infections, ob-
structs the pancreas and stops natural enzymes from helping the body break
down and absorb food. In the 1950s, few children with cystic fibrosis lived to
attend elementary school. Today, many people with the disease can expect to
live into their thirties, forties, and beyond.

35. Andrea Eisenman, comments at Limmud screening of her film trailer,
January 15, 2005, author's transcript.

36. Dianne Cohler-Esses, "In God's Image?" *Jewish Week,* December 2006, 17.

37. Barbara Kirshenblatt-Gimblett, "A Parable in Context: A Social
Interactional Analysis of Storytelling Performance," in *Folklore: Performance
and Communication,* ed. Dan Ben-Amos and Kenneth S. Goldstein (The
Hague: Mouton, 1975), 107; see also 123. The term "parable of possibility" has
been used in quite different contexts, for instance, by the economist Russell
Roberts in his novella about the virtues of the free market and the creativity of
the American economy: *The Price of Everything: A Parable of Possibility and
Prosperity* (Princeton: Princeton University Press, 2008). It also appears in the
literary scholar Terence Martin's study of the American literary fixation with
"beginnings." See Terence Martin, *Parables of Possibility: The American Need for
Beginnings* (New York: Columbia University Press, 1995).

38. http://www.prayingwithlior.com/directorsstatement.html.

39. Quote from author's notes taken at postscreening discussion, February 1,
2008.

40. Ibid.

41. Ibid.

42. See Caryn Aviv and David Shneer, *New Jews: The End of the Jewish
Diaspora* (New York: New York University Press, 2005).

43. The independent living movement has been an important part of this
   broader movement for disability rights. It is based on the premise that people
   with even the most severe disabilities should have the choice of living in the
   community. This can be accomplished through the creation of personal as-

sistance services allowing an individual to manage his or her personal care, to keep a home, to have a job, go to school, worship, and otherwise participate in the life of the community. The independent living movement also advocates for the removal of architectural and transportation barriers that prevent people with disabilities from sharing fully in all aspects of our society.

Although there were earlier experiments with this concept, it wasn't until 1972 that the first Center for Independent Living was founded by disability activists in Berkeley, California. (introduction to *The Disability Rights and Independent Living Movement,* http://bancroft.berkeley.edu/collections/drilm/introduction.html)

44. Randi Sherman, "Setting the Wheelchairs in Motion," *Jewish Week,* March 12, 2008, http://www.thejewishweek.com/viewArticle/c36_a4850/News/" New_York.html#.

45. Quoted in Carolyn Slutsky, "Getting Reel on Disabilities," *Jewish Week,* January 23, 2008, http://www.thejewishweek.com/viewArticle/c36_a3543/News/New_York.html#.

46. See Gina Kolata, "Parents Take Charge, Putting Gene Hunt onto the Fast Track," *New York Times,* July 16, 1996, http://www.nytimes.com/1996/07/16/science/parents-take-charge-putting-gene-hunt-onto-the-fast-track.html; Susan Lindee, *Moments of Truth in Genetic Medicine* (Baltimore: Johns Hopkins University Press, 2008). For the most up-to-date information on FD, see http://www.familialdysautonomia.org/history.htm#history.

47. For more information on the Make-a-Wish Foundation, see http://www.wish.org/.

48. For more on Samantha's Make-a-Wish experience, see http://samanthamyers.typepad.com/. For more on her bat mitzvah and fund-raising efforts, see http://www.familialdysautonomia.org/Fammat/winter03_samantha_myers.htm.

49. See, for instance, Robert Bogdan, *Freak Show: Presenting Human Oddities for Amusement and Profit* (Chicago: University of Chicago Press, 1990); Rosemarie Garland Thomson, *Extraordinary Bodies* (New York: Columbia University Press, 1997).

50. Along with parent-activists who worked in the mainstream media such as Emily Kingsley, a writer for *Sesame Street,* whose son Jason was the first child with Down syndrome to appear on television, there were people such as Mary Johnson and Cass Irvin, who in 1980 founded the alternative journal *The Disability Rag.* Barnett Shaw, ed., *The Ragged Edge: The Disability Experience from the Pages of* The Disability Rag (Louisville, Ky.: Advocado, 1994).

51. See, for example, Nancy Burson and Michael L. Sand, *Seeing and Believing: The Art of Nancy Burson* (San Francisco: Twin Palms, 2002), which accompanied the exhibition of the same name at the Grey Art Gallery, New York University, February 12–April 20, 2002. One of the longest-running disability film festivals in the United States is SuperFest Film Festival (started in 1998) in Berkeley, California: http://www.culturedisabilitytalent.org/superfest/sf2009

.html. For a helpful listing of disability film festivals worldwide, see http://nadc
.ucla.edu/filmfest.cfm.

52. Rapp and Ginsburg, "Enabling Disability."

53. For a discussion of these forms of mediation, see Faye Ginsburg, "Found in Translation," March 28, 2007, http://mediacommons.futureofthebook.org/imr/2007/03/28/found-in-translation.

54. The January 2007 meeting attracted over five hundred Jews from all walks of life, multiple generations, and a range of backgrounds, who came to take part in lectures, workshops, text-study sessions, discussions, exhibits, performances, and much more—all planned by a community of volunteers.

55. Program for Limmud, New York: Learning without Limits, 2005, http://apps.zebra.limmudny.org/lny_2005/limmud_pub_schedule/schedule_v1.pl?op=p&id=40, 5.

56. According to Jewish law, there are specific times when this prayer should be said. However, it is also recited when people experience something unique, new, and good for the first time: "Baruch Atah Hashem, Elokeinu Melach Haolam,shehechiyanu,v'keyamanu v'heigeanu lazman ha zeh" (I am grateful to the source of life, that I have been kept alive and brought to this moment so that I may share life with those I love and experience the blessings and goodness that life has to offer).

57. While one anonymous reader suggested that this claim is exaggerated, I would argue that the resignifying of racist and imperial film and photo archives is now widespread, with Nazi archives and films made on indigenous people being the most notable in this movement for repatriation of such materials. This work includes that of scholars such as Crane ("Choosing Not To Look") and Eigen ("*Liebe Perla,* Memento Mori") as well as the outstanding work on the repatriation of indigenous images by Jane Lydon (*Eye Contact: Photographing Indigenous Australians* [Durham: Duke University Press, 2005]) and Elizabeth Edwards (*Raw Histories: Photographs, Anthropology, Museums* [London: Berg, 2001]), to name two exemplary cases. A recent dramatic example is the extraordinary documentary *A Film Unfinished* (2010) by Israeli director Yael Hersonski, who subjects a Nazi propaganda film "documenting" Jews in the Warsaw ghetto to a critical deconstruction thanks to recently discovered additional materials that show how numerous scenes of Jews appearing to have great wealth in the ghetto were completely fabricated. As one reviewer wrote:

> Like the flickering shadows in Plato's Cave, these images were subjected to a radical rereading with the appearance of another reel in 1998: 30 minutes of outtakes showing the extent to which scenes had been deliberately staged. Over and over, in multiple takes, we see well-dressed Jews enter a butcher's shop, ignoring the children begging outside. . . . Moving methodically reel by reel and acknowledging the "many layers of reality," the director creates a palimpsest of impressions from multiple, meticulously researched sources representing both victims and oppressors. (Jeanette Catsoulis, "An Israeli Finds New Meanings in a Nazi Film," *New York Times,* August 17, 2010, C1)

HAMID NAFICY

Accented Filmmaking and Risk Taking in the Age of Postcolonial Militancy, Terrorism, Globalization, Wars, Oppression, and Occupation

INTERSTITIONALITY AND INEVITABLE RISK

Accented filmmaking by exilic, diasporic, and ethnic filmmakers inherently involves taking risks, risks that sometimes are integrated into the film's narrative and style and often provide the focus for the film's extratextual material in the form of a filmmaker's biography, interviews with the filmmaker, film reviews, film lore, blogs, Web sites, and social-networking portals. Risk taking is inevitable for these filmmakers, particularly for those in political exile, because they are often situated in the interstices and across the borders both of local, national, and transnational spaces and of filmmaking practices. Thus situated, the mere existence of the filmmakers can pose a challenge to normative formations and institutions. The resulting risks are compounded by these filmmakers' tendency to challenge, even critique, the generic, narrative, and aesthetic norms of filmmaking through their filmmaking practices.

Crucially, it is not just the filmmakers who take risks and sometimes suffer the consequences. Their subjects, too, do so by trusting the filmmakers, particularly the documentarists working on politically sensitive topics. The filmmakers may, for example, fail to reflect the views of their subjects accurately, may fail to disguise their identities sufficiently (through blurred images and distorted voices), and may as a result expose them to reprisals from governments and adversaries. Every act of cinematic risk taking involves placing trust in someone else. Potentially each such act involves not only personal, physical, and material consequences but also ethical ones, as filmmakers and subjects may mutually implicate and endanger one another. In this chapter I concentrate on exploring the risk strategies of accented filmmakers, and the consequences of these strategies for the filmmakers themselves and for their films. I thus leave the impact of the filmmakers' risk taking on their film subjects to another time and place.

BORDER FILMMAKING

Accented filmmaking, particularly that involving crossing borders, structurally involves significant political, financial, aesthetic, and personal risks. The following cases highlight these risks in different parts of the globe in the past few decades.

A Turkish filmmaker of Kurdish descent, Yilmaz Güney directed *Yol* (The Way, 1982) by proxy from inside a prison in Turkey, where he was serving a long jail term for murdering a judge. Directing by proxy is a form of risk aversion; however, in this case it was not so much to avert risk, as Güney was already in jail, but out of necessity. Making strategic use of the story *Yol* tells, about a liberal furlough program allowing prisoners to leave prisons for a temporary family visit, Güney was able to leave the prison when he had served only seven of his eighteen-year term. Instead of returning to prison, he escaped to Switzerland with smuggled rushes filmed by his friend Serif Goren, which he then edited into the finished film *Yol*. Upon its release, this scathing and profoundly sad film, which critiques the repressive patriarchal and military rules of the country, especially those affecting women and Kurds, evoked two diametrically opposed reactions from outsiders and insiders. The 1982 Cannes Film Festival awarded *Yol*, along with Constantin Costa-Gavras's *Missing* (1982), the Palme d'Or Grand Prize. The military government in Turkey, on the other hand, sentenced Güney in absentia to twenty additional years in prison, revoked his citizenship, and banned all of the many films he had directed, scripted, and acted in. He died in France, of cancer, after completing only one more film, *Duvar* (The Wall, 1983), another prison story. The unavailability of his films and his permanent exile hampered serious studies of his works at home but also helped to mythologize Güney, as did his early death. Once he was stripped of his citizenship, his films (even those made in Turkey before his exile) were considered foreign imports and as such they had to be officially approved for exhibition within Turkey. Attempts by leftist and pro-Kurdish organizations to gain permission to "import" them were denied by the Ministry of Culture for years until an appeal to the Supreme Administrative Court removed the prohibition on *Umut* in the early 1990s.[1] The ban on *Yol* was lifted in 1992, but the film was screened publicly in a dozen theaters in Istanbul only years later, in February 1999, to enthusiastic crowds.[2]

                                    Hamid Naficy

Another Kurdish-Turkish filmmaker, Nezamettin Ariç, who lives in Germany, filmed most of his *Klamek ji bo Beko/Ein Lied für Beko* (A Cry for Beko, 1992) in Armenia in the early 1990s, near the Armenian-Turkish border.[3] As an exile from Turkey, condemned by the government, which had revoked his Turkish citizenship, he could not film his Kurdish nationalist saga in his homeland. However, filming in Armenia presented risks of its own. As there were no processing labs nearby in Armenia, he had to ship the exposed footage to Leningrad. For various reasons, the lab did not deliver the footage in time, forcing Ariç, who was operating under a tight temporal and financial budget, to continue filming without seeing any of the dailies until long after the cast and crew had left the location—all this during his directorial debut! The telltale signs of such production risks are the traces they sometimes leave on films, which show that certain look and feel of "imperfection" that signifies, or allegorizes, the condition of exile and of interstitial production.[4]

Kurdish-Iranian director Bahman Ghobadi put Kurdish cinema as a "national cinema" on the map of world cinema with his award-winning *Zamani baray-e masti asbha* (A Time for Drunken Horses, 2000), which was followed by a series of equally distinguished films. According to Ghobadi, this is the "first Kurdish-language movie in the history of the world" (the dialogue is spoken largely in Kurdish, with some Persian).[5] Ghobadi is a "border filmmaker" par excellence, for most of his films are about the Kurds (the largest population in the world without a national homeland), their way of life, and their national and personal aspirations. Kurdish language and music perform significant and signifying functions in his films, and the stories unfold in borderlands, usually between Iran and Iraq, pointing to the personal investment of the director as well as that of Kurdish people in the wounds and freedoms of borders. "I learned the meaning of 'border' from childhood." Ghobadi said. "I was born in Baneh, Iran's closest border town to Iraq. . . . It had the highest Iranian casualties both in internal conflicts as well as during the war with Iraq. The village where I then took refuge for three months was where I later shot *A Time for Drunken Horses*."[6]

Making border films, however, is not risk free. Ghobadi's *Niwemang* (Half Moon, 2007), about a legendary aging Kurdish musician in Iran embarking on a trip to Iraq to perform a long-planned celebratory concert, was banned in Iran, apparently due to the inclusion of female singers, which the Islamic Republic considers illegal. If he ran into censorship on his home turf, in Iraq he was free to film anything he wanted. However, there he was saddled with other burdens of interstitial and border filming: "In Kurdistan, both here and in Iran, they don't have film professionals to fine-tune the script, or good assistants or location managers. You have to do everything yourself. You're performing the functions of 15 people. I had to roam around in the back alleys of villages to find actors." Iranian authorities not only banned *Half Moon* but also refused Ghobadi permission to work on his next film.[7]

Interstitial and border filming has also caused difficulties on the other side of the world. Mexican American filmmaker Gregory Nava filmed his immigration saga, *El norte* (1983), in the borderlands of Mexico and the United States and of Guatemala and Mexico, which posed a series of harrowing personal and aesthetic risks. The critic Pauline Kael called the work "an epic of the independent and underfinanced film movement, which means that moviegoers have to be willing to settle for humanistic aims and considerable amateurishness."[8] For accented films, however, amateurishness is not a liability but a distinguishing feature. The film's interstitial and artisanal production mode forced the filmmakers to re-create the Guatemalan scenes in Mexico (in Chiapas, bordering Guatemala), to hire non-Guatemalan actors for their leads (both of whom are Mexican), and use Guatemalan nonactors for smaller parts. But if necessity and underfinancing drove the filmmakers to film in Mexico, the political turmoil of the Chiapas which, according to the filmmakers, "was ready to blow," offered them some insight into the oppression that the Mayans were experiencing in Guatemala. It was that oppression that motivated the Mayans' risk taking in connection with illegal entry into the United States. Indeed, the difficulties encountered by the filmmakers turned the film's mode of production from artisanal to guerrilla. Secret agents working for the Mexican government, which was apparently bent on stopping the filming, visited the set carrying weapons. These agents kidnapped the production manager and chased the cinematographer in a car, finally running him down and taking away the exposed negatives at gunpoint. Frightened, Nava and his producer-wife, Ana Thomas, checked out of their hotel and found residence elsewhere using assumed names. After much negotiation with the kidnappers, they agreed upon a cash ransom for their hostage and the exposed film and designated a Mexico City parking lot as their rendezvous point. Thomas explains what happened there: "Two cars pulled up, with guys who had submachine guns and sunglasses, at night. It sounds almost comic but it was very scary. We paid around 1.3 million pesos, around $17,000 at the time. They threw down a metal box and drove away. Although we had another week of shooting left there, we had to get out of Mexico within 24 hours."[9] Filming had to be completed in California.

Despite the flaws stemming from its production mode, *El norte* demonstrates that border crossing—despite its celebration in much of the border literature—leaves physical and psychic scars that may never heal, as well as aesthetic scars on the film. In some accented films, the border is terminal, in others it is a festering wound, and in yet others it is a passage to freedom and new possibilities. Every successful cultural translation and transition exacts a price. There is no risk-free crossing! By being historically situated and culturally specific, and by paying attention to the inequalities of power relations at the borders, the best of border films avoid having their critical thrust neutralized by the hegemonizing and homogenizing celebratory discourses of border crossing and neoliberal globalization.

One of the most contentious borders is that between Palestinian lands and Israel. This border has increasingly been militarized, by Palestinian rocket attacks on illegal Israeli settlements and by Israel's construction of a massive separation wall around and through Palestinian lands and the institutionalization of an invasive checkpoint system that impedes Palestinian commerce, communication, transportation, migration, employment, and travel, turning the Occupied Territories into a giant prison house. Palestinians, like Kurds, form a large and vital population of displaced people in the Middle East, without an internationally recognized national homeland. Because of this fact and the peculiarities of their border with Israel, border concern and aesthetics are prominent among Palestinian films. Michel Khleifi's early film *Urs al-Jalil* (Wedding in Galilee, 1987) offers a powerful rumination on Palestinian life and cultural rituals on the borderline and under occupation, allegorized in the famous sequence of rescuing a mare that has wandered off into a minefield. Elia Suleiman's celebrated *Yadon illaheyya* (Divine Intervention, 2002) deals parodically with a more modern topic of two Palestinian lovers, one from Jerusalem and the other from Ramallah (he plays one of them) trying to establish liaisons across the Israeli checkpoint that separates them.

Another artist dealing with these issues is Emily Jacir, a leading Palestinian American artist-filmmaker who engages in strategies of critical and conceptual concealment and revelation both in her life and in her art—an inevitable outcome of traumatic displacements. Jacir has either refused to identify her real birthplace or allowed it to be named variously as Riyadh, Baghdad, Palestine, Bethlehem, Jordan, Memphis, Chicago, or Houston.[10] Having been born in one country (uncertain), raised in another (Saudi Arabia), educated in yet another (high school in Italy; college in Dallas and Memphis), she now divides her time between Brooklyn, New York, and Ramallah, the West Bank, giving a new transnational dimension to interstitial and border existence and its corollary, interstitial filmmaking. A review of her photographs, installations, and films, most of which revolve around questions of Palestinians' travel, displacement, and exile, points to this ambiguity about her birthplace as a deliberate conceptual art strategy to document, dramatize, and remind her public—and perhaps even herself—of the trauma of Palestinians' continuing displacement and homelessness under Israeli rule and occupation. Her lengthy 130-minute film *Hajiz Surda* (Crossing Surda: A Record of Going to and from Work, 2003) documents the hardship and daily frustration and humiliation of Palestinians at these checkpoints.

Crossing Surda is a record of Jacir's twenty-minute daily commute to and from work, on foot, between Ramallah and Birzeit University over a period of eight days, documenting how she and thousands of others have to go through the Surda checkpoint, which is manned by Israeli occupation army soldiers. She had originally begun filming her commute openly, but when Israeli soldiers noticed her filming her feet with a video camera, they stopped her, asking for ID. "I gave them my American passport and they threw it in the mud," says Jacir. "They told me that this was 'Israel' and that it was a military zone and that no filming was allowed. They detained me at gunpoint in the winter rain next to their tank. After three hours, they confiscated my videotape and then released me" (a soldier slipped her tape into his army pants' pocket).[11] Upon returning home that night, she cut a hole in her bag and put the video camera inside, and thus began her surreptitious filming.

Crossing Surda documents quotidian life, building into a powerful and angry indictment of the checkpoint system that bedevils Palestinians' lives as they wait in lines, sometime for long periods, and are subjected to humiliating questioning and treatment. These scenes are punctuated by the emphatic sounds of the footsteps of the filmmaker carrying the camera concealed in her handbag. The film's point of view is largely at near-ground level, showing endless series of civilian Palestinian feet, shoes, bags, and cars encountering Israeli soldiers, armored personnel carriers, and tanks on their halting march through the claustrophobic space of a militarized checkpoint. Jacir claims, "All people including the disabled, elderly, and children must walk distances as far as two kilometers depending on the decisions of the Israeli army at any given time. When Israeli soldiers decide that there should be no movement on the road, they shoot live ammunition, tear gas, and sound bombs to disperse people from the checkpoint."[12] As Maymanah Farhat states on The Electronic Intifada Web site, *Crossing Surda* and Jacir's other works bear witness to the "tragic yet defiant existence of a nation that remains physically fragmented by occupation but spiritually, intellectually and culturally bound by resistance."[13] Jacir's films have proven to be both controversial and widely appreciated, capped by a Hugo Boss Prize in 2008 bestowed upon her in recognition of her "significant achievement in contemporary art," which included a $100,000 cash award and a solo exhibition at the Guggenheim Museum of her *Material for a Film* (an installation in which the artist works with texts and photographs and with video and sound pieces) on the Israeli intelligence service's assassination of Wael Zuaiter, the Palestinian intellectual and translator of *One Thousand and One Nights* (from Arabic into Italian).

That life under occupation is extremely dangerous is borne out by a diary entry that Jacir's sister Annemarie Jacir, herself a filmmaker, posted on The Electronic Intifada, which begins with this dramatic sentence: "This afternoon I thought we were going to die." It continues, "Four hours ago my sister Emily, her curator Carolyn and I were shot at by the Israeli army. My nerves are still shaky. We've been drinking ever since. My legs are weak. [I] feel I can't stand on them." And it ends this way: "A man disappeared this afternoon. Two men were killed. It won't even make the news."[14] In 2008, Annemarie and one of her films ran into border troubles. Billed in a press release as the "first feature film by a Palestinian female director," *Milh hadha al bahr* (Salt of This Sea, 2008), about the return home of a third-generation Palestinian American female refugee from Brooklyn in search of her roots, had been accepted as an "official selection" of the Cannes Film Festival. As she was attempting to cross Jordan into the West Bank to finish the film, Israeli authorities held her for six hours, interrogated her, took away her cell phone, and finally denied her entry. They placed her on a bus and sent her back to Jordan. She had been trying for nine months to return to the West Bank to film. What this meant was that she was exiled from her ancestral home and some of her film's final scenes had to be filmed outside it—in Marseille, thanks to the French government's assistance. In a CNN program Annemarie Jacir stated, "It is a miracle the film exists. Everything was denied to us. Eighty percent of our locations we were forbidden to film in. Our whole West Bank crew was denied permits to leave Ramallah. Basically our policy was to film until we were stopped."[15]

The structural risks of accented filmmaking involving borders bedevil the films and their makers long after their production, for the films encounter difficulties as they enter the distribution, exhibition, and festival circuits. These difficulties become more personally painful when national representations at festivals are involved, raising anew such vexing questions as to which nation the filmmakers belong and which national cinema they represent.

In the 1970s, scores of films were made by Chilean exiles escaping the military dictatorship of Augusto Pinochet, constituting a Chilean cinema of resistance. This classification, however, excluded certain exilic films, such as Raúl Ruiz's works after *Dialogue d'exilés* (Dialogue of Exiles, 1974), which had critiqued the exiles.[16] The politics of exilic filmmakers, which are usually against their home governments, often forces them into painful positions. For example, because of the revocation of his citizenship, Güney, the most famous Turkish filmmaker who was also a very popular actor, could not represent his country at international festivals. Iranian exilic filmmaker Parviz Sayyad could not enter in the Cannes Film Festival as an Iranian product his film *Ferestadeh* (The Mission, 1983), an anti–Islamic Republic film made in the United States. Instead he was forced to enter the film as a U.S. production. In so doing he effectively admitted that he represented neither Iranian cinema nor Iranians. Unable to represent his home country, and unwilling to represent the host country, the film was in essence made "homeless." In 2002 the U.S. Academy of Motion Picture Arts and Sciences refused to include Suleiman's sardonic allegory *Divine Intervention* in the voting for the Best Foreign Language Film Oscar award. The reason cited was that it originated from Palestine, a place not recognized by the United Nations as a country. This despite the fact that the film had won the International Critics Prize at the Cannes Film Festival in May 2002 and that the same committee had previously recognized as countries, for the purpose of the Oscar consideration, regions the U.N. did not so recognize, such as Puerto Rico, Taiwan, and Hong Kong. "Obviously, we are disappointed," Feda Abdelhadi Nasser of the Permanent Observer Mission of Palestine to the U.N. said. "What it comes down to is that the Palestinian people, in addition to the denial of other rights . . . are now being denied the ability to compete in a competition that judges artistic and cultural expression."[17] A filmmaker without an officially recognized country risks making a film that will be homeless, or orphaned, like its maker.

Artistic homelessness, a profound outcome of the risk of exile, is not limited to third world or non-Western films or to their makers in the West. An increasing number of transnationally financed films and filmmakers have found it difficult to land a home, so to speak. Agnieszka Holland's *Hitlerjunge Salomon* (Europa, Europa, 1990), made in Germany, is an example of a European film threatened with homelessness. The German Export Film Union refused to nominate the film for an Academy of Motion Picture Arts and Sciences Foreign Film Oscar, claiming it was too "international." According to the union, the film's Polish director, French cofinancing, and Russian assistance disqualified it as a German entry. Critics, however, surmised that the real reason behind the government action was that the Germans were uncomfortable with the film's depiction of a young Jew who opportunistically survives in the Hitler Youth.[18] The case of Luis Buñuel's exilic film career, most of it spent in Mexico but also in France and the United States, provides a more complex and long-term view of the

     Hamid Naficy

artistic risk of homelessness, and of its nemesis, internationalization, exile being capable of producing both.

There are accented filmmakers, of course, who take what Mette Hjort calls either excessive or "flamboyant" risks (see her chapter in this volume) as a strategy of display or critique. Some take flamboyant risks as a risk-aversion strategy, to avoid other, riskier outcomes, which produces political and stylistic effects of a different sort in their films.

Flamboyant, Performative Risk Taking

Miguel Littín's *Acta general de Chile* (General Statement on Chile, 1986) is a classic accented film by an exilic director, one involving a complex series of risk-taking strategies with potential life-threatening consequences for the filmmaker and his collaborators. Key among these was flamboyant risk taking for the purpose of demonstrating defiance against the dictatorial regime that had banned Littín from returning to his homeland, Chile. Littín was born in the small village of Palmilla, Chile, in 1942, to a Palestinian father and a Greek mother. He worked as assistant director to Joris Ivens, cofounded the Committee of the Popular Unity Filmmakers, and ran Chile Films, for which he made weekly newsreels.[19] He also directed several important films, including *Por la tierra ajena* (On Foreign Land, 1968) and *El chacal de Nahueltoro* (The Jackal of Nahueltoro, 1969), which catapulted him to the forefront of the New Latin American cinema. Salvador Allende Gossens appointed him director of the national film company, Chile Films, a political and artistic position that, despite its brevity, became a liability in 1973 when General Augusto Pinochet staged a coup d'état that toppled Allende, forcing Littín (and his family) into exile, first to Mexico and later to Spain.

He was not alone, as the coup scattered many Chilean filmmakers to Europe and the Americas, where they used the wealth of films and footage smuggled out of Chile after the coup to mount anti-Pinochet and anti-military junta campaigns.[20] These filmmakers made over 250 feature films and documentaries in exile—far more than were produced in Chile itself up to 1973.[21] Littín's contributions to this exilic "cinema of resistance" include *Actas de Marusia* (Letters from Marusia, 1975) and *Alsino y el condor* (Alsino and the Condor, 1982), both of which were nominated for the Best Foreign Film Oscar.

However, he was not happy in exile, which he described in such painful terms as "tunnel of exile," "twilight of exile," and "plague of exile."[22] In 1985, after twelve years of living in this dystopic purgatory, he took advantage of a hiatus in his work to put into action a long-held desire to return home.

The problem was that his name had appeared on a list of five thousand people permanently barred from returning. The solution he came up with was as dangerous as it was ingenious: return to a militarized Chile, clandestinely and in disguise, accompanied by film crews hired to document the return. What followed is a bravura demonstration of politically motivated exilic doubling and flamboyant and performative risk taking. He adopted the persona of a Uruguayan advertising executive and spent several weeks preparing himself: he shaved his trademark beard, dyed his hair and changed his hair style, shed some twenty pounds, began wearing contact lenses, worked on changing the way he walked and gestured, and practiced a Uruguayan accent. In addition, a false marriage was arranged with a female political activist who was instrumental in realizing the project, and he obtained the passport of a sympathetic Uruguayan national and adopted his name and identity.

With financing from an Italian producer, he hired three foreign film crews (French, Dutch, and Italian) and sent them to Chile to obtain official permissions to film innocuous but plausible documentaries. He practiced the "drama of not being myself" by traveling with his new papers to several European countries, where in answering custom agents' questions he gained confidence in his new identity. He arrived in Chile with his falsified papers and identity and with a pounding heart, but he gained a safe entry. He stayed there for six weeks, traveling from one part of the country to the other, directing each foreign film crew as well as three locally hired crews. He made a point of appearing in his new persona in many of the shots filmed in public places in order to prove that he had been there. His transformation was so radical and his imitation of the businessman so real that his close friends and relatives, including his mother, did not recognize him. Unable for security reasons to reveal his true identity to them (until the very end, and then only to his mother), he resigned himself "to not being me." Suppressing his innermost feelings, he "assumed the strange condition of an exile in my own country, the most bitter experience for me."[23]

The six film crews audaciously filmed the daily lives of Chileans in cities and villages under the watchful eyes of the police (including Pablo Neruda's house and village in Isla Negra and the interior of the renovated presidential palace that had been gutted during the coup). They also filmed interviews with members of the open and underground opposition. Understandably, the film's mode of production was clandestine, improvisational, and artisanal—even guerrillalike. At times, the film crews would carry two sets of equipment, the larger one for confiscation by the police and the smaller one for clandestine filming.[24] Littín himself carried a hidden tape recorder in his pocket to record the voices of ordinary people and passersby for later use as dialogue. During filming, he communicated with his crew by agreed-upon signals. Secrecy was built into all aspects of the project, which operated in a cellular fashion that resembled the structure of the guerrilla groups then fighting oppressive military regimes in the third world. Only the chief of each crew knew Littín and was in on the true nature of the project, and apparently no film crew was aware of the other crews. In addition, no rushes could be viewed during filming, as the exposed footage was smuggled out for processing in Spain. As a result, like the case of Kurdish filmmaker Ariç, there was no possibility of correcting mistakes. All in all, 105,616 feet of film were exposed, which Littín spent six months editing after leaving Chile. The result was *General Statement on Chile,* a four-hour television program broadcast in many European countries. It won accolades at the Venice, Toronto, and Havana film festivals. Subsequently, he edited a shorter, two-hour version for theatrical distribution.

In the context of the ethics of accented filmmaking and of risk taking it is important to note that Littín did not assume his persona of a "bourgeois mummy" willingly. It was forced upon him by his status as a "permanent exile." In addition, his masquerade was multifaceted and profound, involving the transformation of many dimensions of identity and personality, including personal name, legal status, behavior and habits, class affiliation, nationality, country of origin, past history, and marital status. Moreover, there was a very high price to be paid in the event of a slip-up in the camouflage. Not only his own life but also the lives of his film crews and members of the internal resistance movement, who were assisting him, were at stake. He could not afford merely to mimic the Uruguayan businessman; he had to *be* him. In other words, the copy and the original had to match perfectly. As a result, the kind of play and excess that characterize the more voluntary forms of exilic doubling and masquerade, and which tend to reveal a criticism of that which is being imitated, could not develop in this case (at least not while he was in Chile). Consequently, he was enchained, not enchanted, by the doubling process.[25] This became evident to him when he was passing by a movie house he remembered from childhood: "I forgot my clandestine situation and returned for a moment to being myself. I had an irrational impulse to identify myself, to shout out my name, to tell the world that it was my right to be home."[26] Despite the impulse, he did not risk breaking the disguise. Nevertheless, the disguise accomplished its aims, which were to rediscover the country that he had "lost in a fog of nostalgia" and to thumb his nose at Pinochet.[27] His success in entering and leaving the country safely, in filming a scathing record of life under the military regime, and in having it shown widely and internationally constituted a bold act of risky parody and sabotage against the invincible dictator.

This turned the unbearable pain of doubling into welcome pleasure. As he states, making the film was tantamount to pinning a 105,616-foot-long tail on the donkey.[28]

Littín's flamboyant risk taking was complex and contradictory. At the social level he engaged in flamboyant risk taking not so much to stand out but to blend in, to pass as someone other than himself while in Chile. It was at the cinematic level, however, that his flamboyance came into full bloom, for the film showed that he had violated the permanent ban on his return—that he had been there in his homeland, in broad daylight, walking the streets.

FILMING IN CONFLICT ZONES

Filming in conflict zones has always involved extraordinary risk taking on the part of filmmakers. These risks have increased in the age of terrorism and counterinsurgency, particularly for émigré, exilic, diasporic, and ethnic filmmakers who may be making films in countries not their own. Cyrus (Kourosh) Kar, an Iranian-born American filmmaker, and his cameraman, Farshid Faraji, were engaged in filming a historical documentary on the life of Cyrus the Great, the Achaemenian king of ancient Persia, who "championed tolerance and human rights even as he built an empire that stretched across the Near East."[29] Kar had been in the United States since the age of two and had served in the U.S. Navy and the Naval Reserve. He had gone to Iraq to film the archaeological sites around Babylon, the city Cyrus had conquered in 539 BCE, releasing many slaves, including thousands of captive Jews, as a mark of his magnanimity and relocating some of them to Iran. In May 2005, after a taxi that Kar and Faraji took from their hotel in Baghdad was stopped by Iraqi forces, they were arrested because dozens of washing-machine timers, which were used by Iraqi insurgents to make improvised explosive devices, were in the car's trunk. The filmmakers were turned over to U.S. soldiers, who detained them for seven grueling and secretive weeks on the suspicion of involvement with the anti-American Iraqi insurgency. Mark Rosenbaum, Kar's lead lawyer, characterized his detention graphically: "Saddam Hussein has had more due process than Cyrus Kar. This is a detention policy that was drafted by Kafka."[30] The fact that Kar had been a supporter of President Bush and the neoconservatives' policy of exporting democracy to the Middle East at gunpoint did not help him.

The dangers of the Iraqi war zone had not deterred Kar and his cameraman from going there. Kar was apparently zealously determined to make this historical documentary, ignoring impediments and dangers. His sister, Ana, pointed to an important source of his determination for making the film, which is relevant to Kar's exilic context. "He had always been a little ashamed of being Iranian," she stated, ever since the Iranian revolution and the American hostage crisis. In the navy, "He got a lot of racial slurs. But reading about Cyrus the Great, he had felt a real sense of pride in what he thought was the real Iran—this tolerant, benevolent empire. And he started on this quest."[31] For this, his first film effort, Kar had traveled over the previous two years to Germany, Britain, Tajikistan, Iran, and Afghanistan, filming over forty hours of interviews and historical and documentary footage. Even after his release from the U.S. forces' detention, Kar did not go home before completing his filming in Babylon.[32]

The promotional material for his unfinished film, *In Search of Cyrus the Great,* posted on his Spenta Productions Web site, makes a case for Cyrus's human rights innovations and offers speculations that Western democracies and the U.S. Constitution may have been inspired by them. "In fact," Kar's voice-over states, "America's Constitution could be considered a very Persian document," for Xenophon's book on the life of Cyrus, *Cyropaedia,* was apparently required reading for the framers of the Constitution and Thomas Jefferson had a personal copy of it.[33] This is the latest effort by Iranians at corrective self-representation, designed to counter Western bias against acknowledging the contributions of the East, particularly Persia, to Western civilization. It also attempts to counter the representations of Persians by contemporary Western media as cruel and uncultured barbarians, which have gained momentum since the emergence of Islamic terrorism and Western governments' declaration of a "global war on terror." A plethora of movies, such as Oliver Stone's *Alexander* (2004) and Zack Snyder's *300* (2006), and historical re-creations, such as those on the American History Channel, evidence this trend. On his Web site, Kar requests help in financing the remaining $400,000 he needs to complete the latest salvo in the wars of national representation.

Clandestine Filming under Oppressive Conditions

Filming clandestinely has been a strategy of radical filmmaking for a long time, coming to efflorescence during the postcolonial national struggles for independence since the 1960s. Technological innovations such as equipment miniaturization and sync sound recording and filming as well as the emergence of direct cinema and cinéma vérité styles facilitated this efflorescence. Clandestine filming is often motivated by a desire to document, bear witness, testify, and provide evidence for the purpose of publicizing, exposing, or seeking justice both in the court of public opinion and in courts of law. The consequences of risking such filming and their oppositional politics are often grave, as they may include the suppression of the films and the imprisonment, death, or exile of their makers. The cases of the Jacir sisters have already offered some glimpses of these consequences. Others follow.

The monumental 260-minute agitprop documentary *La hora de los hornos: Notas y testimonios sobre el neocolonialismo, la violencia y la liberación* (The Hour of the Furnaces, 1968), directed by Spanish filmmaker Octavio Getino and Argentine filmmaker Fernando Solanas, was filmed clandestinely during the initial stages of what became known as Argentina's infamous "dirty war." The filmmakers had a history of underground filmmaking: in 1966 they had cofounded with Cesar Vallejo the Grupo Cine Liberación to make such films. *The Hour of the Furnaces* documented graphically and with various degrees of insight and bombast a veritable third world war, this time against neocolonialism, waged by oppressed peoples of the third world. A landmark film that embodies both the theory and practice of Third Cinema, this film and the 1974 manifesto "Toward a Third Cinema," which Solanas and Getino coauthored, further secured their place within the emergent militant Third Cinema.[34] The film was not only shot surreptitiously but also screened clandestinely to sympathetic audiences who, taking their cue from the film's tripartite structure and its urgings, interrupted the projection to discuss issues the film raised. Soon after the film was finished Solanas was driven into exile in Paris, from where he began his contemplative musical film about external exile, *Tangos: El exilio de Gardel* (Tangos: The Exile of Gardel, 1985). This period of displacement and disempowerment put Solanas in touch with the deep existential meanings of exile, which he described as "a feeling of absence, a sense of loss," and which profoundly shaped the film, turning it, like *The Hour of the Furnaces,* into a work that embodied both the theory and practice of a new cinema—accented cinema.[35] Whether forced or voluntary, exile is always traumatic; some experience and express this as absence and loss, such as Solanas, while others see it as liberation and artistic gain. Affected deeply by the dirty war and his external exile, soon after he returned to Argentina Solanas made *Sur* (South, 1988), a film about the pains of internal exile. His collaborator on *The Hour of the Furnaces,* Getino, was already in exile when they worked on that film, as he had migrated from his homeland Spain to Argentina in the early 1950s. After the takeover of the generals, he was compelled to migrate once again in the 1970s, this time to Peru, where he taught film. From here he fought Argentina's efforts to extradite him, eventually moving to Mexico. Perennial exile is one outcome of clandestine filmmaking.

     Hamid Naficy

Likewise, Chilean filmmaker Patricio Guzmán made *La batalla de Chile: La lucha de un pueblo sin armas* (The Battle of Chile, 1975), a seminal, lengthy (190 minutes), tripartite film about the September 11, 1973 military coup by General Augusto Pinochet's army that toppled the democratically elected Socialist government of President Salvador Allende Gossens. Guzmán and a team of four also chronicled the ten months of street unrest leading to the coup, some of it filmed clandestinely. It is a bravura act of showing the "minute-to-minute of history," causing one critic to claim that "if Tolstoy had made movies, his work might well have looked like this."[36] By the time of the coup, Guzmán and collaborators had been able to conceal in the Swedish embassy the forty-two thousand feet of film they had shot. This was eventually smuggled out of Chile as diplomatic material, and edited in Cuba and France. The risk of such oppositional film practice was such that the film has never been shown in public cinemas in Chile, despite its international awards and fame and the fact that Chile has had democratically elected governments since the early 1990s. The risk extended to the filmmakers as well. The military regime arrested, tortured, and murdered the cinematographer, Jorge Muller-Silva. Guzmán was arrested by military intelligence officers five days after Allende's overthrow and was interrogated in the infamous national stadium in Santiago for two weeks before his release, whereupon he fled the country into exile. "He was lucky," for while many Allende supporters were "being jailed, tortured and killed, he escaped because he was 'only' a documentary filmmaker."[37] Another price of making such films was a kind of serial national homelessness for its maker, as Guzmán lived in five different countries. A "wandering filmmaker," he called himself. There was yet another price, the one the film subjects would potentially have to pay, subjects who had fearlessly spoken to his camera. "I thought about them all the time," Guzmán stated. "I was always asking exiles, 'This worker at that factory, what has happened to him?' The people in *The Battle of Chile* were well known. So there was reason to worry."[38]

Like Littín, Guzmán returned to his homeland clandestinely, in 1986, while the military was still in power, and secretly filmed *En nombre de Dios* (In the Name of God, 1987), a documentary on the role of the Roman Catholic Church in protecting human rights. He discovered that Chile was no longer home. Permanent exile is perhaps the biggest price he has had to pay for his radical filmmaking. But even this is not without risk, for it is not just the exiles who reject their homelands; often the homelands also reject those in exile and refuse to welcome them back, should they wish and be able to return. "So many Chilean artists, writers and filmmakers still live in exile," Guzmán states. "There is no work for us at home, and there's also a very negative attitude toward the exiles. When I visited, I felt that there were a lot of people who wished I wasn't there."[39]

Surveillance, Sousveillance, and Inverse Surveillance

Surveillance means "watching from above." Sousveillance, a form of inverse surveillance, means "watching from below." While surveillance generally refers to acts of control exerted by authorities and private businesses on their subjects, sousveillance refers to acts of civil disobedience and resistance to being watched, involving subjects documenting their own resistance activities with portable, stationary, or wearable cameras and computing devices.[40] Surveillance involves centralizing and collecting data by governments and private sectors for optimum panoptic control and profit; sousveillance involves decentralizing and dispersing information for the purpose of first-person witnessing, documenting, resisting, providing legal proofs, and ultimately countering external control. The idea is to establish a balance or equivalence (in the words of Ian Kerr and Steve Mann, "equiveillance") between these two forms of surveilling. A prime example of using sousveillance to achieve equiveillance is the strategy of grassroots political activists, such as anti–World Trade Organization globalization groups, and activist media makers, such as Indie media filmmakers, to film their demonstrations and agitprop actions in order to monitor and document police (mis)conduct against them.[41]

With the recent adoption of draconian antiterrorism and anti-immigrant measures in many countries, particularly the creation in the United States of the Department of Homeland Security and the adoption of the Patriot Act, state-sponsored surveillance has penetrated all spheres of life and all sorts of communications, business transactions, artistic activities, and travel, particularly those involving Muslims and Middle Eastern men. The militarization of airports and border posts has turned ordinary travel for them into an unpleasant and risky business. The treatment of Iranian filmmakers during their international travels, recounted at length in my forthcoming book, offers a good case study of such panoptic transnational surveillance.[42] In 2002 renowned filmmakers including Abbas Kiarostami and Bahman Ghobadi, invited to the United States to participate in events celebrating their works, had to wait for several months and travel more than once to a third country in order to obtain a visa to enter the States (and some were denied a visa). Iranian filmmakers had to submit to fingerprinting and photographing long before these practices became more generalized. Some were interrogated and humiliated; others, like Jafar Panahi in 2001 and Hossein Dehbashi in 2002, were handcuffed and deported. Travel proved too risky, humiliating, and cumbersome, forcing some filmmakers to avoid visiting countries regarded as hostile. Kiarostami avoided the United States while others resorted to creative alternatives. In 2008, French-Iranian filmmaker and installation artist Ghazel Radpay, invited as a featured filmmaker to the Virginian Film Festival in Charlottesville, Virginia, ran into so much red tape and humiliation at the U.S. embassy in Paris (before she had obtained her French citizenship) that she gave up on coming to the United States; instead she participated from Paris via live Skype Video, fed directly into a Charlottesville movie house, where I interviewed her live before the spectators, who engaged in a question-and-answer session with her.

Of course, surveillance is not unidirectional. The home countries of accented filmmakers also engage in it, often to a greater degree and in a more violent manner, making the return of these filmmakers very risky, if not impossible. Iranian filmmakers who are political exiles do not typically return home, because of either their opposition to the Islamist regime or their fear of its violence. One who did return encountered a gruesome death. Canadian-Iranian photojournalist and documentarist Ziba Zahra Kazemi returned to photograph. In June 2003, while taking pictures of student demonstrations outside the Evin Prison, she was arrested and imprisoned, and subsequently died under torture.[43] Some filmmakers did not return because they would have had to do so clandestinely—with its risky consequences—or seek official permission—which could have incurred a denial or an arrest upon arrival. The case of one filmmaker living in Europe illustrates the risks of exilic returns by political exiles. As Reza Allamehzadeh tells it, when in 1998–99 he wanted to return to Iran to make a film about the ailing renowned modernist poet Ahmad Shamlu, he applied to the Iranian authorities for permission.[44] Having escaped Iran years earlier, he did not have an Iranian passport; given political asylum in the Netherlands, he had become a Dutch citizen. Iranian officials denied his request for a visa on his Dutch passport because they continued to consider him an Iranian subject, in no need of a visa to return to his birth country. He could not risk obtaining an Iranian passport; that would deny him the protection of Dutch citizenship, protection he would sorely need due to his vociferous anti–Islamic Republic writings and films while in exile. In the meantime, Shamlu's health took a turn for the worse, torpedoing the trip and the film project, which ironically was titled *Vasiyatnameh-ye qoqnus* (The Testament of the Phoenix). The phoenix, the lionhearted aged poet, did not rise again. He succumbed to his diabetes and cancer, burying the exiled director's wish for a grand return for filming.

Politicized or militant émigré communities and individuals also engage in surveillance, sometimes on their own filmmakers and sometimes on the host countries' filmmakers, as part of their patrolling and defending of their national and religious identities. The fate of the rabble-rousing Dutch filmmaker and writer Theo Van Gogh, great-grandson of Theo van Gogh, who was the brother of painter Vincent van Gogh, is a case in point. Van Gogh made the ten-minute film *Submission* (2004) based on a script by writer Ayaan Hirsi Ali, a fiery Somali-Dutch feminist and a member of the Dutch parliament, which provocatively attacked Islam for its violent misogyny. It depicted a naked woman under a see-through black veil praying and complaining to God about having to submit to the men in her family, who abused her sexually and physically. These complaints are emphasized by images of large bruises on her arm and bloody cuts on her face and body, which are punctuated by violent swishing sounds recalling whipping. In addition, from time to time, on her body are projected Arabic words (implying words from the Quran), which in the context of the other forms of violence registered on the woman's body are clearly to be interpreted as violent words, words that hurt (perhaps copying Shirin Neshat's famous *Women of Allah* photographs). Unfortunately, intolerant militant Muslims have perpetrated terrible violence in the name of various schools of Islam, but it is not difficult to take offense at this film's crass Muslim-baiting discourse, particularly given Van Gogh's published inflammatory commentaries in which he regularly refers to Muslims and Islamists in such derogatory terms as *geitenneukers* (goat fuckers). What happened next was an intolerant violent reaction from an inflamed Dutch Muslim citizen of Moroccan descent. After Dutch TV aired the film, both Van Gogh and Hirsi Ali received death threats. After stalking him, on an early morning in November 2004, Mohammed Bouyeri fired eight shots at Van Gogh while he was bicycling to work, assassinating him. Police found a threatening poem and a letter the killer had written pinned with a knife to the murdered body. Bouyeri was sentenced to life in prison without parole. Hirsi Ali, a refugee who had been forcibly circumcised in Somalia as a child and later apparently forced into an arranged marriage before fleeing to the Netherlands, was placed under police protection for years, eventually becoming a fellow of the conservative think tank American Enterprise Institute, working from an unknown location.

The intensification of state-sponsored surveillance of daily life, artistic activities, and travel in both democratic and authoritarian societies, typical of what Gilles Deleuze rightly called "societies of control,"[45] have made life for exilic, diasporic, émigré, and ethnic filmmakers of color harsher, intensifying their burdens and risks of unbelonging, partiality, multiplicity, and hybridity. However, such intensification of repressive state apparatuses has in turn created opportunities for creative countermeasures from accented filmmakers and artists. Some have embarked upon personal sousveillance and inverse surveillance to counter state intrusion into their lives and works. An interesting case in point is that of Bangladeshi American artist, filmmaker, and university professor Hasan M. Elahi, born in 1972 in Bangladesh and raised in a traditional but "quite secular" Bengali family, which emigrated to the United States when he was seven. He currently teaches at San José State University in California.

"Hasan M. Elahi is an interdisciplinary artist whose work examines issues of surveillance, simulated time, transport systems, borders and frontiers," as he himself puts it on his Web site.[46] He is an internationally exhibited artist whose massive and controversial works are discussed widely in the mass media, including an appearance on Comedy Central's popular *The Colbert Report* (May 7, 2008). One of these, "Tracking Transience: The Orwellian Project," is his creative response to his entanglement with the U.S. Federal Bureau of Investigation, which from June to November 2002 subjected him to investigation as a terrorist suspect. As he tells it in an e-mail statement he sent me (September 3, 2009), he had been reported to the police as "an Arab man that had explosives who fled on September 12." Upon returning to the United States on September 19 from a European exhibition, he was met at the Detroit airport by an FBI agent who rigorously interrogated him about his whereabouts and activities. For the next six months he met with agents frequently, undergoing interrogations and "nine consecutive polygraphs." He was eventually cleared and is "officially no longer considered a terrorist threat." This experience was so traumatic that he turned it into an art project, his Orwellian project, whereby he developed a "network device built upon a modified/hacked mobile phone," which opened just about every aspect of his life to the FBI and to the public. The network device generates a database of imagery and locative information that, combined with a Web-enabled companion, tracks him and his points of transits at all times and uploads it to his Web site. This information is archived along with over twenty thousand images showing "which food I have eaten, where I have slept and even which toilets I have used." Also, his financial data, communication records, and transportation logs map his locations since 2004. Elahi's strategy amounts to what might be called "flamboyant risk aversion," and it is fraught with risks of one kind or another. He hoped that by "publicly disclosing every bit of personal information" about him he would achieve two goals: "not only devalue the currency of the FBI by disclosing the information that is held secret in my file, but also make every detail about myself completely transparent to the public to the point where it clearly demonstrates how invasive our new Homeland Security and Patriot Act laws are." The project received wide publicity with colorful headlines, each of which brought out an aspect of its politics and poetics: "Hiding in Plain Sight" (*Yahoo News*), "The 24/7 Alibi" (*New York Times Magazine*), "Spoofing Big Brother" (*Policy Innovations*), "The Visible Man: An FBI Target Puts His Whole Life Online" (*Wired*), "Self-Imposed Surveillance" (CNN), "Life Online" (National Public Radio), "The Transparent Man" (*Forbes*), and "Art in Security and Security in Art" (*Kinship International Strategy on Surveillance and Suppression*).

To the extent that this act of performative inverse surveillance made public the currency of intelligence services, which is secrecy, and thereby made it worthless, his project was counterhegemonic, for it reversed aspects of the state's panoptic system. In this manner he averted risk. However, what he calls his "aggressive compliance" turned the radical potentiality of sousveillance on its head, for it demonstrated to the authorities (and whoever else cared to visit his site) that he was an obedient citizen, fully socialized to behave himself. If visibility diminished his risk in the age of secrecy, national security, and terrorism, and guaranteed his safety, it also robbed him of the radicalism of invisibility, secrecy, and misbehaving, which are the coins and privileges of artists. Of course, Elahi could be selective in reporting his activities and his whereabouts, and he could even misleadingly report them. In that case, he would be countering both the interpellative capacity of his own system and the state's panoptic system.

One of the dilemmas of all minority and oppressed people, including exiles, is how to balance between the desire for visibility and the risk of visibility. Taking risks in order to become visible, to come into representation, is life affirming. It gives meaning to the life of individual filmmakers and the communities they represent. However, the more visible they become, the more they risk opening themselves up to the disciplinary, regulatory, and surveilling regimes of control. Risk taking, if acknowledged and narrativized in the film, can become a source of spectatorial tension and pleasure. However, the risks and benefits of visibility and invisibility are not evenly distributed among the filmmakers, their subjects, and their spectators.

NOTES

1. "Hope Deferred," *Index on Censorship* 20, no. 3 (1991): 11.

2. Hamid Naficy, *An Accented Cinema: Exilic and Diasporic Filmmaking* (Princeton: Princeton University Press, 2001), 181–84.

                                                                                    Hamid Naficy

3. In a feat of accented multitasking, Ariç directed the film, cowrote the screenplay, starred in the production, composed and performed the music, and supervised the makeup and costuming.

4. Naficy, *An Accented Cinema,* 160–64.

5. Quoted in Peter Scarlet, "Kurdish Director, Stuck between Iraq and Iran," *New York Times,* December 16, 2007, 18.

6. Ibid.

7. Ibid. Ghobadi made his *Kasi az gorbeha-ye irani khabar nadareh* (No One Knows about Persian Cats, 2009) about the dynamic underground music scene in Iran without government permission. The government banned the film and he left the country.

8. Pauline Kael, *State of the Art* (New York: E. P. Dutton, 1985), 130.

9. Quoted in Annette Insdorf, "*El norte:* On Screen and in Reality, a Story of Struggle," *New York Times,* June 8, 1984, 17, 26.

10. Michael Z. Wise, "Border Crossings between Art and Life," *New York Times,* January 30, 2009.

11. Emily Jacir, "The Wall and the Check Points," *Darat al Funun,* 2006, http://www.daratalfunun.org/main/activit/curentl/febo6/emily/emily06.html.

12. Ibid.

13. Maymanah Farhat, "Palestinian Artist Emily Jacir Awarded Top Prize," *The Electronic Intifada,* December 15, 2008, http://electronicintifada.net/v2/article10028.shtml.

14. Annemarie Jacir, "A Tale of Two Sisters: Witnessing an Undercover Israeli Operation in Ramallah (1)," November 15, 2006, http://electronic intifada.net/v2/article6041.shtml.

15. See "Inside the Middle East: Award-Winning Palestinian Film *Salt of This Sea,*" http://www.youtube.com/watch?v=oPbR5mk1_As&feature=related.

16. Zuzana M. Pick, "Chilean Cinema in Exile (1973–1986)," *Framework* 34 (1987): 39–57.

17. Quoted in Burhan Wazir, " Palestinian Film Denied Oscars Entry," *Observer,* December 15, 2002, http://www.guardian.co.uk/world/2002/dec/15/film.filmnews.

18. Karen Breslau, "Screening out the Dark Past," *Newsweek,* February 3, 1992, 30; Joseph McBride, "Foreign Oscar Hopeful Tongue-tied," *Variety,* October 1991, 3.

19. Nicholas Thomas, ed., *International Dictionary of Films and Filmmakers,* 2nd ed. (Chicago: St. James Press, 1990).

20. Pick, "Chilean Cinema in Exile (1973–1986)."

21. Richard Peña, "Images of Exile: Two Films by Raoul Ruiz," in *Reviewing Histories: Selections from New Latin American Cinema,* ed. Coco Fusco (Buffalo, NY: Hallwalls, 1987), 136–45.

22. Quoted in Gabriel García Márquez, *Clandestine in Chile: The Adventures of Miguel Littín* (New York: Henry Holt, 1987), 23, 79, 86.

23. Ibid., 34.

24. Ibid., 62.

25. Naficy, *An Accented Cinema*, 279–82.

26. Quoted in Márquez, *Clandestine in Chile*, 18.

27. Ibid., 2–3.

28. Ibid., 114. In the way it deflated the regime of the Chilean junta, Littín's *General Statement on Chile* is similar to Constantin Costa-Gavras's influential film *Z* (1969), which mocked and exposed the ruthless regime of the Greek generals in his home country.

29. Tim Golden, "U.S. Had Held Iranian-American in Iraq since May," *New York Times*, July 6, 2005, A1, A8.

30. Ibid., A8.

31. Ibid.

32. Tim Golden, "U.S. Says It Will Release American Held in Iraq," *New York Times*, July 10, 2005, A10.

33. See: http://www.spentaproductions.com/Cyrus-the-Great-English/cyrus preview_english.htm.

34. "Toward a Third Cinema," in *New Latin American Cinema*, vol. 1, *Theory, Practices and Transcontinental Articulations*, ed. Michael Martin (Detroit: Wayne State University Press, 1997).

35. Quoted in the publicity package accompanying *Tangos*.

36. Claudia Dreifus, "The New Battle of Chile: Keeping Memory Alive," *New York Times*, September 6, 1998.

37. Alan Riding, "Telling Chile's Story, Even if Chile Has Little Interest," *New York Times*, October 3, 2002.

38. Quoted in Dreifus, "The New Battle of Chile."

39. Ibid.

40. Ian Kerr and Steve Mann, "Exploring Equiveillance," January 3, 2006, http://www.anonequity.org/weblog/archives/2006/01/exploring_equiv_1.php.

41. Tish Stringer, "Move: Guerrilla Films, Collaborative Modes, and the Tactics of Radical Media Making" (PhD diss., Rice University, 2006), 271. The practice of installing video cameras in highway police cars in the United States to record for legal purposes the officers' traffic control and arrest incidents can be considered a form of official sousveillance.

42. Hamid Naficy, *A Social History of Iranian Cinema*.

43. See her official Web site: http://www.zibakazemi.org/index.html.

44. Reza Allamehzadeh, *Vasiyatnameh-ye qoqnus* (Teheran: Karevan, 2003/ 1382).

45. Gilles Deleuze, "Postscript on the Societies of Control," *October*, no. 59 (1992): 3–7.

46. http://elahi.org/.

JINHEE CHOI

Multinational Casts and Epistemic Risk

The Case of Pan-Asian Cinema

In Chen Kaige's *The Promise* (2005), Asian audiences see odd interactions among a multinational cast, free from language barriers and unbound by national identities. Set in a mythic space, the film depicts the entangled romances of the slave Kunlun (played by Korean actor Jang Dong-gun), General Guangming (Sanada Hiroyuki from Japan), and Duke Wuhuan (Nicholas Tse from Hong Kong), all of whom pursue Princess Qingcheng (Hong Kong actress Cecilia Cheung). The film *Initial D* (dir. Andy Lau and Alan Mak, 2005), a Hong Kong adaptation of a Japanese manga/anime, features the Japanese actress Ann Suzuki as Natsuki, dubbed into Cantonese. The Korean actor Ji Jin-hee speaks in Mandarin to portray the character Monty in the musical *Perhaps Love* (dir. Peter Chan, 2005). *The Myth* (dir. Stanley Tong, 2005) and *Seven Swords* (dir. Tsui Hark, 2005) showcase casts of actors from various countries—Hong Kong, India, and South Korea. All these films are examples of a significant production trend throughout the region: pan-Asian cinema.

Multinational casting has been a production strategy found in both European art cinema and genre quickies made in Canada and New Zealand, as a result of coproduction and/or with the aim to attract audiences across national borders. Some of the most renowned European art cinema directors, such as Michelangelo Antonioni and Luchino Visconti, created films with multinational casts—*The Eclipse* (1962), *Rocco and His Brothers* (1960), and *The Leopard* (1963), to name a few—that are products of French and Italian partnerships.[1] Darrell Davis and Emilie Yeh view a coproduction trend in East Asia as emerging out of necessity, that is, as a way for Asian producers and filmmakers to resuscitate the regional film industry.[2] The declining industries in Hong Kong, Taiwan, and Japan demanded a means to recapture the hearts of local audiences and expand potential markets with films of high entertainment value and stars with broad appeal.

As a coproduction between South Korea (Show East) and China (21st Century Shengkai Film, China Film Group, Capgen Investment Group), *The Promise* was China's most expensive film to date, with production costs reaching $35 million, but with grosses totaling only $18 million in the People's Republic of China (PRC) and $650,000 in Hong Kong.[3] A distribution deal with the Weinstein Company fell through, and the stateside box office results ($660,000) were rather tepid in comparison to previously released swordplay films such as *Hero* ($53.3 million) and *House of Flying Daggers* ($11.1 million).[4] The industry discourse on such high-budget films as *The Promise* often focuses on the economic necessity and benefits of shifting target audiences/markets from the local to the regional and global. But to what extent does this trend of pan-Asian cinema—as an attempt to manage financial risk within an increasingly globalized film industry—involve and ignore immanent epistemic risk?

A reviewer for *Variety* predicted a reception gap between ethnic Chinese and non-Chinese audiences for *The Promise:* "Although non-Asian audiences will be unaffected by the multinational casting of stars Sanada and Jang . . . Mandarin-speaking audiences have been loudly critical of non-Chinese actors' accents."[5] Should the multinational casts' imperfect command of Mandarin be considered a concession to regional audiences, a marker in a number of "me-too" coproduction swordplay films to emerge after the strong North American box office draws of such films as *Crouching Tiger, Hidden Dragon* (dir. Ang Lee, 2000) and *Hero* (dir. Zhang Yimou, 2002)? Is this an inevitable yet bearable consequence, given the ambitions of regional filmmakers to create a self-sustaining pan-Asian film market? Or do the multinational casts bring to the fore some of the epistemic and aesthetic risks resulting from multinational coproductions? In this chapter, I explore the epistemic risk involved in films with multinational casts. To what extent does pretend communication among multinational casts affect the audiences' aesthetic engagement with film? To what extent does such a practice create epistemic conditions under which audiences with cultural knowledge depreciate the aesthetic value of a work?

The issue of epistemology here concerns the relationship between an artwork and its audience, the conditions under which audiences assess and appreciate a work. The concept of risk—borrowed and refashioned from sociology—underscores the probability, rather than the truth claim, the latter being the concern of philosophical epistemology.[6] Sociologists such as Ulrich Beck and Anthony Giddens approach the question of risk in relation to knowledge, wherein the perception of risk depends upon the access to knowledge—especially in relation to experts' knowledge of technology and the environment in the late modern era.[7] It is claimed that a growing awareness, and/or fear, of one's exposure to hazards and environmental risks, for instance, relies upon the access to "scientific" and/or "statistical" knowledge at hand, however provisional it may be. Nonetheless, the actual occurrence and/or the individual experience of a danger remain predicated upon contingency and uncertainty, rather than necessity and certainty. For example, given the statistics to be found among Asian populations and my personal family history, I may be more aware of my risk for contracting stomach cancer, but the actual chance of my doing so is still contingent upon a number of factors that I have no complete control over.

Such a concept of risk may lack direct applicability to the cultural consumption of coproduction films in question, but it sheds light on the correlation between cultural product, consumption, and knowledge. Awareness of epistemic risk in such consumption depends upon, as will be shown, an audience's uneven access to cultural knowledge, a lack of which would mitigate the epistemic risk present in a work. Epistemic risk, however, should be further differentiated from the "authenticity" of a work, which deals with the relationship between an individual work and the traditions and practices of a genre to which it belongs; "fidelity," which concerns the relationship between the original and a translated text; and "accuracy," which addresses the relationship between the work and the historical, cultural, and political reality of the originating nation-state. Rather, epistemic risk deals with favorable or unfavorable conditions under which audiences can view and determine the authenticity or accuracy of a work.

Target Audiences and Epistemic Risk

Previous approaches to cross-cultural communication have focused on the ideological dimension of cultural translations and transformation. Translation, often employed in a metaphorical sense, refers to the process by which source materials are adapted, transformed, and digested to accommodate the tastes of a target culture. Unequal exchange and power relationships come to the fore, especially when such activities take place between East and West and/or marginal and dominant cultures in their dissemination across the global scene. That is, a foreign culture is exoticized and cropped for the sake of recognition—however insufficient it may be—in the West. Criticisms of "self-orientalism," which were often leveled against Fifth Generation Chinese directors such as Zhang Yimou and Chen Kaige, who were deemed to have "sold out," resonate with such concerns.[8]

Similar criticisms were heard in the heated debate regarding the "Westernization" of the martial arts tradition in such megahit films as *Crouching Tiger, Hidden Dragon*. The film has been at the center of many debates on the globalization of Chinese culture and has been denounced as "inauthentic" by many critics and scholars.[9] It is often pointed out that the film's romance plot is extended to such an extent that it is as prominent as the main action plot. Furthermore, martial arts sequences are narrativized to be expressive of character psychology, in contrast to many martial arts films within the tradition wherein a series of action sequences are pinned together on a thin narrative thread.[10] The lacking cultural knowledge also makes a non-Chinese audience unable to detect the unnaturalness manifest in the non-Mandarin-speaking actors' various accents.[11] Furthermore, English subtitles are less sensitive to the subtleties and nuances conveyed in the original language. The female protagonist's Chinese name, "Jiaolong" (Pretty Dragon), for instance, is translated as "Jen"; this both clouds the contrast cued in the film's title, *Crouching Tiger, Hidden Dragon*, and lessens the masculinity associated with "dragon."[12]

The pressing issue in this chapter may be viewed as a continuation and a fracture of the unequal exchange between East and West, since it embeds an epistemic risk and the corresponding aesthetic consequences in cross-cultural translation and exchange. However, it is distinct from, as well as narrower in its scope than, the concerns expressed above. The question here specifically deals with the verbal communication manifest among characters in pan-Asian cinema, in both commercially driven and festival-oriented films. Translation studies underscore both the domestic "inscription" or "remainder" that is untranslatable and the various ways to acknowledge such a gap during the translation process and within the translated text,[13] but the question here has more to do with the "intelligibility" of communication and the "performance" restricted by language barriers—and their corresponding aesthetic disengagement.

Some of the characteristics of pan-Asian cinema may overlap with those of East-West co-ventures, but the former departs from the latter with respect to both target audience and relative cultural proximity. East and Southeast Asia is a heterogeneous space, both culturally and linguistically, despite the cross-cultural exchanges that have been institutionally facilitated and redirected lately. Changing cultural policies have opened up a new mode of media production, distribution, and consumption in East Asian countries. One must remember, however, that it was only in 2004 that the South Korean government fully lifted its ban on Japanese cinema to allow the theatrical release of Japanese films of all ratings, including adult-rated films,[14] and that both South Korea and the PRC still maintain a screen quota. The former has allotted seventy-three days per year for the screening of homegrown films, while the latter limits the number of imports of foreign films to twenty for revenue sharing and another forty on a flat fee basis per year.[15] In order for a Hong Kong film to be exempt from the import quota, the government of the PRC increasingly demands collaboration with Chinese talent and/or location shooting in China. Furthermore, cultural consumption is not completely free from the political and ideological tensions and conflicts still present among East Asian nation-states. Korea's colonial past is constantly brought to the fore by political debates, such as the ongoing territorial disputes between Japan and Korea. At the level of production, linguistic barriers create further obstacles for both film crews and casts.[16] Even if East Asian audiences do not intimately know a foreign tongue, they can still detect its "foreignness," which could influence their appreciation of Asian coproduction films.

Although multinational casting is closely tied to an emerging trend of coproduction in the East Asian region, it is not a phenomenon exclusive to films with high production value. *Last Life in the Universe* (2003) and *Invisible Waves* (2006), two films by Thai director Pen-ek Ratanaruang, as well as *Breath* (2007) and *Dream* (2008), films by Korean provocateur Kim Ki-duk, all feature protagonists of different nationalities. In *Last Life,* for example, Kenji (Asano Tadanobu, Japan) and Noi (Boonyasak Sinitta, Thailand) communicate in broken English. *Dream* stars Jin (Odagiri Jo) and Ran (Lee Na-yeong) speak in their own tongues—Japanese and Korean, respectively—without any attempt to narrativize the possibility of such mysterious communication.

As Davis and Yeh note, "[F]or producers and audiences alike, pan-Asian is an emerging trend. As the ultimate tactic East Asian screen industries employ to sustain commercial markets, no Asian players, big or small, can overlook it. Everyone wants to play the pan-Asian game, including Hollywood."[17] Davis and Yeh divide pan-Asian cinema into different types, including "intra-Asian co-production," "pan-Chinese co-production," and "pan-Asian program packages," according to budget and target audience. The first two categories are often funded by large corporations in the region, such as Applause Pictures (Hong Kong), CJ Entertainment (South Korea), Kadokawa (Japan), and Raintree MediaCorp (Singapore), targeting multinational markets within Asia.[18] On the other hand, the third category combines "film festival artistry with commercial appeal" and is intended for viewing in the West.[19] This chapter does not aim to challenge the validity of such categorizations or contest specific instances of each category, but rather to investigate the relationship between a target audience and the epistemic risk involved in various types of coproductions—that is, whether the production of a film for a specific target audience sanctions epistemic risk and warrants certain aesthetic decisions.

In traditional aesthetics, especially within the analytic tradition, the perception and appreciation of the aesthetic values of a work are often predicated upon the idea of an "ideal critic," one who has cultivated a sensitivity toward and gained cultural knowledge of a work,[20] as well as an audience's familiarity with the relevant category to which a work belongs.[21] That is, in order to fully appreciate an artwork, certain epistemic conditions should be met: a connoisseur is free from cultural limitations and personal predilections, and is able to contextualize an artwork within its proper historical and artistic traditions. But the focus on film reception in the discourse of contemporary film studies—from textually constructed subject position(s) to real or target audiences—demands both a different approach and a different measure to discuss the epistemology and aesthetics of cultural consumption facilitated by globalization and regionalization. A potentially new target audience member, especially for the films that will be discussed below, departs from the "suitably informed viewer" in that the audience member's knowledge of foreign culture and tradition is not presupposed; priority is instead given to accessibility for those who lack cultural knowledge. How should we evaluate the aesthetic value of a work, then, when its aim is to maximize accessibility?

The Mythic Asia

Kendall Walton, in his article "Categories of Art," asserts that the historical circumstances of a work's origin bear relevance to aesthetic considerations: the aesthetic properties of a work depend upon nonaesthetic properties in that the former need to be perceived relative to the categories to which a work belongs. His position had more theoretical significance back when it was written against New Criticism, which rejects the relevance of historical or contextual aspects of a work in aesthetic criticism. However, Walton's discussion of how to determine a relevant set of categories in discerning the virtues by which an artwork is assessed provides an insight into the contemporary debate on transnational and pan-Asian cinema.

Walton considers four criteria in seeking a relevant category within which an artwork is perceived and appreciated: (1) the degree to which the work adheres to standard features of the category; (2) maximization of aesthetic value; (3) artist's intention; and (4) audience's familiarity/expert's knowledge. In other words, a relevant category proves to be such by the fact that a work manifests the majority of standard features of that category. Furthermore, if everything is equal, finding a relevant category would

　　　　　　　　　　　　　　　　　　　　　　　　　　　　Jinhee Choi

enhance the aesthetic experience and value of the work in question: a work is viewed as "more interesting, or pleasing aesthetically, or more worth experiencing" when considered under that category rather than others. One must also take into account the artist's intention with regard to the relevant category under which a work is to be viewed. Last, the relevant category in which the work is produced should be well established and recognized by the audience.[22]

These four categories often converge. A work manifests the majority of the standard features of a relevant category; therefore, the aesthetic consideration of a work within that category featuring the standards it manifests would maximize the value of the work in question. In many cases, the artist's categorical intention, which often presupposes audience familiarity, guided by an expert's knowledge of the category, would confirm such aesthetic considerations. However, what is interesting in contemporary Asian coproductions—or problematic, depending upon your perspective—is that they yield conditions in which these four criteria are often competing against each other and are sometimes even irreconcilable.

The aesthetic consideration of an artwork, in this case a film, would be made in light of various categories and traditions—be they genre, authorship, style, or mode. Criticisms of films of a self-orientalist bent tend to focus on the fact that they often depart significantly from the conventions and traditions of a genre to which they belong. Such films often both violate the traditions of genre—and are thus inauthentic—and erase the national specificities of the work's origin—and are thus inaccurate. Does pan-Asian cinema inherit problems similar to those of wuxia films aimed at international audiences who were unfamiliar with the genre? With respect to *The Promise, The Myth,* and *Seven Swords,* all three products of Asian coproductions, I will address the following questions: Does an Asian audience's cultural knowledge make it more acutely aware of aesthetic distractions and ruptures, and to what extent does the filmmaker's intentional obfuscation of genre bring about epistemic risks?

Within the wuxia tradition, a national literary as well as cinematic genre in China, historicism and fantasy have been two principal characteristics incorporated and refashioned throughout its history.[23] Wuxia films are sometimes set in specific historical periods, but a mythic setting often provides the most convenient narrative backdrop against which to foreground the genre's fantastic nature without imposing constraints on fidelity and authenticity. The flexibility of the genre also enabled local filmmakers to accommodate various cultural and industry needs. Hong Kong has been producing wuxia films in both Cantonese and Mandarin from the start in accordance with political, cultural, and industry fluctuations and

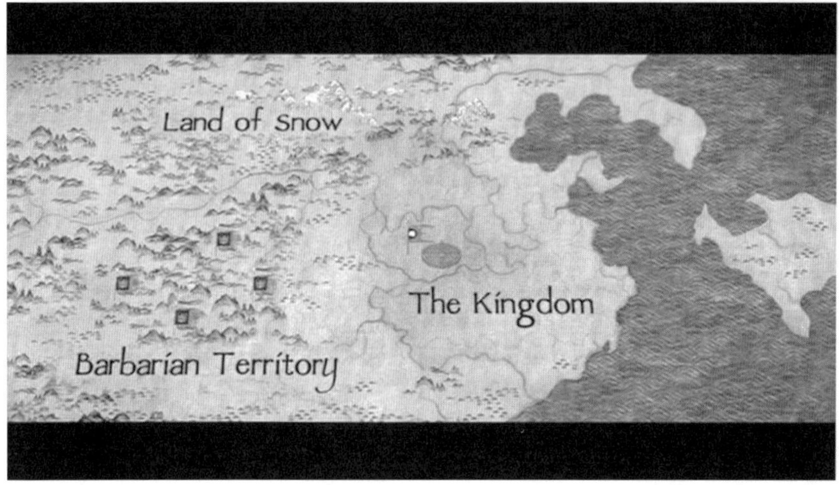

The imaginary geography of *The Promise*.

transformations. Dubbing has also proved to be a useful tool in the industry since the 1960s, providing leeway for production—in both shooting and casting—and in reaching out to overseas Chinese diasporic communities.[24] Many martial arts films were also dubbed into English for export, with the crude sound fidelity of the original intact.[25]

The Promise and *The Myth* are set in ancient Asia, the former in a mythic kingdom and the latter during the Qin dynasty, although in the latter film the locations shift between Qin and contemporary Hong Kong/China. *Seven Swords* tells an epic tale of the efforts of villagers to defend their town in the seventeenth century during the Qing dynasty. The mythic world of *The Promise* makes a convenient setting in which the national identities of actors are erased. The imaginary geography of *The Promise*, divided into three territories—the Kingdom, Barbarian Territory, and the Land of Snow, in which resides a tribe with superhuman powers—is hardly reflective of either ancient Asia or contemporary East Asia. According to Stephen Teo, the film is a "total misfire as a historicist allegory" and amounts only to "an allegory on transnationalism and the need to efface the specificities of cultural nationalism and perpetrate culturalist distortions in the service of transnationalism."[26]

The lack of national specificities at the level of narrative, however, does not seem detrimental to the film. Fantasy in the wuxia tradition *could* exempt *The Promise* from Teo's historicist criticism. Not all wuxia films render a historicist reading, at least an interesting one, nor do they all carry cognitive value. Such should not be the sole criterion by which to evaluate films of the wuxia tradition. Nonetheless, despite such a bland mythic set-

Jinhee Choi

ting, the film cannot completely erase the national differences of its cast. Although regional dynamics and tensions are neither realistically portrayed nor allegorically written into the film's architecture, the differences within the multinational cast are registered through the actors' accents. The foreignness detected in "accented cinema," a term that Sheldon Lu adopts from Hamid Naficy, constantly underscores the non-Mandarin-speaking actors' otherness.[27] The film is filled—excessively so—with various computer-generated and computer-enhanced spectacles and fights, but the emotional center of the film still lies in the love quadrangle between Kunlun, the general, the duke, and the princess. On their way to defend the king, the general and Kunlun are confronted by Snow Wolf, an assassin sent by the duke. The general is injured during their encounter, so Kunlun, disguised in the general's armor, is sent to rescue the king but instead saves only the princess. The princess falls for the general, believing it was he who saved her life, but the mistaken identity proves the accuracy of a goddess's prophecy, announced in the prologue, that love will be always out of the princess's reach. However, the performances of the non-Mandarin speakers fall short of fully exuding the characters' conflicting desires—lust, love, loyalty, and sacrifice— except perhaps for Tse, the only one who stands out among the male leads, as the jealous duke who constantly interferes and complicates things in order to grin at the resulting suffering.

The national specificities of the cast are effaced within the diegesis in *The Promise* except in the accents and performances of the actors. In contrast, both *The Myth* and *Seven Swords* narrativize and signal, although not fully, the different nationalities represented by the actors. A Jackie Chan star vehicle, *The Myth* involves an international romance between General Meng Yi and Ok Soo, a Korean princess turned concubine to the Qin emperor. In the film, Chan plays dual roles: Meng Yi, the ancient general, and Jack, a contemporary archeologist. In the opening sequence, the Korean general Choi, Ok Soo's fiancé, attempts to rescue her, but is thwarted by General Meng Yi. The mise-en-scène cues Ok Soo's nationality through the costumes of her servants in the procession and the *taeguk* symbol—a traditional Korean symbol that represents the harmony of ying and yang, which is also incorporated in the Korean national flag—in front of her carriage. Her "foreignness" is reinforced by the dialogue between her and General Choi, delivered in Korean. This opening sequence, which is framed as Jack's dream only retrospectively, when Jack wakes up in bed, establishes Ok Soo as a princess from "another" country, but does not fully inform the viewer. Kim Hee-sun, the actress who plays Ok Soo, had already gained popularity among audiences throughout the region, so perhaps Stanley Tong, the director, did not feel much necessity to clearly demarcate her nationality.

But with the exception of the opening sequence, Ok Soo speaks Mandarin for the rest of the film, in which romance stirs between her and General Meng Yi.

The prime attractions of *Seven Swords* are the swordfights, although several characters develop multiple romantic subplots, including one consisting of Chu Zhaonan (Donnie Yen) and Green Pearl (Kim So-yeon), a Korean captive of the ruthless villain Fire-Wind. Chu is cast as a Korean-Chinese who was once a slave but earned his freedom. In his interviews during the promotion of the film in Korea, Yen claims that he finds Korean difficult to learn, despite the efforts he made for this film.[28] Derek Elley rates the film's marketability negatively for both Asian and Western audiences, but unlike the *Variety* review of *The Promise,* which expressed concerns about the accents, the voice dubbing in *Seven Swords* (misidentified in Yen's case), is not considered to be a potential distraction.[29]

The awkward conversational style between Chu and Green Pearl may give rise to momentary disengagements and ruptures for viewers, as is evidenced by the grumbling fan reviews at various Web sites. But one may again appeal to the conventions of wuxia films in order to mitigate the imperfect communication witnessed in *Seven Swords.* It may be excused by virtue of the fact that the romantic subplot is relatively minor within both the film itself and the genre as a whole. Zhang Che's wuxia films explore "hard" masculinity, in which heterosexual romantic subplots are either marginal, as in the *One-Armed Swordsman* series, or almost nonexistent, as in his *Five Venoms* series. Within the genre, dramatic performances in general are often subsidiary to martial arts performances.

Reasons for dubbing should vary from case to case, and perhaps the regional fan base of Yen may have influenced Tsui's decision. Post-sync sound and dubbing have been standard practices in the Hong Kong film industry, and Tsui was an advocate of such practices on the set. But in his commentary for the DVD release of *Seven Swords,* Tsui claims that when Yen is dubbed by a Korean voice actor, it seriously breaches character identity: Yen sounds as if he were two different people. Priority is given to the aural continuity of a character over his dramatic performance, but this comes with a sacrifice in the intelligibility of the dialogue, some of which was incomprehensible to Korean audiences (although Tsui insists that Yen's Korean was pretty good!).

The acknowledgment of multinational casts is dealt with more self-reflexively in *The Myth.* Jack has recurring dreams of being the ancient general and finally meets Ok Soo, who has been waiting for Meng Yi for centuries. The romantic reunion between Jack/Meng Yi and Ok Soo is portrayed through their brief aerial embrace in a gravity-free cave, accompa-

   Jinhee Choi

nied by the theme song, "Endless Love," sung by Jackie Chan and Kim Hee-sun themselves, in Mandarin and Korean, respectively. The nondiegetic music—though motivated for various reasons, one being the marketing of the soundtrack in both the Chinese and Korean version—reminds the viewer of the foreignness of the female lead both at the diegetic and extradiegetic levels.

Moreover, during the ending credit sequence, during which in other films Chan shows his own stunt footage and bloopers of action sequences, the audience instead sees Chan and Kim performing in front of a green screen, with special effects to be added later. In additional footage, a Chinese soldier on the battlefield and Kim in a carriage are shown having difficulties delivering their lines in Mandarin. The film ends with Chan's direct address to the camera, aimed at Tony Leung Ka-fai, who played William his scientist friend: "William, you've been lying! Fom de [*sic*] beginning, until today . . . you've been speaking with a Cantonese accent!" This behind-the-scenes footage functions differently from similar footage in Chan's other films, such as *Police Story* (dir. Jackie Chan, 1985), where it serves to underscore the authenticity and physical risks involved in creating spectacles. Instead, here inauthenticity and epistemic risks are foregrounded in a self-reflexive manner.

All three films—*The Promise, The Myth,* and *Seven Swords*—register their production circumstances with varying degrees of self-reflexivity. But to what extent do self-reflexive cues allow the viewer to willfully grant these films concessions? As Antje Ascheid convincingly argues in her discussion of dubbing culture in Germany, defamiliarization is not necessarily a textual effect. The presence or absence of self-reflexive cues, in and of itself, neither necessarily performs a Brechtian function nor assuages alienating effects in the viewer. What is more pertinent in explaining such an effect should be located in the audience's familiarity with film practice and star performance.[30] She claims that the German audience accustomed to John Wayne dubbed into German would feel less jarred by an otherwise amusing clip during an Oscar ceremony of him in his German voice. But these actors in question—Sanada, Jang, and Kim Hee-sun—have all earned regional fandom. Sanada starred in such popular films as *Ringu* (dir. Nakata Hiddeo, 1998) and *The Twilight Samurai* (dir. Yamada Yoji, 2002) as well as in the Hollywood production *The Last Samurai* (dir. Edward Zwick, 2003). Popular Korean television series launched the stardom of many Korean actors, including Jang and Kim, in East and Southeast Asia. Although Korean television series are dubbed into Mandarin for airing on national television in China, the shows are widely circulated in Korea with Chinese subtitles via "unofficial" routes—pirated VCDs, DVDs, and the Internet—facilitating the regional audiences' acquaintance with the actors' true voices and performances. It is ironic that the major reason for casting regional stars is their potential box office draw, yet their regional star status in fact ultimately undermines the audience's appreciation of their performance in a foreign tongue.

These observations still leave the main question of this chapter unanswered: whether a target audience's lack of cultural knowledge can excuse some of the undetected aesthetic defects. If the "target" audience does not imply "exclusivity," then the consideration of market range provides understandable, though not fully warranted, reasons for certain aesthetic decisions and choices, especially those that end up hampering intelligibility and performance. One of the consequences or remedies is to redeem the aesthetic status of such a trend; industry personnel and some film scholars often attempt to forge a "new" category in which the above-mentioned distractions—intelligibility and performance of multinational casts—are permissible. Although critical of the practice, Teo proposes the category of "transnational wuxia," in which the narrative conventions of an indigenous genre are restructured to accommodate the needs of a globalized film industry.[31] Not only have "transnational cinema" and "pan-Asian cinema" become prominent production trends, they also function as aesthetic categories that sanction those aesthetic ruptures and discomforts that would normally be considered aesthetic demerits for an audience with background knowledge.

It is useful here to remind ourselves of Walton's four criteria that help the informed appreciation of an artwork: (1) the degree to which the work adheres to standard features of the category; (2) maximization of aesthetic value; (3) artist's intention; and (4) audience's familiarity/expert's knowledge. Most criticisms of transnational cinema have focused on the first: whether or not transnational wuxia films properly belong to the wuxia tradition. And the common verdict has been negative. Throughout this chapter, I embraced some but not all of the criticisms leveled against wuxia films targeted at regional audiences. "Ambiguity is a part of the film's architecture," says Teo in his critique of *Crouching Tiger, Hidden Dragon*.[32] Ambiguity, considered to be one of the principal characteristics of art cinema,[33] is valued since it opens up a text for multiple points of entry, enriching the text. On the contrary, ambiguity—employed here for the lack of a better term—as manifested in some of these cross-cultural productions fosters an epistemic risk both by obfuscating the categories to which it *used to belong* versus the categories to which it newly *belongs* and by committing the "detectable faux pas." What is at stake is that such a condition demands "untargeted" viewers to take up an epistemically demoted position and bracket their cultural knowledge in order to make the viewing experience more enjoyable and/or maximize the aesthetic value of the work.

I will end this chapter by considering some of the industry implications of the observations made about coproductions and multinational casts. Coproductions can play an important role within a regional industry, not only through the sharing of talent but also through artistic and technological exchanges. But the uneven reception of these films across the region indicates that the "visibility" of multinationalism in these coproductions was not an effective box office draw, although that must not be the sole reason.[34] *The Promise* grossed $4.5 million and $3.6 million in South Korea and Japan, respectively, which is less than half and almost one-tenth of the gross of *Hero* in each country ($10 million and $33 million).[35] Certainly the relatively poor film attendance of *The Promise* as a Chinese-language film in South Korea and Japan has much to do with its distribution[36] and the overall artistic quality and entertainment value of the film, but the audiences' familiarity with the actors of their own nationality coupled with their lack of familiarity with their performances in foreign tongue, may have contributed to it.

Multinational casts should not, however, be ruled out as an aesthetic option in regional filmmaking. The imperfect communication between the protagonists of different nationalities can successfully be incorporated within the subject matter of a film. In *Last Life in the Universe*—a coproduction between Thailand, Singapore, Hong Kong, Japan, and the Netherlands—the communication between the protagonists is far from perfect, as they must speak to each other in a third tongue. But the affection that the two characters feel toward each other despite the language barrier accentuates both their isolation and their romantic longing for someone, if not each other. In *Dream*, Kim makes a bold aesthetic decision to completely disregard language barriers. This grand gesture is worthy of note, compared to his previous approach to the matter. In *Breath*, he has recourse to the conventional tactic of turning a character mute. The voice of male protagonist Jang Jin (played by Taiwanese Chang Chen) is taken away, as he has tried to kill himself with a sharpened toothbrush handle to the neck. Such a strategy has been prevalent within the art cinema tradition, including films such as *A City of Sadness* (dir. Hou Hsiao-hsien, 1989), in which Tony Leung Chi-wai plays a mute character. In contrast, in *Dream* Odagiri's strong performance is palpable, an outcome that would have been jettisoned if he either spoke in or was dubbed into Korean.

Pan-Asian cinema and coproductions no doubt deserve closer industry analysis in and of themselves. However, this chapter attempts to draw out some of the epistemic and aesthetic implications embedded in such filmmaking practices. Films that target regional audiences with multinational casts create rather different epistemic conditions than do films with market ambitions broad enough to include audiences beyond the region. Unlike non-Asian audiences, regional audience members' greater cultural knowledge and familiarity with stars could enable them to spot the heterogeneity of a multinational cast. But regional coproduction films still pose an epistemic risk in that regional audiences are being asked to bracket their cultural knowledge and linguistic sensibilities in order to aesthetically appreciate these films.

NOTES

1. Mark Betz, *Beyond the Subtitle: Remapping European Art Cinema* (Minneapolis: University of Minnesota Press, 2009), 47.

2. Darrell William Davis and Emilie Yueh-yu Yeh, *East Asian Screen Industries* (London: British Film Institute, 2008), 85.

3. Box Office Mojo, "The Promise," http://boxofficemojo.com/movies/? page=intl&id=promise05.htm.

4. Mike Goodridge, "The Promise (Mo gik)," *Screen Daily,* December 23, 2005, http://www.screendaily.com/the-promise-mo-gik/4025600.article.

5. Robert Koelner, "The Promise, aka Master of Crimson Armor," *Variety,* December 29, 2005, http://www.variety.com/review/VE1117929184?ref catid=31.

6. Deborah Lupton, *Risk* (London: Routledge, 1999), 6.

7. Ulrich Beck, *Risk Society: Towards a New Modernity* (London: Sage 1992), 58–59; Anthony Giddens, *The Consequences of Modernity* (Stanford: Stanford University Press, 1990), 7–10.

8. Rey Chow, *Primitive Passions: Visuality, Sexuality, Ethnography, and Contemporary Chinese Cinema* (New York: Columbia University Press, 1995), 182–84.

9. Emilie Yueh-Yu Yeh and Darrell Davis, *Taiwan Film Directors: A Treasure Island* (New York: Columbia University Press, 2005), 185.

10. Christina Klein, "*Crouching Tiger, Hidden Dragon:* A Diasporic Reading," *Cinema Journal* 43, no. 4 (2004): 32–35.

11. Sheldon H. Lu, "Crouching Tiger, Hidden Dragon, Bouncing Angels: Hollywood, Taiwan, Hong Kong and Transnational Cinema," in *Chinese-Language Film: Historiography, Poetics, Politics,* ed. Sheldon H. Lu and Emilie Yueh-yu Yeh (Honolulu: University of Hawaii Press, 2005), 227.

12. Stephen Teo, *Chinese Martial Arts Cinema: The Wuxia Tradition* (Edinburgh: Edinburgh University Press, 2009), 177–78.

13. Lawrence Venuti, "Translation, Community, Utopia," in *The Translation Studies Reader,* 2nd ed., ed. Lawrence Venuti (New York: Routledge, 2002), 484.

14. Kim Jin, "Sexy Japanese Pix Causes Problems in South Korea: Adult Film Raising Eye Brows in Seoul," *Variety*, February 22, 2004, http://www.variety.com/article/VR1117900443?refCatId=19.

15. Patrick Frater, "Outsiders Run into Chinese Regulations: Movie Co-productions May Be Difficult to Navigate," *Variety*, March 15, 2008, http://www.variety.com/article/VR1117985807.html.

16. Hwang Dong-mi and Park Ji-in, *Asia gongdonjejak hyeonhwanggwa baljeon bangan* (Seoul: Korean Film Commission, 2002).

17. Davis and Yeh, *East Asian Screen Industries,* 85.

18. Ibid., 90–91.

19. Ibid., 100–101.

20. David Hume, "Of the Standards of Taste," in *Essays: Moral, Political and Literary,* rev. ed. (Indianapolis: Liberty Fund, 1985), 226–49.

21. Kendall Walton, "Categories of Art," *Philosophical Review* 79, no. 3 (1970): 334–67.

22. Ibid., 357.

23. Teo, *Chinese Martial Arts Cinema,* 5–6.

24. Stephen Teo, "Wuxia Redux: *Crouching Tiger; Hidden Dragon* as a Model of Late Transnational Production," in *Hong Kong Connections: Transnational Imagination in Action Cinema,* ed. Meaghan Morris, Siu Leung Li, and Stephen Chan Ching-kiu (Durham: Duke University Press / Hong Kong: Hong Kong University Press, 2005), 203.

25. Yeh and Davis, *Taiwan Film Directors,* 87.

26. Teo, "Wuxia Redux," 190.

27. Lu, "Crouching Tiger, Hidden Dragon, Bouncing Angels," 227.

28. Derek Elley, "*Seven Swords,*" *Variety*, August 31, 2005, http://www.variety.com/review/VE1117928022?refcatid=31.

29. Ibid.

30. Antje Ascheid, "Speaking Tongues: Voice Dubbing in the Cinema as Cultural Ventriloquism," *Velvet Light Trap* 40 (1997): 36.

31. Teo, *Chinese Martial Arts Cinema,* 173, 177.

32. Teo, "Wuxia Redux," 201.

33. David Bordwell, "The Art Cinema as a Mode of Film Practice," *Film Criticism* 4, no. 1 (1979): 56–64. Reprinted in *The European Cinema Reader,* ed. Catherine Fowler (New York: Routledge, 2002), 94–102.

34. Jinhee Choi, "China Inc. Limited," *In Focus Forum: China's Rise, Cinema Journal* 49, no. 3 (2010): 144–49.

35. Box Office Mojo, "The Promise"; "Hero," http://www.boxofficemojo.com/movies/?page=intl&id=hero02.htm.

36. Choi, "China Inc. Limited," 147.

MICHAEL POKORNY AND JOHN SEDGWICK

The Financial and Economic Risks of Film Production

It would generally be accepted as self-evident that the film industry provides a very unstable environment for the development of a coherent investment strategy. Indeed, realistic investors in film production should expect their returns to be in the form of reflected glamour and kudos, rather than in strictly defined balance sheet profits. Even hardheaded investors would allocate only a small proportion of their investment funds to film production, ensuring that the remainder of their investments generate sufficient profits to compensate for the film losses that are likely to be generated.

For the one brutal constant in the film industry, from its very beginnings in the late nineteenth century, is that only a relatively small proportion of films ever make profits. Even in the case of Hollywood, the world's consistently dominant film producer from the 1920s, only about half of its films have been profitable. And in the case of these profitable films the vast majority has been only modestly profitable, with just a handful of films, annually, generating significant profits. Indeed, part of Hollywood's success derives from the perpetuation of the myth that these handfuls of "hit" films represent the norm rather than, in fact, being the very rare exceptions.

In pure investment terms, the low incidence of hit films would not be a problem, if there were a basis or methodology for predicting with any level of accuracy which of the large numbers of films released annually will turn out to be hits. The problem is that such a methodology would not appear to exist—in essence, it is impossible to predict, on a consistent and regular basis, which of the hundreds of annual film releases will turn out to be profitable, the process being to all intents and purposes an apparently random one. It is this empirical regularity that has been pithily captured in screenwriter William Goldman's throwaway line that in Hollywood "nobody knows anything," an observation that has now become part of film industry "wisdom."[1] To be sure, there are many who argue that they have particular insights into the complex process of profitable film production, particularly those film producers who at any point in time are seeking investment funds for their next productions. But in the same way that there are those who argue that they have particular insights into the manner in which stock market prices evolve over time, the empirical support for such claims are weak if not nonexistent. For the paradox is that while film investment is inherently risky, Hollywood is a manifestly profitable industry and has been so for almost a century, albeit within the context of marked profitability cycles. Many of the major studios/distributors that make up Hollywood have been there from its establishment, although these studios have experienced regular changes in ownership and structure.

Our objective in this chapter is to present an overview of the risk environment of film production within the context of Hollywood, and to attempt to identify the various influences on this environment. In turn, we will draw conclusions about the nature of the strategies that might be employed to attenuate the risks of film production, and the implications that these have for the evolution and structure of the industry. Despite its claims to the contrary, the risk environment in which Hollywood operates is not unique—it shares many of the characteristics of other industries in which only a small proportion of outputs are profitable, but sufficiently so to more than compensate for the loss-generating outputs. Examples of such industries are book publishing, music recording, and pharmaceutical manufacturing. What these industries appear to share are research, development, and production processes that are characterized by a seemingly blind and extensive search for success, and failure is not so much an unfortunate consequence of these processes but is integral to them.

The Risk Environment of Film Production

There are two main data sets that will be drawn on here. The first derives from the films released in the North American market between 1929 and 1942 by three of the five Hollywood major studios/distributors at the time, Metro-Goldwyn-Mayer (MGM), Radio-Keith-Orpheum (RKO), and Warner Bros. (WB). The reason that these three studios were used is that their detailed accounting ledgers are now publicly available, but to our knowledge, comparable data for the two remaining studios—Paramount and Twentieth Century Fox—have not come to light.[2] This data set consists of 1,796 films, for each of which data are available on production costs, rev-

   Michael Pokorny and John Sedgwick

enues received by the studio/distributor, and in the case of MGM and RKO, the profits that each of these films generated. In the case of WB, we had to apply a methodology for estimating its film profits. This methodology assumed that distribution costs were a function of both film budgets and film revenues, and by estimating the precise nature of this relationship using the MGM and RKO data, the distribution costs for each of the WB films could be estimated, and estimated film profits thereby derived.

The second data set derives from the 4,164 films released in the North American market between 1988 and 1999. The data set consists of the North American box office revenues generated by these films and estimates of the production costs of just over half of these films. This data set does not contain any profitability data, and we had to estimate profits for the films for which production cost estimates were available. The resulting data set consists of 2,116 films, of which 1,458 were distributed by the major studios. The methodology for estimating film profits was adapted from that used to estimate WB film profits in the 1930s, and again assumed that distribution costs were a function of both film budgets and film revenues, although the higher emphasis on film marketing expenditures during the 1990s was incorporated into the estimation methods. Note that in order to make the profitability data from the 1990s comparable to those of the 1930s, the 1990s data relate to profits generated only from theatrical release and therefore do not include profits generated from all ancillary markets. That is, estimates were made of the revenues generated from ancillary markets for the 1990s, and on the basis of these, the proportion of production costs attributable to theatrical release only could be estimated, and hence the profitability of films due to theatrical release derived.[3]

The first figure below presents a scattergraph of film profits generated in the North American market against film-production costs for the 1930s, and the next presents the equivalent graph for the 1990s. For contextual purposes the titles of a number of the films produced during both periods are also included.

The outstanding and common feature of these two graphs is that the variability of film profits increases as production budgets increase, reflecting the increasing levels of risk that are associated with high-budget film production. The obvious attraction of high-budget production is that it offers the possibility of a single film generating very high profits. However, as is also clear from the figures, high-budget films can also generate substantial losses, and even when profitable, generate profits that are often comparable to those generated by much more modestly budgeted films. However, there are a number of more subtle differences between the two figures. By and large, high-budget film production was relatively unsuccessful in the

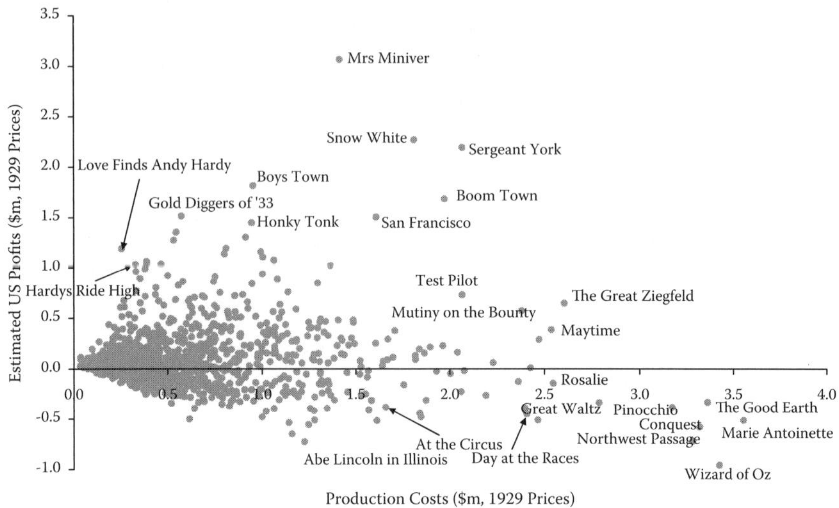

Scattergraph of U.S. Profits against Film Costs, 1929 Prices, 1930–42 (*n* = 1,796).

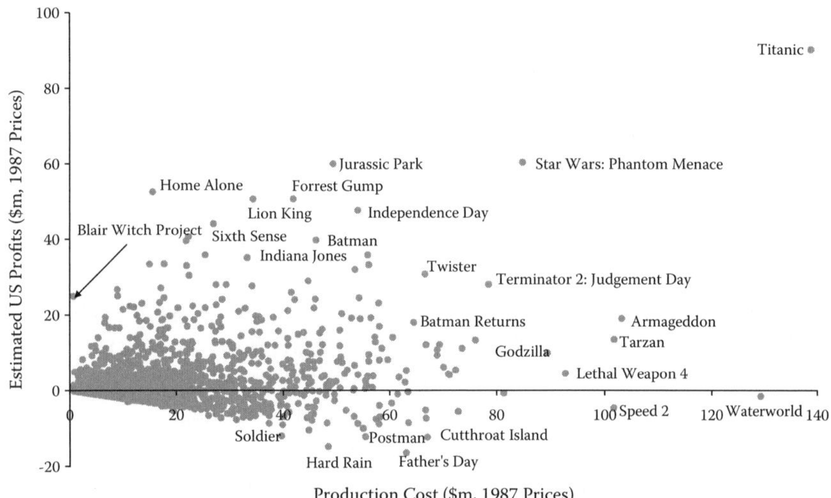

Scattergraph of U.S. Profits against Film Costs, 1987 Prices, 1988–99 (*n* = 2,116).

1930s, whereas it was the main source of profits during the 1990s. Thus the rate of return on high-budget production during the 1930s was less than that on lower-budget production, whereas during the 1990s the profitability of high-budget production exceeded that of lower-budget production. It is not simply that Hollywood became better at producing high-budget films over time (though it did) but that Hollywood recognized that the suc-

     Michael Pokorny and John Sedgwick

cessful production of high-budget films was essential to its survival in the post–World War II period, when the advent of television and other demographic and lifestyle changes resulted in the industry's near collapse. It was only by producing high-budget "event" movies—what today would be termed "blockbusters"—that Hollywood could hope to differentiate its output from that of television and attract audiences back to moviegoing. Starting with developments such as suburban multiplex cinemas in the 1960s, Hollywood developed increasingly sophisticated strategies for maximizing film revenues, and with the continual development and diffusion of a range of movie-consumption technologies the revenues that can be generated by successful movies is now virtually limitless. Such an environment stands in stark contrast to that of the 1930s, when theatrical revenues were the only source of film revenues and, at best, a successful movie had a life of only fifteen months, with most movies being on release for a considerably shorter time.[4]

An alternative means of presenting the profitability data in the two figures above is via frequency distributions—a histogram representation of the data that provides a more explicit reflection of the manner in which profits and losses are spread across the profitability range. These frequency distributions are shown below for the 1930s and for the 1990s. Again, the similarities between these distributions are clear, in particular, the long right-hand tails that both of these distributions exhibit. That is, it is the films that appear in this "long tail"—the blockbusters—that dominate the profit distribution and generate profits that can compensate for the losses made by the large number of films falling in the shorter left-hand tail.[5] Clearly such blockbusters are relatively rare but are crucial for the financial success of the industry, and provide the defining characteristic of the industry.

In order to provide a more detailed interpretation of these long tails, consider the films that generated profits in excess of $0.5 million (1929 prices) during the 1930s, and those films that generated profits in excess of $20 million (1987 prices) in the 1990s. During the 1930s there were ninety such films—5 percent of the films produced—and in the 1990s there were fifty-two such films—3 percent of the films produced. The films that fall into these long tails can be seen directly from the scattergraphs above. In the case of the 1930s, a horizontal line can be drawn at 0.5 on the vertical axis, and all the films lying above this line are those that fall into this long tail. Thus the film lying the furthest to the right in the first frequency distribution chart can be seen to be *Mrs Miniver*, having generated U.S. profits of $3.1 million. In the case of the scattergraph of the 1990s, a horizontal line can be drawn at 20 on the vertical axis, all the films above this line defining

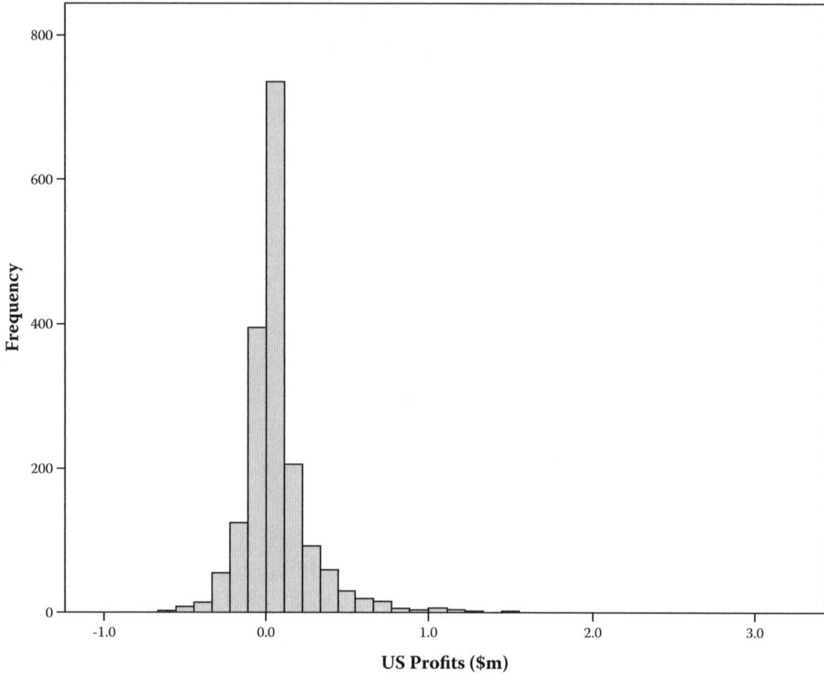

Frequency Distribution of U.S. Profits, 1929 Prices, 1929–41 ($n = 1,796$).

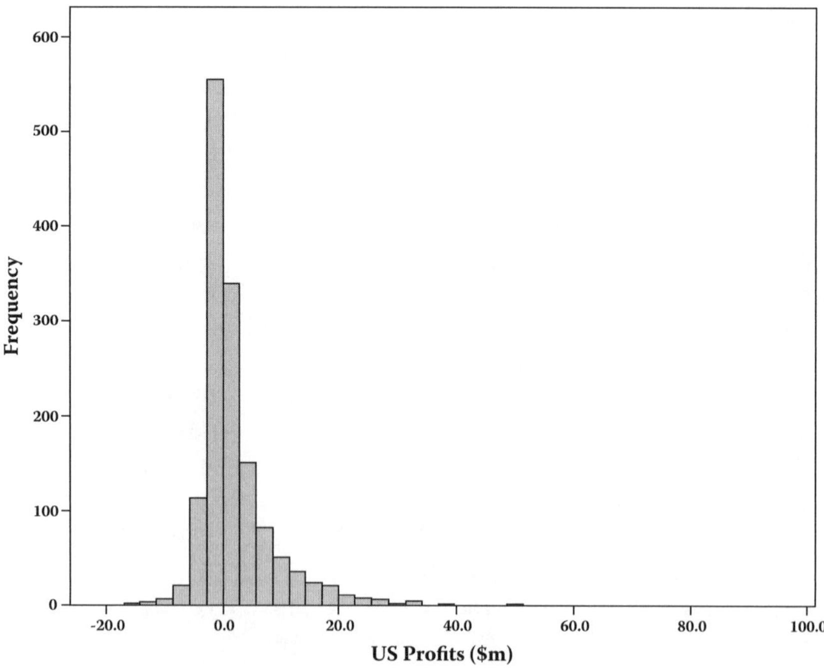

Frequency Distribution of U.S. Profits, 1987 Prices, 1988–99 ($n = 2,116$).

the long tail, with *Titanic* at the extreme right-hand point of this tail, having generated estimated U.S. profits from theatrical release of $90.2 million.

We can compare and contrast these long tails in more detail. However, in order to compare like with like, we will consider only the films distributed by the majors. Clearly these are all the 1,796 films in the 1930s data set, and for the 1990s 1,458 of the 2,116 films for which profits could be estimated fall into this category. Thus consider the top 10 percent most profitable films during both periods, a somewhat more extensive definition of the long tail than used above. For the 1930s these 180 films accounted for 84 percent of the profits generated by all films, and for the 1990s the 146 most profitable films accounted for 85 percent of the profits generated by all the films produced by the majors. So in this regard, the contribution of the long tails was remarkably similar between the two periods. However, there are marked differences in the nature of these top films between the two periods. Thus consider the incidence of high-budget films among the top profit earners—the extent to which strategic decisions on the part of film producers were translated into profitable films, on the assumption that a high level of investment in a film is a direct reflection of the producer's confidence in the quality and appeal of the film. We will here define a high-budget film as one costing more than twice the average cost of all films produced in the film's year of release. According to this definition, 179 high-budget films were produced in the 1930s, 10 percent of all films produced, absorbing 30 percent of production costs, and in the 1990s, 247 of these films were produced, or 17 percent of the total, absorbing 39 percent of production costs, thus confirming the greater extent of high-budget production in the latter period. In the 1930s 46 of these high-budget films—26 percent of the high-budget films produced—were located in the long tail, with a similar proportion lying in the long tail in the 1990s—68 high-budget films, or 28 percent of the high-budget films produced. But note also that these long-tail high-budget films accounted for 26 percent of the long-tail films in the 1930s, but 46 percent of the long-tail films in the 1990s. However, the main difference between the two periods is the contribution to overall profits made by these long-tail high-budget films. In the 1930s, the 46 long-tail high-budget films accounted for only 25 percent of aggregate profits, whereas in the 1990s the 68 long-tail films accounted for 42 percent of aggregate profits. In terms of all high-budget films produced, the 179 produced in the 1930s generated just 17 percent of profits (on 30 percent of costs, with 44 percent of these films making losses), whereas the 247 produced in the 1990s generated 45 percent of profits (on 39 percent of costs, and 33 percent making losses). That is, the focus of profitability in the 1930s was on lower-budget production, whereas the profitability of the contemporary industry derives from higher-budget production.

Clearly, the film producer's objective is to locate his or her film in this long tail, and thereby derive the disproportionate returns that will be generated by so doing. However, as is also clear from the two frequency distribution charts, the likelihood of doing so is minimal. Indeed, the clear implication of all four figures is that any film production strategy based on the success of single, one-off film projects is doomed to failure. Rather, a more sensible strategy for a rational, profit-maximizing film producer is to produce a wide range of films annually, in the hope that at least some of these will produce profits that will compensate for the losses that a large proportion of these films will inevitably generate. That is, we could characterize the successful film studios/distributors as constructing diversified annual portfolios of films, diversified according to production budget and genre, and allocations of stars, directors, and screenwriters. The issue, then, is not so much which of the films in the portfolio are profitable, but simply that the portfolio itself is profitable.[6]

However, this is not to suggest that such a strategy can now render film production riskless—at best, such a strategy can exert some control over the risk of film production, but certainly not eliminate it. But what it does mean is that such a profitable film-production strategy requires considerable financial resources so that a fully diversified film portfolio can be constructed— the successful film producer must have the capacity to absorb significant losses in addition to enjoying the fruits of the profitable films.

It is therefore not surprising that the consistently successful film studios/distributors are large organizations that themselves are often parts of even larger media/entertainment conglomerates, allowing for further opportunities for risk spreading. Conversely, relatively small independent studios/distributors will not have the ability to develop sufficiently diversified film portfolios, nor have the financial strength to absorb the losses that any film portfolio will inevitably generate.

To this point our objective has been to describe the nature of the financial risk environment within which film producers operate. However, we have not made any attempt to identify the factors that influence or determine this risk environment. That is, why is it the case that even highly experienced film producers cannot predict with any reliability how consumers will react to their films, and hence which of their films will make profits and which will generate losses? Our answer to this question derives from the recognition that consumers themselves enter a risk environment when choosing to view a movie, in the sense that while the consumer will have certain expectations prior to viewing a given movie, there will often be

                               Michael Pokorny and John Sedgwick

a divergence between actual experience and expectation. Indeed, it is the possibility of the actual viewing experience markedly exceeding the expectations of that experience that provides the essential stimulus to continued movie consumption. We will now go on to discuss in more detail the nature of the risk environment from the film consumer's perspective.

THE RISK ENVIRONMENT OF FILM CONSUMPTION

One of the essential characteristics of films is that they are "experience" goods: audiences can form a full assessment of the product only when the act of consumption is complete. The standard model developed by Nelson depicts experience goods as a category of good the quality of which can be established only after it has been consumed ("experienced") by the buyer.[7] Thus consumers identify the "best" brand of a given good by repeatedly consuming the range of brands that are available, and on the basis of the experience so derived, decide upon the preferred brand. In consuming a new brand the consumer will form expectations concerning this brand derived from the past consumption of competing brands, together with any information provided by advertising/promotion. But it is only once the act of consumption is complete that a full assessment of the new brand can be made, within the context of the extent to which expectations were disappointed, met, or exceeded. Even if consumers identify a clearly preferred brand, they may still continue to sample/experience competing brands, if for no other reason than to confirm their original choice.[8]

Thus films clearly fall into the category of an experience good—irrespective of the information available to the consumer prior to viewing the film, in the form of word-of-mouth and promotional/advertising messages, such information will be an imperfect substitute for the experience derived from the act of consumption. However, in contrast to most other experience goods, films are generally consumed only once, as the key characteristics that filmgoers seek is novelty—they seek "surprises" and innovation in the film-going experience, and in particular, do not seek exact replications of previous film-going experiences.

Thus in choosing to view a given film the film consumer will have formed expectations of the pleasures that are likely to be generated by the experience. These expectations will derive both from the consumer's previous film consumption experiences and the marketing/promotional activities surrounding the film. However, the consumer will also be aware that these expectations are likely to be confounded, in either a positive or negative sense. Indeed, the definition of a hit film is a film that generates, among the film consuming population, a pervasive and positive divergence between the pleasures derived from actually viewing the film and the expectations of those pleasures prior to consumption. This pervasiveness, typically, would be built up via a word-of-mouth information cascade, as the consistently positive messages relating to the film's qualities are disseminated throughout the population.[9] However, as is clear from the figures above, such hit films are relatively rare. For the dilemma that the film producer faces is that consumer tastes in film are ultimately unpredictable. What the consumer is seeking in the film consumption experience is novelty—"surprises"—but the consumer is incapable of articulating what form such novelty might take, and indeed probably has no interest in doing so. Certainly the consumer will form attachments to specific film "markers" such as stars and genre—that is, consumers will also seek a degree of familiarity in their film consumption experiences—and producers will use these markers in an attempt to perpetuate previously successful film formulas. However, such strategies generally have limited life cycles, and in effect serve the purpose of fully exploiting previous hit formulas only until the next hit emerges.[10]

As a simple reflection of the dilemmas facing the film producer, consider the production just of high-budget films, films for which producers presumably have clear expectations. Now, the budgets of such films allow for the incorporation of high production values, in the form of stars, directors, screenwriters, and cinematography, and as such, producers would hope that these films would stimulate extensive consumer interest, thereby generating high box office revenues, if not profits. Thus we could interpret the size of production budgets as directly reflecting the level of producer expectations concerning film success. Similarly, the extent of consumer reaction to films—the level of satisfaction derived—would be reflected in the box office revenues generated. Were producers able to accurately anticipate consumer reactions, then we would expect there to be a close correspondence between production budgets and film revenues—higher-budget films would generate higher revenues. The simplest way of measuring the extent of this correspondence is via a rank correlation coefficient. That is, if films are ranked according to production budget from smallest to largest, and the films are then ranked according to box office revenue from smallest to largest, then if the rankings by production budget exactly match those by box office revenue, this would produce a maximum rank correlation coefficient of 1. This would mean that the highest-budget film would produce the highest revenue, the second-highest-budget film would produce the second-highest revenue, and so on, down to the lowest-budget film producing the lowest revenue. The implication would be that film producers are able to perfectly anticipate consumer responses, and could always be sure that a high film investment would pay off in terms at least of consumer responses (this does not of course mean that the film would necessarily be profitable—so much may have been spent on production that even the high revenues that such a film generates would not be enough to cover the costs). Conversely, the minimum rank correlation coefficient of -1 would be produced if the production cost ranks were the reverse of the box office ranks—the highest-budget film generates the lowest revenue, the second-highest-budget film generates the second-lowest revenue, and so on, down to the lowest-budget films generating the highest revenue. In such a situation we could interpret film producers as being hopelessly confused with regard to anticipating consumer responses, consistently investing in the wrong film projects. A rank correlation coefficient of 0 would imply a random correspondence between production cost and revenue ranks—a random distribution of high-budget films among high- and low-ranking revenue-generating films (and vice versa).

We can use both our 1930s and 1990s data sets to derive these rank correlation coefficients. We will define a high-budget film, as we did above, as any film costing more than twice the average cost of all films produced in the film's year of release. During the 1930s 179 high-budget films so defined were produced by MGM, RKO, and Warner Bros. In the 1990s the major studios produced 247 high-budget films. The (Spearman) rank correlation coefficients between film-production costs and box office revenues were 0.461 for the 1930s and 0.254 for the 1990s, implying only a moderate correspondence between producer expectations and consumer satisfaction. In turn we would argue that this is a direct reflection of the difficulty producers had in predicting the evolving nature of consumer tastes. However, even if these rank correlation coefficients are interpreted as reflecting reasonable success in producers being able to anticipate consumer responses, within the context of a relatively volatile market, the rank correlation coefficients derived from production budgets and film profits demonstrate the fundamental difficulties facing producers. For the 1930s the rank correlation coefficient between film budgets and film profits was -0.193, and for the 1990s it was 0.059. Thus, while producers might have had some modest success in generating higher revenues from higher-budget films, this success was countered by the fact that such strategies had no impact on profits—in essence, in attempting to stimulate consumer satisfaction through high-production-value films, producers were unable to control these budgets sufficiently to ensure a commensurate impact on profits.

Another way of characterizing the risk environment faced by film consumers can be illustrated by drawing on a simple, albeit unscientific, experiment.[11] This involved the generation of a self-selecting sample of filmgoers,

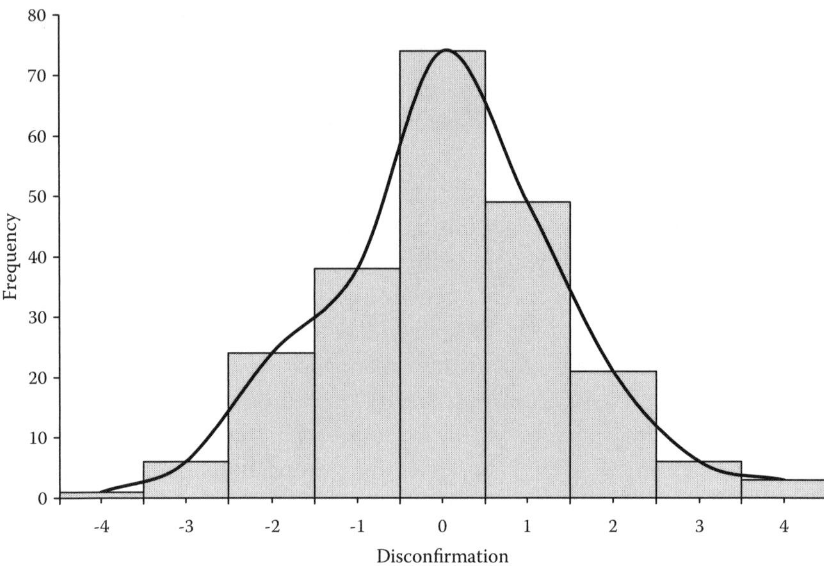

Frequency Distribution of Disconfirmation in a Sample of 222 Film Consumers.

achieved via an invitation to complete a short online questionnaire. The questionnaire was hosted by a specialist online survey Web site,[12] and respondents were made up of friends and acquaintances of the survey's organizers together with respondents produced by links to the questionnaire placed on a number of other film-related Web sites. A total of 222 usable responses was generated.

Apart from providing some basic demographic information and data on film-viewing habits, respondents were asked to evaluate their last movie-viewing experience by indicating, first, the nature of their expectations prior to viewing the movie (on a 5-point scale ranging from "very high" to "very low") and then, second, to indicate the level of satisfaction actually derived once the movie had been viewed (on a 5-point scale ranging from "very satisfied" to "not satisfied at all"). Thus we could interpret the difference between these two 5-point scales as reflecting the extent of divergence between expectations and realizations—the extent of "disconfirmation" of the expected moviegoing experience—with a value of -4 ("very high" expectations "minus" "not satisfied at all") indicating considerable disappointment in the film, and a value of 4 ("very low" expectations "minus" "very satisfied") indicating unexpected pleasures, with a 0 value indicating a close correspondence between expectations and realizations. The figure above presents a histogram of this disconfirmation variable, together with

                                                     Michael Pokorny and John Sedgwick

an interpolated smooth curve fitted to the data. Thus we could conclude that within this sample at least, there is a marked incidence of a divergence between expectations and realizations of the movie consumption experience, and that this distribution is a broadly symmetrical one.

Given the unscientific manner in which these sample data were selected, it is clearly inappropriate to draw any detailed conclusions concerning the population of film consumers. However, this experiment does allow for a degree of speculation to be undertaken. Thus, note first that the data were collected on the basis of the last movie the consumer had viewed, and hence covers a range of different movies. This experiment could be repeated focusing on a single given film, thus allowing conclusions to be drawn with regard to the extent of disconfirmation associated with this film. This would imply that in the case of hit movies, the disconfirmation distribution would be shifted to the right, and in the case of "flops," the distribution would be shifted to the left. That is, we could interpret the word-of-mouth information cascade that builds up around any given film, together with the marketing and promotional strategies undertaken by the film's distributors, as determining the manner in which this distribution evolves over time, with the parameters of this distribution (mean, variance, and skewness) reflecting consumer responses to the film. That is, within the context of the disconfirmation chart, we would expect a hit film to produce a disconfirmation distribution that is shifted to the right, distributed tightly around a relatively high and positive value of disconfirmation, and perhaps with a degree of skewness producing a long, thin left-hand tail— even for a hit film there will be a very small proportion of consumers for whom the film generates disappointment. Conversely, for "flops," we would expect the disconfirmation distribution to be shifted to the left, focused on a low and negative value of disconfirmation (and possibly a long, thin right-hand tail).

Some Conclusions

The key to understanding the risks inherent in film production is to recognize that film consumers are themselves engaged in a risk process when choosing and viewing a film. Consumers seek novelty in the film-viewing experience, or at the very least some combination of the familiar and the novel, but by definition are incapable of defining the form that this novelty, or novelty/familiarity mix, might take—they will "know it when they see it." For those consumers who restrict themselves to particular genres and/or stars, the extent of novelty sought in a new film may only be incremental, but the consumer would still expect something new or novel in the film, otherwise the repeat viewing of films would be much more pervasive than is observed to be the case.

The manner in which film producers have dealt, and continue to deal, with this uncertainty has been to produce large and diversified annual portfolios of films, inducing consumers to consume extensively across these portfolios, thereby allowing the hits of the season to emerge. Such an interpretation explains why cinema admission prices have traditionally been relatively low and invariant across films, a pricing strategy that can be justified in two ways. First, low admission prices stimulate consumption, ensuring that annual film portfolios are sampled widely. And second, discriminatory pricing policies on the part of film distributors/exhibitors—such as higher prices being charged for what are anticipated to be "blockbuster" movies— would, by implication, imply that lower-priced movies are of lower quality, thereby providing a disincentive to the consumption of such movies. Furthermore, the disappointment of consuming unsuccessful high-budget/ blockbuster movies—which, as can be seen from the scattergraphs above, occurs regularly—would be intensified by a high admission price policy for such films. In other words, any attempt at price discrimination would imply that there is a price/quality trade-off in movie consumption, and encourage in the consumer an overly strategic approach to the selection of films to be considered for consumption, thereby inhibiting the emergence of the "unexpected" hits.

Our discussion of the concept of disconfirmation that consumers experience in the film consumption process, illustrated in the discomfirmation chart, also allows for an interpretation to be made of the manner in which the information cascade evolves throughout the period of a film's release. It would seem reasonable to assume that consumers would experience the greatest level of risk at the point at which a film is initially released, when information concerning consumer reception of the film is at a minimum. It is important from the film distributor/exhibitor's perspective that the word-of-mouth information cascade be stimulated as efficiently as possible, an outcome that is achieved by the common practice of blanket releasing films. Thus, film distributors/exhibitors put a great deal of emphasis on a film's performance on its opening weekend, in the hope that this will trigger a pervasive and positive information cascade. However, there is no direct and reliable link between a film's performance on its opening weekend and its subsequent performance throughout its release cycle.[13] Hit films will result from a high incidence of positive disconfirmation among filmgoers, irrespective of the influence that distributors/exhibitors may try to exert, generating a positive word-of-mouth information cascade, and the

        Michael Pokorny and John Sedgwick

converse will be true in the case of "flops." However, it is also important to recognize that once a film is released, film producers can have little influence on the success that the film might subsequently achieve. Indeed, our disconfirmation interpretation of the manner in which films are received by consumers implies that producers should be careful not to overpromote films or make exaggerated claims for them, the potential consequence being that consumer expectations will be unrealistically heightened, and hence (negative) disconfirmation will be intensified and positive word-of-mouth will thereby be inhibited.

Notes

1. William Goldman, *Adventures in the Screen Trade* (New York: Warner, 1983).

2. See Michael Pokorny and John Sedgwick, "Profitability Trends in Hollywood, 1929 to 1999: Somebody Must Know Something," *Economic History Review* 63 (2010): 56–84, for a more detailed description of these data sources.

3. See ibid., appendix, for a more detailed description of the data sets and estimation methodology.

4. See Pokorny and Sedgwick, "Profitability Trends," for a more detailed discussion of these issues.

5. See Chris Anderson, *The Long Tail: Why the Future Is Selling Less of More* (New York: Hyperion, 2006); Eric Clemons, "How Information Changes Consumer Behavior and How Consumers' Behavior Determines Corporate Strategy," *Journal of Management Information Systems* 25 (2008): 13–40; Anita Elberse, "Should You Invest in the Long Tail?" *Harvard Business Review,* July–August 2008, 88–96, for a discussion of this phenomenon applied to Internet retailing.

6. See John Sedgwick and Michael Pokorny, "The Risk Environment of Film-making: Warner Bros. in the Inter-war Period," *Explorations in Economic History* 35 (1998): 196–220; Michael Pokorny and John Sedgwick, "Stardom and the Profitability of Filmmaking: Warner Bros. in the 1930s," *Journal of Cultural Economics* 25 (2001): 157–84, for developments of this idea.

7. Phillip Nelson, "Information and Consumer Behavior," *Journal of Political Economy* 78 (1970): 311–29; Phillip Nelson, "Advertising as Information," *Journal of Political Economy* 81 (1974): 729–45.

8. Rebecca Ratner, Barbara Kahn, and Daniel Kahneman, "Choosing Less-Preferred Experiences for the Sake of Variety," *Journal of Consumer Research* 26 (1999): 1–15.

9. See Charles Moul, "Measuring Word of Mouth's Impact on Theatrical Movie Admissions," *Journal of Economics and Management Strategy* 16 (2007): 859–92, which tests a model estimating the significance of word-of-mouth in forming consumer expectations.

10. See John Sedgwick and Michael Pokorny, "The Relationship between Consumer Risk and Producer Risk," *Business History* 52 (2010): 74–99, for a fuller discussion of these issues.

11. This experiment was carried out by Claudia Domokos, Tobias Pospischil, Karina Sokolova, Richard Wallace, and Michael Zieniewicz, under the supervision of John Sedgwick.

12. See https://www.soscisurvey.de/.

13. For a detailed statistical analysis of this so-called blockbuster strategy, see Arthur De Vany, "Big Budgets, Big Openings and Legs: Analysis of the Blockbuster Strategy," in *Hollywood Economics: How Extreme Uncertainty Shapes the Film Industry* (Oxford: Routledge, 2004): 122–38.

BILL GRANTHAM

Motion Picture Finance and Risk in the United States

Financing commercial motion pictures by its nature involves risk. Such risk is of a different order from that which is intrinsic to the calculations behind whether or not to make a commercial film, such as the strength of the screenplay, the ability of the director, the appeal of the stars, and so on—subjective, even aesthetic considerations that studios and others attempt to correlate to business models of financial returns. This "macro" risk assessment is based on the potential overall success of the picture itself. In this chapter, the focus is on the risks undertaken by different parties involved in the motion picture production and financing process, risks that are not borne evenly or equally and that can be allocated or shifted according to different finance structures. The range of parties is substantial, including producers, distributors, banks, investors (individual and institutional), insurance companies, state and other public instrumentalities, and the people who are paid by film producers: writers, directors, crew, vendors, and so on, together with the bodies that represent them, such as unions or professional guilds, which may have a role in seeking to reduce risk for their members.

The chapter uses a historical perspective to show how models of film financing have evolved over the past twenty-five years or so and how these models have adapted and fluctuated as parties have alternatively accepted risk or declined to do so, and have sought to shift risk to other participants

The author of this essay is an independent scholar and motion picture lawyer in Beverly Hills, California. Opinions expressed are the author's own and not those of any law firm or client with which he is associated.

in the financial chain. The models that will be considered here are fundamentally those of the U.S. film industry. Non-Americans may participate in these models, but the models themselves are driven by the financial and business imperatives of the U.S. market, which is itself largely dominated by production and distribution structures established and dominated by the Hollywood major studios and principal TV networks. Domestic production from, say, France or South Korea would have quite different financial structures and are not considered here.

FRAMING RISK IN MOTION PICTURE FINANCE

If you were thinking of investing in a film production and asked to see a producer's financial prospectus, this is the sort of thing you would read:

> Purchase of the stock involves a high degree of risk as it is impossible to forecast accurately the results to an investor from an investment in the film, since no one can predict with any certainty whether and to what extent entertainment-related (including motion picture) investments will be successful. Investment in the stock is suitable only for persons of substantial means who have no need for immediate liquidity.[1]

Or this:

> The production, distribution and other exploitation of motion pictures are highly speculative, and traditionally have involved a high degree of risk. It is generally believed in the motion picture industry that less than one out of every five feature length films is sufficiently successful to enable the recovery of production costs by an independent producer. The success of motion picture productions is dependent upon a variety of factors over which the Company will have limited or no control such as public taste, critical reviews, promotion and distribution, and the popularity of other motion pictures and other entertainment productions then being distributed. In addition, there are significant risks that could materially delay completion of a motion picture or entertainment production or make completion impossible. Such risks include, but are not limited to, labor disputes, death or disability of a director or star performer, unanticipated changes in the weather and the health of the economy in general in the U.S. Moreover, there can be no guarantee that motion pictures will maintain their current popularity

as public interest in other forms of leisure time activities, particularly those which are participatory in nature, increases.[2]

These are taken from documents that seek to *sell* motion picture investments and are just snippets: a placement memorandum or prospectus can contain dozens of detailed paragraphs like these under the rubric "Risk Factors," the point being to insulate the offeror—the producer seeking investors—from claims that it did not divulge all the things that could go wrong with the investment. For those of us who keep our spare cash in saving accounts or invest it in our homes, in unit trusts or mutual funds, or in "safe" household-name stocks and shares, these types of disclosures would likely annihilate any enthusiasm we might have had for a movie investment: what sane person would take these kinds of risk?

Of course, many outwardly rational—if not entirely sane—people do just this all the time. In 2007, the major U.S. studios in the Motion Picture Association of American (MPAA) spent more than $12.6 billion producing films and a further more than $6.4 billion releasing them in the United States alone.[3] The 179 MPAA pictures were just 30 percent of all films released in the United States that year, although the average production and release costs of the remainder likely were significantly less than the average $106.6 million spent on each MPAA picture in 2007.[4] Nevertheless, if the average production and release costs of each of the 411 non-MPAA pictures released in 2007 was just one-quarter of the majors' expenditures, total production and U.S. release costs of all pictures shown in U.S. cinemas would have exceeded $30 billion. (It's practically impossible to get accurate figures on production costs for non-MPAA pictures in the United States, but the author's examination of many film-finance structures suggests that such costs are substantially lower.) Whatever the prospectuses may say, banks, funds, companies, and individuals provided that money, despite the myriad risks.

In 2007, those 590 MPAA and non-MPAA films earned around $9.6 billion at the U.S. box office. (Worldwide box office, which would have included many but not all of those 590, and many others besides, provided an additional $17.1 billion.) Given that only a fraction of these revenues reaches the producers and distributors of these films because of the substantial box office cut taken by cinema owners, it is clear that even with substantial additional revenues from DVD, television (free and pay), Internet, merchandising, soundtrack, and ancillary exploitation of these movies, recoupment of our notional $30 billion outlay is a tough challenge. Moreover, per-film returns are sharply asymmetrical: in 2007, the top 20 hit films out of the 590 total—less than 3.4 percent—took nearly $4.2 billion at the domestic box office, or one-third of the $12.6 billion total. It is uncontroversial to state that if a small number of movies are making most of the money, a large number of the rest must be loss makers. Conversely, even allowing for such egregious big-budget flops as *Howard the Duck* (1986), *Ishtar* (1987), *Waterworld* (1995), and *Leonard, Part 6* (1987), there may be lower risk associated with higher-cost films.

Moreover, the major studios, with their large production slates and substantial distribution pipelines, are in a position to cross-subsidize the blockbusters against the least successful pictures. While they may not intend any film to lose money, they are reasonably placed to reduce the downside on the flops; indeed, because the majors' distribution arms are able to use their booking strength to secure for even their less successful films reasonably wide cinema releases, they are able to squeeze more out of the box office—and then from video and other markets—than producers and distributors of non-MPAA "independent" films.

In this context, it's important to understand a key financing distinction. The MPAA companies generally raise substantial amounts of money from *corporate* finance, that is, institutional or major investment fund financing of the overall activities of the company. Non-MPAA companies tend to raise money from *project* finance, that is, investor funding of individual films or small slates. Project financing has limited or no potential for cross-subsidy which, as we have seen, may limit downside risk for the majors (while also capping upside potential). In other words, film risk is variable and the degree of risk is subject to structural considerations as well as the greater or lesser degree of "riskiness" inherent in any project's subject matter, or associated with its writer, director, stars, and so on. Put baldly, even a sophisticated, wealthy, well-connected investor has scant chance of taking a piece of a programmed-for-success blockbuster such as *Transformers* or *Avatar:* such a person is going to find him- or herself kept away from the top table and thereby taking greater risk. (Even when, on occasion, such investors have been offered a way into such elite projects, as with the tax-driven limited partnerships used by many Hollywood studios in the 1970s and 1980s, the terms of the investment tended to weigh against the interests of the investors: the "Hollywood accounting" issue—the widely held belief that Hollywood's methods of accounting to its investors do not correspond to general accounting practices and are always to the investors' disadvantage—while not part of the discussion in this essay, is always a matter of concern for those who put cash into movies.) However, even within individual projects, there are means and mechanisms for allocating and shifting risk among players in the financing. To understand these, some film financing history will be helpful.

                                                    Bill Grantham

Presales

In the 1980s, as the home-video business began to increase significantly the potential revenues of motion pictures, new financing approaches began to develop. Independent producers such as the Italian producer Dino Di Laurentiis and the Dutch financier Frans Afman of Slavenburg's Bank in Rotterdam devised structures that allowed banks to provide full production finance for new films with minimal risk. A producer, either alone or with a sales agent, would attempt to "presell" a film project. In a presale a distributor—in France, say, or Argentina—will agree to pay a certain amount for rights in its territory to a film under development at the time of the presale. This payment is usually termed a "minimum guarantee," since it is a minimum advance on royalty income for the film in that particular territory: if it earns more, then the excess, termed "overages," is paid to the producer, in theory at least. Generally, payment on the minimum guarantee is made when the film is completed and delivered to the distributor, although a small portion thereof may be payable earlier.

Once promises of sufficient minimum guarantees have been obtained from presales, the producer takes the signed distributor agreements to a financial institution, usually a bank. The bank assesses the creditworthiness of the distributors: in the case of some distributors it may be prepared to advance amounts close to the total value of the minimum guarantee. In other cases, it may be prepared to advance only a lesser amount, say 50 percent of the minimum guarantee. In the least creditworthy cases, the bank may insist on some backup for the promise to pay, such as a letter of credit. The bank makes a calculation of interest payable, calculates its transaction fees, and then agrees to make a loan that will cover the production costs of the picture. The producer is paid fees for its work that are built into the budget of the picture. It may also earn money from overages and any unsold territories whose minimum guarantees are not factored into the loan. This is very good for the producer: the film is made and money is earned.

At this point, the bank has limited risk by weighing the creditworthiness of the distributors and adjusting the amount it will advance based on this. The distributors agree to pay their minimum guarantees directly to the bank, so the risk of the producer diverting the funds is reduced. The bank also takes an interest in the picture as collateral for the loan: if the loan is not repaid, the bank can foreclose on the picture and attempt to liquidate the debt. However, there is one substantial area of risk still remaining: the minimum guarantees, or a substantial portion thereof, are not payable until the picture has been delivered to the distributor. Production delays may jeopardize delivery and therefore payment. In addition, if the costs of the picture overrun the budget against which the loan has been advanced, the producer may not have the funds to finish the film. Accordingly, the bank needs reassurance that the picture is going to be delivered on time and on budget. This reassurance comes in the form of a completion bond.

The Completion Bond

A completion bond is a type of insurance policy that provides a guarantee of on-time and on-budget delivery. The completion bond company charges a premium that is usually a small percentage of the film's cost and built into the production budget. If the picture overruns its schedule or budget, the bond company has the right to take over its production and supervise its completion and delivery. The bond shifts risk away from the bank: the bond company, like any insurer, assesses risk in calculating the amount of its premium: while 3 percent of the budget amount is not untypical, bond premiums can rise as high as 6 percent. In other words, on a $20-million film budget, the bond cost might range from $600,000 to $1.2 million. Note that the bond company's interest generally is not in how well the film may ultimately perform: its prime concern is that the film be capable of being produced for the approved budget amount by the production team that has been hired for that purpose. As with any insurance policy, the bond company has to pay out only when something goes wrong.

"Gap" Financing

This model—minimum guarantees covering 100 percent of the budget, a single bank lender, and a completion bond to protect against the unforeseen—drove the huge growth in international independent film production in the 1980s and after. It is obvious that it shifts the principal risk to the distributors, since they have to calculate what the minimum guarantee should be, based on their prediction of a film's performance before it has even been produced. If they predict badly, they may find themselves paying an excessive minimum guarantee and losing money on the picture. In such circumstances, in which the bank is repaid, the bond has not been claimed against, and the producer has received fees from the production, the distributor is the only loser and effectively bears the greater part of the risk. However, in the heady days of the 1980s, when new money came into the film business, demand was high, particularly in the video sector, and

   Bill Grantham

competition was intense among territorial distributors, there were plenty of distributors willing to assume such risks.

However, over time this model began to soften. While many hits were financed this way, so were myriad mediocre films. Competition among distributors became less frantic and the willingness to pay high minimum guarantees waned. It became more difficult to obtain 100 percent financing for a film based on a script, a director, and a couple of stars: instead, gaps began to appear in film budgets. And where there was a gap, "gap financing" emerged to make up the difference between minimum guarantees and the film's production budget. With gap financing, an experienced sales agent provided estimates of what it could obtain for the film in the unsold territories—that is, those markets that were not presold—once the film was completed. The bank that was already lending against the minimum guarantees would agree to fund a gap of, say, 20 percent of the budget based on these sales estimates. This involved a greater risk to the bank for two reasons: the sales agent might be unable to collect the estimated amounts, and the length of time to repay would be greater, since the selling of the film in the "gap" territories would only begin following, or close to, the time of delivery. Accordingly, the banks charged higher interest rates for gap financing. However, assuming that the sales agent's estimates were realistic, the risk of gap financing seemed to be manageable.

The problem, of course, was that the estimates were not always realistic. Bank and sales agents often colluded with each other to drum up numbers that would justify the amount of gap financing. And as the consumer market became more discerning, it was often more difficult to obtain predicted returns on the types of pictures that did well in the go-go days of the 1980s—exploitation titles, soft-core, and the like. Ultimately, banks capped the gaps and would fund only a portion of them. This left a further gap to be financed.

"Soft" Money

From the risk perspective, the perfect financier is one who does not seriously expect to be paid back. As gaps widened, producers looked to public funds—dubbed "soft" money—to make up the difference. Pioneered by Canada, France, Australia, Ireland, and other countries, soft money provided a range of mechanisms to producers—tax credits, rebates and refunds, and direct subsidies being the most popular—to make filming in a particular country or region attractive. While many of these schemes, particularly those involving direct subsidies, required some kind of repayment by the producers if the film made money, in reality, the public bodies entitled to such repayments tended to stand behind the commercial money before seeing any themselves; in addition, the institutional impetus to police and audit the accounts from which such repayments would be made was often weak. Soft money became—and remains—a very soft option for producers to finance films, since it greatly reduces the risk of the other players in the financing structure. Even in the United States, which has halfheartedly attempted to use diplomacy to attack European film-subsidy regimes in the early 1990s, soft money emerged in force in the early 2000s, with both a federal tax break to stimulate individual investment in films and a welter of state and city schemes to attract production to, say, New York, Louisiana, Florida, or Michigan. Mechanisms emerged to shift even the small risks of accepting soft money—for instance, tax credits could be traded at a discount so that their value was available to the production up front, and the risk of their being disallowed would be assumed by a third party, for a fee.

By the 2000s, the basic financing model had accordingly evolved: from bank financing against minimum guarantees to minimum guarantee plus gap financing to minimum guarantee plus gap plus soft-money financing. Yet the trend whereby distributors refused to accept the types of risk that they had taken on in the 1980s continued to make film financing problematic. Minimum guarantees became exceptional rather than routine. And sales agents found it hard to meet their estimates: increasingly, distributors sought to impose the risk-sharing model that had been standard before the explosion of the 1980s. That model involved the producer and distributor sharing both the upside and downside of a film's performance, and advance money became scarce.

Private Debt and Equity

Into this mix came various types of private financing. Individuals and investment funds would provide money to films in different ways. These investors might make loans to producers at higher interest rates (and with higher fees) than the commercial banks charged. They might invest directly in the picture and take a premium recoupment—say, 110 or 120 percent of the initial investment—plus a substantial equity ownership position in the film, ranging from 50 percent to 75 percent or more for the providers of 100 percent of the financing. Some structures provided for a combination of equity and debt financing.

The real problem for this private financing was that it tended to take on greater risks than the banks had been prepared to incur in the past. After all, the opportunity for private financing arose only once the combination of minimum guarantees, gap financing, and soft money became insuffi-

　　　　　　　　　　　　　　　　　　　　　　　Bill Grantham

cient to cover the financing of a particular project. The rationale for taking a greater risk was the prospect of a greater return: as we have seen, higher interest rates, privileged recoupment positions, and high transaction fees formed part of these structures. However, as we have also seen, the reason for the retreat from the traditional financing mechanisms was largely determined by the evaluation of what the actual returns were likely to be: for the private investors, the potentially big returns turned out to be merely hypothetical or actually chimerical.

This situation became worse when private investors tried to fit into traditional structures, essentially funding the gaps that the banks were unprepared to loan against. If a bank was prepared to be in a deal at all, it was because the particular project, for a particular reason—the presence of one of the few bankable movie stars, for instance—attracted presales and healthy sales estimates for the unsold territories against the grain of the overall market. But because the banks are always paid off first, the private investors were left trying to recoup from the leftover funds—almost by definition from the less attractive markets—that remained once the banks had taken their share. The appearance of downside protection—by limiting the amount of the investment in relation to the overall budget of the picture— often masked the fact that the investor was taking an even greater risk by restricting the potential for a return to the least attractive revenue sources.

Security Interests and Priority

The various parties to the transactions described above are tied together on a single financing by a network of contracts. Key to these are the creation and prioritization of security interests. A security interest is created when a party provides collateral to secure its contractual obligations to another party. A familiar secured transaction—that is, a transaction involving a security interest—is a mortgage or home loan, whereby the lender takes a security interest in the property against which the loan is made. If the borrower defaults on repayment of the loan, the lender, as the secured party, is permitted to foreclose on the property: in other words, to take possession of it and sell it in order to realize the money owed. As a result of foreclosure, the buyer loses possession and ownership of the property.

In the context of a film's financing, many parties will seek security interests in the collateral offered by the producer—the film and all rights in it. Any bank lender will seek a security interest, as will the completion bond company, other lenders, investors, and even providers of soft money. In addition, large distributors—particularly those providing substantial minimum guarantees—may also seek a security interest, as will the main film guilds, or unions, notably the Directors Guild of America, the Writers Guild of America, and the Screen Actors Guild. In each case, the producer is usually offering the same collateral on each secured transaction. Since there is only one film, and one set of receipts, this multiplicity of security interests contains the potential for conflict between the various secured parties, each of which will ideally want a clear path making it possible to foreclose before the others. These issues—sometimes termed "intercreditor" issues—are dealt with by having the various parties determine among themselves who gets to collect what money in which order upon foreclosure—that is, who has priority as a secured party and in which order.

Even from this brief description it is clear that the security priority question can be viewed as one of allocating risk. The secured party in senior, or first, position—the financier with top priority—is in a better position to collect money owed to it than the junior secured parties, who may have to wait until the senior party or parties have first collected. The willingness of secured parties to subordinate their position to others is usually dictated by party strength. For instance, the guilds generally seek to protect the right of their members to receive payment of so-called residuals—monies from the exploitation of the film in media other than the cinema—which are payable throughout the commercial lifetime of the film, which is to say potentially for many years. If the guilds fail to obtain security interests securing the payment of residuals (among other benefits), they will likely prevent their members from working on the production. This is a threat that nearly always obtains high, if not highest, priority for the guilds. Among other financiers, the willingness to accept higher risk is always hitched to their desire to engage in the transaction. As with the types of financing described previously, parties may have factored in upside benefits, such as higher interest rates and transaction fees, to justify the risk profile. Whether or not these calculations have been well made, the decision to accept a subordinate position always involves an increased appetite for—or, at least, a resignation to—greater risk.

THE FUTURE OF RISK IN FILM FINANCING

The global recession that began in 2008 had a severe impact on all of these funding mechanisms. The existing trend that had already depressed presales and minimum guarantees continued to the point where these were virtually extinguished for all but a handful of major films. A new factor emerged to make distributors even less willing to advance money to film producers: the DVD market, which had driven huge revenues since the 1990s, began to decline while "replacement" technologies, such as online

                                                  Bill Grantham

distribution, failed to provide new revenues sufficient to match the lost DVD money. At the same time, soft money came under pressure as the tax base shrank and public expenditures were squeezed. And, as finance gaps consequently grew, private money became less widely available as investment funds dried up and those investors who still had money switched into lower-risk vehicles.

Despite this, the appetite for making and watching films was largely undiminished. The year 2009 closed with the U.S. cinema box office hitting a new record, thanks to blockbuster hits such as *Transformers: Revenge of the Fallen, Harry Potter and the Half-Blood Prince, Up,* and *Avatar.* Yet at the project financing, as opposed to corporate financing, level, the film model seemed close to broken, requiring private finance to take on most of the risk that distributors and, to a lesser extent, bank lenders had assumed during the minimum guarantee and gap financing days. However, it became increasingly clear that the obvious way of reducing risk—investing less— put the funds actually invested at *greater* risk, since the investor putting up 20 percent or even 50 percent of the production budget could only rarely establish a share of the returns and the priority that would predictably lead to a bare recoupment of the amount invested, let alone a profit. The alternative, to put up a much greater amount of the funds required—perhaps the entirety apart from the soft money—largely eliminated the risks arising from poor interparty or intercreditor positions: nevertheless, the amount of at-risk capital required for such an investment was discouraging to many, if not most, investors.

In retrospect, it can be seen that the single-picture film-financing model pioneered in the 1980s and developed over the past quarter century, as described above, was always unstable, since it relied on the willingness of parties to take on risk that turned out to be unjustifiable. As the consequences of these bad risk assessments became clear, the risk takers retreated, to be replaced by a series of progressively more risk-aversive alternatives. In this context, it is important to point out that while financiers always propose structural business models that appear to justify their involvement in film-financing transactions, there is arguably a substantial psychological aspect to this as well. Unlike more typically fungible "widget" businesses, film financing seems to encourage players to disregard risk to an extent greater than they would elsewhere. The superficial justification for the investment may be the substantial returns that are obtainable on hit films, and in this context, the rare-as-hen's-teeth low-budget movies that become blockbusters are particularly alluring, even if for every *Four Weddings and a Funeral* (1994), *Blair Witch Project* (1999), or *Paranormal Activity* (2007) there are literally hundreds of similarly budgeted, and themed, films that flop. However, it is not fanciful to believe that the driving impulse behind many investments is not always steely business calculation. The old joke about the circus worker who cleaned up behind the elephants comes to mind. "Why don't you get another job?" he was once asked. "What, and give up show business?" he replied. In such contexts, the investment decision may look more like a spree—a conscious (or semiconscious) decision to *disregard* risk. As with most sprees, remorse, alas, may often follow.

In place of this, what would a rational model of film financing look like? The first element would probably involve a hard-nosed appraisal of the risk timeline. The initial appeal of the minimum guarantee model was that everybody involved directly in the financing of a film was repaid in a fairly short time, typically one to two years. Only the distributors had to wait for the revenues to come in to get paid. As we have seen, the distributors lost their appetite for this type of risk, but the financing parties often remain unwilling to contemplate a longer wait for returns. It seems obvious that this will have to change. A second element would be to reduce the complexity of film-financing transactions. Apart from reducing transaction costs—often considerable when the financing puzzle has many pieces—this would arguably restore clarity to the process of risk assessment, clarity that can currently be lost in the welter of interparty and intercreditor issues. However, in order to simplify the financing process, fewer people will have to put up more money. While, as has been seen, the impact of this on the risk calculation is more complicated—and in some ways more favorable— than might at first be believed, it nonetheless involves a more substantial increase in the investment contribution than such generally private parties have previously been prepared to stake. Because of this, it is arguably more likely that the existing models, which have essentially evolved in an improvisational manner as producers trawl around for new financing structures, will continue to develop opportunistically—in other words, with some parties, if not all, making imprudent assessments of risk in order to get their cherished films made.

NOTES

1. From a confidential motion picture prospectus in the author's possession.
2. From a confidential motion picture prospectus in the author's possession.
3. Motion Picture Association of America, *Theatrical Market Statistics 2007* (Los Angeles: MPAA, 2008). All 2007 box office data are taken from this source.
4. Note that the MPAA has not made available the 2008 figures in its annual release of U.S. cinema market data.

Bill Grantham

EVA NOVRUP REDVALL

Encouraging Artistic Risk Taking through Film Policy

The Case of New Danish Screen

Making a feature film is a costly affair. As a filmmaker you are constantly confronted with the economic realities of realizing your creative vision, as you have to persuade a number of people to risk their money on your project. Artistic self-expression or risk taking are rarely the top priority in the financial framework for filmmaking, and the complicated relationship between art and industry is often discussed in all national film cultures. The deep divide between art and commerce is thus in no way unique to Danish cinema, but a small national cinema with a limited domestic market results in some natural limits being placed on the scale and scope of the films produced. Most small national cinemas are dependent on government support to finance feature film production, since the financial risk of making films for a limited domestic market is otherwise simply too great.

This chapter analyzes the cultural arguments and film policies underlying the state-subsidized film industry in Denmark, focusing on the notions of financial and artistic risk taking. In this context, film practitioners are understood to engage in artistic risk taking when they step outside traditional comfort zones, trying new approaches with outcomes that are to some extent uncertain. Historically, the focus of Danish film policy has shifted from artistic concerns in favor of support for an art- *and* industry-based approach to government support. However, in 2003 a subsidy scheme called New Danish Screen was created to encourage the further development of film's idiom and narrative techniques, the ultimate goal being to sustain the vitality and diversity of Danish film. New Danish Screen, that is, is a targeted strategy aimed at ensuring innovation in Danish film by creating a space for artistic risk taking. The rationale behind the scheme is not an industrial one in any obvious or immediate sense, inasmuch as no requirements with regard to box office performance are made, as has otherwise increasingly been the case in Danish film policy in recent years.

Using New Danish Screen and the production of its first feature film, Pernille Fischer Christensen's *En soap* (A Soap, 2006), as a case, this chapter discusses the ways in which cultural policy issues have an impact on the film production of small national cinemas. The chapter analyzes how issues of "institutional trust," and the role of the film consultant as sparring partner rather than traditional gatekeeper, can help to create a space in which both emerging and established directors feel that they have the artistic freedom to pursue their personal cinematic visions and to take artistic risks.

THE NORDIC CULTURAL MODEL

The postwar cultural policies of the Nordic welfare states point to the Nordic countries' largely overlapping interests in promoting art and culture with a view to ensuring artistic freedom and cultural democracy.[1] These cultural policies tend to subsidize culture more generously than do most other countries, and to focus more strongly on welfare commitments to artists.[2] In Denmark, the reasoning behind the creation of a Ministry of Cultural Affairs in 1961 was based on ideas about what has been called a "democratization of culture."[3] The advent of the welfare state made the political and cultural education of citizens a matter of national interest, and in connection with the goal of democratizing culture, funding for the arts—and for cultural activities more generally—was seen as crucial. The Danish Arts Foundation Act established major support schemes for professional artists in 1964. This tradition of direct state support for individual artists is often highlighted as a key feature that differentiates the Nordic model from other models of public support for artists in Europe.[4]

Danish cultural policy is based on the so-called architect model, whereby the state designs the framework for supporting the arts and determines the overall objectives.[5] Traditionally in this model, artists and institutions depend on public-sector funding rather than commercial revenue generated through ticket sales or patronage and sponsorships. Another important element is "the arm's-length principle," which is meant to ensure that politicians are not directly involved in concrete decisions about arts funding.[6] These decisions are made by independent councils, the Danish Film Institute in the case of film.

While the early reasoning behind state support focused on ensuring art and culture of high quality as well as cultural diversity and equal access

                                                    Eva Novrup Redvall

to culture, the focus gradually became far broader, encompassing amateur activities, local initiatives, and a generally inclusive and participatory attitude toward cultural production.[7] Over the years, the primarily educational and aesthetic objectives have also been challenged by a more social and economic rhetoric, emphasizing the possibility of art and culture as instruments capable of furthering noncultural aims like creating jobs and strengthening the identity as well as economic growth of regional and rural areas.[8]

Several scholars have analyzed how this new emphasis has led to an increased focus on the economic dimensions of artistic production and the cultural industries, now often referred to as the creative industries.[9] Within the Nordic cultural model, this tendency has been regarded as a form of "political colonization," based as it is on a fundamental change of attitude at the level of the political establishment, which now articulates cultural policy in relation to an ideology of economic growth instead of in relation to ideals of public enlightenment, equal access to cultural products, cultural diversity, participation, and artistic freedom.[10]

As I will now discuss, the increased economic focus has influenced the overall framework of Danish cinema. However, New Danish Screen is an attempt to secure the existence of a space where artistic experimentation and risk taking are encouraged without regard to box office performance. New Danish Screen can be seen as a return to a more narrow, and in many ways elitist, focus on an artistically oriented, aesthetic rationale for support of the arts. The support scheme underlines the importance of freedom of artistic expression—freedom not only from the demands of the commercial market and dominant cultural policy ideas at any given time but also from narrative standards and accepted forms of cinematic expression.

The Two-Pronged Danish Film Policy: Art and Commerce

The present structure of state support for film production in Denmark was established with the Danish Film Institute (DFI) in 1972. The DFI was financed directly through the fiscal budget, and the so-called consultancy scheme was set up to secure the existence of "artistically valuable films." Independent commissioners allocate support based on their personal views of artistic quality. As discussed by Mette Hjort, this structure is thus not a liberal gatekeeping function, with projects judged on the basis of multiple assessments; rather, the commissioners act on ideas and visions as individuals, supporting what they personally regard as the best projects.[11]

A recent report on competency development for Nordic film commissioners clearly states that the basic concept behind this individual decision making is "that the decision to support a film should be grounded in a personal, professionally competent quality assessment and not be marked by consensus decisions, which tend to gravitate toward safeness and entail a risk of blocking the most daring and visionary projects." The reasoning is that since quality cannot be measured, no objective foundation for assessment can be attained. Thus, any assessment will invariably be subjective, but must be based on a professionally competent analysis and rise above private preferences and personal tastes.[12]

In 1989, the consultancy scheme was supplemented with a second support scheme, the commercially oriented 50/50 scheme (now the 60/40 scheme), named after its financing structure: the DFI allocates support of a maximum of originally 50 percent and now 60 percent of a film's budget. In this scheme, the assessment of projects is made by external assessors following predefined quality parameters concerning the film's potential to attract an audience of at least 175.000 viewers.

The setup of a commercially oriented scheme with a quality parameter of projected ticket sales is of course based on economic and industry arguments rather than artistic rationales. The "nobody knows factor" of filmmaking makes the financial risk of any given project considerable. In a small national film culture with a limited domestic market, the conditions of filmmaking are hard, and thus state support for most small film cultures aims not merely at securing the existence of films of high quality but at, quite simply, ensuring that films in the national language will be produced. What is at stake, essentially, is the very existence of a national film industry. The two-pronged support system for Danish film has generally been praised for allowing a national film culture and film industry to flourish throughout the 1990s: artistically ambitious films, as well as commercial ones, kept the wheels of the industry turning.[13]

As a result of the new economic priorities discussed above, the implementation of film policy has been subjected to so-called performance contracts since 1999. Moreover, since the end of the 1990s, politicians, the DFI, and the press have all tended to emphasize the box office figures. A reason for this is that Danish film started to perform well at the domestic box office in the wake of Dogma 95 and highly popular domestic comedies. From 2001 onward, local films have had an impressive domestic market share, ranging from 24 percent to 32 percent, so expectations are generally high. In keeping with such tendencies, a recent report, *Film in the Danish Experience Economy*, discussed the success of Danish film in terms of its contributions to economic growth, rather than in terms of the cinematic experiences it provides.[14]

                                    Eva Novrup Redvall

It is reasonable to assert that the overall paradigm of economic growth and the newfound taste for financial success have had an impact on the rhetoric associated with Danish cinema. However, the subsidy scheme New Danish Screen, launched in 2003, in many ways goes against the stream.

New Danish Screen: Risking the Interesting Failure

New Danish Screen (NDS) has been presented as a deliberate political initiative to secure the future success of Danish film. Vinca Wiedemann, NDS's first artistic director, has explained the scheme as a strategic countermove to "the inherent risk of inertia quickly setting in [in] any form of government support."[15] Wiedemann finds that the remarkable run that Danish film has enjoyed since Dogma 95 can easily become a problem: filmmakers may copy strategies that have previously been successful, and filmmakers may assume that the production of a hit entitles them to a bigger subsidy the next time around. With a limited number of subsidies to grant, NDS aimed to encourage directors to pursue artistic risk taking, instead of repeating successful formulas and seeking bigger budgets. As Wiedemann has stated: "We found it important politically to create something for the new generation as well as for the more experienced filmmakers who feel cornered or always feel that they are making the same kind of films and want to try new things."[16] Thus, NDS is not only a talent scheme but also a scheme for reinvention.

The declared aim of New Danish Screen is to

> promote and inspire the development of film language and story-telling, so that Danish cinema will sustain and strengthen its dynamics and diversity. It must be ensured that new generations of filmmakers do not fall back on conventional, handed-down forms but continually strive to push the limits and create new experiences for audiences, whether they are found in cinemas or in front of the TV screen. The subsidy scheme should know how to utilise the energy and direction of talents rather than guide them in certain directions.[17]

NDS is supposed to support what is called "manifested talent," a term that encompasses both emerging and established filmmakers who seek to develop their talents as film practitioners. NSD, in short, targets film practitioners who are interested in trying out new ideas or in changing course in relation to their earlier productions.[18] The funding is risk capital and is allocated by the DFI without any recovery requirements. The capital in question thus provides the opportunity to test new material instead of funding seemingly safer, more conventional projects.[19] NDS does not impose or work with strict genre limitations. Experimentation can be pursued through form, concept development, hybridizing approaches to fictional and nonfictional filmmaking, and so on. As the guidelines explicitly state: "Conventional thinking is not a priority."[20]

Unlike the consultancy scheme or the 60/40 scheme, NDS focuses less on the product and more on the process. Attention is paid to the importance of exploring new paths. As Wiedemann has explained, NDS offers artistic freedom and a framework for a focused dialogue among practitioners with a strong interest in creativity and innovation, since there is "nothing to sell": "the whole idea is to explore your material in a process of artistic clarification."[21] This line of reasoning has been continued by Jakob Høgel, NDS's artistic director since 2007; he finds that a special element in NDS is that the role of the commissioner actually consists of two very different roles blended into one: the role of sparring partner (someone with whom one can have friendly arguments and discuss ideas and approaches to a project with the purpose of enhancing its quality) and the role of über-judge (someone who decides what projects will eventually move from development to production). It can be hard to navigate, both as an applicant and as a commissioner, when the roles are blended like this, but Høgel insists that this blending of roles is a strength. According to him, it is crucial that the focus be not only on allocating support but also on having a dialogue with the filmmakers, since the applicants are constantly in a state of tension, caught between the desire to throw themselves into a process of artistic discovery and the awareness that they have to prove the worth of their project.[22]

The commissioner is actively involved in encouraging filmmakers to run the risk of exploring new ground, aiming at being a sparring partner in this process of exploration. This involvement in the creative process challenges the traditional view of commissioners as gatekeepers, as analyzed by the sociologist Sara Malou Strandvad in a study of NDS as an institutionalized facilitation of creativity within the context of the creative industries.[23] Strandvad sees the role of the NDS commissioner as that of an organizational representative who conducts an initiative to enhance creativity instead of focusing only on the selection of projects. In her view the concept of intermediary is appropriate in this case, its use allowing for the possibility of seeing art-funding decision makers as more than gatekeepers. In 2009, this line of reasoning was in fact supported by the report on the Nordic film commissioners; part of the definition of the commissioners' role is their "double role: they are constructive dialogue partners, striving for open, trusting dialogue with applicants, but they are also the judge of the projects and, if you will, the 'axeman.'"[24]

Wiedemann has underscored the extent to which the NDS commissioners understand their role in terms of a willingness to take the risk of supporting what may become an "interesting failure." She further argues that the thinking behind NDS's approach to film subsidy must, necessarily, lead to failure in some instances. Things will inevitably go wrong sometimes if filmmakers, as she puts it, have been urged to aim high enough.[25] This openness toward cinematic experiments that just might fail, not only economically but also artistically, is a defining feature of NDS, as is the understanding of the commissioner's role.

Artistic Risk Taking and the Importance of Trust

An openness to risk taking and dialogue is often considered crucial in creative processes. In her analysis of creative collaborations, Vera John-Steiner has described risk taking "as a particularly urgent concern for young artists who are faced with the challenge of gaining recognition while also testing their own sense of worth and promise."[26] The willingness to take risks, including the risk of failure, has often been described as a personality trait characteristic of creative people.[27] As Gary A. Davis puts it: "The creative person must dare to differ, make changes, stand out, challenge traditions, make a few waves, and bend a few rules. Creative people tend to have an internal locus of evaluation, rather than being swayed too easily by external influences and opinions."[28] However, since filmmaking is expensive, external evaluations play a bigger part in the filmmaking process than in most other art forms, making the *institutional* tolerance for risk taking an important aspect. Yet, institutional tolerance with regard to risk taking is at odds with more general tendencies, and must thus, as in the case of NDS, be explicitly built into the protocols of film policy. That NDS, with its tolerance for risk, has an important role to play is beyond doubt, for as any number of Danish directors have pointed out, trust, as it relates to artistic vision, is undermined by a system that emphasizes project evaluations, commercial promise, and marketability instead of concepts of intrinsic value and the potential of a still-developing idea to evolve into a product of high artistic quality.[29]

Lily Kong has explored the sociality of the cultural industries based on an analysis of the film industry in Hong Kong. She concludes, among other things, that trust is important as a constitutive element of the framework for cultural industries policies. This is so, she argues, because "the risks faced at various steps of the production, marketing and distribution process are ameliorated by trust relations, built up through time between social actors in spontaneous ways."[30] Kong foregrounds the way in which various cultural policy initiatives attempt to provide a means of managing risks, while they fail to properly recognize the importance of social knowledge and mutual trust in the risky film business. Mark Banks et al. have studied aspects of risk and trust in the cultural industries, and their conclusions point in a similar direction. They suggest, more specifically, that "senses of risk are constitutive and often pivotal to the whole economic and social basis of cultural entrepreneurship."[31] What is more, they identify trust as a crucial means of *facilitating* as well as countering, offsetting, or managing risk.

While trust in these cases is primarily discussed as a relationship between individual players in the industry, I would argue that what one could term "institutional trust" is also at play in a state-subsidized film industry. As emphasized by scholars from the field of organizational psychology, with a focus on measuring creativity and innovation in organizations, elements like trust and a tolerance for risk taking are important when trying to measure the level of creativity in what Göran Ekvall has termed "an organizational climate."[32] NDS provides a framework, or "institutional climate," that allows the commissioner, as an intermediary rather than a gatekeeper, to create a space of trust in which alternative projects can be given the freedom to evolve without having to constantly prove their worth along the way.

Less (Money) Is More (Freedom)?

One reason that NDS can have this trust in applicants with different types of ideas is that funding for each project is limited to a relatively modest amount. As Wiedemann has explained, NDS is not only a talent scheme but also "a low budget scheme built on the Danish tradition that having a small amount of money doesn't prevent you from making a good film, as long as the artistic quality is there. Films, however, have to have a strong personal mark and the director should have something at stake."[33] This essentially low-budget thinking behind initiatives to further new talents has been discussed by Mette Hjort as an example of creating *zones of limited risk* in which "young novice filmmakers should be given every opportunity to prove their promise; and the risk involved in allowing novices to perfect their skills and refine their artistic vision constitutes a legitimate gamble with public monies if the relevant budgets are kept within clear limits."[34] Hjort also discusses the forerunner of NDS, New Fiction Film Denmark

(NFFD), which was established in 1994 to provide a stepping-stone from the National Film School to professional filmmaking. However, NFFD supported only productions limited to sixty minutes and had a clear emphasis on young filmmakers.

Since NFFD had been a success in many ways and even supported productions that "grew" into breakthrough feature films like Jonas Elmer's *Let's Get Lost* (1997), there was initially a widespread skepticism toward NDS. It did not help that NDS had a complicated beginning—it was boycotted by members of the industry who considered the ceiling of support to be so low as to essentially undermine official union agreements.[35] Negotiations with producers and an increase in the maximum amount of funding helped get the first projects off the ground.

Many directors working within NDS have described the relief resulting from a significantly limited financial burden as an important factor that allows them to take far greater risks. Also, a number of directors have found the limited budget to be a constructive creative constraint that led to new ideas and original solutions. Following the Dogma manifesto that was considered inspiring by many directors, talk of the value of constraints is not uncommon in Danish cinema.[36] Similarly, research on creativity and constraints has discussed the possible value of both self-imposed and imposed constraints in the arts.[37] Economic constraints rather than self-imposed artistic ones can, of course, be problematic if the idea and the budget are simply too far apart. However, in NDS the concrete financial aspect of making a given film is always at play during the very process of developing the idea for the film. In this way a reasonable relationship between guiding ideas and budgets is made possible.

To illustrate what the process of developing a project within the context of NDS can be like, I will now turn to *A Soap*.[38] In what follows I draw on my own interviews with Pernille Fischer Christensen and screenwriter Kim Fupz Aakeson, interviews that focused on their development of *A Soap* through a collaborative process, from the original idea to the finished screenplay.

A Soap is the story of the thirty-two-year-old Charlotte (Trine Dyrholm) who becomes the upstairs neighbor of the transsexual Veronica (David Dencik) after moving away from her boyfriend. The shy Veronica prefers to keep to herself with her little dog and a romantic soap show on TV, while the outgoing Charlotte prefers company, including one-night stands. An assault, a new bed, and some white curtains bring the two of them together in a story that plays with the classic romantic expectations of traditional love stories.

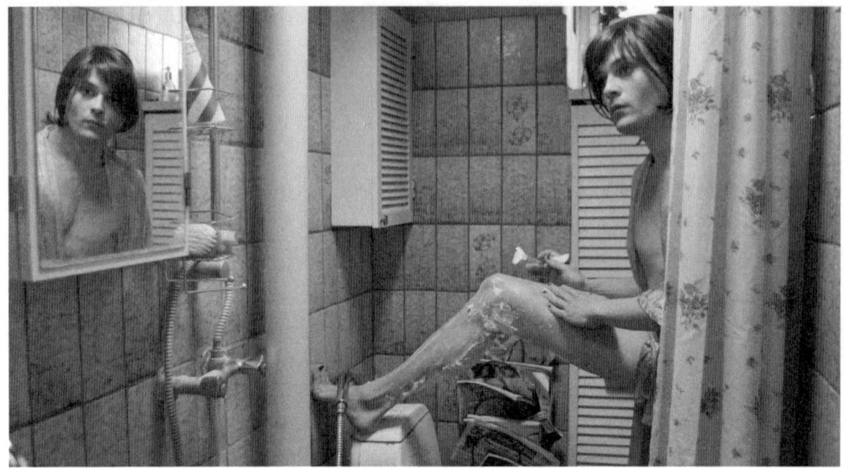

David Dencik as the transsexual Veronica in Pernille Fischer Christensen's *A Soap*. (Photography: Lars Wahl.)

A Soap: A Case Study

After making the promising diploma film *Indien* (India) at the National Film School of Denmark in 1999, Pernille Fischer Christensen spent a number of years trying to get her first feature film project off the ground. She made the award-winning short *Habibti min elskede* (Habibti, My Love, 2002), but has described the period following film school as exhausting and shaped by her constantly thwarted desire to work as a director:

> You feel happy at school, since you are just floating around in honey. You are allowed to be creative all the time and you are constantly in the process of investigating. When you then leave school, you spend most of your time trying to get permission to work as a filmmaker. Imagine a painter or a musician begging to get a brush or a guitar. Imagine having constantly to run around telling people how great you are, so as to get a guitar and be allowed to play it.[39]

Christensen doubts that she would ever have made it to the feature film level had it not been for NDS. She describes herself as an artist who is curious, who likes to test and push boundaries, and who is always searching for something new. She believes that spotting the new instead of the known is always difficult, and she is grateful to Vinca Wiedemann for taking a chance on her.

Christensen's experience is that the creative process is often very "messy," in the sense of her initially being fascinated by the idea of explor-

                                              Eva Novrup Redvall

ing a number of themes and questions without knowing how to make them come together, or even why it might be meaningful to do so. The initial phase is a period of asking all sorts of questions about both story and form. In the case of *A Soap,* questions abounded: What is the difference between men and women when it comes to love? What happens if one changes one's sex? How does the film sound? What colors might be in it? According to Christensen, this phase of asking questions rather than having all the answers can often lead gatekeepers to shut down projects, since they don't understand the *process* of developing an idea. In NDS she found that "the mess" was allowed, even encouraged, the result being a great sense of freedom.

Many theories of the nature of creative processes highlight the importance of problem definition in the front end of a problem-solving or creative effort.[40] Some insist on singling out the first step of the process as "mess finding," involving aspects like the personal orientation of the problem solver and the setting in which the work is to take place, since "the creative opportunity or challenge in a task pertains as much or more to what might be unknown, uncertain, or unclear than to the agreeable facts of the situation."[41] Most often, film ideas are not presented to commissioners or financers until they are in the state of a synopsis or a first draft produced after most of the initial mess finding. However, in NDS applicants are encouraged to approach the funding scheme at an early stage and, as in the case of *A Soap,* this demands a high tolerance for the often fragile and confusing process of understanding a still-evolving idea.

After months of exploring different strands of ideas and formulating many possible storylines in what Kim Fupz Aakeson has described as the crucial "dumb room" where everything can be said and tried out, Christensen and Aakeson developed the first draft in close collaboration. Christensen finds that one of the strengths of working with Aakeson is his talent for structuring what she describes as "the chaos" generated by all the questions and the many different pitches. Aakeson also convinced her to develop the story further with the actors in the film, which takes place only in the apartments of the two main protagonists and employs only a handful of actors.

Evaluating the process, Christensen thinks that it was creatively stimulating to make her first feature through NDS. The limited budget was not a problem but instead a constraint conducive to creativity. She recalls having tried to use the restrictions creatively by thinking minimalistically from the outset. The limited budget also helped to make the process "extremely fearless since I was able to say, 'If it does not turn out very well it will be all right, because it is only a little film costing 6 million DKK, and at least we will have tried something new.'"[42] To Christensen's mind, NDS is about freedom of speech for artists, and the limited budget is an important element in securing that freedom:

> It costs a lot to make a film, and that is a problem you always face as a director. Many people assess your film in terms of its acceptability to others. For instance, with *A Soap,* the distribution company asked me to change Veronica's profession, as the view was that her being a prostitute would offend some people. I did no such thing, and in my view the talent scheme creates a space where freedom of speech for the artist becomes possible. The less money you spend making a film, the more freedom you have: the more you're able to say something personal and to subject certain attitudes to scrutiny, without having to pander to people.[43]

In sum, Christensen regards NDS as a scheme that allowed her to explore her own personal vision through a process in which a certain messiness and doubt are accepted. She found that she was able to establish a trustful relationship with the commissioner, who served as a sparring partner. She felt that she was able to risk telling a story with the kind of controversial content that she no doubt would have been required to relinquish had she worked with investors with a more commercial outlook.

According to Christensen, she actively tried to create a story that matched the limited budget. Inasmuch as the budgetary restrictions of NDS were understood as limiting financial risk, they also provided a sense of relief, by lowering the stakes. Yet, budgetary restrictions can also become a personal problem for a director. Christensen invested her own salary in the film, and during some periods of developing the film she was forced to work as a cleaner in the morning to make ends meet. This is, of course, a disadvantage when you, as she puts it, want to invest yourself completely in your film.

NDS allocated 4 million DKK to the film, making the scheme the biggest investor. Christensen praises the structure for facilitating a setup that made it possible for her to deal with only one investor, in this instance Wiedemann (representing NDS), rather than a host of different people or funding schemes, each with their own views or priorities. For Christensen, the sustained dialogue about the project was an especially rewarding experience since this process was supportive throughout; she was encouraged to engage more and more deeply with her ideas. Christensen's description of her exchanges with the commissioner supports Strandvad's claim that the

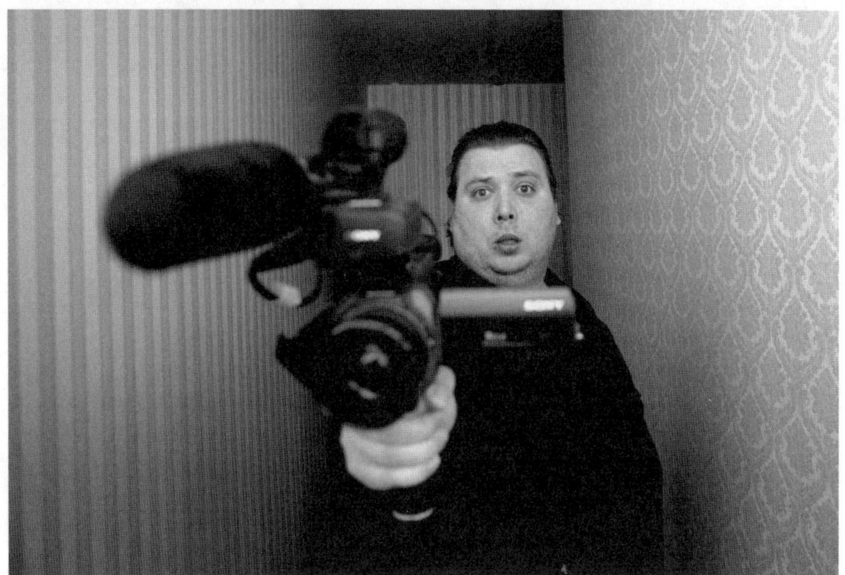

Nicholas Bro with the film camera in Christoffer Boe's *Offscreen*. (Photography: Hr. Boe & Co.)

role of the NDS commissioner is very different from that of the traditional gatekeeper. What we are dealing with here, rather, is a dedicated mediator and facilitator who is involved in the creative process itself.

The final film was ultimately deemed to have genuine artistic qualities. *A Soap* won both the prize for best debut and the Jury Grand Prix at the Berlin International Film Festival in 2006. In addition, the film received a Bodil in 2007 as the best film of the past year from the Danish Association of Film Critics. However, in spite of the success in Berlin and laudatory Danish reviews, the film had a limited audience of 29,000 people when it opened in April 2006. Similarly, the second and third feature films supported by NDS drew small audiences later that year: Anders Morgenthaler's *Princess* sold 9,763 tickets when it opened in June; Christoffer Boe's *Offscreen*, opening in August, was seen by fewer than 5,000 people. Even by small-nation standards, these figures are very low indeed.

Yet, the international and critical success enjoyed by these three films has repeatedly been foregrounded as legitimating the scheme's continued existence. NDS has since produced Christian E. Christiansen's Oscar-nominated short *Om natten* (At Night, 2007), Omar Shargawi's Rotterdam winner *Gå med fred Jamil* (Go with Peace, Jamil, 2008), and a number of other shorts and features. With an expanded mandate in the Film

Agreement for 2007–10 also to support documentaries, NDS has produced a wide variety of films in recent years.

Concluding Comments

Danish cultural policy has in recent years shifted, with a move from purely artistic and educational justifications toward including social and economic rationales. A similar development has taken place in Danish film policy, in which a commercial funding scheme has supplemented the consultancy scheme for artistically valuable films since 1989. Since 1999, the DFI has entered into performance contracts with the Ministry of Culture, and overall, there has been an increased focus on box office returns, national market shares, and festival prizes since the late 1990s.

However, since 2003 NDS has existed as a haven for artistic experiments and risky projects. The scheme focuses on the artistic process rather than the finished product and makes room for what has been termed "interesting failures." In many ways, NDS can be regarded as a return, albeit with some important and innovative differences, to the kinds of schemes that have long been viewed as a defining feature of the Nordic cultural model, schemes that supported individual artists rather than specific projects.

In the official mission statement governing NDS there are no specific performance indicators that have to be met. What we find instead, quite simply, is a stated desire to sustain and strengthen the dynamics and diversity of Danish cinema. Several of the films produced have opened to critical and international acclaim, but they have not found a big national audience. However, there seems to be no expectation that the films produced through a scheme that gives priority to talent and experimentation should be box office successes. The hope, rather, is that the scheme might foster innovative strategies, allow for the emergence of new film practitioners, and facilitate the creation of new companies, all with an eye to the future. Innovation is a buzzword in much of the talk that surrounds the creative industries, and in 2009—with negotiations for a new Film Agreement fast approaching—both the CEO of the DFI (Henrik Bo Nielsen) and the Minister of Culture (Carina Christensen) independently expressed the view that NDS is an excellent initiative that should be maintained.[44]

NDS has also won the attention of international film scholars. David Bordwell has written about successful examples of risk and renewal in Danish cinema, highlighting how efforts toward renewal have gained important institutional support in the form of NDS funding for what he terms "noncommercial features." The point, he argues, is to "maintain creative

                                                        Eva Novrup Redvall

innovation as central to the historical identity of this national cinema."[45] There is no doubt that Danish cinema post-Dogma would love to find new talents and approaches that will prove as stimulating and successful as the acclaimed manifesto asking filmmakers to run the risk of not using the traditional tools of cinematic storytelling and the technically sophisticated apparatus that normally goes with them. There seems to be a general consensus among practitioners, politicians, industry players, and film scholars that NDS would be the best place to foster new talents and approaches, and that it is thus worth putting risk capital into more experimental projects and into the nurturing of a talent pool.

Even though artistic risk taking is the main issue, money will of course always be a matter for discussion in a public funding scheme. The current artistic director, Jakob Høgel, has openly stated that it is important to make sure that the economics of any given production is not so bad that the incentive to try new things disappears in the industry.[46] Even with support from NDS, production companies still run a financial risk in allowing a filmmaker to try a different idea. Also, as the producer of *A Soap*, Lars Bredo Rahbek, has remarked, the scheme is not for everyone, precisely because of the limited budgets. He believes that you have to be both an idealist and quite canny to be able to make good creative use of the opportunities the scheme provides. In Rahbek's opinion, the necessity of minimalist solutions can itself become a problem over time, leading to many of the films produced by NDS resembling each other to a significant degree.[47]

No matter how you look at it, artistic and financial risk taking will usually be closely intertwined in filmmaking. However, NDS is a rare example of an institutional willingness to allocate money to artistic risk taking with no financial strings or performance criteria attached. The trust that the NDS commissioner is institutionally authorized to invest in the chosen applicants is another defining feature of the scheme and an important part of the contribution that it makes, not only in relation to specific projects but as a model for understanding the creative aspects of the filmmaking process and as a potentially transferable example of innovative film policy.

As an example of a targeted strategy to further artistic risk taking, the scheme provides inspiration on a national as well as international level at a time when risk management and the economic and social value of creative production are much more on the agenda than is the encouragement of creative art that does not simply repeat known formulas. The case of NDS suggests that a more unconventional understanding of how to structure cultural policy initiatives may be needed if, as the NDS guidelines put it, conventional thinking is not a priority.

This essay has benefited from Mette Hjort's encouragement, thoughtful editorial comments, and stylistic changes, for which I am very thankful.

1. Peter Duelund, ed., *The Nordic Cultural Model* (Copenhagen: Nordic Cultural Institute, 2003).

2. Per Mangset, Anita Kangas, Dorte Skot-Hansen, and Geir Vestheim, "Nordic Cultural Policy," *International Journal of Cultural Policy* 14, no. 1 (2008): 1–5.

3. Peter Duelund, "Nordic Cultural Policies: A Critical View," *International Journal of Cultural Policy* 14, no. 1 (2008): 14.

4. Merja Heikkinen, "The Nordic Model of Promoting Artistic Creativity," in Duelund, *The Nordic Cultural Model*, 277–303.

5. The architect model is one of the four cultural policy models defined by Harry Hillmann-Chartrand and Claire McCaughey in "The Arm's Length Principle and the Arts: An international Perspective—Past, Present and Future," in *Who's to Pay for the Arts?* ed. Milton C. Cummings Jr. and J. Mark Davidson Schuster (New York: ACA Books, 1989), 43–80.

6. Peter Duelund, "Cultural Policy in Denmark," in Duelund, *The Nordic Cultural Model*, 63.

7. Duelund, "Nordic Cultural Policies," 16.

8. Reports like *Denmark's Creative Potential* (2001) is an example of emphasizing the economic potential of the cultural industry as a contributor in the business landscape, as discussed by Darrin Bayliss in "Denmark's Creative Potential," *International Journal of Cultural Policy* 10, no. 1 (2004): 5–28.

9. For example, John Hartley, ed., *Creative Industries* (Oxford: Wiley-Blackwell, 2005); Nicholas Garnham, "From Cultural to Creative Industries," *International Journal of Cultural Policy* 11, no. 1 (2005): 15–29.

10. Duelund, "Nordic Cultural Policies," 7.

11. Mette Hjort, *Small Nation, Global Cinema* (Minneapolis: University of Minnesota Press, 2005).

12. Vinca Wiedemann, *The Art of Individual Decision Making* (Oslo: Nordisk Film & TV Fond, 2009), 5.

13. Ib Bondebjerg, "The Danish Way: Danish Film Culture in a European and Global Perspective," in *Transnational Cinema in a Global North*, ed. Trevor Elkington and Andrew Nestigen (Detroit: Wayne State University Press, 2005), 111–39; Pil Gundelach Brandstrup and Eva Novrup Redvall, "Breaking the Borders: Danish Co-productions in the 1990s," in Elkington and Nestingen, *Transnational Cinema in a Global North*, 141–63. Finding the balance between artistic and commercial rationales is often delicate, as discussed in Albert Moran, ed., *Film Policy* (London: Routledge, 1996).

14. Rikke Wümpelmann, *Film i den danske oplevelsesøkonomi* [Film in the Danish Experience Economy] (Copenhagen: Imagine, 2008).

15. Kim Skotte, "New Danish Screen," *FILM* 50 (2006): 3.

   Eva Novrup Redvall

16. Annika Pham, "Directors Should Have Something at Stake," Cineuropa .org, October 2, 2006.

17. The Danish Film Institute, introduction to *New Danish Screen*, http://www.dfi.dk/Service/English/Funding/New-Danish-Screen/Guidelines-Fiction-and-Documentary.aspx.

18. Ibid.

19. New Danish Screen is founded on a partnership between the Danish Broadcasting Corporation DR, TV2, and the DFI. The funding over the accord term, 2007–10, is roughly €20 million. Around one-third of the budget comes from DR and TV2, while the rest is provided by the DFI.

20. The Danish Film Institute, *New Danish Screen: Guidelines Fiction and Documentary*, http://www.dfi.dk/Service/English/Funding/New-Danish-Screen/Guidelines-Fiction-and-Documentary.aspx.

21. Skotte, "New Danish Screen," 3.

22. Eva Novrup Redvall, "Laboratorium for åbenhed og mod" [Laboratory for Openness and Courage], *FILM* 59 (2007): 20.

23. Sara Malou Strandvad, "New Danish Screen—An Organizational Facilitation of Creative Initiatives: Gatekeeping and Beyond," *International Journal of Cultural Policy* 15, no. 1 (2009): 107–21.

24. Wiedemann, *The Art of Individual Decision Making*, 8.

25. Skotte, "New Danish Screen," 4.

26. Vera John-Steiner, *Creative Collaboration* (Oxford: Oxford University Press, 2000), 79.

27. For example, ibid.; Robert J. Sternberg, ed., *Handbook of Creativity* (Cambridge: Cambridge University Press, 1999).

28. Gary A. Davis, *Creativity Is Forever* (Dubuque, IA: Kendall Hunt, 2004), 88.

29. Mette Hjort, Eva Jørholt, and Eva Novrup Redvall, eds., *Danish Directors 2* (Bristol: Intellect, 2010).

30. Lily Kong, "The Sociality of Cultural Industries," *International Journal of Cultural Policy* 11, no. 1 (2005): 61.

31. Mark Banks, Andy Lovatt, Justin O'Connor, and Carlo Raffo, "Risk and Trust in the Cultural Industries," *Geoforum* 31 (2000): 453.

32. For example, Göran Ekvall, "Organizational Climate for Creativity and Innovation," *European Journal of Work and Organizational Psychology* 5, no. 1 (1996): 105–23; Göran Ekvall and Lars Ryhammar, " The Creative Climate: Its Determinants and Effects at a Swedish University," *Creativity Research Journal* 12, no. 4 (1999): 303–10.

33. Pham, "Directors Should Have Something at Stake."

34. Hjort, *Small Nation, Global Cinema*, 15.

35. Marianne Krogh Andersen, "Madpakkefilm" [Lunch Bag Films], *Weekendavisen*, July 1, 2005.

36. For example, Mette Hjort and Scott MacKenzie, *Purity and Provocation: Dogma 95* (London: British Film Institute, 2003); Hjort, *Small Nation, Global*

Cinema; Mette Hjort, ed., *Dekalog 01: On* The Five Obstructions (London: Wallflower, 2007).

37. For example, Jon Elster, *Ulysses Unbound* (Cambridge: Cambridge University Press, 2000).

38. This is not an attempt at a detailed analysis of the relationship between the organizational forms and the working practices associated with the cultural industries that Hesmondhalgh and Pratt, among others, identify as a missing dimension in academic work on cultural industries and cultural policy (David Hesmondhalgh and Andy C. Pratt, "Cultural Industries and Cultural Policy," *International Journal of Cultural Policy* 11, no. 1 [2005]: 9). It is, nevertheless, a step in the direction of insisting on the importance of analyzing the actual implementation and consequences of different policies and the need to know more about how practitioners think and what influences their choices in their creative work.

39. Eva Novrup Redvall, "Anerkendt talent" [Acknowledged Talent], *Information,* February 22, 2006.

40. As summarized in Scott G. Isaksen and Donald J. Treffinger, "Celebrating 50 Years of Reflective Practice: Versions of Creative Problem Solving," *Journal of Creative Behavior* 38 (2004): 75–101, this focus on the front end of a problem-solving process is especially prevalent in theories and models from the field of creative problem solving (CPS). Scholars with an interest in understanding creative processes in art have often highlighted the importance of problem finding, not only of problem solving, as in Mihaly Csikszentmihalyi and Jacob W. Getzels, *The Creative Vision: A Longitudinal Study of Problem Finding in Art* (New York: John Wiley & Sons, 1976).

41. Isaksen and Treffinger, "Celebrating 50 Years of Reflective Practice," 82. For a discussion of filmmaking as problem finding and problem solving, see Eva Novrup Redvall, "Scriptwriting as a Creative, Collaborative Learning Process of Problem Finding and Problem Solving," *Mediekultur* 46 (2009): 34–55.

42. Redvall, "Anerkendt talent."

43. Ibid.

44. Andreas Relster, "Filmens mosaik" [The Mosaic of Film], *Information,* April 2, 2008; Carina Christensen, "Ministerens mening: Filmisk identitet" [The Opinion of the Minister: Filmic Identity], the Ministry of Culture, March 2009, http://www.dfi.dk/Nyheder/FILMupdate/Filmupdate-arkiv/Film-staar-hoejt-paa-kulturministerens-dagsorden.aspx.

45. David Bordwell, "Risk and Renewal in Danish Cinema," *FILM* 55 (2007): 16–19.

46. Eva Novrup Redvall, "New Formats, New Talents, New Companies," *FILM* 64 (2008): 30.

47. Ibid.

　　　　　　　　　　　　　　　　　　　　　　Eva Novrup Redvall

MICHELLE L. WOODWARD

After the Decisive Moment

Moving beyond Photojournalism's High-Risk Mode

Since the early years of the new 35 mm photojournalism in the late 1930s, a dominant visual mode of depiction has gradually developed that privileges close-up shots of action and interaction, particularly when reporting from conflict zones. Specific historical conditions such as technological change, social and cultural trends and beliefs, and professional competition have contributed to the emergence and salience of this look, which has become increasingly dramatic and emotionally charged. The change in photojournalistic images—from distant and static in the early twentieth century to highly engaged and full of action in the present day—has helped create a culture of photojournalism that valorizes, and necessitates, the taking of ever more dangerous risks. Yet, how does this strategy of creating visual drama influence what viewers learn about a given situation? Close-ups and action create emotional intensity and a sense of immediacy, and are thus attractive. But they also simplify the narrative embedded in the frame by focusing attention on fleeting moments, which may add to our knowledge of the texture of conflict but do nothing to illuminate the particular politics at play.

The relationship between risk and visual style in photojournalism is rarely discussed, but these phenomena are intimately connected, as this essay aims to demonstrate.[1] The risks taken by photojournalists today are not only physical but also psychological, financial, and ethical. The profession is more dangerous than ever before, according to photographers and professional groups such as the Committee to Protect Journalists (CPJ). Due to the dominance of high-risk photojournalism, it is difficult to imagine alternative modes, but photojournalism was not preordained to privilege the capture of moments of dramatic action. This essay will demonstrate how the look of photojournalism was constructed over time by outlining some of the historical forces that have created a visual mode made possible only through taking great risks. The experiences and opinions of individual photojournalists will be used to illustrate the role of risk in the professional practice of photojournalism. The influential photography agency Magnum Photos has played an important role in the shaping of photojournalism since its founding in 1947, and so will be considered at points in the essay. Particular cases and examples will focus on photojournalism of the Middle East, for reasons having to do with the centrality of that region in the news today (as a particularly dangerous arena for photographers) and my own expertise.

At the end of the chapter I will consider how visual modes in photojournalism are changing. While many photojournalists today find themselves competing to produce the most dramatic image, it is becoming increasingly common for photographers to choose another vantage point by depicting aspects of everyday life, or the aftermath of violence, instead of violence itself. Rather than take up-close photographs from the midst of action, these photojournalists attempt to illuminate the political and social forces that provoke or maintain conflict. The focus on civilians in times of war within photojournalism is not new. However, a visual mode that privileges everyday experience, or focuses on large-scale political forces that are visible only as traces in various urban, industrial, or environmental landscapes, is gaining space in magazines, Web sites, books, and exhibits.

This visual mode entails the taking of far fewer physical risks than the dominant mode. Although photojournalists are not consciously seeking lower-risk practices, there is a growing awareness that taking ever greater risks may not be leading to greater insights. As the famous war photographer Don McCullin commented on visual journalism, "I feel I totally wasted a large part of my life following war. . . . Have we learned any lessons from the countless pictures of pain and suffering? I don't think we've learned anything. Every year, there's *more* war and suffering."[2]

Historical Development of a High-Risk Mode of Photojournalism

The famous war photographer Robert Capa is often quoted approvingly as saying, "If your pictures aren't good enough, you're not close enough."[3] Early members of the Magnum Photos agency such as Capa, David Seymour, and George Rodger helped pioneer a new kind of war photography during the Spanish Civil War and World War II that emphasized

                                           Michelle L. Woodward

close-up shots of action as well as sympathetic images of civilian suffering. Previously, war had been photographed at a relatively safe, and visually dull, distance. Technological changes enabled the creation of a highly engaged practice of photographing war, which soon became the norm in photojournalism, as the photographer used small, fast cameras to move ever closer to scenes of conflict.[4] Members of Magnum were among those who, in the 1930s, first switched from bulky glass plate cameras, which exposed one frame at a time, to the compact, lightweight 35 mm format, which used long strips of film. They effectively exploited their new cameras' capacity to produce a spontaneous new look based on natural light rather than a bright flash. Often called candid camera photography, this style of photojournalism relied on sensitive film that could capture the subject both unaware and unposed as it was advanced frame by frame, and in a mere instant. Photojournalists took advantage of the camera's small size and fast mechanics to capture revealing gestures and expressions close up. For example, Capa's photographs of Allied troops landing in Normandy on D-Day in June 1944 were clearly taken from a position in the surf, along with the advancing troops. The photographer's implicit position in the midst of the action dramatizes events through his—and thus the viewer's—proximity to the unfolding events. Dramatic photographs of war, suffering, and disaster pull in the viewer through a sense of heightened immediacy, but they involve considerable risk taking on the part of the photographer.

Conventional notions about the connection between truth and the eyewitnessing of events have also helped normalize a high-risk mode of photographic practice. When covering and viewing conflict and tragedy, photographers and viewers respectively often summon the mantra of needing to "bear witness" as a means of calling attention to problems in society. Commentators often trace this concern to the reformer Lewis W. Hine, who photographed child labor in the early twentieth century and is quoted as saying. "I wanted to show the things that had to be corrected. I wanted to show the things that had to be appreciated."[5] The philosophy of humanism—which emphasizes the rights and needs of the individual—has given photographers another impetus to focus on fleeting human encounters and events rather than the depiction of macro forces that shape societies. Cornell Capa, Robert Capa's brother, coined the term "concerned photographer" in the 1960s to describe many Magnum and other photojournalists whose overriding concern was for humanity, using Hine's quote to convey what he meant. Photojournalism is predicated on the belief that a focus on specific moments of individual human experience can reveal the essence of a given state of affairs. The photographer, it is assumed, needs to be talented enough only to know which moment this is and how to capture it with the camera. This belief was bolstered by Magnum Photos' founding member Henri Cartier-Bresson's famous concept of the "decisive moment." He described the idea in his 1952 book by the same name as "the simultaneous recognition in a fraction of a second of the significance of an event as well as of a precise organization of forms which gives that event its proper expression."[6] Generations of photographers have thus been inspired to attempt the capture of an exact moment that expresses a fundamental understanding of a particular situation.

The capturing of unique, fleeting moments in time keeps the viewer's attention focused narrowly on the symptoms of conflict, inequality, and oppression, but does not reveal much about the deeper political and structural forces that underlie them. The convention of focusing on individuals also suits the staging and arranging of publicity events for the camera, which take up much of a daily news photographer's time. However, some photojournalists who are now pursuing new visual modes are doing so in an attempt to get beyond the superficial, discrete moment in time in order to depict the forces that provoke or sustain conflict. Since the conception of photojournalism's subject as moments in time is so entrenched, these photographers often find it difficult to place their work with magazines and newspapers, and thus tend to rely on art galleries and books as a means of reaching audiences.

In addition to technological changes and social beliefs in the importance of witnessing moments of conflict directly, economic trends encouraged the development of a high-risk visual mode of photojournalism. Dramatic scenes of action capable of attracting viewers are important to commercial publications that need to entice advertising dollars with large circulation figures. The new mode of photojournalism that began in the 1930s was developed in tandem with the mass-circulation picture magazines, most notably in Germany but also in France, Britain, and the United States, such as *Vu, Picture Post,* and *Life.* The picture magazines enhanced the photographs' drama and novelty by publishing them in a large format and in great numbers as extended photo essays. Big-font headlines added to the drama, with statements such as "This Is War!" Photographers' and agencies' financial well-being was closely linked to the popularity of these magazines until their decline in the 1960s, thus providing photographers with incentives for meeting the need of editors for close-up, engaged images.

As an example of how photojournalism's visual mode has developed into a look that entails increasing risk to the photographer, it is useful to look at the changing depiction of conflict between the Israelis and Palestinians.[7] Photographic coverage in magazines such as *Time* and *Life* of

                                    Michelle L. Woodward

the fighting in 1948, as the state of Israel was established, consisted primarily of the aftermath of conflict between Jews and Palestinians or of static moments between fighting, such as the inspection of troops or captured prisoners under guard. *Life* magazine emphasized pictures over text, often spreading photos across two pages. A double-page spread in the June 7, 1948 issue starts on the upper-left side of the page with Arab Legion trucks advancing along a narrow Jerusalem Old City street. The end frame, placed on the right at the bottom, shows a wounded Arab legionnaire being carried away by volunteers. In between are photographs that show the Arab troops crouching with guns and sandbags along the top of an Old City wall, Palestinian civilians crowding together at the Church of the Holy Sepulchre to hear battle bulletins, and explosions around Jewish-held buildings seen from a distance.

The visual mode used in all of these photographs conveys a sense of an impartial witness standing apart from the events through the use of normal lenses that approximate human vision, a straightforward angle of view, and placement of subjects in the middle or background. Surveying a broad scene from a distant, standing perspective, rather than in close-up or at an angle, was the conventional style in photojournalism during this era, and it is still often visible in standard news photography, especially that distributed by wire agencies such as Associated Press, Reuters, and Agence France Presse. This neutral appearance gives the impression of a simple observation of facts, even though it is just as constructed as any other style.

By October 2000 and the beginning of the second Palestinian intifada, or uprising against Israeli occupation of the West Bank and Gaza, these early stylistic conventions had been all but abandoned by most ambitious photographers. *Life* magazine was defunct and double-page spreads in *Time* featured one close-up photo bringing the viewer into the middle of the action. A photograph from the October 23, 2000 issue of a Palestinian man arguing with an Israeli soldier emphasizes the physicality of their confrontation through photography at extremely close range.[8] The soldier's arm, pointing to the right, shoots across the entire photograph, threatening to break out of the frame, while the Palestinian man's fists on the soldier's chest push in the opposite direction, creating a dynamic, tangible tension. The use of color instead of black and white, high-resolution digital technology at the point of capture and reproduction, and automatic focus lenses have enabled the creation of a sense of immediacy and intimate involvement that was lacking in photographs from earlier decades. The emphasis now is on capturing emotionally charged scenes not seen in the coolly distant photos of 1948. Use of a wide-angle lens with the compositional technique of tightly filling the frame with action demands close physical proximity to the subject, which entails taking the risk of getting caught up in conflict.

The visual intensity created by the technique of photographing from within the middle of an unfolding event has since become the norm in *Time* magazine's depiction of the Israeli-Palestinian conflict. The former Magnum photographer James Nachtwey often supplied these action-filled photographs. As a five-time winner of the Robert Capa Gold Medal for "best published photographic reporting from abroad requiring exceptional courage and enterprise" by the Overseas Press Club of America, Nachtwey's high-risk practices are often celebrated as the epitome of what it means to be a photojournalist covering conflict.[9]

The trend in depictions of the Israeli-Palestinian conflict to get ever closer to the action is mirrored in the broader field of photojournalism. Photographers who participate in the U.S. military program of embedding with troops in Iraq and Afghanistan do so with the hope of getting as close as possible to conflict. Nachtwey himself was injured by a grenade attack in 2003 while riding with U.S. army troops in Iraq. However, as Ed Kashi—an acclaimed freelance photojournalist since 1979—explains, the physical risk facing photojournalists has become more sinister over time: "The calculus has changed dramatically. It's not the fear of getting hit by random violence or being in the wrong place at the wrong time. Now it's the issue of actually being hunted down by forces who want to hurt me physically, kidnap me for money or both." Kashi made the calculated decision not to continue covering Iraq after April 2004: "This is partly due to my personal calculations for risk taking, the fact I have a young family, plus the type of work I excel in and relish. My work is predicated on intimacy and access. In Iraq it has become impossible to attain either of those qualities due to the dangers, lack of trust and a general paranoia and anger towards people from the West, particularly Americans."[10]

The increased risks involved in conflict photojournalism are not only physical but financial. In the era of mass-circulation picture magazines, most photographers were either on staff or were employed by agencies that could sell the same package of photographs to multiple publications around the world. As the picture magazines declined in circulation in the late 1960s, photojournalists began to lose important venues for their work. When *Life* ended its weekly publications in 1972, budgets and space for photography at many magazines were shrinking, pushing them to cut the number of staff photographers with full-time contracts. Television was an additional pressure on photojournalism as it lured advertisers away from picture magazines, compelling print publications to cut budgets or close

                                          Michelle L. Woodward

altogether. But around the same time as its decline in print publications, photojournalism began to garner respect in the art world. The photography exhibit On the Line: The New Color Photojournalism, which traveled to at least seven art venues in the United States beginning in 1986, heralded a new era in which some photojournalism was seen to have elements of visual style, to use color in an artistic manner, and to warrant a second life on a museum wall beyond its original purpose as news.[11] For many ambitious photojournalists today, having a gallery show or publishing a book is the best way to communicate with an audience on the photographer's terms. However, while they may add to the photographer's prestige, gallery shows and books do not bring in much revenue.

As space for photographs in newspapers and magazines shrinks and numerous small-niche publications appear on the Internet, many photojournalists are working freelance. They operate without the financial security provided by a steady income and the benefit of the legal resources and political connections enjoyed by salaried employees at the large media organizations.[12] The CPJ reports on its Web site that as of December 2009, almost 45 percent of jailed journalists are freelancers who lack "the legal and monetary support that news organizations can provide to staffers."[13] In pursuit of dramatic stories that will appeal to editors in a narrow market for photojournalism, freelance photographers are often determined to enter locations and situations that are unstable and difficult to access, and thus have not been saturated with media attention. Recent technological changes such as increased Internet access and affordable digital cameras enable freelancers with no institutional affiliation and little experience or money to work in high-risk conflict zones in an attempt to jump-start careers.[14]

THE CURRENT SITUATION: A MULTITUDE OF RISKS

Risk is a significant and accepted part of the practice and culture of photojournalism, from local crime reporting to international coverage of war and conflict. Many photojournalists see taking risks as intrinsic to the job, even an indicator of the importance of the story. As Anne Holmes, a young photojournalist who has worked in Afghanistan, says, "Chances are, if there is risk involved, it's a story worth telling, though not always."[15] Sometimes taking risks is seen as part of an ethical obligation to one's subjects. Iason Athanasiadis, a photographer and writer based in Istanbul, considers the risks he took to cover the Iranian elections and demonstrations in June 2009 "a classic case of the ethical responsibility of bearing witness," and he would take those risks again, even though he was arrested and spent three weeks in Evin prison for his work.[16] Yet, others say that the risks have become so great that they now impede their ability to pursue a story. Kashi says, "There are many issues, places and subjects I cannot cover anymore due to the physical dangers. These dangers always existed but now they are more focused and dangerous. In general, and I'm sorry to have to say this, working in the Muslim world has become the most risky and tricky place to work today."[17]

According to analysts and photojournalists, political circumstances in conflict zones have made the profession more dangerous than ever before as journalists have increasingly become targets for suspicious combatants and repressive government forces. Publications with tight budgets are relying more frequently on freelancers, who lack the protections of money and lawyers that come with institutional affiliation.[18] But in addition, editors, publishers, and public tastes have over time encouraged—wittingly or not—greater risk taking by creating a demand for dramatic, action-filled photographs.[19] When a photographer is unwilling to take the risks necessary to create a suitably dramatic image, there is usually another photographer who will. Editors say they encourage photographers to take precautions and to value their own safety, but this rhetoric cannot compare with the competitive pressures of the shrinking marketplace for photojournalism. The dilemma was illustrated in a November 2009 *New York Times* story. The paper reported that, according to Rodney Pinder of the International News Safety Institute, "several large broadcasters tried to reach an agreement not to buy video from unassigned, unaffiliated freelancers, so as to discourage excessive risk-taking. But that collapsed when it became apparent that no news organization would actually turn down images from a major news event."[20]

The risks facing a photojournalist in the Middle East vary depending on the particular environment and situation as well as on the photographer's work practices and perceived identity. Indigenous photographers confront a different set of risks than foreigners, who in turn will face different risks depending on whether they have flown in for a short assignment or are based locally for the long term. Risk in photojournalism appears in a multitude of different forms. Those most celebrated are physical risks of injury or death from operating close to conflict. Photographers who take such risks are lauded as heroic and encouraged by awards such as the Robert Capa Gold Medal. Most photographers do not romanticize the risks they take, often preferring not to discuss them unless prompted by events or questioning. External commentators, on the other hand, often glorify risk taking. In writing about the release of journalists who were taken hostage in Gaza in 2006, *Washington Post* columnist Howard Kurtz wrote, "[I]t's

                                    Michelle L. Woodward

worth remembering that there is a hardy band of reporters, producers, cameramen and photographers who risk their lives and put their families through great stress simply to tell the rest of us what is transpiring in far-away lands."[21] Even the language Kurtz uses—"hardy band" and "faraway lands"—creates a romantic, swashbuckling picture of foreign correspondents that is echoed in much public discourse. However, the most risky photojournalism is not done in "faraway lands." The CPJ has found that those at greatest risk are local journalists covering crime and corruption: "While the killings of U.S. journalists generate intensive media coverage in the United States, they are not very common; of the 366 journalists killed in the last decade, only 13 were Americans. In fact, most of the journalists killed were local journalists who were murdered in their own countries."[22]

Women photojournalists in the Middle East confront risks specific to their gender as well as those common to all photographers. The first Saudi female photojournalist to work for a local newspaper, Mona al Jeddawi, explains some of the difficulties she has faced: "There are many stories and risks especially in this line of work, some of which have caused me to visit police stations and to be subjected to investigations for example when I took pictures of the building belonging to the Department of Education for Women in Jeddah where a security man arrested me and accused me of taking pictures of the building 'in order to bomb it,' adding that he had never heard of a Saudi female photographer."[23] Eman Mohammad, a young freelancer, was featured, along with three other women, in an article on female photojournalists in Gaza. The article reports that "she feels highly unappreciated for her work and receives little encouragement from her male peers. She says they have been hindering her work. 'Palestinian society is a patriarchal society and prefers men working rather than women.'"[24]

Other risks, often downplayed or ignored, include psychological harm, such as post-traumatic stress disorder (PTSD) suffered by those who cover war and tragedy, damage to personal relationships due to stressful working conditions, and potential danger to family members when the photojournalist is covering crime, war, or violence in his or her own community. The risk of harm to subjects, translators, and drivers associated with journalists or foreigners is an ethical quandary that must be seriously considered by photographers. Ed Kashi explains how this can affect one's work: "I know for certain that in the past individuals have been hurt by their associations with me. This is why I rarely go against their advice or push past the limits they deem acceptable. I have become acutely aware of the risks local individuals take in working with me and show the utmost respect for that dynamic."[25] In addition, subjects are also vulnerable after the photojournalist has returned home. As Holmes explains, "There used to be this notion that when western journalists went to far away places they could bring back photos and publish them and no one in the said country would ever see them. But the internet has changed everything now." After photographing women in Afghanistan who tried to commit suicide by self-immolation, she says, "I have been extremely careful about publishing [the photographs] and have always made explicit stipulations about the text that goes along with it, disabling comment sections, because often people write in to say offensive things. But it's out of my control once they are on the internet. Anyone can copy them, republish them on a blog and there is no way for me to track this."[26]

Freelancers face financial risks when they produce work on the speculation of being able to sell it in the future, while searching for the next job, or by working for less reputable clients who may not pay on time or at all. Photojournalists regularly face the risk that photographs may be used for purposes not intended or approved by the photographer, and the possibility that their ability to work may be obstructed by those threatened by their coverage. For example, freelancer Zoriah Miller's embedded position with the U.S. Marine Corps in Iraq was terminated in July 2008 after he posted photos of dead soldiers.[27] A fairly new risk among photojournalists is that of losing journalistic credibility by working for organizations, such as nongovernmental human rights groups, that pursue additional agendas beyond reporting.

Currently, the burden of managing risk is shouldered by the individual photographer almost entirely alone. The institutional infrastructure surrounding the practice of photojournalism is not configured to substantially mitigate most risks to the photographer. Some news organizations provide their journalists with specialized training before they enter conflict zones, but freelancers must rely on their own resources.[28] Advice on reporting in hazardous situations is provided by organizations such as the CPJ, the International News Safety Institute, and the Dart Center for Journalism and Trauma. Some material support is available for injured freelance reporters and their families through groups such as the Rory Peck Trust, which also provides funding to train those working in hostile environments. Photojournalists generally view risk as a personal responsibility and seem reluctant to involve editors in the process of making decisions regarding risk. As Kashi says, "The risks I take are entirely of my own making. I rarely discuss these risks with my editors. It is tacitly understood they care about my welfare and they trust the calculations I make in deciding what to do, where to go, etc."[29] Holmes concurs: "My current agency leaves the level of risk I am willing to take up to me. My previous agency had no real interest in what I had to do to get the pictures, but I never complained and they

　　　　　　　　　　　　　　　　　　　　Michelle L. Woodward

never asked me to do anything I didn't want to do. Editors generally seem to be completely oblivious to what we do so [long as] they can print their paper and get a pay check."[30] Athanasiadis expresses the unstable position of the freelancer when he explains that "my editors seldom check on the risks I undertake, they just accept or turn their noses up at the end offering."[31]

Preparing for work in conflict zones such as Iraq and Afghanistan is a laborious process, as photojournalists must learn first aid, buy protective gear such as body armor, and be proficient with digital technology in the form of cameras, computers, and satellite phones.[32] Some learn languages, study local behavior and dress, and do extensive research on local politics and security conditions. Once on location, photojournalists in the Middle East now find they must regularly alter their daily patterns, limit political conversations with locals, and even assess the distance of a hotel room from the road in case of car bombs.

Changing Modes

Although the wars in Iraq and Afghanistan, the conflict between Israelis and Palestinians, and now war in Libya provide opportunities for dramatic, up-close—and risky—photojournalism, alternative visual modes achieved through less risky practices have been steadily emerging. Photojournalists pursuing these other modes believe that working on conceptual projects away from the drama of violent interactions allows for a deeper perspective, one capable of illuminating the underlying causes of conflict. For example, Ziyah Gafic, a young photojournalist who has won numerous prestigious photography awards, writes on his Web site describing his project Troubled Islam: "This is a series of photo essays on the aftermath of war and violence in the daily life of people living in societies in Europe, Africa and Asia. I aimed to . . . compare [these societies] and to try to understand the circumstances and the political environment that can lead a country to its disintegration and above all to record the consequences for the human condition in these places."[33] Some freelancers are also finding that stepping back from depicting violence entails less direct financial risk. By securing funding from art or photography organizations prior to beginning the project, they no longer need to risk wasting their own resources on work they may not be able to sell to news publications.

There are two major visual trends in contemporary photojournalism that eschew the high-risk, close-up action mode and yet seek to address the subjects of violence and conflict—a documentary-style focus on people and a conceptual focus on landscapes. Laura Junka, a Finnish photographer and PhD candidate in cultural studies in London, struggled with how to depict

Palestinians without relying on the simplistic tropes of victim or terrorist and so spent the summer of 2003 taking photos of Palestinians at leisure, especially on the beach in Gaza.[34] Her intention, however, was not to elide the presence of violence in their lives but to create multilayered images that would capture the quotidian as well as the traces of Israeli occupation. For example, in a photo of a family in a tent at the beach, there are layers of important information that are available only through explanatory captions. The family borrowed the tent from their neighbors, who received it from the Red Cross when their house was bulldozed by the Israeli government in retaliation for one son's involvement in violent resistance to occupation. Knowing this adds a new dimension to the scene, creating a complex sense that everyday happiness and pleasure is mixed with tragedy and loss.[35]

Rula Halawani, a Palestinian photographer based in Jerusalem, worked for the agency Sygma and then Reuters, covering news events in the dominant high-risk mode until 1999 when she started her freelance work and began to develop a new visual mode. She explains the difficulties of her work in comparison to other photographers: "Besides the fact that I was a woman and there were very few other women working, there were even fewer Palestinians working as photojournalists. Most of the others were westerners or Israelis. . . . I was trained like they were to 'get the picture' . . . The problem for me was that the picture was not a separate thing or event to document, but the pictures I was taking were part of me, and I was part of the pictures I was taking." After a boy she knew and had photographed was killed in the street while throwing stones at Israeli soldiers, she made her choice to change directions. "After witnessing his death, I decided I could not continue as a photojournalist, after 9 straight years of photojournalism, I realized I couldn't just keep documenting kids growing up and getting killed. . . . I didn't want to be a photojournalist but I still wanted to take pictures, the problem was I had to find a different way to relate my photography to how I was feeling, to being Palestinian in Palestine."[36] She still considers herself a photojournalist, but one who no longer covers news. In her new projects she rejects the language of traditional photojournalism by refusing to depict dramatic confrontations, strong emotions, or conflict. For example, in Intimacy (2004) she instead focused her lens on the hands of Palestinian civilians and Israeli soldiers as they interact at the Qalandia checkpoint between Jerusalem and the West Bank, the point being to reveal the exercise of power in everyday interactions through the system of military occupation.

Others are attempting to reveal forces of power that lie beyond the control of any individual by showing the traces they leave on the landscape. This mode in particular rejects the pursuit of a "decisive moment." Simon

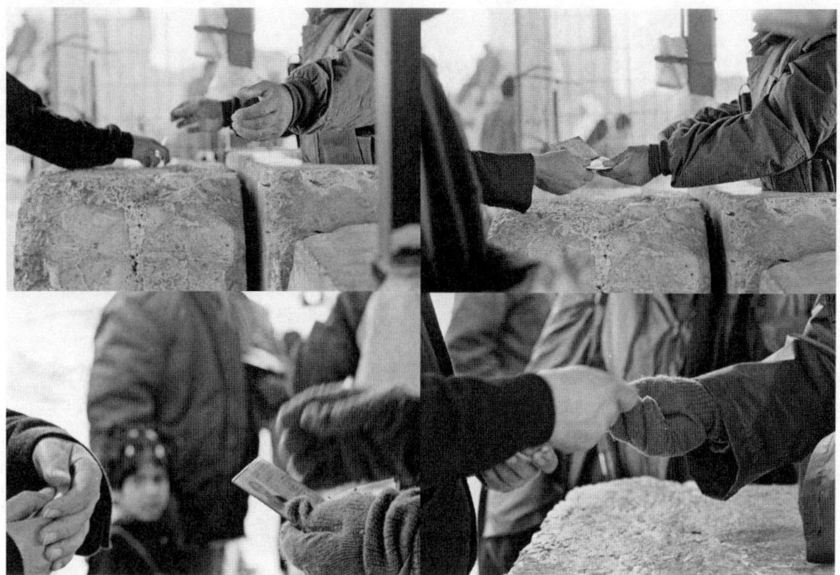

Rula Halawani's Intimacy (2004): Qalandia checkpoint between Jerusalem and Ramallah.

Norfolk is not a traditional photojournalist, since his work appears mainly in the Sunday magazine sections of newspapers, art galleries, and museums, but his subjects—war and genocide—are those of photojournalism. He describes the subject of his photographs as "the way war makes the world we live in. War shapes and designs our society. The landscapes that I look at are created by warfare and conflict."[37] Unlike most photojournalists, he avoids photographing people and events. In describing his project of photographing supercomputers and other military technology used for warfare and surveillance, he explains on his Web site, "Traditional war reporting risks irrelevance if it only concentrates on what can be seen, what can be photographed and filmed when the 'real' war is taking place elsewhere. In the 21st century, war is being visualised in the language of the 1950s, and that is bad for journalism and, ultimately, bad for democracy."[38]

Dirk-Jan Visser is a Dutch freelance photojournalist for the news media who also pursues his own projects. One of these, Blocked, renounces the usual depiction of Israel and Palestine as sites of dramatic confrontations between individuals. Instead Visser has chosen to reveal a more mundane and insidious aspect of the conflict. In a typological and neutral style, with the subjects seen in the middle distance from a uniform straight-on standing perspective, he photographed some of the more than five hundred roadblocks currently placed throughout the West Bank. This project is a departure from the normal visual mode used for depicting conflict, a mode

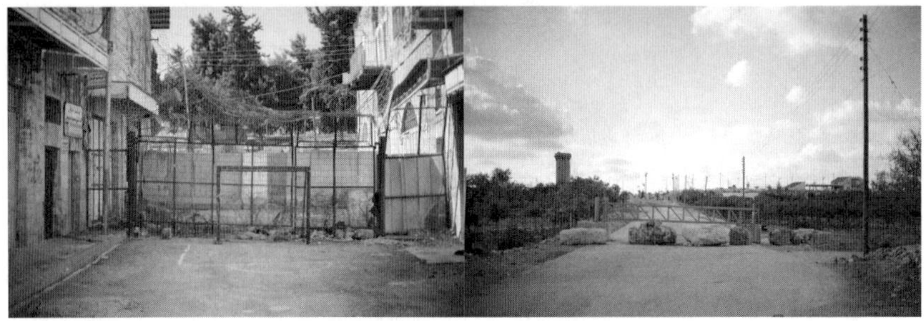

A fence blocking the entrance of Palestinians to Al Sahle Street in the old city of Hebron has been turned into a soccer goal.

The main road is blocked between the Palestinian villages of Bir Nabala and Al Jib, both located in the seam zone between the separation wall and the Green Line, north of Jerusalem.

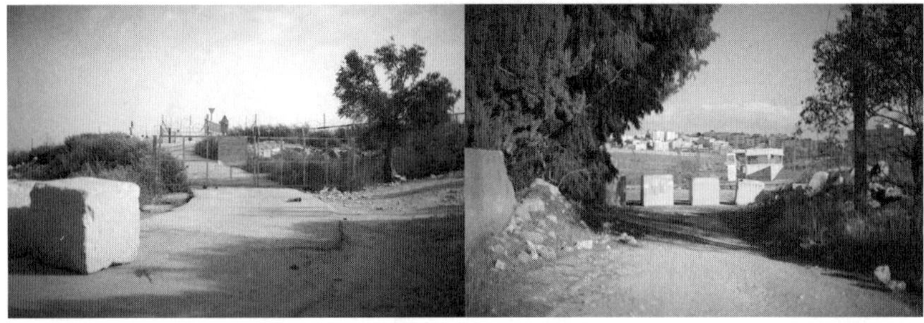

A road blocked near 'Anin in the northwestern West Bank.

The road blocked between Qalandia refugee camp and the village of Qalandia. A three-minute journey now takes twenty-five minutes.

Dirk-Jan Visser's Blocked (2008): roadblocks in the Palestinian West Bank.

that has saturated viewers with images of action. Instead Visser quietly depicts the obstructions without visible people and in the context of the surrounding landscape.

The Israeli photographer Shai Kremer's project Infected Landscape attempts to "reveal how every piece of land has become infected with loaded sediments of the ongoing conflict. Instead of confronting the subject of the Israeli occupation in the way the world is absorbing it through the news, I approach it in a more subtle way. . . . One does not need to shock the audience in order to make an impact. I would rather challenge the viewer to think, using the landscape as a platform for discussion."[39] Kremer has photographed subjects such as military ammunition storage areas, training zones, and Palestinian olive trees chopped down for security reasons in an impassive, unemotional style.

Most of the work of these photographers is presented in art venues, books, or magazines rather than newspapers, and indeed the range of

Michelle L. Woodward

photographs considered to be photojournalism is slowly expanding. As the publication for professional photographers *Photo District News* noted about British photographer Tim Hetherington's project Sleeping Soldiers, "It may be the best photojournalism project we can't show you: A powerful three-screen audio-visual presentation about the war in Afghanistan. The difficulty is that it requires a theater rigged with three projectors."[40] Hetherington, a contributing photographer for *Vanity Fair,* was embedded with U.S. troops in Afghanistan numerous times in the past few years. In addition to more conventional photojournalism (for which he won the 2008 World Press Photo award), he photographed soldiers as they slept and also documented their experiences through audio and video recording. He collected his materials together into multimedia presentations, books, and films such as the Academy Award–nominated documentary *Restrepo.* On April 20, 2011 Hetherington and another acclaimed war photographer, Chris Hondros, were killed by an explosion during heavy fighting in Misurata, Libya. Ed Kashi also creates multimedia slide shows for the Internet and is exploring new ways to engage audiences and enlarge the scope of photojournalism beyond its traditional focus on discrete moments of action.[41]

CONCLUSION

The historically constructed emphasis in photojournalism on capturing a "decisive moment" or "getting the picture" that supposedly conveys the essence of a situation or event has encouraged the creation of a visual mode that fills the frame with up-close, dramatic action. The development of the 35 mm camera in the 1930s and the influential example of driven and daring Magnum photographers such as Robert Capa and later James Nachtwey have gradually enabled and pushed photojournalists to make ever more emotional and engaged images and to take ever greater risks. Risk—physical, psychological, financial, and ethical—in today's world of reduced staff positions at news publications and of increasing freelance work is often shouldered by the photographer alone. Physical risks are valorized within photojournalism and romanticized by the public, while other risks are often downplayed by photographers, lest they be a liability in finding work.[42]

Competing to capture the most intimate, startling, and moving image obscures quieter realities. Focusing on single, dramatic moments pulls attention away from the broader political and structural forces that underlie crisis, conflict, and oppression. Documentary photography, which entails a long-term, slow exploration of a single issue or place, is a mode of visual depiction that can complement the speed and haste characterizing most photojournalism, and that thus can provide insights into both micro and macro levels of society. Even during the "golden age" of picture magazines, from the 1930s through the 1960s, there have rarely been adequate platforms for the mass distribution of documentary images that challenge the status quo or deepen the public's understanding of core issues. Photojournalism, ubiquitous in print publications and on the Internet, is still the genre of photography that most people rely on for visual information about the state of our world.

Since photojournalism privileges the capture of dramatic moments, photographers will always be expected to rush toward conflict, tragedy, and disaster. However, some photojournalists are questioning the prevailing risky visual mode on the grounds that emotional, dramatic images do not illuminate what causes and maintains conflict, poverty, and other social problems. While different visual modes—such as a quiet focus on the everyday and mundane, or on landscapes that show traces of macro forces—may or may not prove to be more informative, these ambitious efforts to find new visual languages for photojournalism are a positive and long-overdue development.

Notes

1. Style in photography is created by the interaction of formal visual elements such as light, color, focus, angle of view, and composition, which are the result of the photographer's choices and skills in using particular equipment. These choices are shaped by changing trends within the professional and social world of photography, technology, markets, and working conditions. Ultimately, style creates meaning and guides audiences in their interpretations.

2. Quoted in David W. Dunlap and James Estrin, "From the Archive: Not New, Never Easy," Lens: Photography, Video and Visual Journalism blog, posted September 23, 2009, http://lens.blogs.nytimes.com/2009/09/23/archive-5/.

3. Howard Chapnick, *Truth Needs No Ally: Inside Photojournalism* (Columbia: University of Missouri Press, 1994), 346.

4. I argue elsewhere that the photography agency Magnum Photos was influential in creating a certain visual style that has played a crucial role in defining what is considered exemplary photojournalism. The institution promoted a style characterized by the aesthetics of drama, documentary realism, narrative, and artistic expression to craft highly ordered, clearly arranged compositions emphasizing a revealing moment, expression, or gesture that implies an important understanding of a given situation. See Michelle Woodward, "The Construction of Photojournalism: Visual Style and Branding in the Magnum Photos Agency" (master's thesis, Massachusetts Institute of Technology, 2002).

5. Cornell Capa, introduction to *The Concerned Photographer,* ed. Cornell Capa (New York: Grossman, 1968).

6. Henri Cartier-Bresson, *The Mind's Eye: Writings on Photography and Photographers* (New York: Aperture Foundation, 1999), 42.

                                    Michelle L. Woodward

7. For an extended analysis of how photographs of this conflict have changed over time, see Michelle Woodward, "Photographic Style and the Depiction of Israeli-Palestinian Conflict since 1948," *Jerusalem Quarterly*, no. 31 (2007): 6–21.

8. Image taken by a unidentified stringer/Reuters, captioned "An Israeli border policeman and a Palestinian scream at each other in the old city of Jerusalem, October 13, 2000, as the Palestinian is refused entry to the Al-Aqsa Mosque for Friday prayers," *Time*, October 23, 2000, 34–35.

9. A documentary film about his work is titled simply *War Photographer*, produced and directed by Christian Frei (2001).

10. Ed Kashi, e-mail message to author, December 6, 2009.

11. Nancy Roth, "The Elements of Style," *Afterimage*, 14 no. 3 (1986): 6.

12. Brian Stelter, "A World of Risk for a New Brand of Journalist," *New York Times*, June 15, 2009, B1.

13. Committee to Protect Journalists, "CPJ 2009 Prison Census: Freelance Journalists under Fire," December 8, 2009, http://www.cpj.org/reports/2009/12/freelance-journalists-in-prison-cpj-2009-census.php.

14. Ian Austen, "For Novice Journalists, Rising Risks in Conflict Zones," *New York Times*, November 30, 2009, B7.

15. Anne Holmes, e-mail message to author, October 26, 2009.

16. Iason Athanasiadis, e-mail message to author, November 21, 2009.

17. Kashi, e-mail message to author.

18. Fareed Zakaria, "Attacks on the Press, 2009: Preface," Committee to Protect Journalists, February 16, 2010, http://cpj.org/2010/02/attacks-on-the-press-2009preface.php.

19. However, limits remain on the actual content of photographs of war. American editors in particular have long rejected images of American or allied casualties. Photojournalists balk at this limitation and sometimes attempt to push the boundaries, risking their access to the battlefield. For a discussion of recent examples, see Michael Kamber and Tim Arango, "4,000 US Deaths and a Handful of Images," *New York Times*, July 26, 2008.

20. Austen, "For Novice Journalists, Rising Risks in Conflict Zones."

21. Howard Kurtz, "Journalism's Rising Risk Factor: Hostage Release Underscores Dilemmas of News Gathering," *Washington Post*, August 28, 2006, C1.

22. Committee to Protect Journalists, "On Assignment: Covering Conflicts Safely: Guide for Reporting in Hazardous Situations," February 2003, http://cpj.org/reports/2003/02/journalist-safety-guide.php.

23. Ali Sharayah, "Q&A with Saudi's First Accredited Female Photojournalist, Mona Al Jeddawi," *Asharq Al-Awsat*, March 24, 2008, http://www.aawsat.com/english/news.asp?section=5&id=12199.

24. "Breaking the Lens That Binds you—Gaza's Women Photojournalists," Menassat, July 30, 2009, http://www.menassat.com/?q=en/news-articles/6983-breaking-lens-binds-you-gazas-women-photojournalists.

25. Kashi, e-mail message to author.

26. Holmes, e-mail message to author.

27. Daryl Lang, "Disembedded: Marines Send a War Photographer Packing," *Photo District News,* July 17, 2008, http://www.pdnonline.com/pdn/esearch/article_display.jsp?vnu_content_id=1003828935.

28. Charlotte Sector, "Intense Training Prepares Journalists for War: Week-long Courses Offer Realistic Take on Hostile Environments," ABC News, January 30, 2006, http://abcnews.go.com/International/story?id=1557505.

29. Kashi, e-mail message to author.

30. Holmes, e-mail message to author.

31. Athanasiadis, e-mail message to author.

32. For an example of what photojournalists find they need for operating in dangerous or remote locations, see this discussion on Lightstalkers, a networking site for photojournalists: http://www.lightstalkers.org/posts/gearing-up.

33. Ziyah Gafic, Troubled Islam, http://www.ziyahgafic.ba/photo.php.

34. Junka's writing on photography is also insightful. See Laura Junka, "Camping in the Third Space: Agency, Representation, and the Politics of Gaza Beach," *Public Culture* 18, no. 2 (2006): 348–59; and Junka, "The Politics of Gaza Beach: At the Edge of the Two Intifadas," *Third Text* 20, nos. 3–4 (2006): 417–28.

35. Alexandra Avakian, Laura Junka, and Michelle Woodward, "Regional Survey on Photography in the Middle East," webinar on OPEN-i, November 25, 2009, http://open-i.ning.com.

36. Rula Halawani, "Arts and Politics in Palestine through My Photographs," ArteEast, April 2005, http://www.arteeast.org/virtualgallery/apr05_halawani/arteeast-vg-halawani-4.html.

37. Geoff Manaugh, "War/Photography: An Interview with Simon Norfolk," BLDGBLOG blog, posted November 30, 2006, http://bldgblog.blogspot.com/2006/11/warphotography-interview-with-simon.html.

38. Simon Norfolk, "Ascension Island: The Panopticon," http://www.simonnorfolk.com.

39. Shai Kremer, "Statement," Julie Saul Gallery, http://www.saulgallery.com/kremer/statement.html.

40. Daryl Lang, "Tim Hetherington Tackles the Emotions of War with 'Sleeping Soldiers,'" *Photo District News,* May 27, 2009, http://www.pdnonline.com/pdn/content_display/photo-news/photojournalism/e3i780ed1bb3c22fbcd545403517d76b877.

41. For example, see his project on oil in the Niger Delta. Ed Kashi, Curse of the Black Gold, http://www.curseoftheblackgoldbook.com.

42. For example, some photojournalists who covered the World Trade Center collapse on September 11, 2001 have said they are reluctant to admit to PTSD or other health issues lest they damage their careers by seeming less capable to employers. See the excellent article by Anthony Depalma, "Suffering in Silence: Ground Zero's Other Victims," *Columbia Journalism Review,* March–April 2009.

                                        Michelle L. Woodward

ROD STONEMAN

Chance and Change

THE ROLE OF CHANCE IN FILM

Alea iacta est (The die is cast).

Our understanding of abstract concepts is often inflected through work-ing with them in the rough-and-tumble of concrete experience. Arriving in Maputo, Mozambique, in November 1990, just after the feature film *Child from the South* had commenced production, I discovered that over 90 percent of the money in the contingency section of the budget (normally 10–15 percent of the total) had been spent by the second day of the shoot, and I could immediately see that the production was in trouble. When the producer tried to reassure me that there would be no need for further con-tingency spending for the rest of the shoot—"because nothing else is going to go wrong"—I found myself trying to outline and define a conceptual basis for the essentially contingent nature of experience, which is inevitably subject to unforeseen circumstances or chance effects. This would be true in relation to a film being shot in much easier conditions, let alone one with problematic logistics, transport, and communications in a place with limited periods of electricity most days and where we were warned not to travel beyond city limits after nightfall as armed groups of RENAMO[1] were lurking on the outskirts of Maputo and the civil war raged on.

Beginning with some reflections on the functions of chance, representing uncontrollable and often unpredictable factors in filmmaking, I will try to connect these thoughts to my experience in commissioning television and

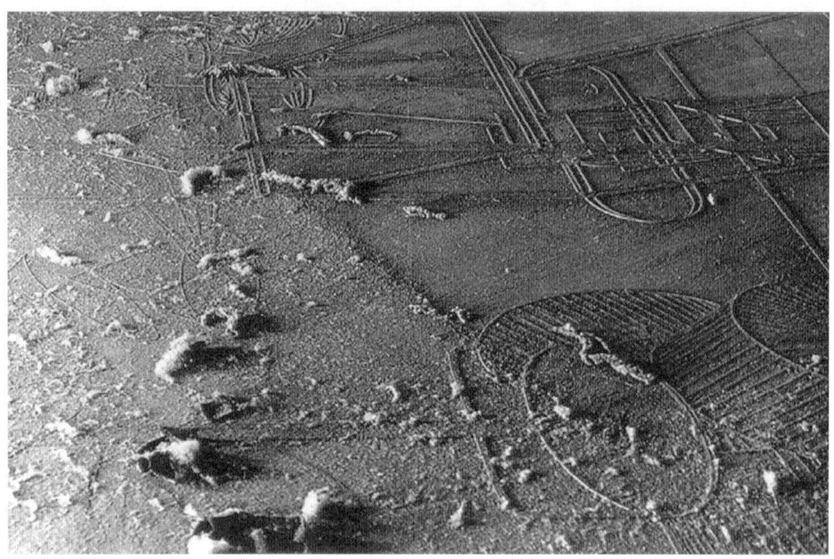

Marcel Duchamp and Man Ray, *Elevage de poussière* (Dust Breeding, 1920).

film in Britain and Ireland over twenty years. I worked for Channel 4 from 1983 to 1993, during the first ten years after it was set up as an innovative British television station and as one of the first European "publisher broadcasters" to commission independents to make all the programs it transmitted. In 1993 I moved to Ireland to help set up the Irish Film Board, a newly reconstituted national film agency. Inevitably, there were many differences between these roles and organizations, but they had much in common regarding the concept and practice of working with risk. To face the risk involved in making any film is to acknowledge the role of chance in the uncertainties of the world.

Chance always has an important role in film, and sometimes it is deployed in benign and generative ways in creative work. Avant-garde explorations in the visual arts have consciously used procedures that draw chance into focus, as in the work of the French artist Marcel Duchamp, who had some association with the Surrealists.[2] In his *3 stoppages étalon* (3 Standard Stoppages, 1913–14), he dropped three one-meter lengths of string from a height of one meter onto a horizontal plane; the cord, "distorting itself as it pleases," created "a new shape of the measure of length." Duchamp recorded the random undulating positions of the strings, describing them as "a piece of canned chance."[3] This work anticipates his *Elevage de poussière* (Dust Breeding), in which he allowed dust to collect on the glass surface of *La mariée mise à nu par ses célibataires, même* (The Bride Stripped Bare by

                                                    Rod Stoneman

Her Bachelors, Even, 1915–23). Man Ray photographed the dust in 1920, registering the passage of time, the chance accumulation of secretions.

The shapes of the "Standard Stoppages" are transposed and used as templates for the contours of the "Capillary Tubes" that transmit the "illuminating gas" from the "Malic Moulds" to the conical "Sieves," which are delicately colored with the accumulated dust, which was fixed with spray adhesive on the glass—Duchamp explained each of the complex elements of *The Bride*, also known as *The Large Glass*, in a set of facsimile notes in *The Green Box*. Indeed, the accidental played another unanticipated role in this major work. In 1926, badly packed and laid flat for transport, it bounced on a long truck ride from the Brooklyn Museum to Connecticut; after the journey the glass was found to be shattered in great symmetrical arcs. When the owner, Katherine Dreier, brought herself to tell Duchamp about the disaster, he accepted the breakage as a "chance completion" and declared that the piece, which had taken him eight years to make, was finally finished.[4]

In historically disparate periods modernist projects have continued to experiment with and examine the parameters of the process of drawing chance forward as a structuring factor in making artworks. Recalling the eighteenth-century Romantics' Aeolian harp, which made music as the wind played gently upon its strings, in *Seven Days* (1974) Chris Welsby placed a camera on an equatorial stand and set in train a pattern of image and sound controlled by the specific local weather conditions as they happened. Systemic films like Malcolm LeGrice's *Berlin Horse* (1970) or Mike Leggett's *Shepherd's Bush* (1971) ran loops of different lengths in motion together in order to create and discover the final pattern of their interaction. This paralleled adjacent work in minimalist music by composers like Steve Reich and Terry Riley. John Cage's conceptual pieces invited unpredictable factors into their composition and performance. Cage conceived *4'33"* in 1952; often called *Silence,* it actually focuses our awareness on the unpredictable role of ambient sound in public spatial environments. He explained its provenance: "Many people in our society now go around the streets and in the buses and so forth playing radios with earphones on and they don't hear the world around them."[5]

Whether in music or in film, this time-based work was unique in its embrace of the aleatoric, characterized by accidental or indeterminate elements, allowing the entrance of enhanced chance factors to make a form. Some of the experimental film was labeled "structural materialist," and many exemplary and systematic pieces were created within the interactive and discursive context that existed around the London Filmmakers' Co-op in the 1970s. Made for smaller audiences, some of the more acute examples

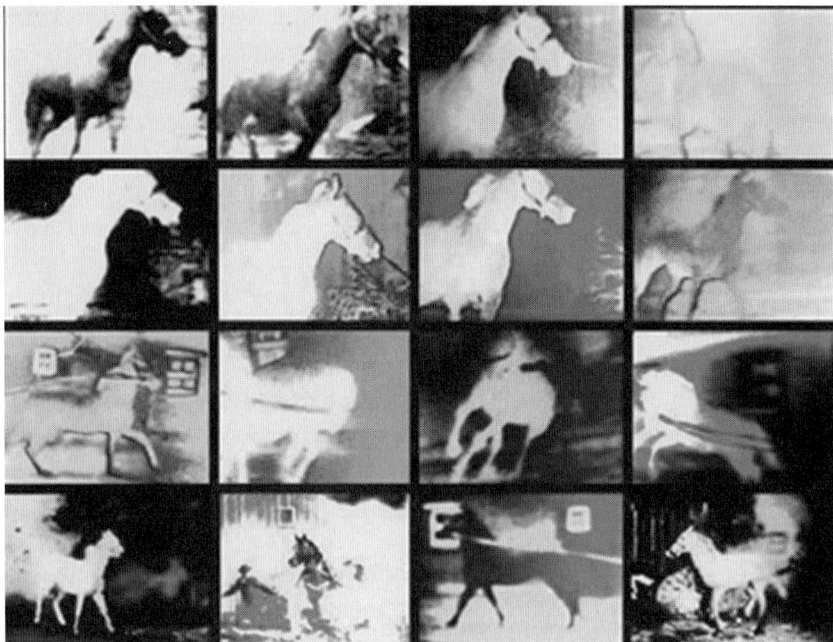

Malcolm LeGrice, *Berlin Horse* (1970).

of experimental art explicitly drew the role of chance and thus nonauthorial elements into focus within "open works."

Leaving aside experimentation by practitioners of the avant-garde, there should be some degree of openness to chance even when filming the largest-budget work, as these budgets allow more resources to exercise control over the aleatoric. While the element of chance can be limited or reduced by filming under controlled conditions in a studio rather than on location, there are so many factors and determinations on the fine distinctions of sound and image that pass in front of the camera and microphone in the moment of recording that even highly controlled conditions encounter a complex of unexpected nuances. This is the unruly, perverse, obstinate, or unmanageable texture and shape of the real, referred to by Noel Burch in his chapter "Chance and Its Functions" in *Theory of Film Practice* as the "refractory nature of film material."[6] Anyone who has worked with editing processes will have glimpsed both the plasticity of sound and image and also their occasional recalcitrance.

Historically there are filmmakers who specifically embraced a conscious degree of improvisation in their method of realization: Roberto Rossellini, while filming *Viaggio in Italia* (Voyage in Italy, 1954) in Naples was contacted when the newly discovered imprints of bodies were exca-

                                                    Rod Stoneman

vated from beneath the volcanic ash in nearby Pompeii. He constructed a scene that integrated the (re)staged unveiling of the plaster casts of the bodies of a male and female, presumed to be lovers who died together, in front of Ingrid Bergman and George Sanders, the actors playing Mr. and Mrs. Joyce,[7] whose relationship has reached a crisis and is in danger of disintegrating. The glimpse of the ancient lovers who died in each other's arms in AD 79 emerging from the ashes of centuries is emotionally pivotal in the finished film narrative.

John Huston specifically threw himself into the arms of the aleatoric: as he put it himself, "I court accident."[8] For *Beat the Devil* in 1953 he assembled a cast and headed for Italy with a draft scenario described candidly by Peter Viertel, who cowrote it with Anthony Veiller, as "[l]acking a central plot. The dialogue was good and the characters were unusual, but the structure was lacking."[9] Humphrey Bogart, who invested in the film, initially saw it as "a chance to make some real money,"[10] but then Huston warned him, "We haven't got a script, and I don't know what the hell is going to come of this. It may be a disaster. In fact, it's got all the earmarks of a disaster." He was relieved by Bogart's irrefutable response: "Hell, it's only money."[11] They arrived in Italy with a cast and budget but no script or scriptwriter, apparently finding Truman Capote "on the street in Rome," after which they all decamped to a villa in Ravello, a small town south of Naples, to make the movie.

By all accounts the shoot was a bunch of friends having an extended party. Approaching the film on a highly improvisational basis, those involved in the production process essentially made it up as they went along. With production manager Jack Clayton, Huston developed a number of ruses, withholding scripted dialogue from actors until the moment before they had to perform on the pretext that he wanted them to remain fresh by not anticipating their lines. This gave him time to write the lines en route. Arriving on set in the morning, Huston made use of delaying tactics: devising elaborate setups, laying track for complex camera movements, removing walls and setting lighting: maneuvers that would divert and preoccupy the crew. In the meantime he would go upstairs with Capote to script the scene to be shot later that day: "We worked very hard and tried to keep ahead of the picture." This inventive strategy embodied an openness to the aleatoric, the role of chance; Huston wrote that actors, if "given time and freedom, will fall naturally into their places, discover when and where to move and you will have your shot."[12]

There is visible evidence of dramatic interaction with chance when filmmakers take production into environments that are beyond their control. In *Medium Cool* Haskell Wexler placed his lead actress (wearing a bright

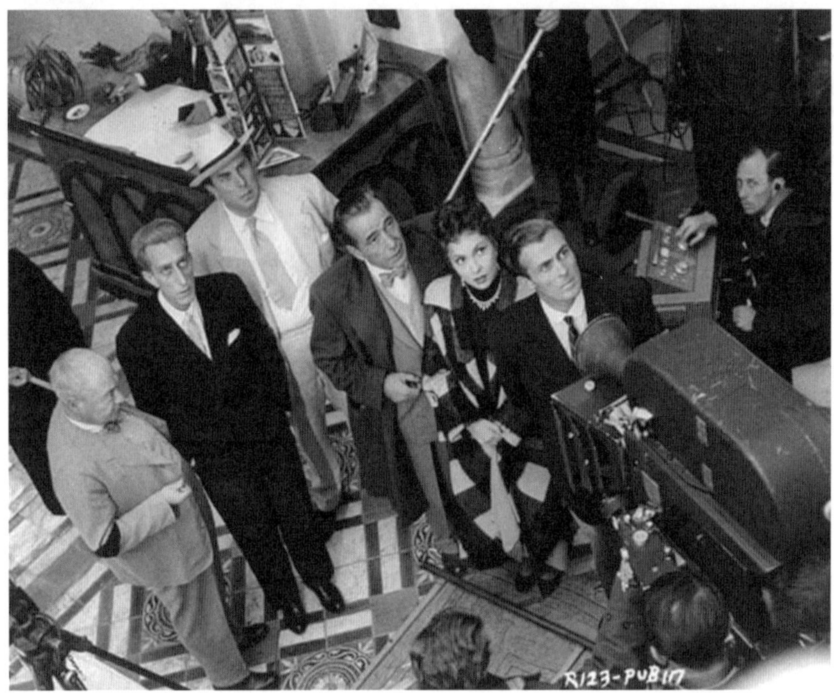

John Huston, *Beat the Devil* (1953).

yellow dress so that she could be seen in the mêlée) in the demonstration staged in front of the Democratic convention in Chicago on August 28, 1968. A sketchy narrative plays through a situation that rapidly and spectacularly became what many witnesses described as a "police riot," with substantial indiscriminate use of state violence. The filmmaker, dissolving those permeable boundaries between documentary and fiction, took his fictional protagonist, playing a journalist, and inserted her into a factual situation that was evidently and dramatically a long way beyond his control.[13]

One can see the experimental domain as a space for research taking place outside the mercantile pressures of commercial film, but there is considerable continuity between these works and the examples of larger-scale feature enterprises that work through different degrees of openness to chance and develop diverse ways of bringing this process to the foreground. They share an approach to creativity that welcomes the dynamic of improvisation and elicits fast and inventive responses—a dialectical interaction between unforeseen, unpredictable factors and planning and anticipation. The intrusions of "natural" contingencies set up patterns of interference between the controlled and the accidental. Artists' use of chance is a small-

                                   Rod Stoneman

scale encounter with the aleatoric, and what we know as "risk" takes place within chance, for the operation of factors outside prediction or control may lead to either harmful or fortuitous results.

Boethius, writing *The Consolation of Philosophy* in AD 524, refers to Aristotle in defining chance as an "unexpected result from the coincidence of certain causes." As he makes clear, it may be unforeseen but that does not mean that it is random or outside causality.[14] Thus chance is understood as the noncontrolled and often unexpected factors that can be invited into filmmaking as beneficial elements, or guarded against as negative or even dangerous intrusions. American underground filmmaker Kenneth Anger condemned the imposition of "rigid intellectual control" leading to works that become "'ends in themselves'—exercises in highly refined style but lacking the irreplaceable qualities of improvisation."[15] Clearly chance can be catalytic in the stimulation of new forms of image/sound and narrative play; "homo ludens"[16] finds different ways of operating within the oxymoron of "controlled chance."

Industrial Experience

Slightly or nearly indecent.

—*Definition of "risky" in The Penguin English Dictionary, 1965*

Television

The unlikely experience of emerging from *Screen* theory into commissioning programs for the newly set up Channel 4 television in 1983 certainly involved coming to operational terms with actual risk in film-production processes, although this was never posed as a dilemma or reason for trepidation at the time. There were of course wrong calls, miscalculations, and mistakes that I made, risks that I took that didn't come off at all well. Yet, somehow the complex reflexivity of the structural theory I had encountered as a student and as a member of the *Screen* board was helpful in trying to understand the process of film commissioning.[17]

The foundational principles in Channel 4 began with a radical pluralism that embraced range and diversity. "There will be some diamonds, but also some dogs," was a phrase from those times that pointed toward an understanding that supporting an increasing multiplicity of independent production and taking greater risks would inevitably lead to some programs and films that just didn't turn out well. I worked in the Department of Independent Film and Video,[18] and we were at the further edge of the station's constitutional remit to support "innovation in form and content," pushing the boundaries of what was available on British television. We absolutely did not see it as our job to "play it safe."

Of course we could easily have reduced risk and saved money by commissioning a smaller proportion of new programs and by using our budget to purchase a much larger proportion of finished films. If one goes to a festival or a market and sees films that can be bought and transmitted, what one is acquiring is completely clear and fixed in advance. This approach would also have made the budget go much further—paradoxically, the market logic inverts a reasonable rationale—for purchases were significantly cheaper than presales or commissions. Committing support to a film before it was made would cost five to ten times more than purchasing the same film as a known quantity, as a finished product. But we were all clear that the hazardous business of commissioning and making new programs and films kept our screen lively and energetic, fresh and topical.

Dangers and risks took many forms. An example from the political domain arose when I commissioned *Mother Ireland,* a documentary directed by Anne Crilly, who was a member of the Derry Film and Video Workshop, located in the nationalist Bogside in that city—a clear, if implicit, position in every sense. From our point of view in Channel 4, the workshop represented direct speech from a community often talked about but rarely able to speak directly or to air its own views through its own programs. But a dramatic and entirely unforeseen transformation in *Mother Ireland'*s fortune occurred when, within days of the delivery of the completed program on March 2, 1988, Mairéad Farrell, one of eleven people interviewed in it, was shot by the British Special Air Service in Gibraltar. I remember seeing her photograph on the front page of the *Sunday Times* and vaguely recognizing her, eventually working out that I must have seen her interviewed in the rough cuts of the documentary (which would not have had names or captions) I had viewed in the previous months. Her status as interviewee was instantly transformed from an ex-prisoner, who had become a Sinn Fein activist while studying at Queen's University Belfast, to someone who had clearly rejoined the Irish Republican Army on release and who had been killed on active service. In an unprecedented procedure the entire board of Channel 4 watched this now problematic program and, to cut a long story short,[19] this unexpected turn of events led to a change in the status of the program and extensive delays. It was eventually transmitted three years later in *Banned,* a season about censorship.

Issues of politics leading to the dangers of censorship were not the only unexpected risks that could intercept transmission. Calculation of the potential transgression of the parameters of sexual mores often necessi-

                                              Rod Stoneman

tated careful discussion with the filmmaker in advance. We approached the excisions and reductions necessary to make a film transmittable with the intention of keeping as much as possible of the meaning and integrity of the work while frankly softening some of the impact of its deliberately aggressive transgressions. I would normally achieve this by decreasing the duration of the incident or by covering over specific images. Apart from the principle of cutting with the filmmaker's consent, I always tried to use black rectangles to blank out offensive parts of the frame in order to make cuts overt—to show what we couldn't show. In order to be able to transmit Dusan Makavejev's classic 1971 film *WR misterije organizma* (WR Mysteries of the Organism), the director superimposed gently moving goldfish over the tumescent genitals depicted in the (faked[20]) Sexpol newsreel in the opening sequence and a psychedelic spiral over the plaster caster's work with the editor of *Screw* magazine.

This version of the practice of censorship also arose in relation to *Salt, Saliva, Sperm and Sweat,* for example. Made in Australia during 1987 by Philip Brophy, it espouses an aggressive strategy of shock in order to attack the repetitious, alienated routines of office work and everyday life. The hour-long film was constructed with rhyming sections organized by the alliterative bodily fluids of the title. The necessity of editing a version that could be shown on television had been discussed in advance and agreed in principle with the director, as it had been clear enough from the most cursory glance that the complete uncut version could not be transmitted. The parameters of the avant-garde, bad taste, and perversity exceeded the limits of what was broadcastable in Britain at that time by a wide margin. Editing to achieve a transmittable "television version" was carried out at Channel 4 with the filmmaker present: we obscured a scrotum shot from behind during intercourse, removed a turd dropping into a transparent toilet bowl, excised the verbal exclamation "Sprog of fucking Jesus!" (in response to food in the office canteen), and softened the protagonist's incestuous stare (angle/reverse/angle) directed toward his younger brother's buttocks being dried after a bath. Transmitted at 11 p.m. on a Monday night, long after the "family viewing threshold," the film was preceded by a presentation announcement specifically warning the audience that it was about to see a "television version" of a film that still "may offend some viewers." There was no significant discernible reaction from the viewing public.[21]

Over the first ten years of Channel 4's existence I witnessed the sad slow process of tightening and standardizing the systems of production and truncating the range of content that appeared on-screen. Cost controllers couldn't understand how precarious, low-budget projects came through and were invariably completed—the personal, political, and artistic

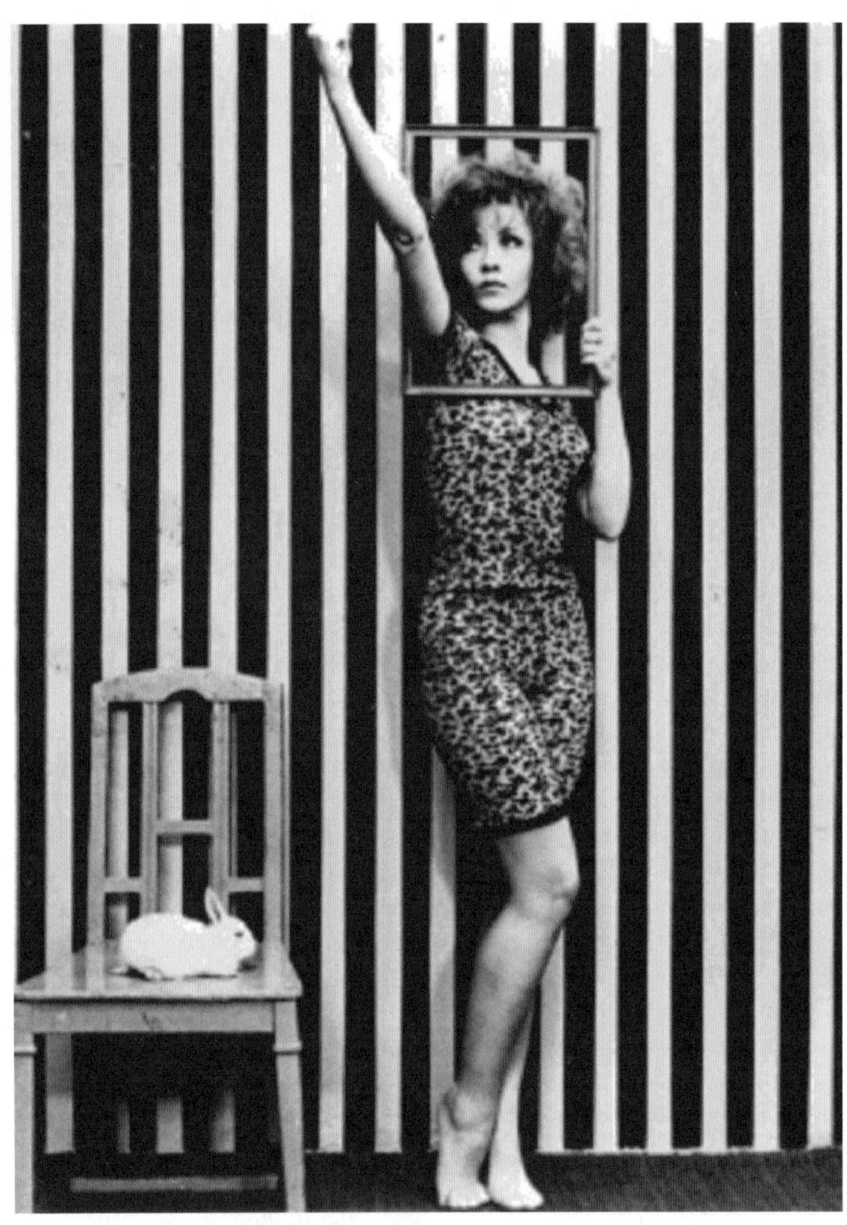

Dusan Makavejev, *WR misterije organizma* (WR Mysteries of the Organism, 1971).

motivations and determinations of an artisanal independent working on a small production were unfamiliar to the average television financial executive, who would thus begin to seek to impose an "executive producer" with more experience. This procedure was rarely efficacious and generally wasted too much of the already tight budget allocated for the program. But the apparatus felt more secure with the delusory safety of a known name (known to the Channel 4 cost controller) "supervising" the project. In fact, the evolution of the channel in the ten years I was there saw the virtual eradication of programs produced by artisanal filmmakers "out of their front rooms." A growing professionalization required that any individual director's bright and original idea for a film be housed in established independent production companies that supervised production and took sections of the budget and the eventual production fee (previously used to finance speculative research for new projects). Smoothing out some of the rough edges of personal program making no doubt reduced the number and nature of the "dogs" in the schedule, but it also eliminated a significant proportion of the "diamonds."

The bravery of Channel 4's period of initiation gradually receded, and concurrent with tighter supervision of production there was an introverted movement toward our own conception of our needs. Commissioning meetings stopped being about asking independents the question "What idea for a program do you have that's fantastic?" Instead the possibility of production was increasingly posed as "Can someone develop a format that will introduce young people to gardening? We're thinking about thirteen times twenty-six minutes, to be scheduled midweek in the early evening?"

At some point preceding the slow descent of Channel 4 the founding chief executive Jeremy Isaacs proffered me some specific advice, writing the Latin adage "Suaviter in modo, fortiter in re" (Soft in approach, hard in deed) on a scrap of paper. Risk taking was the center of our commissioning activity, and it was somewhat protected as an accepted and inevitable dimension of the complex and sometimes awkward work that it was our role to encourage. There had to be some explicable basis for making a judgment or taking a decision; institutions demand something more of a rationale than, in Michael Grade's apocryphal phrase, "It seemed like a good idea at the time."[22] As individuals making commissioning decisions we had to be something like fearless, but not reckless. I remember withdrawing tentative support from a project when it became clear that a young Croatian filmmaker intended to place herself in jeopardy while filming the 1991 siege of Dubrovnik during the breakup of Yugoslavia and the foundation of Croatia. We were not a current affairs department and there was no reason to encourage someone deliberately to put herself in physical danger to achieve a program that could be broadcast.

Sometimes people constructed their explanations after the event. I came across a rare example of defensive documentation being manufactured retrospectively when, after an educational series had not worked well and received a bad reception at the weekly internal program review meeting, an assistant showed me a colleague's backdated and unsent memo warning the independent producer that he foresaw serious problems with the series of programs. There may have been considerable pressure on those executives who sought advancement in their careers, but I came from a different and more critical perspective outside television and at some level was surprised to be there anyway. There was always a sense that risks were taking place over the horizon, but, like Alfred E. Newman,[23] I always felt, "What—me worry?" or, in Gertrude Stein's version: "Anything scares me, anything scares anyone but really after all considering how dangerous everything is nothing is really very frightening."[24] It seemed to me that as long as there was a reasonable explanation for the original commitment, we could deal with the eventuality of a film moving into crisis or coming off the rails.

I remember ringing the RUC (Royal Ulster Constabulary) when, during the making of *Hush-a-bye Baby* (1990), a feature film being directed by Margo Harkin, another member of the Derry Film and Video Workshop, a leading actress was arrested during the shoot. She had already been extensively filmed and for continuity reasons was essential for the filming of further scenes. It was clear from the brief dialogue I had with a rather dry RUC Special Branch policeman that we came from very different worlds:

"I'm from Channel 4 and we are supporting the production of a low-budget feature by the Derry workshop. Your arrest of Rosena Brown earlier today is a big problem for us as she is one of the main actresses in the film and her continued detention is threatening our production schedule."

"Well, it may not have occurred to you, but we are fighting a war here . . ."

Pause.

"Would it be possible to give a specific time or date for her release from questioning in the near future so that we can factor it into the schedule for filming?"

"We find in general that indicating the precise end of the interrogation process in advance renders that process less effective."[25]

When he took over from Jeremy Isaacs in November 1987, Michael Grade made a liberating remark to commissioning staff on his accession; speaking in the small basement studio, he said pointedly, "I would rather

                                          Rod Stoneman

you made the wrong decisions than no decisions." His affirmation was a necessary release for overcautious commissioners who might hover hesitantly around a swathe of possible proposals, and it was helpful for independent producers who were held indefinitely in limbo while waiting for commissioning decisions to be made.

Too often in our department we felt we were an alibi for the channel as a whole—a high proportion of still images from our programs illustrated the annual report as examples of innovation, and yet we always found it difficult to extend our overall budget or airtime. However, gradually we supplemented those transmissions in the tundra of the schedule for *The Eleventh Hour* and *Midnight Underground* with mid-evening magazine formats like *Out, South, The Media Show,* and *Critical Eye,* and occasionally there were examples of our most audacious programs taking center stage. During the 10 p.m. transmission of Derek Jarman's *Blue* by Channel 4 and Radio 3 on September 19, 1993, the television screen radiated a pure, Yves Klein blue into living rooms while a cluster of voices circled the filmmaker's desperate predicament—going blind through retinal deterioration brought about by AIDS. As with Claude Lanzmann's *Shoah* (1985), it was understood that this particular film could not be interrupted with ad breaks, and so the station took the brave decision to forego the advertisements and revenue for the duration of the program.

Cinema

Moving in 1993 from television to film-production funding when I was appointed CEO of Bord Scannán na hÉireann (the Irish Film Board), the reconstituted Irish national film agency, I saw some continuities in the approach to different scales of exposure, although there were also some differences and specificities as a result of working for a government semistate agency in Ireland at that time. I tried to formulate something specifically about the risk taking involved in these roles in section 6 of an essay on the differences involved in these two media, "Nine Notes on Cinema and Television," published in *Big Picture, Small Screen:*

RISK

Novitatem meam contemnunt ego illorum ignaviam /
They despise my novelty, I their timidity.

In their different ways the commissioners and financiers of film and television nearly always avow some commitment to taking high risks, working with first time filmmakers, making films without well-known actors or stars. Everyone manifests a predisposition toward the new, the innovative. Indeed television uses cinema to provide it with new ideas, new material, to take risks for it. The desire to "bring in new talent" has led to the proliferation of a plethora of short film schemes. It is also a way of cordoning off and placing troublesome new talent in a safety net: surrounding a tyro director with the scaffolding of experience—"they can't go too far wrong with a brilliant cinematographer in front, an experienced editor alongside, an established producer behind."

But, despite good intentions, it is very difficult to achieve consistent risk-taking under sustained pressure. Hesitancy, timidity and conservatism take different forms in cinema and television. Television is governed by the ineluctable algebra of *high risk equals low audience equals lower levels of investment.* Actually it can be argued that the opposite is true: first-time directors need significantly larger budgets to support longer preparation, an editor working alongside them from an earlier stage, and five- rather than six-day weeks in order to take pressure off the process of the shoot. But this would be to invert the logic of the market. However there are some advantages in working with lower budgets because there is less pressure on this production space.

The television micro debate about innovation and risk takes place following the dangerous change in climate that has occurred over the last decade in European public service broadcasting. The insertion of commercial pressures has had an inevitable long-term effect on editorial postures even in some non-commercial stations.[26]

Setting up the new operation of the reconstituted Irish Film Board, we would generally provide 30–50 percent of the budget of feature films, and the biggest dangers often arose around closing the convoluted, many-layered coproduction agreements as production began. Somehow the pressure of the commencement of the shoot was necessary to push the final formal legal and financial agreement through, a distracting problem for all involved while the film lifts off. Once the financing was closed, the film was fully insured or "bonded." As with traditional forms of insurance, there was a calculation of financial risk and redemption within the specific terms of any claim, but bonding companies worked closely and cooperatively with financiers at all stages. As the completion bond was not valid until all the interlocking contracts (sometimes the paperwork would be two or three feet thick) were closed, this was a moment of real jeopardy. The fact that

                                          Rod Stoneman

it took place in the demanding first week of the shoot was a potential distraction, and this at a time when everyone should have been concentrating on the intricate and multifarious effort of making a film work. More than one project collapsed in preproduction or the first weeks of production in this period—with extremely negative side effects for casts and crews, who worried about being paid, and for potential cofinanciers, who were nervous about losing their investment. For these reasons we at the board were involved in the strenuous exertions to avoid films collapsing in this period, although these attempts stopped short of bailing a film out by pouring extra film board money into its budget.

At Easter 1994 the Irish-language fiction, *An Gobán Saor,* started production in Feakle, County Clare, with only a small proportion of its finance in place. Initially disconcerted by the startling irresponsibility of engaging a cast and crew and beginning the production of a film without the money to make it, I drove out to the location on Easter Monday, April 5, 1994, and found that it had been left to me to explain the seriousness of the situation to a very disgruntled crew during the lunch break in the bus used for location catering. I promised the crew that the film board would use its best endeavors over the next seven days to pull the rest of the funding together.[27] It actually took ten days; the film came very close to collapse after seven, and I learned not to make promises and offer deadlines that I could not deliver.

We became used to the delicate and difficult question of how much cash flow we should advance to a production that had not stabilized: not enough means the oxygen of production is cut off, while too much takes pressure off finding solutions, and it would be difficult to justify having advanced large amounts if the production grinds to a halt. It was always necessary to limit the board's exposure in case a project collapsed before it was fully funded; it would have been irresponsible to overcommit (taxpayers') money to an unstable production that might end in disaster.[28]

Sometimes we were party to the miscalculation of cash-flow needs; a few years after *An Gobán Saor,* Deborah Warner's *Last September* (a much bigger feature project) was in great jeopardy in the second week of its shoot in October 1998. As one of the producers, Nik Powell, was working with lawyers to interlock and make two complex national tax incentive schemes compatible in the financial structure, the electricians (a crew of sparks imported from Britain) threatened to abandon the production unless they were immediately paid. Searching for €10,000 in cash, Neil Jordan, an executive producer on the project, turned to me with the half-joking but memorable remark, "Do you know any drug dealers?"—presumably they might be a source of ready cash. I had to admit that I had no such relevant acquaintances, and in the end it was said that the urgently needed money was borrowed late that night via Paul McGuinness (manager of U2) from the safe of the Clarence, a Dublin hotel owned by the group.

These financial and production issues are separate from what one might term aesthetic or formal risk, although they have effects on it. They play into and eventually interact with the myriad factors that lead to what appears on the screen and, at a later stage, in some ineffable way, they impact on the factors that determine cultural or commercial success. A film is as strong as its weakest element, not its strongest, and lining up consistent and correct choices of scripting, casting, shooting, editing, and music is necessary for a film to succeed in its own terms. An attempt at creating a balance sheet of the one hundred feature films we were involved with over ten years will indicate a good number and spread that "worked," if we can define that in terms of lucid intensities, films that are coherently themselves at various levels of budget. It is because films are more artisanal than industrial that there is no simple relationship between financial investment and return in European cinema.[29]

We had an average ratio of one film going into production for every ten that we had provided with development funding, and there were those who suggested that the higher attrition rate of Hollywood's twenty-to-one development ratio would lead to more commercial films and better returns. I argued the opposite—that as some would-be commercial projects were receiving €50,000 or even €75,000 in long, drawn-out development periods, we should deploy equivalent sums to encourage the notionally much riskier process of ultra low-budget films being "developed in the camera" as part of an improvisatory and artisanal production process.

It was essential for a national film agency like the Irish Film Board that there be some combination of success in both cultural and commercial domains. Film agencies and institutes in the 1960s and early 1970s had more of a purely cultural remit, but the neoliberal economistic discourses of the later 1970s and 1980s provided pressure for economic performance. In Ireland the Coopers and Lybrand Report of 1992 argued for the reconstitution of the film board, which had been dissolved in 1987, on the grounds that it would stimulate economic activity and thus employment. Of course these were important arguments to make, and we produced figures to show the economic effects of our support for production. However, we were concerned to maintain a judicious equilibrium among cultural, social, and financial motives; there are always reasons for "thinking of the audience"— if one is to avoid solipsistic or unthought-through forms of filmmaking practice.

It was important to keep the relentless financial tendencies at bay by balancing them with cultural arguments and so I wrote polemical comments like "In all its forms film is at its most innovative when it is experienced as unexpected, challenging social norms and complacencies of taste, extending the boundaries of the possible" in the annual report.[30] In 2003 we came up with a mission statement: "We intend to encourage bravery and embrace creative risk. Paradoxically, in cinema, the further you push artistically the more genuinely commercial you can be."[31] Uttering these "neither/nor" verbalizations and myriad other oxymoronic policy formulations seemed like indispensable discursive maneuvers and the only way to absorb and deflect the implacable pressures of increasingly economistic discourses. Utilizing public monies for the expensive business of film needed justification as right-wing public representatives and a hostile tabloid press were always pleased to indulge in a feeding frenzy the minute we failed to maintain a robust sense of purpose allied with some quick footwork.

The fall of the Berlin Wall and the disintegration of global versions of "currently existing socialism" at the end of the 1980s led to the public sector being pushed toward increasingly market-led approaches, in all areas of its operations. This general shift led to extreme, macho commercialist stances being taken by some film-funding agencies in the late 1990s, the UK Film Council or the Australian FFC (Film Finance Corporation), for example. Posing as commercial with public money is a contradiction in terms—real commercial activity is different and should be left to itself. As Sergio Leone put it in a 1984 interview, "American studios have a way of facing problems that is very realistic, very drastic and very hard, because the product is money and money must be protected. . . . However, in my view, they often forget that we are dealing with an artistic work and that artistic values must contribute to the defense of the product."[32]

The Terms of Timidity

The Middle of the Road is a Very Dead End.

—Alexander Kluge, 1974

The development of discourses surrounding the idea of risk has taken place within a set of material determinations and a specific historical context. Encouraged by contemporary mercantile mentalities, there is the sense that the performance of discursive routines will eliminate uncertainty and unpredictability. On the whole, present-day attitudes and approaches are models of containment that attempt to enclose and restrain risk taking. A crisis of governance in a government department leads to journalistic exclamations calling for "a major overhaul of risk management procedures to ensure taxpayers get better value for money."[33] This is a voiced diversion and a disingenuous euphemism as improved planning procedures may well be a good idea, but it is unlikely that they will preempt and preclude venality and corruption. The development of different versions of risk aversion in different spheres of public life attempts to coerce film production into less adventurous forms. It becomes even more difficult openly to embrace the fundamental risk taking of the artistic imagination.

In Los Angeles in September 2008 I could hear the sound of the machinery of commerce in action; I remember hearing the admiring phrase "They can run the figures so accurately now" from many different people. It was the moment of the release of *Prince Caspian*, the second in the trilogy *The Chronicles of Narnia*, and the media city was admiring the level of precision of calculation and financial modeling currently possible in "franchise movies": the succession of sequels in blockbuster trilogies and series are sometimes also referred to as "brand-based properties."[34] This film was made for a high budget of $225 million with something like $100 million spent on marketing, but it earned $55 million from the saturation release in four thousand theaters across the United States on its opening weekend. The total domestic box office of this film was $141 million, while the foreign was $278 million; and with total box office receipts of $419 million one can assume a profit of something like $100 million during the first year of distribution. This is an industrial cultural process with a high proportion of return on investment and the scale of the machinery ensures that there is little risk involved.

In cinema, marketing has come to dominate production and the researched premonition of audience taste has now become powerful and preemptive. Thus to some extent, across time, marketing works as a self-fulfilling prophecy. It is a mechanism increasingly deployed to reinforce patterns of desire in which the audience asks to receive that which it expects it should want. At worst this becomes a closed loop, replicating learned forms and received formulas. Clearly, despite careful testing, publicity and advertising cannot achieve success for each and every specific product, for there is still a degree of risk that the thoroughly checked and verified version will not succeed. Nonetheless, a cumulative and pervasive effect is produced by the process, and it works to make occasional failure less likely.

These shifts in cultural formation invoke a relevant adjacent political movement whereby since the early 1980s (the launch of the short-lived Social Democratic Party in England would be a key example),[35] political parties began to research their policies in advance of arguing for them. Instead of developing, proposing, and convincing people about ideas and politics, parties now start with procedures employing focus groups, with

                                             Rod Stoneman

research polls designed to "see what people want." With the results of these market-research methods, the new policies, which have thus already been tested, are formulated. Of course, this kind of process easily becomes a preemptive forecast whereby ideology moves around in a circle to reinforce itself.

While such procedures are the basis of most commodity manufacture and distribution, and function proficiently in the context of the introduction of myriad new domestic products and FMCG (fast-moving consumer goods), there are problems in applying them to different domains. In the field of film and culture they have the predictable and deleterious effect of reducing diversity and of creating a less variegated cultural landscape. What may not be a problem for a breakfast cereal becomes detrimental for a television serial as marketing changes taste across time and induces a persistence of formulas and repetition.

Different motives lead to the same end—conservative risk aversion in commercial companies parallels well-established pusillanimous attitudes in the public sector. Civil servants are long used to inhabiting an organizational culture of inertia or indecision: "Better not to take a decision in case it might be a mistake." This is not an encouraging environment for clarity and decisiveness. "We must protect our minister" is a phrase I have heard many times in government departments, and one English civil servant even confided to me his technique of calling for the relevant file and sitting on it—"Action cannot be taken without the file."

The public sector in Europe has been subject to modernizing reforms based on policies and practices with a provenance in MBA (master's in business administration) programs. These courses were developed in American colleges in the 1960s and were motivated by a perceived need to formulate new templates to analyze, plan, and manage very different types of businesses and organizations. However, the clear benefits of these powerful tools can also lead to problems when MBA-style analytical formulations are applied clumsily by those who do not have an adequate grasp of the specificity of a particular area of work such as film. To be effective, business analysis needs to be coupled with a feeling for the nuances and specificities of the arts. At its worst, half-digested jargon is wielded as a weapon and well-paid consultants conduct risible seminars on risk management. At a Institute of Public Administration briefing session for semistate agencies held in Dublin in 2001, the following were listed among twenty-one "risks" for any organization: "15) coming in under budget, 16) coming in over budget . . . 19) not recruiting high quality staff."[36]

In the context of contemporary media-production education, students are now taught new replicas and grids of risk modeling for their projects.

Risk analyses, quantification, and management, when they are not stating the absolutely obvious, offer formulas for false comfort by containing and denying the unpredictable aspects of the creative process. Risk quantification subjects organic processes to the misconception of the metrical. Although the "Probability/Impact Matrix" (*sic*) of risk calculation should notionally include positive outcomes—opportunities—it is symptomatic that it dwells only on negative possibilities—threats. The delusion that uncertainty can be systematically managed may offer a reassurance to those who lack the confidence or the competence to face, let alone embrace, the existential reality of artistic processes, but it does not alter that reality.

The mirage of protection from exposure is reinforced at an educational level, as over the last decades media institutions have moved toward craft-based vocational training that leads to industrial assimilation and mimetic production. If the aim is to train for independent thinking, to train critical practitioners, then the educational process should be devised in a very different way and should involve a different approach to understanding risk.[37] Creating a new generation of technicians with craft skills but unused to reflection will not encourage genuine artistic exploration, and intelligent imaginative adventure is the only basis on which to create something striking or original enough to attract an audience whose taste has been formed elsewhere.

Embracing Risk

Control is an illusion.

—Apocryphal feminist maxim

It is often worth reminding oneself that in film production there is always and only risk; although producers work to minimize certain dangers, every batch of newly made low- and medium-budget films in Europe serves to indicate how undependable even the biggest, most "bankable" names turn out to be. Filmmaking should be careful, and it may be calculated, but it ultimately involves facing factors foreseen and unforeseen; in Donald Rumsfeld's notorious formulation: "There are known unknowns . . . but there are also unknown unknowns."[38] If we needed reminding that comprehensive foresight is not available to us, the terrible movement of the earth's tectonic plates in Lisbon in 1755 and Haiti in 2010 indicate that the ground on which we stand is not entirely secure.

Most people do not look for the hazardous for its own sake, but there is a sense that moments of mortal danger provide exhilarating existential

   Rod Stoneman

stimulation. One evening during the filming of *Beat the Devil*, John Huston left an all-night poker game and stood swaying on the terrace of the house he had hired near Naples. In a reverie, martini in hand, he found himself falling through the air. Luckily, a tree broke a forty-foot fall, and Huston survived another of the close encounters with mortality he had celebrated throughout his life, adding to his near-death experiences with waterfalls, cars, explosives, tigers, and sea snakes recounted in his autobiography, *An Open Book*.[39] In John Huston's case his psychological dalliance with danger was consonant with a wider trust in chance, with his "courting accident" in an open creative process.

Outside film production, the concept of risk plays a role in the framework of social judgment placed on adventurous individuals: unsuccessful equals reckless, successful equals brilliant. Although the general climate encourages risk aversion, there are formations of generally individualized risk that are supported or proposed by dominant representational regimes. These specifically include spectacular individual danger: the heroic mountaineer, the extreme sportsman or explorer. *Touching the Void* (dir. Kevin MacDonald, 2003) is a recent example of British derring-do or daring action restaged for the camera. Such exploits are generally an extension of an expansive and for the most part masculine ego, although female variants, such as aviatrix Amy Johnston, do occur. The film *Man on Wire* (dir. James Marsh, 2007), about the Frenchman who walked a tightrope between the Twin Towers in 1974, is disingenuous as it takes its meaning from the unspoken context of 9/11. His motivations, as the documentary reveals, are personal and psychological, but the making and reception of the film at this time are influenced by other factors. It is not that this deed did not embody extraordinary and heroic risk taking, but the eventual film hides the way in which its poetry and significance are entirely and inevitably embedded in the post-9/11 implications of the buildings he walked between. American invulnerability was destroyed with the towers and in the film Philippe Petit's feat is a reassertion of the pride of the West in its quirky, but ultimately triumphant, bravery. There is always one soldier in the foxhole in a war film who is eccentric but, finally, courageous. These representations function ideologically: in Britain the quiet heroism of the dangerous risks taken by "our boys" in Afghanistan is stressed by the media as a conduit for support for untenable foreign policies. These people in peril are exceptional, and the images of danger and hazard faced by others in society are precisely far enough away to comfort us during our quieter quotidian experience.

It is astonishing to discover the way in which a pervasive image system crosses the globe, reiterating authorized narratives that disclose events deceptively. This socialized representational background constantly impinges on the arena of creativity in film. There is a pervasive context, shaped by the discursive hegemony of a stable image system and a centripetal process, and this context reduces the variations of taste. Of course cinema is a subsidiary element in this complex image system that works to stabilize subjectivities and social formations, themselves the domain of the dominant illusions, falsities, and selectivities that sustain our culture. Some of these happen intentionally (conspiracies), many are determined unconsciously (ideologies), and some are even the result of the passage of chance. Most representations are the result of the specific interactions of these three factors. The third factor of the accidental is rarely seen from outside and is often incalculable, but although it plays a significant role, it is the most difficult to integrate into the model and also the least discussed.[40] Unfortunately, the understanding of reciprocal reinforcement of symbolic and social systems is not widely developed and does not seem to lead to any imminent prospect of change.

We need to be open to the spaces of dangerous creation, to films made in a brief passage where cinema can embrace the risk involved in the imaginative process. Now, with the pervasive emphases on industrial modes of production, the forces of mechanical repetition have increased their dominance. In a climate of risk aversion, the written scenario moves from constituting a firm base for singular filmmaking to a way of avoiding an encounter with the uncertainties of both art and the world. There is a danger of a veritable tyranny of the script (in contemporary Bollywood, apparently, it is known as "the bound script") as the only basis for gathering production monies. Increasingly, the script is becoming an editorial gatekeeper that focuses creative movement on particular ways of fabricating fiction films.

Creating a space where a greater range of calculated risks might be taken is essential for the project of pluralism. Health and safety precautions reduce the likelihood of negative outcomes from potentially dangerous actions, but they do not stop the activities taking place. A desire to embrace adventurous ways of working is a starting point for opening the envelope of the possible. Pluralism is the space of difference and challenge through other potential orders. As William Blake wrote, "Without contraries [there] is no progression." There should be contention between a very wide diversity of styles and subjects, for this makes it possible to recognize the extent to which chance is a portal for many aspects that we cannot control and do not know. We need to encourage and maximize the dynamic of the daring, the possibilities of the perilous, in order to enable the realization of new images and sounds that may contribute to social and cultural transformation. In a recent interview, Eric Hobsbawm suggested:

                                                    Rod Stoneman

"Historically, communities and social systems have aimed at stabilization and reproduction, creating mechanisms to keep at bay disturbing leaps into the unknown."[41]Aesthetic modes that face an encounter with chance suggest more dynamic means of bringing about change. Perhaps the variegated range of films achieved by artistic risk taking will also in its way help to sustain radical and imaginative solutions to the urgent human and political developments we face.

NOTES

1. Mozambican National Resistance/Resistência Nacional Moçambicana.

2. It could be argued that the Surrealist embrace of chance was a premonition of later modernist work. They used games like the Exquisite Corpse, assembling sentences and images by chance procedures as routes to the unconscious. The point was to achieve "[t]hought dictated in the absence of all control exerted by reason and outside all moral or aesthetic preoccupations," as André Breton's formulation in the *Surrealist Manifesto* of 1924 indicated. André Breton, *Manifestos of Surrealism* (Ann Arbor, MI: Ann Arbor Paperbacks, 1972), 26. Ironically, when they turned to film, they had to involve a basic level of planning; making *Un chien andalou* (An Andalusian Dog, 1929) or *L'âge d'or* (Age of Gold, 1930) involved a cast and crew assembling at an agreed time and place with appropriate costume and props—constraints not involved in the immediacy of games or automatic writing.

3. "This experiment was made to imprison and preserve forms obtained through chance, through my chance." Notes in *The Box of 1914*, in *The Writings of Marcel Duchamp*, ed. Michel Sanouillet and Elmer Peterson (New York: Da Capo, 1973).

4. Dawn Ades, Neil Cox, and David Hopkins, *Marcel Duchamp* (London: Thames & Hudson, 1999), 94.

5. Brandon LaBelle, *Background Noise* (New York: Continuum, 2007), 10.

6. Noel Burch, "Chance and Its Functions," in *Theory of Film Practice* (London: Secker & Warburg, 1973), 114. The work was first published in French in 1967.

7. In reference to James Joyce, as the film has an intertexual relationship with Joyce's short story "The Dead."

8. James Goode, *The Making of the Misfits* (New York: Limelight Editions, 1986), 46.

9. Peter Viertel, *Dangerous Friends* (London: Viking, 1991), 174.

10. Ibid., 172.

11. John Huston, *An Open Book* (London: Macmillan, 1980), 246.

12. Lesley Brill, *John Huston's Filmmaking* (Cambridge: Cambridge University Press, 1997), 238.

13. The demonstrations that ended the Ceauşescu regime in Romania in December 1989 are utilized by Robert Dornhelm in *Requiem for Dominic.*

14. Anicius Manlius Severinus Boethius, *The Consolation of Philosophy*, trans. W. V. Cooper, 1902, book 5, section 142, available from Electronic Text Center, University of Virginia Library, http://etext.virginia.edu/etcbin/toccer-new2?id=BoePhil.sgm&images=images/modeng&data=/texts/english/modeng/parsed&tag=public&part=5&division=div1.

15. Kenneth Anger, "Modesty and the Art of Film," *Cahiers du cinéma*, no.5, September 1951.

16. Johan Huizinga, *Homo Ludens: A Study of the Play Element in Culture* (London: Routledge, 2003).

17. I attended the University of Kent at Canterbury, 1972–75, and the Film Unit, Slade School of Fine Art, University College London, 1976–78. I was a member of the *Screen* editorial board from 1980 to 1985.

18. With Alan Fountain and Caroline Spry from 1983 to 1993.

19. See Derek Jones, ed., *Censorship: A World Encyclopaedia* (London: Fitzroy Dearborn, 2001), 593–94, for a more detailed account.

20. Although they are black-and-white (tinted puce), and grainy and integrate plausibly with the Wilhelm Reich material from the 1930s, the images of the couple making love in the open air were actually shot on video during the Woodstock music festival.

21. Jones, *Censorship*, 357–58.

22. Michael Grade, *It Seemed Like a Good Idea at the Time* (London: Macmillan, 1999). There is a 1976 film and at least twelve other books with this phrase in the title.

23. The supposed founder and figurehead of *Mad* magazine.

24. Gertrude Stein, *Everybody's Autobiography* (London: Heinemann, 1937).

25. Rosena Brown was charged with playing another role that would have involved acting—as a Mata Hari in a "honey trap" allegedly gathering information about a senior prison officer who was later killed by the IRA. She was sentenced to twenty years' imprisonment and released under the Belfast agreement.

26. Martin McLoone and John Hill. eds., *Big Picture, Small Screen* (Luton: University of Luton Press, 1996), 118–32.

27. As we were driving back from the location, after a long silence, my six-year-old son, Adam, sitting in the back of the car, chirpily remarked, "Those people in the bus, Daddy, they weren't very happy, were they?"

28. This same approach is evident in relation to the film board financing of a documentary production: Rod Stoneman, *Chávez: The Revolution Will Not Be Televised* (London: Wallflower, 2008), 26.

29. Rod Stoneman, "Under the Shadow of Hollywood: The Industrial versus the Artisanal," *Irish Review*, Institute of Irish Studies, Queens University Belfast, no. 24, Autumn 1999, 96–103.

30. Irish Film Board, *Review/Athbhreithniú 1993* (Galway: Bord Scannán na hÉireann, 1993).

 Rod Stoneman

31. Irish Film Board, *Review/Athbhreithniú 2000,* (Galway: Bord Scannán na hÉireann, 2000); "Icons of the Imagination," in *Ten Years After,* ed. Kevin Rockett (Galway: Bord Scannán na hÉireann, 2003), vi–vii.

32. *Italy: The Image Business,* directed by Rod Stoneman, 1984, made as part of the *Visions* series for Channel 4.

33. "Spending Watchdog's Report Highly Critical of FAS Controls," *Irish Independent,* February 29, 2010.

34. "H'W'D Slashes Final-Cut List," *Variety,* January 25–31, 2010, 6.

35. Led by the "Gang of Four"—Labour Party "moderates" Shirley Williams, Roy Jenkins, David Owen, and Bill Rodgers—from 1981 to 1988.

36. "Risk Management and Governance" (presentation at the briefing session organized by the Institute of Public Administration, Dublin, December 18, 2001).

37. In 2003 I left the Irish Film Board and have since been involved with setting up the Huston School of Film & Digital Media at the National University of Ireland, Galway.

38. Rumsfeld's comment was originally made at a U.S. Department of Defense briefing on February 12, 2002. He used a fuller version in June that year: "Now what is the message there? The message is that there are known 'knowns.' There are things we know that we know. There are known unknowns. That is to say there are things that we now know we don't know. But there are also unknown unknowns. There are things we do not know we don't know. So when we do the best we can and we pull all this information together, and we then say well that's basically what we see as the situation, that is really only the known knowns and the known unknowns. And each year, we discover a few more of those unknown unknowns." Donald H. Rumsfeld, "Secretary Rumsfeld Press Conference at NATO Headquarters, Brussels, Belgium," U.S. Department of Defense, June 6, 2002, http://www.defense.gov/transcripts/transcript.aspx?transcriptid=3490.

39. Huston, *An Open Book,* 248.

40. Perhaps this recalls E. H. Carr's account of the role of unpredictable events (his example is Trotsky taking a duck-shooting weekend away from Moscow at exactly the moment when Stalin moved to take control of the Soviet state) in the broad sweep of history understood through economic and social determinations. E. H Carr, *What Is History?* (London: Penguin, 1961).

41. Eric Hobsbawm, "Interview—World Distempers," *New Left Review* 61 (2010): 150.

RICHARD MAXWELL AND TOBY MILLER

Film and the Environment

Risk Offscreen

When you think of film and the environment, does your mind turn to how cinema has depicted nature and pollution?[1] Do you revel in Adorno's conceit that cinema can provide an "objectifying recreation" akin to dreaming about landscapes, as if that would prettify urban existence?[2] Isn't "representation" what turns film academics on? Or perhaps your mind turns to how filmmakers use their celebrity status to draw public attention to related causes. Hollywood stars love to add "carbon footprints" to their lists of enviable personal traits. Small is finally fabulous, and the ecorazzi (paparazzi on the eco-celebrity beat) oblige with nonstop, if sometimes rather arch, coverage, especially since the advent of the Environmental Media Association's awards and the 2007 "Hollywood Goes Green" summit meeting.[3] For example, *Hollywood Today* boasts that actors give green gifts of "vintage-inspired" camisoles and recycled jewels, but MSNBC.com admonishes that although "the Prius reigns supreme as the current status symbol" in Hollywood, "trucks that carry equipment from studios to locations and back continue to emit exhaust from diesel engines," as do generators on set.[4]

The MSNBC story suggests that a scholarly focus on just representation or celebrity isn't, pardon the trope, sustainable. A study of Hollywood's environmental impact has disclosed massive use of electricity and petroleum and the release of hundreds of thousands of tons of deadly emissions each year. In fact, the motion picture industry is *the biggest producer of conventional pollutants* in the Los Angeles area. Municipal and statewide levels of film-related energy consumption and greenhouse-gas emissions (carbon dioxide, methane, and nitrous oxide) are about the same as the aerospace and semiconductor industries.[5] Film consumers are also major producers of pollutants, from auto emissions en route to the theater and chemical runoff when parked there to the energy powering home-entertainment devices.[6]

What would happen to the discourse on film if, rather than yet more textual analysis or promotional dross, it confronted the fact that, for example, millions of cartridges of Atari's failed electronic game adaptation of *E.T.: The Extra-Terrestrial* (dir. Steven Spielberg, 1981) were buried in a New Mexico landfill, broken up by a heavy roller, and covered in concrete to consign them to history?[7] What would it mean if those involved in cinema studies and journalism were required—as an ordinary part of their work—to evaluate motion picture production ecologically?[8] What would they make, for example, of *The Beach* (dir. Danny Boyle, 2000), in which (textually) a modern-day Eden suddenly turns nasty for jaded tourists?

Thai environmental and pro-democracy activists publicized the arrogant despoliation they experienced when Fox was making *The Beach* in Maya Bay, part of Phi Phi Islands National Park. Natural scenery was bulldozed because it did not fit the company's fantasy of a tropical idyll: sand dunes were relocated, flora rearranged, and a "new" strip of coconut palms planted. The producers paid off the government with a donation to the Royal Forestry Department and campaigned with the Tourism Authority of Thailand to twin the film as a promotion for the country. Meanwhile, the next monsoon saw the damaged sand dunes of the region collapse, its natural defenses against erosion destroyed by Hollywood bulldozers. All the while, director Boyle claimed the film was "raising environmental consciousness" among a local population that was allegedly "behind" U.S. levels of "awareness."[9] And those levels would be? Hadn't Boyle learned from Fox's earlier confrontation with the people of Popotla, in Baja California, whose village was cut off from the sea and local fisheries by a walled "movie maquiladora" built to keep them away from the production of *Titanic* (dir. James Cameron 1997)? After Fox's chlorination of surrounding seawater "destroyed a crop of sea urchins that Popotla had fished for decades" and reduced overall fish levels by one-third, the Popotlanos demonstrated *their* "environmental consciousness" by decorating the wall with rubbish to ridicule the filmmakers and call for *mariscos libres* (freedom for shellfish).[10]

The wider background to this ecologically destructive filmmaking was the message of economic structural adjustment peddled by the World Bank, the International Monetary Fund, the World Trade Organization, and the sovereign states that dominate them. This neoliberal clerisy had encouraged a turn away from subsistence agriculture and toward tradable goods, beyond manufacturing capacity and in the direction of service exchange.

     Richard Maxwell and Toby Miller

In much of Southeast Asia, structural adjustment pushed people to littoral regions in search of work, and fish-farming corporations created a new aquaculture, displacing the natural environment of mangroves and coral reefs that protect people and land. And the requirement for the third world to constitute itself as a diverting heritage site and decadent playground for the West has seen Thailand, Indonesia, and Malaysia undertake massive construction projects of resorts located at the point where high tides lap, attracting more and more workers and decimating more and more natural protection (areas that had not been directed to remove natural barriers suffered dramatically fewer casualties in the 2004 tsunami).[11]

Such questions barely appear on cinema studies' agenda, even when the discipline examines the film industry via political economy and policy approaches.[12] Nor are they part of popular film criticism or publicly available fan discourse. In this chapter, we seek to address these largely neglected matters, arguing that an environmental perspective is crucial to understanding film commerce, culture, and politics throughout history. We begin by establishing our theoretical coordinates, focusing on Ulrich Beck's concept of "risk society" (*Risikogesellschaft*) and the science studies work of Bruno Latour. Then Hollywood comes into view.

Risk (and the United States)

According to Beck, democratic industrialized societies are characterized by "institutions of monitoring and protection" that aim to bring order to a chaotic world. A risk society "organises what cannot be organised" by creating institutions to protect people from "social, political, economic and individual risks." If early modernity was about producing and distributing goods in a struggle for the most effective and efficient forms of industrialization, with devil-take-the-hindmost and no thought for the environment, risk society is about enumerating and managing those dangers via probabilistic, or scenario, thinking that imagines a range of possible outcomes. Rather than being occasional, risk is now part of what it means to be modern. This second modernity is characterized by ever-more sophisticated mechanisms for measuring risk, even as the range and impact of risks grow less controllable with the proliferation of technologies and markets that "improve" life while adding unforeseen harm.[13] We can see instances of this in capitalism's imposition of time discipline over working-class life, which improved the productivity of industrial labor but posed new potential and actual risks to workers' minds, bodies, and communities. The increasing velocity of production, with an unprecedented variety and volume of commodities, fostered a new fetishism and engendered the modern detachment from the natural environment. Risks posed by an unruly nature and proletariat were disciplined in the service of growth and progress.

Risk society also resides in the public-safety surveillance operations that regulate modern life: electronic monitoring of traffic at intersections for safer crossing of pedestrians and vehicles in densely populated cities; air-traffic control; credentialing trained drivers, pilots, or food and drug makers; centralized monitoring of private economic activity, such as banking, tax payments; and so on. It embodies and propels the desires of capital and state to make sense of and respond to problems, whether of their own making or not. As governmental and commercial knowledge aggregates statistics to define, measure, and model populations in the interest of social control and productivity in advanced industrial/postindustrial societies, it also induces massively increased feelings of risk in people. Risk societies admit and even promote the irrationality of the economy—as a means, paradoxically, of governing populations—by naturalizing despoliation, global labor competition, cyclical recession, declining life-long employment, massive international migration, overreaching communications technologies, and the rolling back of welfare-state protections.

We have seen this combined with a "cultural logic of computation" that makes inequality and income redistribution toward the wealthy axiomatic.[14] Denizens of postindustrial societies are factoring costs and benefits into everyday life as never before, while their sense of being able to determine the future through choice is diminished. Ironically, the future orientation of the risk society lacks the revolutionary sensibility of forward-thinking politics. Risk thinking has weakened ideological commitments to Marxism, feminism, and anti-imperialism. Unlike the notion of a broad Left that once infused such struggles, political and social issues are delinked from a central organizing critique, such that a position adopted on ecologically sound consumption says nothing about a position on popular democracy. The taming of chance worsens the odds for radical change.[15]

The United States is *the* risk society, with 50 percent of the population participating in stock market investments. Risk is brought into the home as an everyday ritual, an almost blind faith (sometimes disappointed) in mutual funds patrolling retirement income. The insurance costs alone of September 11, 2001 have been calculated at $21 billion. In 2005, U.S. residents spent $1.1 trillion on insurance—more than they paid for food, and more than one-third of the world's total insurance expenditure. The industry's global revenues exceed the gross domestic product of all countries bar the top three. At one level, this represents a careful calculation of risk, its incorporation into lifelong and posthumous planning—prudence as a way of life. At another, it is a wager on hopelessness and fear. As dangers mount,

    Richard Maxwell and Toby Miller

safeguards diminish, and statisticians become the new mavens of risk management within corporate and government sectors.[16] So whether we are discussing nuclear power plants or genetically modified foods, the captains of the respective industries argue that they pose no risks, but insurance companies decline to write policies on them for citizens—because they are risky. Much of this relates to the deregulatory intellectual and policy fashions of the last three decades, which have aided the historic redistribution of income upward by opposing the universalization of Medicare, reducing labor protection, and ideologizing against collective action other than in the private sphere—at the same time as people confront spiraling health costs and multiplying economic changes.[17]

So where do motion pictures take their place in risk society?

RISK AND HOLLYWOOD

Historically, risk in Hollywood has meant financial risk. From the first time a script was used, movie making entered into the risk-reduction business. Financiers could get a foretaste of what they were paying for; shots could be ordered, schedules made, and shooting days organized; budgets could be tamed by the elements on the page—the number of actors, elephants, street scenes, bathing beauties, makeup people, electricians, camera operators, and sets all entered into a ledger. Risk diminished with the establishment of movie theaters, which made film viewing less haphazard, film demand more predictable, and film distribution less chaotic. Financial risk could also be reduced by establishing market dominance. Examples include Edison Company and Biograph using patent protections to fight foreign film's dominance of U.S. screens in the early 1900s, until antitrust laws caught up with them; studios simultaneously owning movie theaters to guarantee with near certainty audiences, until regulators said this was illegal in the 1940s; Hollywood's distribution cartels reducing the risk of foreign competitors' success, to retain some certainty in overseas dominance; and film-stock monopolies creating better odds of controlling demand but also of defining what passed as proper skin tone.[18]

The surveillance of film audiences may be the most influential, if reviled, method of risk reduction in the motion picture industry, growing in status from the earliest days when exhibitors began to ask for feedback to the current wizardry associated with a billion-dollar market research business.[19] "Demand uncertainty" remains the driving force behind the ongoing investment in market research.[20] Until now, such uncertainty, alongside perpetual risk of financial failure, has defined Hollywood's place in risk society. The humanities' latest fetish, "creative industries," institutionalizes this kind of service to business, in keeping with its dedication to neoliberal discourse.[21] One of us well remembers being invited to a conference on film economics at a large university in the Midwest where the papers were all about risk and how to reduce it in terms of producers' financial investments. To speak of the public good, or workers' interests, or anything else, was to be outside the discourse, outside the conference, and in the wilds of St. Louis. It was to be beyond risk and film.

However, in recent years a new specter of risk has provoked a subtle but significant shift in Hollywood's business strategy. As we'll show, Hollywood is profoundly complicit in the world's ecological crisis. To counter that risk, we must see it as an *environmental participant,* not merely a signifying agent of information and pleasure. Movies are not just things to be read; they are not just coefficients of political and economic power; and they are not just industrial objects. Rather, they are all these things—hybrid monsters, coevally subject to rhetoric, status, and technology, to text, power, and science: all at once, but in contingent ways.[22]

Since the 1960s, environmental risks have slowly become central public and academic concerns, with the rise of environmental science and public policies protecting air, water, and soil. The United States has seen a doubling in membership of environmental groups between 1980 and 2000, with numbers rivaling membership in political parties.[23]

Meanwhile, calls for interdisciplinary efforts to confront the eco-crisis have grown within the academy as more and more disciplines have acknowledged their failure to undertake relevant work.[24] In this essay we latch onto the momentum of environmentalism to offer a new, greener direction for cinema studies by identifying some key environmental risks associated with filmmaking and consumption. We acknowledge the difficulty of expanding cinema studies to encompass environmental issues, in particular as these emerge from an analysis of political/economic arrangements that have until recently stifled efforts to build green strategies into Hollywood production.

Moreover, it is hard to break away from the dominant discourse of cinema studies, which theorizes the history of film through a predictable set of idealist moves: a drive toward artistic realism; the desire for pleasurable spectacle; a passion for profits; the genius of systems; and the talent of inventors. For example, André Bazin, the twentieth century's most influential film theorist and journalist-critic, tells us that film derived from the imagination, which attained its physical realization in subsequent technological developments. Cinema was "an idealistic phenomenon," with economic and social relations following the lead of a desire for realism. Artists' and audiences' desires drove technological innovation.[25]

                                        Richard Maxwell and Toby Miller

We want to complicate this story by digging a little deeper into economic and political connections between motion picture technologies, the environment, and film form. For example, the development of film stock privileged certain skin tones over others (that would be white over black) via the selection of specific chemical dye couplers, such that a particular kind of whiteness was reproduced much more easily with most industrial and domestic filmmaking technology than darker-toned skin. All this was the outcome of aesthetic, chemical, commercial, and racist choices—not a merry march to realism. And why did 3-D film emerge and then collapse? Not because people liked the concept but not the reality. Its appearance and demise were about Polaroid challenging Eastman's hegemony over film stock and being defeated because exhibitors were unwilling to incur the costs of refitting theaters.[26] Similarly, the technical capacity to bring sound to moving pictures existed long before it occurred. War and its associated technologies and bureaucracies stimulated research into the possibilities, but then the power of the telephone corporations after World War I saw sound technologies focused on interpersonal speech rather than visual recordings.[27] Yet Bazin's idealist rhetoric remains at the center of cinema studies. There has been little room for what you are about to read, as we illustrate how film's history is closely linked to a widespread pattern of the culture industries as magisterial polluters.

The type and volume of chemical waste emitted into the air and waterways by large-scale raw film production can be traced to the chemical process for extracting cellulose from cotton and wood pulp that was invented in the 1800s. Guncotton, or cellulose nitrate, was the first synthetic commercial plastic and the first celluloid base, upon which an emulsion of light-sensitive silver crystals was applied to make film for photography and motion pictures. Cellulose nitrate was originally marketed as imitation ivory for making billiard balls, combs, and sundry personal items. But raw film manufacturing became the defining application for cellulose nitrate. The equally raw early twentieth-century film industry developed techniques for mass production, financed the techno-scientific research to improve its quality, and set standards for the development of plastics.[28]

Cellulose nitrate was closely linked to explosives through nitrogen-based chemistry, and film stock was famously combustible. Many precautions were put in place from the earliest days of its production, transportation, and exhibition, including the fireproof enclosure of projection rooms and projectionists trained in handling flammable materials. This film base would eventually be replaced by triacetate and polyester. A substitute of cellulose acetate, a less flammable product known as safety film, was available in the 1920s and prescribed for screenings in "homes, schools, churches, factories, lecture and assembly halls" and lightweight 16 mm filmmaking.[29]

The chemical-mechanical process for manufacturing cellulose nitrate film required large volumes of clean water and a variety of chemicals, including alcohol, sodium hydroxide (lye or caustic soda), camphor, and nitric and sulfuric acids. By 1926, Eastman Kodak's raw film plant at Kodak Park in Rochester, New York, was churning out two hundred thousand miles of film annually, sucking more than 12 million gallons of water daily from Lake Ontario and spewing the used water, along with chemical effluents, into the Genesee River.[30] At the end of the century, when it supplied 80 percent of the world's film stock, Kodak Park was using 35 to 53 million gallons of fresh water a day. By then, Eastman Kodak had become the primary source of pathogens (mainly dioxin, a carcinogen) released into New York State's environment. Rochester had been "ranked number one in the US for overall releases of carcinogenic chemicals" for the preceding thirteen years—this despite the fact that most of the wastewater was collected in a treatment plant built in the 1970s to comply with the Clean Water Act.[31]

The main ingredients of cellulose nitrate film manufactured after 1890 were cotton and silver. Cotton supplies were abundant in the United States, rising very rapidly in the early decades of the twentieth century.[32] Eastman Kodak consumed 5 million pounds of cotton in 1926, and almost twice that amount in 1936.[33] While most commercial manufacturers of cellulose nitrate used cotton-mill waste, it is not clear whether Eastman Kodak used mill waste or a mix of available supplies.[34] To remove impurities, the cotton was bleached with sodium hydroxide (the same stuff used in wood-pulp bleaching). The treated cotton was then submitted to the nitrating process. It was immersed in nitric and sulfuric acids as it rotated in large perforated vats that allowed the acids to be drawn off. After this acid wash, the nitrated cotton was put into large centrifugal washers that rinsed the remaining acids with large quantities of water, a process repeated over weeks. Once the water was spun off, the cotton was fed into mixers that added a solvent of camphor and alcohol to produce a paste with the viscosity of honey. The camphor was used as a softener or plasticizer that kept the film from becoming brittle. With the substitute of acetic acid and other chemicals, cellulose acetate film was made in a similar way.

The silver arrived at Kodak Park in forty-two-pound bars of bullion, and the company was already processing three tons of silver a week at the turn of the twentieth century, and five tons by 1936.[35] The silver bars were dissolved in nitric acid to obtain pure crystals of silver nitrate, which were mixed into an emulsion with potassium iodide, potassium bromide, and gelatin (the latter made from cattle bones and hides). The emulsion was

                                        Richard Maxwell and Toby Miller

then applied to the film base.[36] By 1926, Eastman Kodak had become the second-largest consumer of pure silver bullion, after the U.S. government mint, and remained one of the largest purchasers of silver in the world even after 2000, when it began to focus on digital photography.[37]

Working conditions in Kodak Park exposed employees to acids and acid vapors as well as other irritants. The waste from this process also sent bleaches, traces of silver, and acids into the Genesee. Silver is not considered dangerous to humans, although high levels of it are toxic to fish and other aquatic life, but workers at the Eastman Kodak plant were exposed to abnormal levels of silver dust or fumes, which can irritate the upper respiratory tract and eyes.[38] Workers exposed to cotton dust also risked daily irritation of their respiratory systems, and if exposed constantly to high levels, they may have contracted byssinosis, or "brown lung," which could reduce lung capacity. Byssinosis was recognized as an occupational hazard in Britain by the 1940s, but not in the United States until the 1970s, largely because cotton-mill owners had moved operations to nonunionized southern states, where worker protections were weak.[39] Workplace hazards and toxic by-product waste were common at Eastman's chemical plant in Tennessee, set up after World War I to produce solvents, cellulose acetate, and plastics.[40]

The competition effect of capitalism—the tendency toward monopolization—propelled environmental exploitation and despoliation in the raw film business as much if not more than rising commercial demand for film stock. For example, George Eastman was very keen to maintain his monopoly in raw film supply. He worried that German and French competitors might capture part of the market with improved film stock, in particular nonflammable cellulose acetate film, which French Pathé and the German firms AGFA, Bayer, and BASF were developing between 1904 and 1909. So Eastman infringed patent rights to acetate film held by his European rivals. Rather than settle for a cartel arrangement offered by the German companies, he leveraged his contracts and credit deals with European customers to obstruct sales of German film stock, especially from AGFA, which he saw as his main competitor (AFGA expanded during World War I, and survived to reestablish its business with European customers).[41]

Eastman experienced less competition for his control over the supply of silver, which was solidly in the hands of U.S. and British interests. In the interwar years, Mexico, the United States, Canada, and Peru were the largest producers of silver ore, and the United States controlled 73 percent of refinery production (including ownership of Mexican refineries by the Guggenheim Exploration Company). China and India were large consumers. China was on the silver standard, which made it vulnerable to U.S.

silver interests. The latter eventually won a favorable purchasing and subsidy agreement from the Roosevelt government in 1933, forcing China into political crisis.[42]

Camphor was another story. By 1932, 80 percent of its world supply went into film and celluloid products. At that time, virtually all camphor came from Formosa (Taiwan), which Japan colonized between 1895 and 1945. Japan set up a government monopoly for the camphor industry, fixing prices to maintain its dominance of the market against growing competition from synthetic camphor producers. Natural camphor would eventually be replaced by synthetic camphor, derived from turpentine in a process developed in Germany.[43] By the end of the twentieth century, Taiwan had become home to Formosa Plastics, the world's largest producer of the plastic polyvinyl chloride.[44]

By the start of twenty-first century, Kodak, the largest supplier of film stock in the world, was dumping "methylene chloride concentrations as high as 3,600,000 parts per billion" into New York groundwater. That was 720,000 times the permissible levels of this pulmonary and skin irritant that humans metabolize into carbon monoxide. The company halved this by 2003 as a result of pressure from regulators and its own desire to reduce celluloid film production and expand its digital media business. Three years later, the ties of film and print came full circle when Kodak announced a process for high-speed digital printing that could be customized by publishers. This new process includes one of the first commercial applications of nanotechnology in the media sector. *Business Week* called it "as important an evolution in printmaking as movable type."[45]

Today's silver halide film stock is under threat by the imminent move to digital printing/filmmaking ("imaging" in marketing lingo). Film will be around as long as millionaire aesthetes and movie moguls insist on its superiority,[46] but digital production is fast becoming the new standard. It brings with it a new ecological context for filmmaking and film studies. The question is whether the ecological conditions of the digital transition provide a way for motion pictures to become less ecologically destructive.

We have heard the prophecies of digitalism before. Since the early 1970s, the information-based technologies of the "new" economy have been pitched as clean businesses, promising endless gains in productivity, competitive markets, and a brand-new green day for workers, consumers, and residents, where the by-products are code, not smoke. Is the digital transition to green film production just another one of these empty corporate promises?

We are already seeing a range of unforeseen environmental risks flowing from some very basic technical problems associated with digital media

                                   Richard Maxwell and Toby Miller

production, distribution, and storage. The root of the problem resides in the computer/electronics industry's familiar business strategy of planned obsolescence, which designs a short lifespan into computer systems (drives, interfaces, operating systems, and so on) along with questionable integrity of the physical media (for example, glitches in recording systems). This has fostered high levels of electronic garbage and energy use, with related waste, pollution, and dangerous working conditions.[47] Making semiconductors requires hazardous chemicals, including some known carcinogens. The accumulation of electronic hardware throughout the world has caused grave environmental and health concerns that stem from the chemical and material composition of these commodities and their potential seepage into landfills, water sources, and the bodies of workers. Electronic waste (e-waste) is the fastest-growing part of municipal cleanups around the first world. E-waste salvage yards have generated serious concerns regarding worker health and safety wherever plastics and wires are burned and circuit boards leached with acid or grilled, then dumped in streams, to minimize the volume of waste and retrieve valuable items. There are serious implications for local and downstream land and water as well as for residents. Much of the recycling work is done in the third world by preteen Chinese, African, and Indian girls, picking away without protection of any kind at discarded first world televisions and computers in order to find precious metals, then dump the remains in landfills. The metals are sold to recyclers, who do not use landfills or labor in the first world because of environmental and industrial legislation against the destruction to soil, water, and workers that is caused by the dozens of poisonous chemicals and gases in these dangerous machines.[48]

RESPONSES

There are signs of hope. Back in 2004, the Political Economy Research Institute listed media owners at numbers 1, 3, 16, 22, and 39 on its *Misfortune 100: Top Corporate Air Polluters in the United States.*[49] These firms are clearly feeling the pressure. Today, nearly every major film company has some program of corporate responsibility aimed at saving money and the planet simultaneously.

Fox, the studio that made *The Beach,* is vigorously reexamining its disastrous environmental record, thanks to an unlikely source of progressive thought—Rupert Murdoch. In 2007, he convened a meeting of all News Corporation employees across the world. The sole agenda item was his goal of making the company carbon-neutral by 2010, despite its annual usage of almost 650,000 tons of such fuels. Murdoch told his employees that "[i]f we are to connect with our audiences on this issue, we must first get our own house in order," and "[c]limate change poses clear, catastrophic threats."[50] Even Fox's far-right-wing vigilante television show *24* got involved. It became the first carbon-neutral U.S. TV drama in 2009, with offsets calculated against the impact of car chases, air travel, and use of coal-generated electricity, and use of wind and solar power from India where feasible.[51]

For its part, Time Warner's 2008 *Corporate Social Responsibility Report* proclaimed "Energy Efficiency at the Studio Lot since 2002," announcing that it had saved "over 8 million kilowatt-hours of energy and approximately $1 million annually" via efficient lighting, heating, and air-conditioning; occupancy sensors and timers; and so on. The corporation even undertook a carbon-footprint analysis in 2007 to determine the greenhouse-gas impacts of DVD manufacture and distribution.[52]

Other major studios have initiated programs that include installing low-energy light-emitting diodes to illuminate buildings, studios, and outdoor signage; reducing paper use; composting organic waste; retrofitting buildings with computer-controlled air and heating systems and environmentally friendly materials; paying for reforestation out of production budgets to mitigate a film's overall pollution; teleconferencing; recycling wood, paper, recording media, metals, film stock, electronics, and printer and toner cartridges; managing chemical use and disposal; reducing or eliminating hazardous materials; eliminating and recycling wastewater; installing solar and other renewable energy sources; and networking with green suppliers and organizations like the Greencode Project (funded by the National Film Board of Canada) and the Producers Guild of America's greenproductionguide.com, a database of environmentally friendly products and services from vendors across the United States.[53]

Various governmental and professional trades initiatives support such activities. For instance, the UK Film Council created an "Environmental Strategy" to help "trade bodies and individual companies" reduce the environmental impact of the U.K. film industry, where so many nominally Hollywood products are made.[54] It remains to be seen whether such policy innovations will continue, given the British government's decision to shutter the council, announced in mid-2010. And the Science and Technology Council of the U.S. Academy of Motion Picture Arts and Sciences is pressing for industrywide models to deal with aspects of the digital transition that could alter Hollywood's relation to the environment in positive ways. Though their recommendations do not explicitly mention the environment, they are indirectly linked to environmental risks posed by Hollywood. They reject the current "store and ignore" and "save everything" attitudes of producers and studio managers and plan to reduce wasteful

                                              Richard Maxwell and Toby Miller

practices through better-organized responses to technical obsolescence (for instance, standardization and nonproprietary technical collaborations using open-source systems that would help extend the utility of digital platforms).[55]

So there is some good news at the frontier of moviemaking, as risks to the environment are factored into spreadsheets and location shoots, eliminating Styrofoam cups and generating headlines. Now we just need the academic study of cinema to awake from its seemingly risk-free slumber and contribute to the debate! It is essential that manufacturers, regulators, and scholars establish a broader dialogue about e-waste by advancing regulatory options and spurring debate in the midst of new policy-making initiatives. Drawing on Beck's risk analysis, film scholars can relink progressive issues that have been decoupled through the beguiling magic of neoliberalism; and, borrowing from Latour's insistence on multivariate analysis, they can transcend their idealist methods. They will not be alone—much of this work is under way by members of the Environmental Communication Network (www.esf.edu/ecn/), for instance.

And it's worth the effort to rethink the discipline. Since we began talking about these issues in 2003, we've been stunned by the response. We've seen our op-eds in Latin American newspapers reprinted; school pupils rush forward after our talks; graybeards undertake to revise their curricula; and indigenous folks get caught up in a critical enthusiasm. None of this appears to have compromised their (or our) enjoyment of cinema.

Scholars outside film are doing marvelous work on the core areas we should make our own, such as star studies of environmentalism and the impact of documentaries and feature films on audience awareness and understanding of climate change, while the research we have drawn on to reconsider film history virtually all comes from beyond the field and by scholars whose work is rarely or never cited by it.[56]

So each time we write about a film, let's be alert to the environmental burden of production practices, attitudes, and technologies—mise-en-scène has a carbon footprint. Let's endorse celebrity environmentalism for what it is, but move beyond the snide swipes at it from the likes of MSNBC—which ought to know better because General Electric, which owned it until 2011, holds the record for carcinogenic polychlorinated biphenyls dumped into U.S. waterways. Let's become more engaged with critical work on technology and the environment as a vital area of film studies and its future—let our debates about analog versus digital aesthetics also speak of phthalates (a poisonous plastic softener), dioxin, and biodiversity.[57] Each time we support state assistance to the cinema, let's ask that such a policy also guarantee ecologically sound production practices and working conditions. And each time we go to a movie or watch one at home, let's remember that our impact as spectators spills over into our air, water, and soil. To do otherwise would be . . . unsustainable.

NOTES

With thanks to Bob Stam for stimulating Toby's interest in film and technology, to Bill Grantham and Virginia Keeny for advice on legal citation, and to the editor for her helpful remarks.

1. Jhan Hochman, *Green Cultural Studies: Nature in Film, Novel, and Theory* (Moscow: University of Idaho Press, 1998); Gregg Mitman, *Reel Nature: America's Romance with Wildlife on Film* (Cambridge, MA: Harvard University Press, 1999); David Ingram, *Green Screen: Environmentalism and Hollywood Cinema* (Exeter: University of Exeter Press, 2000); Pat Brereton, *Hollywood Utopia: Ecology in Contemporary American Cinema* (Bristol: Intellect, 2005); Sean Cubitt, *EcoMedia* (Amsterdam/New York: Rodopi, 2005); Deborah A. Carmichael, *The Landscape of Hollywood Westerns: Ecocriticism in an American Film Genre* (Salt Lake City: University of Utah Press, 2006); Cynthia Chris, *Watching Wildlife* (Minneapolis: University of Minnesota Press, 2006).

2. Theodor W. Adorno, "Transparencies on Film," trans. Thomas Y. Levin, *New German Critique* 24–25 (1981–82): 201.

3. Dan Brockington, "Powerful Environmentalisms: Conservation, Celebrity and Capitalism," *Media, Culture and Society* 30, no. 4 (2008): 551–68; Alessandra Stanley, "Sounding the Global-Warming Alarm without Upsetting the Fans," *New York Times,* July 9, 2007, E1; Bryan Walsh, "Living with Ed—in a Green Hollywood," *Time,* November 30, 2007, time.com/time/health/article/0,8599,1689569,00.html; Charles J. Corbett and Richard P. Turco, *Sustainability in the Motion Picture Industry* (Los Angeles: University of California, Institute of the Environment, 2006), personal.anderson.ucla.edu/charles.corbett/papers/mpis_report.pdf, 5; visit ecorazzi.com for "The Latest In Green Gossip."

4. Gabrielle Pantera, "Hollywood Goes Green," Hollywoodtoday.net, May 6, 2009, hollywoodtoday.net/2009/05/06/hollywood-goes-green; Michael Ventre, "It's Not Easy Being Green, Hollywood Discovers," MSNBC.com, April 23, 2008, msnbc.msn.com/id/24256817/ns/business-going_green.

5. Corbett and Turco, *Sustainability,* 11–14.

6. Kurt W. Roth and Kurtis McKenny, *Energy Consumption by Consumer Electronics in U.S. Residences* (Arlington, VA: Consumer Electronics Association, 2007); Stacey Mitchell, *Big-Box Swindle: The True Cost of Mega-Retailers and the Fight for America's Independent Business* (Boston: Beacon, 2007), 117–19.

7. Pete Engardio with Kerry Cappell, John Carey, and Kenji Hall, "Beyond the Green Corporation," *Business Week,* January 29, 2007, 50–64.

8. Corbett and Turco, *Sustainability*, illustrate the complexity of such research and provide examples of greenish production practices in Hollywood film production.

9. Toby Miller, Nitin Govil, John McMurria, Richard Maxwell, and Ting Wang, *Global Hollywood 2* (London: British Film Institute, 2005); also see Rodanthi Tzanelli, "Reel Western Fantasies: Portrait of a Tourist Imagination in *The Beach* (2000)," *Mobilities* 1, no. 1 (2006): 121–42; Lisa Law, Tim Bunnell, and Chin-Ee Ong, "*The Beach,* the Gaze and Film Tourism," *Tourist Studies* 7, no. 2 (2007): 141–64.

10. "Popotla vs. *Titanic,*" rtmark.com/popotla.html; Miller et al., *Global Hollywood 2,* 165; for photos see rtmark.com/popotlaimages.html.

11. Praful Bidwai, "Prevent, Prepare and Protect," Rediff.com, January 4, 2005, in.rediff.com/news/2005/jan/04bidwai.htm; Devinder Sharma, "Tsunamis, manglares y economía de mercado," trans. Felisa Sastre, Rebelión.org, January 14, 2005, rebelion.org/noticia.php?id=10010; Vandana Shiva, "Lecciones del tsunami para quienes menosprecian a la madre tierra," Rebelión.org, January 15, 2005, rebelion.org/noticia.php?id=10045.

12. But see, within film studies, Robin L. Murray and Joseph K. Heumann, *Ecology and Popular Film: Cinema on the Edge* (Albany: State University of New York Press, 2009); Nadia Bozak, "The Disposable Camera: Image, Energy, Environment" (PhD diss., University of Toronto, 2008); and the physiocratic critique of Harri Kilpi, "Green Frames: Exploring Cinema Ecocritically," *WiderScreen* 3, no. 7 (2007).

13. Ulrich Beck, Anthony Giddens, and Scott Lash, *Reflexive Modernization: Politics, Tradition and Aesthetics in the Modern Social Order* (Stanford: Stanford University Press, 1994), 5; Ulrich Beck, *World Risk Society* (Cambridge: Polity, 1999), 135.

14. David Golumbia, *The Cultural Logic of Computation* (Cambridge, MA: Harvard University Press, 2009).

15. Ian Hacking, *The Taming of Chance* (Cambridge: Cambridge University Press, 1990).

16. Steve Lohr, "For Today's Graduate, Just One Word: Statistics," *New York Times,* August 6, 2009, A1.

17. Toby Miller, *Makeover Nation: The United States of Reinvention* (Columbus: Ohio State University Press, 2008).

18. Bill Grantham, *"Some Big Bourgeois Brothel": Contexts for France's Culture Wars with Hollywood* (Luton: University of Luton Press, 2000), 44; Candace Jones, "Co-evolution of Entrepreneurial Careers, Institutional Rules and Competitive Dynamics in American Film," *Organization Studies* 22, no. 6 (2001): 911–44.

19. Miller et al., *Global Hollywood 2,* chapter 5; Gerben Bakker, "Building Knowledge about the Consumer: The Emergence of Market Research in the Motion Picture Industry," *Business History* 45, no. 1 (2003): 101–27.

20. Barry R. Litman and Hoekyun Ahn, "Predicting Financial Success of Motion Pictures: The Early '90s Experience," in *The Motion Picture Mega-Industry*, ed. Barry R. Litman (Boston: Allyn & Bacon, 1998), 172–97.

21. Anna M. Dempster, "An Operational Risk Framework for the Performing Arts and Creative Industries," *Creative Industries Journal* 1, no. 2 (2009): 151–70.

22. Bruno Latour, *We Have Never Been Modern,* trans. Catherine Porter (Cambridge, MA: Harvard University Press, 1993).

23. Russell J. Dalton, "The Greening of the Globe? Crossnational Levels of Environmental Group Membership," *Environmental Politics* 14, no. 4 (2005): 441–59.

24. Deborah B. Rose and Libby Robin, "The Ecological Humanities in Action: An Invitation," *Australian Humanities Review* 31–32 (2004), lib.latrobe.edu.au/AHRarchive/issue-April-2004/rose.html; American Psychological Association, *Psychology and Global Climate Change: Addressing a Multi-faceted Phenomenon and Set of Challenges; A Report of the American Psychological Association, Task Force on the Interface between Psychology and Climate Change* (n.p.: American Psychological Association, 2009).

25. André Bazin, *What Is Cinema?* trans. Hugh Gray (Berkeley: University of California Press, 1967), 17–18, 21.

26. Brian Winston, *Technologies of Seeing: Photography, Cinematography, and Television* (London: British Film Institute, 1996), 40–43; Brian Winston, "Let Them Eat Laptops: The Limits of Technicism," *International Journal of Communication* 1 (2007): 170–76; Peter Wollen, "Cinema and Technology: A Historical Overview," in *The Cinematic Apparatus,* ed. Teresa de Lauretis and Stephen Heath (Basingstoke: Macmillan, 1985), 19. The secondary sources on this come from a valuable if maverick figure within screen studies (Winston) and a valuable if maverick moment within screen studies (when Althusserians and others briefly undertook archival research projects on technology).

27. Paul Virilio, *War and Cinema: The Logistics of Perception,* trans. Patrick Camiller (London: Verso, 1989); Steve Neale, *Cinema and Technology: Image, Text, Ideology* (Chicago: University of Chicago Press, 1985).

28. Julie A. Reilly, "Celluloid Objects: Their Chemistry and Preservation," *Journal of the American Institute for Conservation* 30, no. 2 (1991): 145–46.

29. George A. Blair, "The Development of the Motion Picture Raw Film Industry," *Annals of the American Academy of Political and Social Science* 128 (1926): 50–53.

30. Ibid.; George Eastman House, "Pumping Station at Kodak Park Connected with Private Water Supply System of 12,000,000 Gallons Daily Capacity," Still Photograph Archive, Catalog Record 87:0026:0029.

31. Eileen Bowser, *History of the American Cinema,* vol. 2, *The Transformation of Cinema, 1907–1915* (New York: Charles Scribner's Sons, 1990), 21–36; Great Lakes Commission des Grands Lacs, "Liquid Asset: Great Lakes Water Quality and Industry Needs," 1992, glc.org/docs/liqasset/liqasset.html;

          Richard Maxwell and Toby Miller

Michael I. Niman, "Kodak's Toxic Moments," Alternet.org, May 29, 2003, alternet.org/story/16030/; *Atlantic States Legal Foundation v. Eastman Kodak Co.,* 12 F.3d 353 (2d Cir. 1994).

32. Louis H. Bean, "Changing Trends in Cotton Production and Consumption," *Southern Economic Journal* 5, no. 4 (1939): 442–59.

33. "Twilight City—Where Snapshots Are Born," *Modern Mechanix and Inventions,* February 1936, 84–86, 122.

34. Blair, "The Development"; Reilly, "Celluloid Objects,"147.

35. "Twilight City."

36. Blair, "The Development"; Reilly, "Celluloid Objects."

37. Blair, "The Development"; United States Department of the Interior, *2006 Minerals Yearbook, Silver,* United States Geological Survey (n.p.: United States Department of the Interior, April 2008).

38. Dartmouth Toxic Metals Research Program, *The Facts on Silver,* Dartmouth College, Center for Environmental Health Services, dartmouth.edu/~toxmetal/TXQAag.shtml.

39. Sue Bowden and Geoffrey Tweedale, "Poisoned by the Fluff: Compensation and Litigation for Byssinosis in the Lancashire Cotton Industry," *Journal of Law and Society* 29, no. 4 (2002): 560–79; W. Kip Viscusi, "Cotton Dust Regulation: An OSHA Success Story?" *Journal of Policy Analysis and Management* 4, no. 3 (1985): 325–43.

40. "Test-Tube Love Seat," *Time,* February 26, 1940, time.com/time/magazine/article/0,9171,763265,00.html.

41. Carlos Bustamante, "AGFA, Kullmann, Singer & Co. and Early Cine-Film Stock," *Film History* 20, no. 1 (2008): 59–76.

42. Institute of Pacific Relations, "Memorandum on Silver," *Memorandum* 2, no. 22 (1933); "The Smelter Trust and Mexican Silver—Believed the Complete Control of the Silver Mining Industry of Mexico Is Contemplated," *New York Times,* April 27, 1903, 2; Dickson H. Leavens, "The Distribution of the World's Silver," *Review of Economics and Statistics* 17, no. 6 (1935): 131–38; Milton Friedman, "Franklin D. Roosevelt, Silver, and China," *Journal of Political Economy* 100, no. 1 (1992): 62–83.

43. Walter A. Durham Jr., "The Japanese Camphor Monopoly: Its History and Relation to the Future of Japan," *Pacific Affairs* 5, no. 9 (1932): 797–801; Reilly, "Celluloid Objects," 149.

44. "Formosa Plastics: A Briefing Paper on Waste, Safety and Financial Issues, Including U.S. Campaign Finance Abuses," n.d., Waverly, MA: Strategic Counsel on Corporate Accountability.

45. "Kodak Rewrites the Book on Printing," *Business Week,* September 4, 2006; Niman, "Kodak's Toxic Moments"; Vance McCarthy, "Kodak—A Picture of Nano-Driven Innovation," Nano Science and Technology Institute, Austin, 2007, nsti.org/news/item.html?id=179.

46. "Moguls to Direct Film's Future," *Financial Times,* November 29, 2006, 14.

47. Science and Technology Council of the American Academy of Motion Picture Arts and Sciences, *The Digital Dilemma: Strategic Issues in Archiving and Accessing Digital Motion Picture Materials* (Los Angeles: Academy Imprints, 2007), 33–50.

48. Basel Action Network and Silicon Valley Toxics Coalition, "Exporting Harm: The High-Tech Trashing of Asia," 2002, http://www.ban.org/E-waste/technotrashfinalcomp.pdf; Basel Action Network, "JPEPA as a Step in Japan's Greater Plan to Liberalize Hazardous Waste Trade in Asia," 2007, http://www.ban.org/Library/JPEPA_Report_BAN_FINAL_29_Aug_071.pdf; Xin Tong and Jici Wang, "Transnational Flows of E-Waste and Spatial Patterns of Recycling in China," *Eurasian Geography and Economics* 45, no. 8 (2004): 608–21; Coby S. C. Wong, S. C. Wu, Nurdan S. Duzgoren-Aydin, Adnan Aydin, and Ming H. Wong, "Trace Metal Contamination of Sediments in an E-Waste Processing Village in China," *Environmental Pollution* 145 (2007): 435, 441; Manas Ranjan Ray, Gopeshwar Mukherjee, Sanghita Roychowdhury, and Twisha Lahiri, "Respiratory and General Health Impairments of Ragpickers in India: A Study in Delhi," *International Archives of Occupational and Environmental Health* 77 (2004): 595–98; O. Osibanjo and I. C. Nnorom, "The Challenge of Electronic Waste (E-Waste) Management in Developing Countries," *Waste Management and Research* 25 (2007): 489–501; Richard Maxwell and Toby Miller, "Green Smokestacks?" *Feminist Media Studies* 8, no. 3 (2008): 324–29; Martin Medina, *The World's Scavengers: Salvaging for Sustainable Consumption and Production* (Lanham, MD: AltaMira, 2007).

49. Political Economy Research Institute, *The Misfortune 100: Top Corporate Air Polluters in the United States* (Amherst: University of Massachusetts, 2004).

50. News Corporation, "0 by 2010," newscorp.com/energy/index.html.

51. Leslie Kaufman, "Car Crashes to Please Mother Nature," *New York Times,* March 2, 2009, nytimes.com/2009/03/02/arts/television/02twen.html; Dan Glaister, "Jack Bauer Saves the World Again: *24* Goes Carbon Neutral," *Guardian,* March 3, 2009.

52. Warner Brothers Studio, "Environmental Initiatives," wbenvironmental.warnerbros.com.

53. For a list of "best practices," see Emma Gardner, *Developing an Environmental Strategy for UK Film* (n.p.: UK Film Council, 2007).

54. Ibid.; UKfilmcouncil.org, "Environmental Strategy," ukfilmcouncil.org.uk/environmental.

55. Science and Technology Council of the American Academy of Motion Picture Arts and Sciences, *The Digital Dilemma,* 51–54.

56. Maxwell T. Boykoff and Michael K. Goodman, "Conspicuous Redemption? Reflections on the Promises and Perils of the 'Celebritization' of Climate Change," *Geoforum* 40 (2009): 395–406; Peter Wells and Liz Heming, "Green Celebrity: Oxymoron, Fashion or Pioneering Sustainability?" *International Journal of Innovation and Sustainable Development* 4, no. 1 (2009): 61–73; Andrew Balmford, Andrea Manica, Lesley Airey, Linda Birkin, Amy Oliver, and

     Richard Maxwell and Toby Miller

Judith Schleicher, "Hollywood, Climate Change, and the Public," *Science* 305 (2004): 1713.

57. W. L. Liu, C. F. Shen, Z. Zhang, and C. B. Zhang, "Distribution of Phthalate Esters in Soil of E-Waste Recycling Sites from Taizhou City in China," *Bulletin of Environmental Contamination and Toxicology* 82 (2009): 665–67.

Contributors

Jinhee Choi is a lecturer in film studies at King's College London. She is the author of *The South Korean Film Renaissance: Local Hitmakers, Global Provocateurs* and the coeditor of *Horror to the Extreme: Changing Boundaries in Asian Cinema* (with Mitsuyo Wada-Marciano) and *The Philosophy of Film and Motion Pictures* (with Noël Caroll).

Faye Ginsburg is director of the Center for Media, Culture and History and codirector of the Center for Religion and Media at New York University, where she is also the David B. Kriser Professor of Anthropology. Author/editor of four books—most recently *Media Worlds: Anthropology on New Terrain* with Lila Abu Lughod and Brian Larin—she is also the recipient of numerous awards and honors, including a MacArthur "genius" grant. She was a Phi Beta Kappa scholar in 2008–9.

Bill Grantham is an entertainment attorney in Los Angeles. He is the author of *"Some Big Bourgeois Brothel": Contexts for France's Culture Wars with Hollywood* and a number of articles on law, cinema, and culture.

Mette Hjort is the chair professor and head of visual studies at Lingnan University in Hong Kong, an affiliate professor of Scandinavian studies at the University of Washington–Seattle, and an honorary professor at CEMES, University of Copenhagen. She is the author of *The Strategy of Letters; Small Nation, Global Cinema; Stanley Kwan's "Center Stage"*; and *Lone Scherfig's "Italian for Beginners."* She is the editor or coeditor of *Rules and Conventions, Emotion and the Arts* (with Sue Laver), *Cinema and Nation* (with Scott MacKenzie), *Purity and Provocation* (with Scott MacKenzie), *The Postnational Self* (with Ulf Hedetoft), *The Cinema of Small Nations* (with Duncan Petrie), *Dekalog 01: On* The Five Obstructions, and *Instituting Cultural Studies: Creativity and Academic Activism* (with Meaghan Morris). She has published two interview books with film directors, most recently *Danish Directors 2* (with Eva Jørholt and Eva Novrup Redvall).

Paisley Livingston is the chair professor and head of philosophy at Lingnan University in Hong Kong. He is the author of numerous books, including *Cinema, Philosophy, Bergman, Art and Intention: A Philosophical Study, Literature and Rationality: Ideas of Agency in Theory and Fiction,* and *Literary Knowledge: Humanistic Inquiry and the Philosophy of Science.* He is coeditor of the *Routledge Companion to Philosophy and Film* (with Carl Plantinga) and *The Creation of Art: New Essays in Philosophical Aesthetics* (with Berys Gaut).

Sylvia J. Martin earned her PhD in anthropology from the University of California–Irvine in 2009. She is currently a Fulbright Scholar at the University of Hong Kong, where she is conducting ethnographic research on cultural production across the Pacific Rim region. In 2009–10 Dr. Martin was a visiting assistant professor of media studies at Babson College. She has published on film/TV production processes, cultural identity, and globalization.

Richard Maxwell is a professor and chair of the Department of Media at City University of New York–Queens College. He is the author of *Herbert Schiller, The Spectacle of Democracy: Spanish Television, Nationalism, and Political Transition,* the coauthor of *Global Hollywood 2* (with Toby Miller, Nitin Govil, John McMurria, and Ting Wang), and the editor of *Culture Works: The Political Economy of Culture.*

Toby Miller is distinguished professor of media and cultural studies at the University of California–Riverside. He currently directs the University of California's study-abroad program in Mexico. He is the author of numerous books, including *The Well-Tempered Self: Citizenship, Culture, and the Postmodern Subject, Contemporary Australian Television* (with Stuart Cunningham), *The Avengers, Technologies of Truth: Cultural Citizenship and the Popular Media, Popular Culture and Everyday Life* (with Alec McHoul), *Global Hollywood* (with Nitin Govil, John McMurria, and Richard Maxwell), and *Cultural Policy* (with George Yúdice). His edited or coedited books include *SportCult* (with Randy Martin), *A Companion to Film Theory* (with Robert Stam), *Film and Theory: An Anthology* (with Robert Stam), and *A Companion to Cultural Studies.*

Hamid Naficy is the John Evans Professor of Communication, teaching screen cultures courses in the Department of Radio, Television, and Film at Northwestern University. His areas of research and teaching include documentary and ethnographic films; cultural studies of diaspora, exile, and postcolonial cinemas and media; and Iranian and Middle Eastern cinemas. He has published extensively on these and allied topics. His English-language books are *An Accented Cinema: Exilic and Diasporic Filmmaking, Home, Exile, Homeland: Film, Media, and the Politics of Place* (editor), *The Making of Exile Cultures: Iranian Television in Los Angeles, Otherness and the Media: The Ethnography of the Imagined and the Imaged* (coeditor), and *Iran MediaIndex*. Forthcoming is the four-volume *A Social History of Iranian Cinema*. He has also published extensively in Persian, including a two-volume book on documentary cinema theory and history, *Film-e mostanad (Entesharate-e daneshgah-eazad-e Iran)*. He has lectured widely internationally, and his works have been translated into many languages, including French, German, Turkish, Italian, and Persian.

Michael Pokorny is a lecturer in economics and statistics at Westminster University. His coauthored articles, with John Sedgwick, have appeared in the *Economic History Review, Journal of Cultural Economics*, and *Explorations in Economic History*. He is the coeditor, with John Sedgwick, of *An Economic History of Film*. Pokorny's research interests include student performance in higher education in the United Kingdom.

Trevor Ponech is an associate professor of English at McGill University in Montreal and the author of *What Is Non-fiction Cinema?*

Eva Novrup Redvall is an assistant professor in the Department of Film and Media Studies at the University of Copenhagen. She holds a PhD in screenwriting as a creative process and has published on different aspects of Nordic cinema in books and journals. She coedited *Danish Directors 2: Dialogues on the New Danish Fiction Cinema* with Mette Hjort and Eva Jørholt. Since 1999 she has served as film critic for the daily Danish newspaper *Information*. She is currently working on a three-year project, funded by the Danish Research Council, on the production practice behind the making of Danish public service television drama series.

John Sedgwick is the head of the Centre of International Business and Sustainability at London Metropolitan University, where he lectures on economics. He was awarded a Leverhulme Research Fellowship in 2000 to investigate the reasons for, and the consequences of, the dramatic decline in film going in the United States in the postwar period (1946–65). The results of this research project were published in the *Journal of Economic History* in 2002. He has also published research articles on the film business in *Cinema Journal* and, with Michael Pokorny, in the *Economic History Review, Journal of Cultural Economics,* and *Explorations in Economic History.* He is the author of *Filmgoing in Britain in the 1930s: A Choice of Pleasures* and the coeditor of *An Economic History of Film* (with Michael Pokorny). Recently, Sedgwick has been conducting research in Australia and New Zealand on film-going patterns during the Depression era. This research is funded by a Sir Robert Menzies Bi-centennial Research Fellowship and British Academy award.

Rod Stoneman is the director of the Huston School of Film & Digital Media at the National University of Ireland, Galway. He was chief executive of Bord Scannán na hÉireann/the Irish Film Board until September 2003 and previously a deputy commissioning editor in the independent film and video department at Channel 4 Television in the United Kingdom. He has made a number of documentaries, including *Ireland: The Silent Voices, Italy: The Image Business, 12,000 Years of Blindness,* and *The Spindle,* and has written extensively on film and television. He is the author of *Chávez: The Revolution Will Not Be Televised; A Case Study of Politics and the Media* and the coeditor of *"The Quiet Man" . . . and Beyond: Reflections on a Classic Film, John Ford and Ireland* (with Seán Crosson) and *Scottish Cinema Now* (with Jonathan Murray and Fidelma Farley).

Michelle L. Woodward is the photo editor of *Middle East Report,* a quarterly published by MERIP (Middle East Research and Information Project). She holds a SM degree in comparative media studies from the Massachusetts Institute of Technology and has lived and worked in the Middle East, including as a photographer for Agence France Presse in Jordan. She is the author most recently of "Creating Memory and History: The Role of Archival Practices in Lebanon and Palestine," *Photographies* and "Photographic Style and the Depiction of Israeli-Palestinian Conflict," *Jerusalem Quarterly.*

INDEX

Note: Italicized page numbers refer to illustrations and their captions.

Bro, Nicholas, *221*
Brophy, Philip, 253
Brown, Rosena, 256, 268n. 25
budgetary restrictions: as constructive creative constraint, 216–17, 219–20; stunt doubles and, 102, 110
Buñuel, Luis, 150–51
Burch, Noel, 248
Burma VJ, 17–18
Burmese video activists, documentary portrait of, 17–18
Business Week, 280
byssinosis (brown lung), 279

Cage, John, 247
calculated risks, creating space for, 266
Cameron, James, 272
camphor, in raw film manufacturing, 278, 280
Cannes Film Festival, 144, 149–50
Capa, Cornell, 229
Capa, Robert, 228, 229
capitalist industries, risk-taking practices, 97–99, 105–6
Capote, Truman, 249
carbon footprints, 271, 281–82
Cartier-Bresson, Henri, 230
"Categories of Art" (Walton), 170–71
cautionary tales, use of term, 120
celebrity crips, 131
celebrity environmentalism, 283
cellulose acetate (safety film), 277–78
cellulose nitrate, in raw film manufacturing, 277–78
censorship, at Channel 4, 252–53
El chacal de Nahueltoro (Littín), 151
Chan, Jackie, 8, 28n. 17, 173–75
Chan, Peter, 165
chance: as catalyst in stimulation of new forms, 251; in completion of *Dust Breeding*, 247; Huston and,

249; role in arts, 245–51; role in creativity, 266–67
Chang, Michael, 6–7
Channel 4, British television, 251–57
Chaplin, Charlie, *74*, 76
Chen Kaige, 20–21, 165–66, *172*, 172–73, 177
Cheung Tit Leung, 15
children with disabilities, medical experiments on, 120–21
Chile, cinema of resistance, 149–51
China, 6–7, 166, 168–69, 279–80
China Documentary Film Festival, 15
Chinese culture, globalization of, 168
Chinese directors, Fifth Generation, 167
Chinese opera, as training ground for stunt workers, 109
Chinese People's Political Consultative Conference (CPPCC), 21
Choi Eun-hee, 20
Christensen, Carina, 222
Christensen, Pernille Fischer, 217–18, *218*, 220–21
Christiansen, Christian E., 221
cinema: Irish Film Board, 257–61; terms of timidity, 261–64
cinema of resistance, Chile, 149–51
cinemas, 185, 194
cinema studies, 4, 13–14, 170, 273, 276, 283
cinematic authorship, 17–20
cinematic fiction, 73, 78–84
cinematic model of irrational risk inadvertence, 61–68
cinematic style, 8–11
A City of Sadness (Hou Hsiao-hsien), 177
clandestine filming: by Jacir, 148–49; by Littín, 152–54; motivations for and consequences of, 155–58
Clash of Egos (Villum Jensen), 32
Clayton, Jack, 249

environmental damage, in film production, 272
environmentalism, 283
Environmental Media Association, 271
environmental risks, 20–21, 26, 276, 280–81
epistemic risks, 167–70, 175–76
equity ownership, in film financing, 204
equiveillance, meaning of term, 158
ethical issues: in accented filmmaking, 148–49, 151–54; in documentary films and filmmaking, 44, 47; in photojournalism, 229–30, 233–34; in risk-taking displays, 42
eugenics, new genetics vs., 117
eugenics projects, documentation of, 119
e-waste recycling, 281
excessive risks, meaning of term, 39
exile and exiles, 149–52, 156–59
exilic doubling, 152–54
experimental art, role of chance in, 248, 250–51
extreme expressionism, 45–46
eyewitnessing of events, 229–30, 233–34

Familial dysautonomia (FD), 130–31
family histories, unnatural, and parables of possibility, 116
fantasy and fantasies, 56, 93–94, 135, 172
Faraji, Farshid, 154–55
Farrell, Mairéad, 252
FD (Familial dysautonomia), 130–31
Fearless (Weir), 75–76
Ferestadeh (Sayyad), 150
Fermat, Pierre de, 2
fidelity, epistemic risk differentiated from, 167
Fifth Generation Chinese directors, 167

film commissioners, 211–12, 214–15, 251–52, 257–58
film consumers: divergence between expectations and realizations, 192–93; and epistemic risk, 167–70; frequency distribution of disconfirmation in, *192;* lack of cultural knowledge and undetected aesthetic defects, 176; as pollutant producers, 272; premonitions of taste in, 262; risk in choosing to view movies, 188–89; surveillance of, as method of risk reduction, 275; unpredictable tastes of, 190. *See also* spectators
film criticism, 167–68, 170–71, 176
film distributors, and film financing, 201–3, 205
film economics conference, 276
film festivals, 14–15, 130, 141–42n. 51, 144, 149–50, 159
Film festival Yearbook series, 14–15
film financing: avowed commitment to risk in, 257–58; commercialist stances in 1990s funding agencies, 261; distinction between MPAA and non-MPAA companies, 200; financial risk in, 201–2, 275–81; framing risk, 198–200; future of risk, 206–8; impact of global recession on funding mechanisms, 206–7; intercreditor issues, 206; investment-returns relationship, 260; "nobody knows factor," 212; pan-Asian cinema, 169; private, 204–5; public monies in, 261; rational model, elements of, 208; risk assessment process, 208; U.S. models, 197–98, 201–4, 207
film industry: cost of risk-aversive tendencies, 14; regional, in East Asia, 165–66; as unstable environment for investment, 181–82
film institutions, 11–15

Hong Kong, 7–8, 28n. 17, 98, 171–72, 174
La hora de los hornos (Getino and Solanas), 156
Hou Hsiao-hsien, 177
The Hour of the Furnaces (Getino and Solanas), 156
Huguenard, Amie, 67
Hui, Ann, 100
Hu Jie, 51
Hush-a-bye Baby (Harkin), 256
Huston, John, 249, *250*, 265

imagined communities, 118
imagining seeing, 78
improvisation in film, 248–49
inauthenticity, in behind-the-scenes footage, 175
Independent Living movement, 129–30, 140–41n. 43
India (Christensen), 217
India, as silver consumer, 279–80
individual agency model, 34, 37
inevitable risk, meaning of term, 39
Infected Landscape project (Kremer), 240
information-based technologies, 280
In G-d's Image: You, Me, and Everyone We Know (Limmud program), 132–33
Initial D (Lau and Mak), 165
In Search of Cyrus the Great (Kar), 155
institutional trust, in state-subsidized film industry, 216
insurance costs, in U.S., 274–75
interdisciplinarity, 22
International Monetary Fund, 272–73
In the Name of God (Guzmán), 157
Intimacy project (Halawani), 238, *239*
inverse surveillance, performative, 161–62

Invisible Waves (Pen-ek Ratanaruang), 169
Iranian filmmakers, 155, 158–59
Iraq: filming in, 154–55; U.S. military program of embedding with troops in, 232
Irish Film Board (Bord Scannán na hÉireann), 257–61
irrational risk inadvertence, cinematic model, 61–68
Irvin, Cass, 141n. 50
Isaacs, Jeremy, 255–56
Iser, Lynne, 128
Islam, in *Submission,* 160
Israel, 147
Israeli intelligence service, 149
Israeli-Palestinian conflict, 230–32, 238–40
Italian for Beginners (Scherfig), 16, 19
Ivens, Joris, 151–54

Jacir, Annemarie, 149
Jacir, Emily, 147–49
The Jackal of Nahueltoro (Littín), 151
Jackass films, 52
Jackson, Peter, *76*
Jang Dong-gun, 175
Jansen, Billeskov, 18–19
Jarman, Derek, 257
Jeddawi, Mona al, 235
Jefferson, Thomas, 155
Jensen, Tomas Villum, 32
Jewish community, 115–18, 120, 124–25, 126–27
Jewish Disability Empowerment Center, 129
Jewish Genetic Disease Consortium, 118
Jewish identity, 116–17
the Jewish question, 116–18, 136n. 4
Jews: Ashkenazi, 118, 124, 130, 137n. 13; New, 129; Orthodox and Hasidic, 125–26

reflexive modernization, risk and, 35
religious teachings, and understand-
    ing value of difference, 128
research questions, 4, 23–26, 32–33
residuals, 206
Restrepo (Hetherington), 241
Reynaud, Bérénice, 6–7
risk: agents' exposure and ability to
    cope with, 37; anthropism of, 60–
    61; approaches to, 33–38, 166–67;
    concept of, 23, 31, 57–61, 64, 98–
    99; discernability in film, 23–24,
    34, 38–42; embracing, 264–67;
    identification and classification,
    59, 73–78; of imagining, 134;
    inevitable, interstitionality and,
    143–44; inference of, in film, 38–
    39; management, 1, 22, 263–64;
    modeling, 263–64; perception of,
    56, 58, 62–63, 167; representation
    of, 9–10, 68, 78–84, 91–94; shift-
    ing, 12–13; social construction of,
    60; types of, 36–39; the U.S. and,
    273–75; and value-bearing conse-
    quences, 58; of visibility, 115–16.
    See also specific types of risk
Risk and Culture approach, 35
risk assessment, 200
risk attitudes, 41–42, 97, 110–11
risk attribution, 77
risk aversion, 14, 161–62, 262–63,
    266
risk blindness, 67
risk inadvertence, 61–68, 70
risk narratives, 68–70
risk positions, 44, 49–50
risk realists, beliefs of, 60
risk research, traditions of thought in,
    33–36
risk running, 73–76
risks: calculated, creating space for,
    266
risk societies, 35–36, 273–74
risk studies, 2, 26–27

risk-style relationship, 8–11, 227–28,
    242n. 1, 242n. 4
risk taking: artistic, and the impor-
    tance of trust, 215–16; to attain
    subjectively valued end, 58; banal,
    and false display, 48–51; in com-
    missioning at Channel 4, 255–56;
    in context of capitalist industries,
    99; cultural attitudes toward spec-
    tacle of, 41–42; difficulty under
    sustained pressure, 258; displays
    of, 52; by film practitioners, 37–38,
    50–51; in financial framework for
    filmmaking, 209; models of con-
    tainment and, 261–62; as person-
    ality trait of creative people, 215;
    physical, conversion of fear into
    adrenaline, 108–9; risk running
    vs., 73–76; spectators and, 15; by
    teenagers, 16; voluntary, 36. *See
    also* artistic risk taking; flamboy-
    ant risk taking
Robert, Yves, 92
Robert Capa Gold Medal, 232, 234
Rodger, George, 228
Rosenbaum, Mark, 154–55
Ross, Gary, 85–91
Rossellini, Raffaella, 88
Rossellini, Roberto, 248–49
Rozen, Shahar, 122–25
Ruan Lingyu, suicide of, 6–7
Ruiz, Raúl, 149–50
Rumsfeld, Donald H., 269n. 38

Sabbath Vision (Bellocchio), 85–
    91, *87*
sacrifice, rhetorical force of, 44
Sa'iq al-Shahinah (The Truck
    Driver), 13
Salahi, Asad, 14
Salt, Saliva, Sperm and Sweat
    (Brophy), 253
Salt of This Sea (Jacir), 149
Samura, Sorious, 42–45, *43*, 50